Sanctuary Cinema

Sanctuary Cinema

Origins of the Christian Film Industry

Terry Lindvall

NEW YORK UNIVERSITY PRESS
New York and London

NEW YORK UNIVERSITY PRESS
New York and London
www.nyupress.org

Library of Congress Cataloging-in-Publication Data

Lindvall, Terry.
Sanctuary cinema : origins of the Christian film industry / by Terry
Lindvall.
p. cm.
Includes bibliographical references and index.
ISBN-13: 978-0-8147-5210-4 (cloth : alk. paper)
ISBN-10: 0-8147-5210-1 (cloth : alk. paper)
1. Motion pictures—Religious aspects—Christianity. 2. Christian
films—United States—History and criticism. 3. Motion pictures in
Christian education. 4. Silent films—United States—History and crit-
icism.
I. Title.
PN1995.9.R4L56   2007
791.43'6823—dc22   2006033344

New York University Press books are printed on acid-free paper,
and their binding materials are chosen for strength and durability.

Manufactured in the United States of America

10 9 8 7 6 5 4 3 2 1

This book is dedicated to the vision of Barbara Newington, Babsy Newington, and Adelia "Dolly" Rasines, wonderful friends whose lives shine with grace, joy, and beauty.

And to my parents, John and Mae Lindvall, incarnate images of God's faithfulness and loving kindness, and who wisely made me go to church a lot—where, sometimes, they showed movies.

Contents

A photo insert follows p. 116.

Acknowledgments

One cannot even begin such a work without the support of an editor who not only believes in the project but also has the wisdom, skill, and grace to discipline its author. Jennifer Hammer has been such an astute critic and generous sponsor, one who adroitly cleared a path for me to follow, but also allowed me to wander off into the forest at times. With a rapier skill for editing, Jennifer proved to be an expert trainer of thought and word. A distant friend and informal editor, Cynthia Read, gave hope and initial pruning to the project. I am also indebted to John Lyden and those anonymous, insightful reviewers who astutely critiqued earlier drafts. So, too, I thank a friend who has a talent for hearing nonsense as well as detecting errata, Pam Robles. I consider Vinnie Rossini, a former doctoral student, more as an archeological colleague in opening up hidden vaults of primary materials. His work in ferreting out significant articles and letters deserves praise from the housetops.

I thank Diane Clark and Suzanne Morton for surreptitious help during some dark seasons. And during my journey in the vocational wilderness, I must thank those who welcomed me into their scholarly oases, fed me manna, and offered cups of cold water, the hilarious saints at Duke University School of Divinity, the College of William and Mary, and Virginia Wesleyan College. So, too, I hold my former colleagues, Ben Fraser, John Lawing, Bill Brown, Dennis Bounds, Gil Elvgren, and Mark Steiner, who meet for coffee and muffins every Thursday morning, in a deepest debt of gratitude. From lively debates on theology to musings on life and assorted holy and bawdy subjects, we have gathered faithfully as fellow Christians and friends. Foremost are dear friends, Andrew and Juliet Quicke, coauthors of a sequel to this volume, *Sermons on Celluloid*. Through the tumults of university life, Andrew has remained a rock and source of deep inspiration and Juliet has tried to keep us both honest and on task. I would also express my deep gratitude to Frank and Aimee Batten Jr., who graciously provided a special sanctuary for me to teach.

Finally, I thank my wife, Karen, who merrily mocks my tendencies to scribble in pedantic jargon and whose love and friendship bolster all I do. And I thank my two effervescent and cheerful children, Chris and Caroline, for all their welcome interruptions to the endless tasks of writing, and who would chase me off the computer for their own serious work, play, and music.

Introduction

Underground films, political films, avant-garde, experimental, educational, and documentary films—these renegade films bubble up and flow against the tide of dominant Hollywood products. Made in spite of a paucity of funding, resources, and support, and despite dim prospects of finding channels for distribution and exhibition,[1] they try to represent alternative ways of looking at life, to offer ideological or pedagogical perspectives that have been overlooked by the dominant media corporations, and to provide a viable alternative to Hollywood's commercialized offerings.[2]

One neglected case among these frequently marginalized modes of independent nontheatrical filmmaking, of films not produced for general theatrical release, has been a fragmented, "lowbrow" network that confesses and professes to a distinctly sectarian vision. Its function is predominantly didactic. Its ideology is unapologetically theological. Its audience is a vast congregation. I call this network the Christian Film Industry.

Christian films are films of, by, and for the people of the church, not aspiring to high aesthetic values nor aiming for economic profit, but seeking to renew, uplift, and propagate. They are tribal films, told and retold within their own community to carry on its traditions and values. The makers of these films go against the grain of mere entertainment to produce a genre of religious cinema that is remarkably political: political because it subverts the secular city by envisioning, however inartistically or superficially, the City of God.

One enduring characteristic of this tribal people's art may well be that it strikes a popular art industry as artless: rough, unpolished, unsophisticated, even kitschy, suggesting a stubbornly peculiar mind set: "It may be bad art, but it is ours." However, just as icons were fashioned not to draw attention to their craftsmanship but to draw spectators into worship, so

Christian films have been crafted primarily to preach rather than to entertain, to emphasize moral and religious concerns rather than aesthetic delights.

Christian filmmakers frequently saw themselves as struggling to be in the world but not of it, wrestling with the classic dilemma articulated by church father Tertullian, namely, "What has Athens to do with Jerusalem? What concord is there between the Academy and the Church?" Jerome echoed this sentiment in the fifth century, asking: "What has Horace to do with the Psalms, Virgil with the Gospels, Cicero with the Apostles?" Trained as a classical rhetorician, Jerome suffered a vision in which he was called before divine judgment and condemned as more of a Ciceronian than a Christian. In a strangely parallel experience, filmmaker George Lucas dreamed that he stood before the Almighty, who looked down on him and said: "Get out. You blew it." Here the question arises: "What has Hollywood to do with Jerusalem?"[3] Or even, what has film history to do with religion? In contrast to studies of class, ethnicity, gender, and other cultural variables in film, religious affiliation is significantly ignored. If film history is to traverse other histories, as critic Lee Grieveson put it, or to become part of a larger, integrated collaboration, as historian Donald Crafton has encouraged, it must intersect with a social history of religion.[4]

In what might serve as a classic paradigm for the religious filmmaker, liberation theologian Gustavo Gutierrez laid the biblical groundwork for a culture of resistance, for those people who wished to sing their own songs, write their own poetry, dance and joke according to their own rhythms and humors, design their own artistic works, and speak boldly for what they saw as good, true, and right. In his aptly titled *We Drink from Our Own Wells,* Gutierrez warned people not to imbibe the poisonous and noxious values of the multinational corporations that concocted a shiny, commodified culture for consumption by an unsuspecting and undiscerning people.[5] His liberating discourse was marked by a concern for marginalized and exploited people, for their need for dignity and justice, and for locating a true and passionate prophetic voice to organize a spiritual resistance to a deeply insidious consumerist culture.

Some corners of Christian filmmaking, particularly those associated with various orders of the Roman Catholic Church, sought to be voices crying in the wilderness, or at least in church basements and school auditoria, in distinct educational and prophetic ways. They saw themselves as standing on their own "sacred" and separate values, identifying themselves through what they define as signs of difference. The Christian film industry's great potential was to propose an alternative way of seeing and to offer a means of guiding pilgrims along the media way. Yet from its earliest years, its filmmaking was assimilated by the capitalist Hollywood system itself, and tagged as a conformist, rather than a transformational, imitator.

In general, while the early Christian filmmakers held beliefs, values, and priorities markedly different from their secular counterparts, they did not consistently separate themselves from the American entertainment culture, contrary to what we might expect.[6] They did not often question the capitalist system as such, but instead warned against the seven deadly sins, campaigned against Prohibition, and made direct appeals for salvation. Perhaps most surprising, they adopted classical Hollywood cinematic techniques and often populated their films with attractive actors and actresses. While often marked by a lack of subtlety, sublimity, and mystery, their films nevertheless communicated effectively with their intended sectarian audiences; these films belong to a particular communal world of which the artists are significantly a part. Granted, these films were preaching to the choir. Yet some were remarkably effective in evangelistic propaganda, historical instruction, and moral edification, drawing in converts through the emotionally and spiritually resonant themes and images of their films.

The purpose of this book is to illuminate the earliest years of Protestant filmmaking—the era of silent films. Remarkably, as we will see, the church functioned as one of the most visionary and effective nontheatrical agencies in the country, experimenting with shows to attract crowds, succor youth, and illustrate the power of the Gospel message. It was a powerful force in both promoting and shaping the new medium and in using the technology to draw in adherents and spur social change even as the burgeoning field of mass media in turn shaped the methods and message of the church.

Today, the recent emergence of this cottage industry into the public eye raises the question of whether the movement has attained some wider legitimacy or has been compromised. In December 1999, *Entertainment Weekly* featured a two-week special report on Christian entertainment.[7] In 2003, director Mel Gibson shocked Hollywood insiders with his independently financed "blockbuster" Christian spectacle, *The Passion of the Christ*. The industry took note that there were profits to be made in this alternative world of cinema. Hollywood discovered a vast untapped market of religious people. Not only in the medium of film, but in print and music as well, God and mammon are cooperating in fruitful joint ventures.[8] But these strange bedfellows began negotiating their relations at the beginning of the previous century.

Our first task is to define (and limit) the objects of our study, Christian films. In her inquiry into "What Makes a Film Christian?" critic Anne Henderson-Hart wanted to include films that have the power to inspire, educate, and mold minds, films that stretch the category.[9] But such an all-encompassing approach requires a highly subjective judgment as to which films inspire or educate. I define Christian films as films made by Christians with a particular goal in mind that relates to the work and ministry of the church or religious community. Limiting ourselves to films made by Christians for religious purposes unfortunately precludes the inclusion of many praiseworthy and spiritually provocative (and some of my personal favorite) silent films, such as *Sparrows, The Disciple, The Gaucho,* and *The Passion of Joan of Arc.* However, other critical studies have dealt insightfully with these and others like them. Our restrictions also allow us to avoid grappling with the quasi-religious silent film spectacles of Cecil B. DeMille.[10]

The definition opens the study primarily to nontheatrical films that preach, teach, and evangelize. My focus keys in on Protestant film industries as inclusion of early Roman Catholic activity would require a bigger book. My task here is much more than identifying such Christian films. The historiography of the early Christian film industry encompasses a rich diversity of themes: how did the church, historically suspicious of graven images and the theater, come to embrace the showing of films from its very pulpits? Were films merely art and entertainment, or could they do holy work? Would technological inventions, distribution and exhibition practices, and the politics of egos contribute to the church's place in society? The early-twentieth-century church recognized the growing importance of the visual mass media in shaping culture and aiding its mission. One underlying question asks how the visual media influence, if not define, religious experiences and understandings of the Gospel message, particularly situated in a Protestant tradition that historically opted for the word over the image. Thus my overarching inquiry focuses upon the impact of silent moving pictures on Protestant churches during the early twentieth century.

Preview of Coming Attractions

In chapter 1, I examine how historical religious debates regarding graven images prefigured the controversies surrounding the acceptance of the use of film as a religious tool. I continue with an investigation of the aesthetic roots of Christian filmmaking and of cultural predecessors such as the magic lantern, the spiritual landscape paintings of the Hudson River School, illustrated stereopticon sermons, and the technological origins of religious films.

Chapter 2 details the development of a sanctuary cinema, introducing its foremost revolutionary apologist, the Reverend Herbert Jump, and culminating in film's emergence as a useful art for uplift in the stupendous 1919 Methodist Centenary. Chapter 3 considers the most notable divine shows, the *Photo-Drama of Creation* and *The Stream of Life,* as well as the ordinary sectarian films that flooded the market. Chapter 4 details the nonsectarian business of making, distributing, and exhibiting nontheatrical religious films and chronicles both the quest for better pictures and the eventual decline of religious filmmaking at the end of the silent film era. In conclusion I argue that the assimilation of film into churches altered the religious culture itself, as film established its own cult. Film became a rival and competitor to the churches. It became another religion, one that has proliferated into the twenty-first century.

In Giuseppe Tornatore's masterly *Cinema Paradisio,* Alfredo, an old grizzled projectionist of a small movie theater in a Sicilian village sits under the supervision of a meticulous censor, a vigilant Roman Catholic priest, Father Adelfio. In this post-World War II era, the cleric previews and scrutinizes each film before it is shown to a raucous public clamoring for pictures of thrills and kissing. During the showing of the films, the priest wanders about the theater with a little bell that rings to warn of any objectionable material, inappropriate images, or immoral behavior. Such a humorous image of religious authority overseeing and policing the viewing habits of impressionable audiences persists as the reigning representation of church-film relations.

Many believe that from the beginning of moving pictures, the Christian church constantly viewed film as the devil's camera, a moral leprosy, or an incubator for sin. Watching films was akin to flirting with the devil;

thus a priest must guard that no vile thing should come before the eye.[11] While some religious reformers did make these accusations, they were not as prevalent in the early days as one might think. Far from a posture of hostility and suspicion, the church welcomed the advent of the medium as providing new opportunities for reaching the unchurched. In fact, in 1907 Jane Addams of Hull House prophesied regarding uplift films— films that ennobled the human spirit and taught moral principles—that "in time moving pictures will be utilized quite as the stereopticon is at present for all purposes of education and entertainment and that schools and churches will count the films as among their most valuable equipment."[12] The churches believed their mission was to educate and uplift the masses and many embraced this richly optimistic hope. Many churches anticipated establishing a home for the moving picture in the sanctuary and assumed that it would play a suitable and strategic role in their mission.

In time, fears that film would corrupt the church by introducing non-Christian values helped to erode efforts to exploit the medium for evangelical purposes. Suspicion arose that trafficking in images would open the door for a reversal of authority and influence. The mid-1920s brought a shift in terms of the relationship of church to the mass popular arts, with the embodiment of an emerging secular American civil religion which proclaimed a self-saving ideology that began to displace the evangelical sensibility that churches had sought to promote. Ultimately the advent of radio attenuated organized religion's involvement in film, leading to an alternative relation with the mass media that eclipsed an early vital one with the moving picture.

But the relationship of the church to the moving picture in the first two decades of the twentieth century was engaging, vital, and robust. Educational and uplift films championed by the moving picture industry press (e.g., *Nickelodeon, Moving Picture World,* etc.) boosted the mission of the churches, prompting them to modernize their communications systems while simultaneously ameliorating the piety and enthusiasm of their congregations.[13] This relationship between Christian goals and the development of silent film as a significant aspect of American popular culture has yet to be fully explored. This book aims to demonstrate how Protestant churches partnered with the new technology of moving pictures to achieve their mission of attracting new audiences, of instructing and entertaining their congregations, and of exploiting nontheatrical films to serve the Kingdom of God and their parishes.

The moving picture emerged as the paramount amusement industry of the early twentieth century. Its technical sophistication, its mass appeal, and its amazing novelty made it the most desirable modern mode of recreation. Nickelodeons attracted immigrant and child audiences, often provoking reformers' concerns about such viewing publics being exposed at such a "formative and impressionable stage."[14] By the end of the first decade, stars appeared, mostly unnamed but recognized by an adoring public, and were identified with such monikers as "the Biograph Girl." By 1910, the transformation of cinema occurred with movie palaces replacing storefront nickelodeons, multireel features being exhibited, and stars like Charlie Chaplin and Mary Pickford emerging. Production companies developed their own distinctive styles, directors, stars, and genres. Vitagraph Studios, for example, developed their biblical, literary, and historical Quality Films in an attempt to attract middle-class and highbrow audiences. In the early 1910s, the Italians exported impressive epics such as Giovanni Pastrone's *Cabiria*, Enrico Guazzoni's *Quo Vadis?* and Torquato Tasso's script of the four-reel *Jerusalem Delivered*, an uneven classic showing the "plotting of the powers of darkness against the success of the Christian cause in the Crusades" that could be best presented through "the lecture with music."[15] Producer-actor Gilbert M. Anderson of Essanay Studios reinvigorated the western with his creation of his popular hero Broncho Billy, and simultaneously reaffirmed the durable values of a Victorian society. The simple story lines also stressed the distinct Protestant themes of sin, repentance, and conversion, creedal beliefs shared by many middle-class audiences in the early 1910s.[16] As social historian Lary May has pointed out, most of the early film producers, like Thomas Edison, were Protestants, but they were quickly surpassed by imaginative independents from an assimilated Jewish heritage, whose savvy sense of audience taste enabled them to build the Hollywood empire.[17]

Alongside the development of the moving picture industry, there grew a visionary recognition of the possibilities of the nontheatrical motion picture, particularly in religious and educational fields. As early as 1898, evangelist Colonel Henry Hadley incorporated *Passion Play* photodramas for his revival campaigns in Atlantic City. Salvation Army Commander Herbert Booth shot his own movies to feed the imaginations of the poor and attract them to his sermons on salvation. With very few prejudices attached to the medium, the revivalist, evangelical church was as likely to use films as the more liberal, modern churches. The positive reception of film marked both groups as they envisioned grand opportunities to animate the messages of the Gospel for personal salvation or for social reform, respectively. Yet coincidentally, religious leaders envisioned the possibilities of the religious film just as exhibitors and critics found such tableau features as *From the Manger to the Cross* dull. Uplifting films lacked an edge. They belonged in the more respectable and dignified (and lackluster) environs of churches or schools. Exhibitors complained that advertising a religious piece meant "an off day in the box office."[18]

Complicating the question of historical church-film relations is the fact of diversity, of various Christian denominations and their peculiar responses to film. While geography, theological doctrine, and church polity regarding culture shaped the variegated responses to motion pictures, most early responses to film were generally positive across an ecumenical board, among both liberals and fundamentalists. Various Protestant denominations had welcomed precursors of the moving pictures, with lantern shows given at Methodist, Episcopal, and Lutheran churches and panoramas exhibited for Presbyterian and Baptist congregations.[19] The progressive Congregationalists established the vanguard of seeing a vital engagement with film as a means to translate biblical stories into the vernacular of visual communication. Religious apologists like George Anderson and Herbert Jump articulated ways and means to discover the religious possibilities of film. Congregationalists from New England, the Midwest, and the West Coast envisioned progressive uses of film for political and social issues, such as for suffrage, as film historian Kay Sloan has capably catalogued. By exploring the lines between silent film and the progressive movements and economic and cultural problems of the era, we can better trace the significant cultural roles played by the church and religious leaders, particularly in the context of the Progressive era, as they sought to upgrade living conditions for the poor and immigrants.[20] Anderson, writing for the *Congregationalist* journal in 1910, spelled out his hope that the motion picture business would prove a worthy effort for "social justice" and universal brotherhood.[21] Progressive Congregational churches like one in Appleton, Wisconsin, combined special lectures with photoplays to promote health concerns or woman's rights (e.g., *Votes for Women*).[22]

While less broad than the Congregationalists, the Methodists' vision centered on educational and evangelical films. In the political forefront of the Temperance, Sabbatarian, and uplift movements, Methodists embraced the Victorian moral cinema of their own southern Methodist "missionary" filmmaker, D. W. Griffith. His *A Drunkard's Reformation*, for example, warned of the harmful consequences of drink and helped to rescue immigrants from the saloon and poorhouse. Such a film echoed the Methodists' opposition to alcohol and suggested that the art of drama could be used to reform sinners. (The film industry press tactically reinforced the notion that the movie house was replacing the saloon.) Griffith, as well, held to a fuzzy postmillennialism, with a belief that filmmakers, being the artists of a new "universal language," would usher in the imminent Kingdom of God. Of all the groups, the Methodists demonstrated the greatest institutional enthusiasm for film, culminating in their 1919 Centenary in Columbus, Ohio, which would erupt into a revival of church-based motion picture exhibition.

Historian William Romanowski's groundbreaking denominational study of the Christian Reformed Church ably connected ecclesiastical responses to the debate regarding highbrow and lowbrow art. By the late 1920s, as religious support for film began to diminish, the Christian Reformed Church's newsletter accused film of being associated with the lower classes of humanity, appealing to corrupt tastes, and giving a "false view of life." Films were deemed culpable for ruining family life, as women neglected duties to children and husbands while they ran off to see movies. Nevertheless, church members frequently voiced positive opinions and did attend movies. Other groups of Presbyterians were likewise cautious, but readily welcomed the 2000 projectors given the denomination by Eastman Kodak in 1920, and sought to make practical use of them in home and foreign missions and Sunday schools. Presbyterians, as will be seen, also experienced enormous growth in their Sunday evening and Sunday school programs by incorporating moving pictures.[23] Episcopalians were frequently involved in promoting elite forms of educational and cultural recreations such as the travelogue shows of E. Burton Holmes, Lyman H. Howe, and others. In the highbrow cultural tradition of the lecture platforms and educational talks of the Chautauqua Institute, Episcopalians, the denomination of Matthew Arnold and the culturally affluent, as one wag put it, would sponsor such privileged high-cultured delights that would educate as much as entertain. In Norfolk, Virginia, Christ and St. Luke's Episcopal Church designed and built its community hall into a film exhibition auditorium in 1919.

Alongside Protestant involvement, scores of large Roman Catholic churches in New York and Boston conducted their own moving picture entertainments as early as 1910, eliciting a pronouncement from the editor of the *Moving Picture World* that such favorable usage demonstrated that "clergymen as a whole are not antagonistic to motion pictures."[24] Robert Molhant's synoptic *Catholics in the Cinema* laid out a short early history of the role of the OCIC, the International Catholic Church Organization for Cinema, illustrating the immense activity within the Roman Catholic Church to appropriate the new technology as an instrument for the apostolate.[25]

Baptists were divided by geography as much as cultural postures. Northern Baptists often paralleled their stubbornly independent cousins, the Congregationalists, in the innovative use of film. Southern Baptists, who would come to radically denounce many amusements, were not as separatist and divisive as one would expect, at least in the first two decades of the twentieth century. In his study of religion, recreation, and masculinity in the rural South at the turn of the century, Ted Ownby expertly pointed out how moviegoing, like the phonograph, was much more salubrious and sanctified than some other macho amusements, from cockfighting to moonshine drinking. As Ownby observed: "Evangelicals had no reason to consider such experiences [of moviegoing] morally objectionable." In fact, they hoped that these early forms of technologically sophisticated entertainments would bring more opportunities for religious messages, such as in the early versions of *The Passion Play* and a film entitled *The Shadow of Nazareth,* noted for its "due reverence for its sacred theme."[26]

Most denominations baptized the use of moving pictures in the first two decades of the twentieth century, with a few of them fully immersing themselves in adapting it to ecclesiastical and pedagogical purposes. These religious bodies correlated faith, learning, and morality with the health of civilization, and showed thoughtful (and optimistic) discernment when it came to the role of the moving picture in promoting such health. Interdenominational differences did occur, especially in regard to religious subjects such as *The Nun,* a film that raised Protestant eyebrows due to its blatantly sectarian nature. However, other more salient theological and social issues demanded the attention of church leaders. In this age of Reform, passionate concerns over blue laws, Sunday shows, and temperance stemmed from both the holiness tradition that shaped many religious bodies and the abuse of alcohol among poorer social classes.

The ascent of Roman Catholics as a numerical and cultural presence corresponded with the waning influence of mainline Protestants. At the turn of the century, the massive immigration of Irish, Italian, and Eastern European people brought a decidedly Roman Catholic flavor to a Protestant-dominated society. Certain religious issues came to the forefront, primarily manifested in a nativist battle for the Lord's Day and the controversy surrounding the Temperance movement. For most of Protestant America at the time, the Lord's Day was intended as a civil institution ordained for public peace, stability, rest, and the recreation of body and soul. To protect the sanctity of the day, its strict Sunday observances were extended to amusements such as the moving picture, unless its shows could be shown to be harmless entertainments that educated or advanced the sacred life of the community. Roman Catholics generally disregarded the Puritan Sabbath of a Protestant society, a holiday that closed all amusements and social activities and even sought to restrain Sunday automobiling and baseball. Such an austere and repressive prohibition ran contrary to the Continental Sabbaths, replete with festivities, drinking, and play, of not only Roman Catholics but of Lutherans and Episcopalians as well. Likewise, the Temperance movement set the continental Roman Catholics, with their hearty appreciation of God's gifts of the vine and grain, against the hegemony of the abstemious American Protestants. Both the Sabbatarian and Temperance movements, born of cultural religious differences, would haunt and shape the early American moving picture industry. Ironically, by the mid-1920s, the moving picture would unite these two disparate groups in common cause, *via negativa*, in protest against the perceived immorality of Hollywood. One could argue that the moving picture was indirectly responsible for significantly promoting religious ecumenical cooperation in the United States for the first time.

Several other theological movements defined this Age of Reform. An overriding concern for the poor and the unenlightened resulted in the optimistic growth of the Social Gospel and the Missionary movements. Into the urban population centers teeming with immigrants arrived the Social Gospel, a movement that augured harmony between the working poor and management. German American Baptist, Walter Rauschenbusch, and Congregational minister, Washington Gladden, sought to bring justice and social equality to many oppressed by misery and poverty and to build a Kingdom of God on earth. Backing the rights and interests of workers, the Social Gospel movement found that sin existed in social institutions such as industrial capitalism, and not just within the individual. The church had a responsibility to practice a social ethic that would redress the needs of the poor and transform society, not merely to preach salvation and advance personal holiness, as Victorian Protestantism had emphasized. Social and political reformers sought to usher in an immanent

Kingdom of God and would use any means possible, even films, to alleviate social problems (from sanitation to prohibition), to educate, and to promote the brotherhood of all men. To minister to the poor, churches acknowledged the need to attract them. Alongside soup kitchens, a prime means of attraction would be the moving picture. Curiously enough, it was General Herbert Booth of the Salvation Army, who not only offered soap, soup, and salvation to slum dwellers, but also inaugurated a fledgling film industry in Australia. His Salvation Army movement of both evangelism and social gospel would be comically, but kindly, represented in numerous silent films, such as Charlie Chaplin's *Easy Street,* Douglas Fairbanks's *Flirting with Fate,* and Harold Lloyd's *Speedy.* Many early films would be directed toward these poor, immigrant urban audiences and would serve to "Americanize" them into the dominant culture. As a central civilizing institution, churches would frequently aid in this cultural and moral enterprise.

Recognizing the explosion of the poor dwelling within the tenements of the large urban centers, YMCA mission work and denominational home mission societies developed to complement foreign missions. Looking at the cramped unhealthy conditions exacerbating social problems, progressive churches equipped themselves with gymnasia, libraries, lecture rooms, social clubs, and religious education facilities. The new architectural church building designs often included the striking feature of motion picture exhibition sites. An ethic of reform was evident in the 1897 publication of popular author Charles M. Sheldon's *In His Steps,* giving added impetus to social gospel. His writings, as well as numerous devotional and theological works costumed in a Western genre, popularized the notion of a practical faith that eventuated in good works. In contrast, by 1925 the Gospel of success according to advertising genius Bruce Barton, *The Man Nobody Knows,* would update Jesus as Rotarian businessman, a go-getter, and a sort of Babbitt on Main Street. Revivalism and camp meetings continued from the nineteenth century, particularly in the South and the Bible Belt. The evangelistic tradition of Dwight L. Moody and others was passed on to more flamboyant revivalists like Billy Sunday and Aimee Semple McPherson, both of whom would extol the potential benefits of the motion pictures.[27]

The Progressive Era emboldened Americans to help their neighbors. Such an altruistic motive resulted in one of the greatest missionary movements of church history. Against an antimissionary complaint of imperialism underlying missionary movements, with missions being accused of foisting not only a Christian God on pagans but of promoting American propaganda, moving pictures also helped to show the need to contribute food and medicine, to build hospitals, and to contribute to the betterment of humanity. For missionaries, moving pictures were worth a thousand words, both on the foreign field and in home churches, where they sought to quicken the conscience of home congregations to contribute money and service to world missions. In 1910, the World Missionary Conference in Edinburgh, along with the YMCA and Student Christian Movement, brought together churches of different faiths to work for this progress. Strong missionary movements circled the globe, with the Student Volunteer Movement seeking to win "the World for Christ in this Generation." At their Centenary in the summer of 1919, the Methodists identified one of the key tactics for evangelism as the global use of film. The missionary impulse was so great that in the inaugural issue of the film trade periodical, the *Nickelodeon,* the editors showcased the increased use of film depicting missionary work.[28]

The new century inspired and bolstered the optimism of Protestants, so much so that a magazine called the *Christian Oracle* changed its name to *Christian Century.* Its editor, George A. Campbell, Jr., believed that the coming a hundred years would unveil the triumph of mainline Protestant Christianity in solving the most pressing problems of society.[29] However, the Progressive Era chronicled a sharp division along two lines of theological emphasis. Fundamentalists and modernists would break openly in the 1920s, with Presbyterian scholar and Princeton professor J. Gresham Machen expressing the essential "fundamentals" of an orthodox faith. The publication of his 1923 *Christianity and Liberalism* attacked the creeping theological modernism and higher criticism of his Presbyterian Church. Film scholars William Uricchio and Roberta Pearson have pointed to the way this deep schism between fundamentalists and liberals effected Vitagraph Studio's filmed story of *The Life of Moses,* as theologians "fervently espoused opposing positions on the 'truth' of the Bible."[30] The nadir of the fundamentalists' image would come in the Scopes "Monkey" Trial in Dayton, Tennessee, in 1925, contributing to a radical break by conservatives with modern cultural trends, such as film. However, by the late 1920s liberal and Roman Catholic churches would join fundamentalists in challenging what they all viewed as the incipient immorality and secularity of the cultural media.

Yet beneath the whirl of ecclesiastical activity, churches still assimilated the new technology of moving pictures. During this Progressive Era, the Protestant Church sought to maintain its authority as the arbiter of morality and taste; however, as it saw the loosening of its grip on the Hollywood industry, it hoped to create its own holy places to show and make suitable films. It aspired to create a Sanctuary Cinema that would reflect its spiritual and moral ideals and enhance its mission to a public slipping away into a mass culture of silent dreams. Whether Pandora's box, Trojan horse, or golden calf, as some feared, the moving pictures invaded sacred realms. What they would prove to be in the early twentieth century was a brazen serpent, a kinetic and iconic set of dramatic narrative practices that churches would embrace and fear, adopt and denounce. By the early 1920s, with several scandals erupting in Hollywood, such as the murder trials of comedian Roscoe "Fatty" Arbuckle, the church began to look more askance at the place of movies within its holy boundaries. With innovations in sound moving pictures, mounting production and exhibition costs, limited film products appropriate for religious settings, and the prospect of a novel medium, radio, ideally suited for preaching, the Church generally abandoned nontheatrical film ministry as outmoded and futile. It would alter its posture vis-à-vis film from creative force to critical judge and lose its place as a viable influence for decades to come.

This volume charts these many levels of interface between American religious communities and their own commercial motion picture industry, seeking to define the impact of film on religious practices and to show how churches assimilated film into their specific missions. The Progressive Era saw the rise and fall of a Sanctuary Cinema movement, a remarkable cultural trend that brought together two modes of re-creation/recreation. Shunted to the margins of mainstream cinema like exploitation, propaganda, documentary, pornography, and art films, nontheatrical religious films embodied different conceptions of the possible function of cinema. Ultimately their conflicts and compromises illustrated a struggle between Christian community and consumer culture/corporate America for the attention of the American middle- and working-class audience. This conflict, however, was not new. It was rooted in historical responses of the church communities to previous means of communication, such as the image and the theater. Ambivalent religious attitudes to both these spheres of representation and communication would shape religious attitudes toward the acceptance, adoption, and rejection of the religious moving picture movement.

1

The Brazen Serpent

Who first seduced them to that foul revolt?
Th' infernal Serpent; he it was, whose guile
Stirred up with envy and revenge, deceived
The mother of mankind . . .

John Milton *Paradise Lost* I, 33–37

Positive church relations with the moving pictures did not spring forth overnight. A history of theological resistance to images and amusements colored the uncertain reception that church leaders gave to the novel invention. Before the early-twentieth-century church embraced the possibilities of motion pictures, biblical and ecclesiastical notions of graven images and brazen serpents shaped its reluctant affections. Moving images were theologically problematic for many adherents of the second commandment. Of particular relevance was a conception of film as a serpent, of a beguiling intruder into a good, moral life. The origins of the Christian film movement point back to this image, both as a caveat against movies and as a vision for them.

As early as 1909, Garnet Warren, a writer for the *New York Herald*, noticed that film had a certain hypnotic effect on members of the nickelodeon audience. He marveled at how the moving pictures had for these persons the "obscure fascination of some serpents."[1] His conception of the silent cinema appearing as a legendary cockatrice whose mesmerizing gaze would stun, daze, and devour its victim proved a curious prophecy. Likewise, the witty George Bernard Shaw described the storytelling power of the cinema, unreeling images to the illiterate as well as to the literate, as rhetorical means to keep its "victim (if you like to call him so) not only awake but fascinated as if by a serpent's eye."[2] Shaw recognized in 1914 that the English mind and ideals, nay, even the entire human conscience, would be shaped by the mesmerizing, serpentine force of cinema.

Ben Hecht, the irreverent screenwriter who mocked Hollywood even as he financially exploited it, confirmed this perception of the cinema in his jaded writings. In a collection of stories entitled *1001 Afternoons,* he offered wry accounts of the doings of the celebrities of the 1920s. He spoofed the ubiquitous publicity ploys of the industry and likened them to the dastardly deed of "selling the celluloid serpent." Rather than viewing film as "ribbons of time" or some other romantic notion, Hecht stripped away the fanciful illusions of the blustering idol-making industry, revealing the dead, empty skin of a dangerously seductive snake and a subsequent huckster marketing of snake oil.[3] The winding, charming, mesmerizing, spell-inducing serpent was indeed an apt metaphor for the hypnotic art of the motion picture. Reflecting in the early 1950s over his participation in such a suspect vocation, Hecht claimed it was a dishonest industry that too facilely solved problems of politics, labor injustice, or domestic conflict with a "simple Christian phrase or a fine American motto."[4]

Others viewed the snake as that most heinous of seducers that slithered into the Garden of Eden seeking to poison all humankind. American dramatist Walter Prichard Eaton contributed an article in the *Freeman* on the "Trail of the Celluloid Serpent," warning of the widening effects of this popular educator in shaping the mores of young audiences.[5] Like the serpent, the moving pictures were condemned for being manipulative and compelling, even winding their way into the safe haven of homes and gardens.

In contrast to this nest of evil snake metaphors, I derive my use of the analogical concept of the brazen serpent from the peculiar biblical narrative in *Numbers* (21:4f) regarding the death of some of the children of Israel in the wilderness. When these people grumbled and complained about the lack of food and water (not only was the food miserable and loathsome, but there wasn't enough of it either), the Lord sent fiery serpents that fatally bit the people. When Moses interceded for them, the Lord, who had previously commanded that His people neither make nor worship any graven image, instructed his servant Moses to make a fiery serpent and set it on a standard so that anyone who looked at it would live. The bronze serpent thus became, for a season, a symbolic vehicle of healing, of rescue, of life. One could pick up serpents and not be hurt, but healed. In what Sir James Frazer called sympathetic magic, a connection existed between serpents and healing that extends back to Aesculapius, the Greek god of healing whose own symbol was a serpent.[6]

This curious narrative provides an appropriate theological backdrop for our study of Christian filmmakers, because, first of all, it stands in stark contrast to the imposing second commandment brought down on a tablet of stone from Mt. Sinai, a law that cemented and quarantined the place of the visual arts, seemingly setting them outside the communal life of God's chosen people. At the very moment when Moses was dutifully engaged in receiving this law amid smoke and thunder on the mountain, Aaron was down on the plain uneasily constructing an idol in the Egyptian form of a calf, gathering the necessary funding for its production, coordinating the various artisans, and celebrating its completion with fitting sacrificial ceremonial rituals.[7] Coming down the mountain to this wild, even orgiastic, gathering of idolaters, Moses brought the Decalogue, which dampened the festivities considerably. Already the first two commandments had been broken, specifically the prohibition against making "a graven image, or any likeness of what is in heaven above or on the earth beneath or in the water under the earth. You shall not worship them or serve them; for I the Lord your God, am a jealous God."[8]

From its reception of this commandment, an inclination to idolatry seemed to plague Israel, an inclination that only increased after they had conquered and settled down amidst the Canaanites, the Philistines, and other pagan nations of ancient Palestine. The specious promises of the cults with their deified idols seduced the Hebrews. Humanly constructed gods rushed in to fill a void of human longing and desire by insinuating a power to satisfy human needs. What the cultic image could do was arouse instincts and trigger emotions that belong to the realm of worship, even though the graven simulacra could never fulfill the desires they stirred.[9] Cults of the nature gods and nude goddesses set upon the high places and beside phallic poles provided adherents with the experience of living in a sort of frenzy of the visible. Baal, at least according to Erasmus, transmogrified into the Babylonian snake god, commanding worship from superstitious and wanton adherents.[10] Shrines to fertility and prosperity frequently connected them to an unbridled, licentious immorality.[11]

The desire for vision was paramount, with adherents of the faith wanting to see and thereby know the power of the gods. One sought to see the heavens by means of the world's materials, an idea that leads to both idolatry and the Incarnation: *invisibilia per visibilia*. The devotion and worship of that which is seen could easily lapse into covetousness and moral decline. What is looked upon and seen commands either worship or want.[12] Female idols like the Asherim aroused idolatry in wayward Hebrews. Film scholar Scott MacDonald equated erotic idolatry with a repressed and spiritual form of adultery; as Jesus admonished, inasmuch as you look upon a woman with lust, you have committed adultery.[13] The phenomenon of idolatry works to seduce faith from its true object to artistic productions, resulting in their gaining power over the viewer. One surrenders, as it were, to the principalities and powers behind a desirable material or sexual graven image. Images become charged with presence, invested with power, brimming with the tease of spurious gratification, so that we find, as David Freedberg astutely put it, that "god is in the image."[14] Freedberg argues for a belief in the efficacy of pictures, whereby both pious and lascivious images call for imitation. Imitation stems from one's perception, contemplation, and then an ascent or descent into the suggestion of the image. He suggests that the fear of idolatry is rooted in (the often repressed) power of images to arouse and provoke.[15] Within a discussion of Nicolas Poussin's painting of *The Dance Round the Golden Calf*, that stands as the *loci classici* of idolatrous image worship, in which the prohibition against graven images is contrasted with the incontrovertible visible evidence of debauched sensuality, Freedberg playfully notes that "the *erection* and invocation of a material image invariably engages the senses." He argues, convincingly, that images *do* have such powers, and while many, especially theologians, seek to repress that idea, pagans are fully aware of the erotic possibilities of the material constructions of their idols.[16]

In sum, Israel's problem with idolatry previews the caution and suspicion of the moving image prevalent in many Christian communities. The opportunities and hazards of the medium of the visual rooted in the brazen serpent would inspire and trouble those who wrestled with it. The question for Christian filmmakers would become, in part, whether they could move beyond the idolatry and voyeurism of pagan graven imagery to develop the potential of the visual as spectator sites for religious truth, spiritual healing, and moral discourse. As we shall see, apologists like St. John of Damascus tried to theologically correct and balance judgments by the Church, arguing that such pagan abuses do not make the "veneration of images loathsome. Blame the pagans who made images into gods! Just because the pagans used them in a foul way—that is no reason to object to our pious practice."[17]

Aesthetic Roots

> To See Is to Believe
> Rev. J. C. Eason[18]

Numerous clergy gathered in the hushed and reverent environs of the Eden Musee on February 15, 1898 to watch a film version of *The Passion Play*. One minister, the Reverend R. F. Putman, was so moved that on his return home, he sat down and immediately wrote a letter to the editor of the *Home Journal* regarding the screen presentation of so holy a story:

> [To] these pictures there can be no objection. One might as well object to the illustrations of Dore and other artists in the large quarto Bibles. Intensely realistic they are, and it is this feature which gives them truthfulness and makes them instructive. Painful they are necessarily to sensitive and sympathetic souls, and so are many of the pictures which surmount some of the altars of our churches. I cannot conceive of a more impressive object lesson for Sunday school scholars.[19]

Connecting the religious moving picture to pious historical religious illustrations extended legitimacy and credibility to the novel medium. Of the many mediated foundations upon which the art of the religious film evolved, two in particular posed unique opportunities, problems, and controversies for the Church. In partial response to scholar Janet Staiger's call for more comparative social histories aiming to uncover marginal influences on film history, and to Steven J. Ross's summons to more fully contemplate audiences and their reception of media, we must focus on the ways in which the advent of the moving picture was understood within the context of previous types of art. By illuminating earlier social and historical contexts we can better understand twentieth-century religious responses to film.[20] The first historical challenge for making sense of religious communication resided in the image/icon as a visible means of communication. As the image would form the ontological basis of cinema, the Church struggled with its immediate impact and spectacle. When the photographic image was taken up in the cinema, audiences came to see realistic images dancing upon a screen and joined a public spectacle of visual attractions. Whether the moving picture as a technological mode of visual communication could, legitimately and effectively, be used by the church depended in part upon the acceptance of the image by the historical church.

The other aesthetic root for Christian filmmakers lay in the institution of the public theater, with its pagan ritual of mimesis. Both Greek and Roman civilization established a central place for their dramatic storytelling artists to explore moral themes and notions of fate, to vivify history and myth, and to mock social conventions and authorities. However, by the time the church spread throughout the Roman Empire, the moral quality of dramatic spectacle had declined precipitously, a fact duly noted by early church patriarchs. Dramaturgical modes of communication were suspect and would have to wait until the Middle Ages to be comfortably assimilated into religious culture. Nevertheless, the theater would provide a model for creative teaching and inspiration that the early-twentieth-century church would find heuristic and practical in its ventures into filmmaking. Examining the reception of the cinema within the context of these two ancient ways—theater and image-icon—of communicating religious messages enables us to escape a temporal entrapment and chronological snobbery, of thinking that all responses are novel and unique.

The Priority and Problem of the Visual

While for many evangelicals and conservative Protestants film flickered against the conscience as a technological form of graven images, this was not the case for Orthodox and Roman Catholic Christians. The latter are marked as the aesthetic descendents of the Greeks, with their celebration of the body/Body; Protestants are more closely aligned to the Hebrew, being a people of the ear (the Word) rather than the eye.[21] Looking at these two sets of religious communities, film scholar Ingrid Shafer drew a helpful continuum between those who critiqued, rejected, and sought to reform culture on the one hand, and those who adopted, embraced, absorbed, and adapted it on the other. Finding both poles of the continuum necessary and valid, she saw the two balancing themes emphasizing the doctrines of the Fall and the depravity of the human, fractured and bent by sin, and of Creation, celebrating the original goodness of life. While not mutually exclusive, the emphases of these aesthetic categories of "Protestant" and "Roman Catholic" still shaped the differing ways in which certain groups of people tended to see reality.

Dr. Robert Hellbeck conceded in 1931 that it was "harder for Protestantism than for other confessions to take up a positive attitude as regards the film because the illustration of the Protestant idea by means of pictures naturally appeared extremely problematical and delicate to a church founded on the 'Word.'"[22] Historian T. J. Jackson Lears described Protestants at the end of the nineteenth century as suspicious and distrustful of Roman Catholic forms of art, even viewing them as forms of pagan pageants with a barbarous sensuality that would "keep the senses captive."[23] Barbara Nicolosi, founding director of Act One, an educational organization for training Christian film writers, noted distinct differences between Roman Catholic and evangelical film screenwriters. She found that Catholic film scripts were strong visually, but that evangelicals believed that it was doctrinal truth expressed in and through words that transformed lives. Nicolosi explained that Catholics were typically cynical about such a verbal approach. Citing the Pope's observation that when "artists have no faith, the only thing they're certain about is the dark side of human nature," she concluded by pointing out the bottom line: "If you want to be a good Catholic filmmaker, you have to be a good Catholic."[24]

More than the Orthodox or Catholic, Protestants have been historically aligned with the Hebrew tendency to focus on *hearing* the Word of the Lord, and have preferred the verbal text as a trustworthy means for artistic expression and communication. Archbishop Trench articulated this contrast when in 1862 he compared Greek and Hebrew forms of art. For the Greek the dominant element was aesthetic, the quest to satisfy a balanced sense of beauty, form, and proportion.[25] The Greek position, expressed succinctly by Horace in his *Ars Poetica,* held that "the mind is more slowly stirred by the ear than by the eye."[26] The appeal to the eye is more immediate and rousing. Whereas words take time to be cognitively processed and sink in, images impact immediately, directly, and tactlessly, assaulting the senses. Different media encourage different ways of thinking. According to media critic Neil Postman, the printed word requires sustained attention, an active imagination, and logical analysis. But the more kinetic visual arts, with fast-moving images, encourage a limited attention span, immediate visceral responses, and mostly disjointed thinking. Thus as he put it, "The God of the Jews was to exist in the Word and through the Word, an unprecedented conception requiring the highest order of abstract thinking." The Hebrew thus insisted on the primacy of language and unwaveringly averred the centrality and necessity of the religious idea being communicated in and through the vehicle of the verbal symbol. Whether its outward appearance found favor and allowance at the bar of aesthetic taste was quite a secondary consideration. In fact, Archbishop Trench suggested that for the Hebrew the aesthetic dimension could be "confidently affirmed not to have been a consideration at all."[27] The Hebrew was cautious about the visual art, although the visual had its sacred place in the worship of God. Even the Tabernacle, however, in all its abstract glory, giant cherubim, and symbolic splendor, is overshadowed by Hebrew poetry, histories, laws, prophecies, love songs, proverbs, and theological ruminations. And the Hebrew "seers" would usually announce: "Thus saith the Lord," or, in other words, "Hear this!" not "Watch this!"

Visual spectacle was a central concern for the theological and ironic journalist Soren Kierkegaard, the Protestant Woody Allen of nineteenth-century Denmark, who italicized tensions within a hierarchy of aesthetic, ethical, and religious modes of discourse. For Kierkegaard, ambivalence toward the aesthetic experience was rooted in its tendency to promote a disinterested appreciation toward an object, even if that object/subject were divine. Kierkegaard illustrated this thought in a discussion about showing a child a sequence of pictures: first one of noble men on horses, then of William Tell shooting an apple, and then climactically, an illustration of the crucifixion. The child could not enjoy the execution of the good and loving Man, because the facts of the picture demand a religious choice rather than aesthetic distance. In contrast, those who beheld the picture from an aesthetic perspective ("whether it is a success, whether it is a masterpiece, whether the play of colors is right, and the shadows, whether blood looks like that, whether the suffering expression is artistically true") would act as a gaggle of distant admirers rather than as passionate disciples.

For Marxist Walter Benjamin, the camera's technological reproduction of art dispelled its "aura," leveling and eviscerating beauty.[28] Although believing in the revolutionary potential of photography, Benjamin found that the pitiless eye of the camera, like capitalism itself, stripped the "halo" from every occupation.[29] The heritage of these foregoing religious conflicts with the visual—both ancient and modern—creates an inescapable tension for Christian filmmakers; that each must come to grips with the nature and functions of the image, potentially stripping the holy from their art. This friction calls into question the entire visual basis of the craft of filmmaking, and finds its theological argument from church history. Reformers Ulrich Zwingli and John Calvin, for example, disputed the range of religious uses to which the image could be put; their arguments led some adherents into a destructive and rabid iconoclasm.[30]

Various scholars have taken up the task of reconsidering the neglected significance and relevance of the Second Commandment as it bears upon our image-saturated society. Lionel Kochan approaches the Second Commandment seriously and with utmost reverence in his *Beyond the Graven Image: A Jewish View*.[31] Exploring the biblical prohibition against the use of images as a means of worship, Kochan probes the theological perception of the Jews as a people of the ear rather than of the eye, and, simultaneously, as a people historically tempted to make and worship false idols. Through its appeal to the eye, the graven image attracted worshipers and endowed false gods with a spurious power and presence, provoking the wrath and jealousy of God. It solidified and entombed the seemingly transcendent.[32] What is physically constructed and embodied can be dangerously confused with what it signifies, becoming idolatrous. One is grateful in this context for such satirists of dumb idols as prophets like Isaiah who openly mocked their futility.

The deluded conception that stone, wood, and other brute matter are dynamic and symbolic of the divine still is, for Jewish scholar Kochan, "the greatest conceivable error of which man is capable." This is the delusion against which the prophets railed. Along with the self-inflicted deception that images can mediate between man and the holy, this is the danger to which the eye exposes the worshiper. The artifact conceals the reality that it purports to reveal. As a result, for some critics like M. Darrol Bryant, churches exhibit an uneasy mind concerning movies because movies are competitors; they offer rival forms of "popular religion deeply rooted in the spiritual aspirations of technological civilization."[33] Movies, as a latent form of idolatry, have the potential to seduce even the faithful away from the faith and into the temporal and material realms.

Thus, as we have seen, the Hebrew prophets repudiated idolatry as a form of rebellion, in that the idol was fashioned by humans as a repository and agent for human hopes, desires, and fantasies. For Kochan, this constitutes no more than a form of self-worship. God, on the other hand, addresses His people in direct, personal ways, eschewing plastic, symbolic mediation of all kinds, including sphinxes, sacred groves, Asherim, and the like. The ideal was, and is, direct oral communication between God and His creatures. Standing in contrast to material images, monuments, and mummies is the Mouth Who speaks to the ears. His servants, like Jeremiah and other prophets, mostly introduced their material as oracles or heard prophecies.[34]

Jacques Ellul and others have pointed out the affinities between the failure to maintain that hierarchy of the ear over the eye and the new demons of visual technology.[35] Following the insights of Marshall McLuhan on the pervasive presence of media technology and its tendencies to supplant ideas, Mitchell Stephens warns that technology will elevate the image with a corresponding fall of the word.[36] Cultural critic Richard Stivers unveils the potentially darker regions of technology by suggesting that contemporary film and television are extensions of ancient pagan festivals of sex and violence, inducing an orgiastic postmodern culture in which one participates daily rather than during intermittent festivals. The present temptation is to cultivate habits of sexual and spiritual masturbation, to separate sex from relationship and the spirit from community, and to dwell in the realm of the erotic simulacra.[37]

A further criticism of the visual is grounded in the prohibition of the second commandment against images that are sculpted, engraved, or impressed upon surfaces. In engraving work, the engraver was one who would carve, construct, or indelibly impress images onto the surfaces of concrete materials, similar to a filmmaker recording nature upon silver nitrate film stock. Each image pointed to a spiritual power or principality, and spirits, gods, and demons haunt the images, even if it is only the god of human piety and pride in the Temple of Vesta or in the "godlike spirit of Man" in H. G. Wells.[38] It is often the artist who perceives this supernatural dimension. In "Der Uberfall," a short story by Manford Hausman, a young religious artist has a radical experience of God and then experiences a crisis of faith, questioning whether he, a dealer in the illusory, can really be a servant of God. This spiritual quandary has pierced the consciences of religious artists throughout history, with a tradition of suspicion that today challenges and rejects visual arts such as the theater and image making. Since cinema itself was fertilized in the ground of these two imaginative visual modes of communication, it behooves us to consider their historical status among various church leaders.

The Iconoclastic Controversy

As we have seen, the suspect nature and ambiguous effects of the graven image suggested spiritual danger. The notion of the idolatry of images lay at the heart of one of the most significant crises in church history, the iconoclastic controversy of the eighth century. Around 730 A.D., iconoclasts appeared to rid the holy church of graven images. Emperor Leo III, the Isaurian, demanded that all Roman subjects swear a hatred of images and an acceptance of iconoclasm. He was followed by his son, Constantine V, who also condemned pictures because they allegedly drew "down the spirit of man from the lofty adoration of God to the low and material adoration of the creature."[39] A virulent and fanatic response occurred with bands of image-breakers smashing holy images wherever they could find them. By the eighth and ninth centuries, this wave of iconoclasm had spread out over the Byzantine Empire.[40]

Pope Gregory III finally excommunicated the Iconoclasts and pronounced that the image was a vital means of communication for the church, writing that: "Pictures are for the illiterates what letters are for those who can read." The vital distinction made by the Seventh Ecumenical Council ultimately hung on the difference between honoring and worshiping icons.[41] The scandal of the visible was resolved at the Council of Nicaea in 787 that decreed that pictures, the cross, and the Gospels should be given their due salutation and honorable reverence, but not the true worship which pertains alone to God. From the eleventh through twelfth centuries, Pope Gregory's articulation of a comprehensive apologetic for holy aesthetics, namely, that painting can teach as well as illustrate religious ideas, diffused throughout Europe. As art historian E. H. Gombrich pointed out, "Images lived on in the minds of the people even more powerfully than did the words of the preacher's sermon."[42] In the thirteenth century, Saint Bonaventura carried on the legacy of Pope Gregory and the Council and summarized the pontiff's defense of using images in churches. He offered three reasons for the indispensable worth of images:

1. They were made for the simplicity of the ignorant, so that the uneducated who are unable to read scripture can, through statues and paintings of this kind, read about the sacraments of our faith in, as it were, more open Scriptures.
2. They were introduced because of the sluggishness of the affections, so that men who are not aroused to devotion when they hear with the ear about those things which Christ has done for us will at the least be inspired when they see the same things in figures and pictures, present, as it were, to their bodily eyes. For our emotion is aroused more by what is seen than by what is heard.

3. They were introduced on account of the transitory nature of memory, because those things which are only heard fall into oblivion more easily than those things which are seen.[43]

This triad of functions served as cures for human weaknesses: for ignorance, sloth, and forgetfulness.[44] Images in the churches were the *libri idiotarum,* the books of the illiterate, a truth repeatedly emphasized by Pope Gregory III: "We do no harm in wishing to show the invisible by means of the visible."[45]

From this point on, the doctrines of the church and the ideas of the transcendent were increasingly conveyed through images: through panel paintings, illuminations, calendar manuscripts, brass fonts, and even candlesticks. An apologetic for religious imagery slowly but surely developed within the Roman Catholic tradition. This was not the case, however, for the reformers who split from the church in the early sixteenth century. In 1523, the admission of graven images into the ecclesiastical culture of the Roman Catholic Church proved to be a momentous and incendiary event that riled and radicalized several sects of the Reformation. The growing ferocity against images would be unparalleled and it was perhaps this moment in Zurich, Switzerland, that irreparably damaged potentially beneficial relations between the Protestant Church and visual artists. Contentious factions led by Huldrych Zwingli rose up in Zurich protesting the artistic tendencies of the Roman Catholic Church, particularly as they contributed to what Zwingli saw as the constitution of cults that worshiped and venerated saints as means of grace. According to Zwingli, any practice or thing not mentioned in the scriptures should be anathema to the truly reformed church.

Unrestrained zeal and severity soon marked the actions of Zwingli's disciples, who destroyed all images of the Virgin Mary and many statues and images of the saints. By June 15, 1524 the Council of Zurich issued an official decree calling for the abolition of all images from its churches, and, in swift succession, murals were scraped off walls, statues broken up, altars stripped of vessels, crucifixes eliminated, and walls whitewashed. Zwingli exclaimed triumphantly: "In Zurich we have churches which are positively luminous; the walls are beautifully white!"[46] The unity of art and the church, which for centuries had been a vibrant source of higher culture, was now shattered. Protestants would bear the burden of a suspicious relationship to images throughout the next centuries. Ironically, a statue of Zwingli was dedicated in Zurich in 1885.

Their ardent pursuit of holiness stirred the fanatic followers of Swiss reformer Ulrich Zwingli to whitewash chapels and destroy all statuary and religious images. Courtesy Don Monteaux.

To a certain extent, the theological ideas of his predecessors redressed and tempered some of Zwingli's iconoclasm.[47] John Calvin's 1543 manifesto, *The Necessity of Reforming the Church*, scorned certain justifications for the use of images (i.e., that they are the books of the uneducated), and he reminded his followers that "Man's nature is a perpetual factory of idols."[48] However, the founder of Presbyterians did argue for the place and value of beauty, particularly that of nature, as a gift bestowed by God. Calvin herein set forth a principle that shaped Protestant art for centuries, when he wrote that only those things which the eyes are capable of seeing, such as landscapes, farms, windmills, portraits, and historical scenes are to be sculpted, painted, or represented in material form.[49]

John Eck and Martin Luther took more reasoned views and sought to stop iconoclastic vandalism. Eck responded to the extremists' objection that such cultic art "not only seduces simple laity into idolatry but sometimes stimulates them to erotic fantasies" by distinguishing between such lascivious subjects and more sacred ones. Reform historian David Steinmetz observed that for Eck images were "licit due to being sensible signs pointing to transcendental reality."[50] Luther's pamphlet "Against the

Heavenly Prophets in the Matter of Images and Sacraments" explained that the scriptures forbade the worship of images, rather than the mere making of them.[51] His principles inspired and influenced such grand Lutheran artists as Lucas Cranach and Albrecht Durer. One must remember that for the sixteenth-century church, relics and paintings were spiritual and devotional, rather than aesthetic, artifacts. For monks like Martin Luther, the popular and vernacular culture supported the liturgy and work of the church that functioned as a social and educational center as well as theater and picture gallery.[52] These two churchmen sought to find a strategy of moderation, neither abolishing nor venerating images but holding them in that delicate balance where they could be temperately appreciated and used.

As Gutenberg printed more Bibles and printed translations of the Holy Writ became more readily available, the word waxed as the suspect image waned, at least for Protestants. The Puritan distrust of the artifice of visual imagery was to linger for centuries, but at least the chains of iconoclasm had been loosened. The stage was set for an embrace by both Protestants and Roman Catholics of the educational and sacred moving images of the screen.

Church and Theater

Nineteenth-century Congregationalist minister Henry Ward Beecher attacked those Christians who attended the theater, telling one popular tale of a Christian boy attending the theater who was kidnapped by the devil. A holy monk reproached the devil for stealing the lad, to which the wicked one promptly replied: "I found him on my premises, and took him."[53] Beecher vividly portrayed the consequences of sin, spreading from the theater, seeing the social impact of the depravity of human nature upon his contemporary society. "Upon the outskirts of towns are shattered houses, abandoned by reputable persons. They are not empty, because all day silent; thieves, vagabonds, and villains haunt them, in joint possession with rats, bats, and vermin."[54]

The troubled relations between the Christian faith and theater began primarily with the Greek and Roman forms of the drama. The young church of the first century viewed the underlying influence of Dionysus as a dangerous diversion from a serious call to religious life. In his *De Spectaculis*, African church father Tertullian (155–225), condemned the theater as a house of idolatry and denounced its actors as creatures of the Devil.[55] The church father was convinced that the theater stirred up filth leading to sin in several ways: first, its lewd spectacles had originated in the worship of idols and consequently their stage, the amphitheater, served a temple of false gods and demons. Second, Christian morality was undermined by the violent passions of anger, grief, and frenzy that the pagan theater aroused: comic and satyr performances were like drippings of honey from poisoned cakes and spectacles like wrestling confirmed the "devil's own trade. . . . Its very movements are the snake's, the grip that holds, the twist that binds, the suppleness that eludes."[56] Thus for Tertullian the entertaining snake, with all its brazen charms, was the devil's own killer.[57]

The artificial emotions induced by the theater likewise spurred St. Augustine to repent of reading Virgil's tragic narrative of Dido and Aeneas—poetry whose literary pathos moved him to tears even when his own sins did not. He regretted wasting his youth in carnality and sensuality, visiting gladiator and circus games of violence, indulging in fortune telling, pornography, luxury, and violence, and finally, "enjoying" stage plays that provoked a miserable madness. (And to top off these idle sins of youth, he also confessed to neglecting his studies.)

A generation later, Cyprian of Carthage studied the works of Tertullian and also castigated the shameless corruption of the stage. What amazed Cyprian about the comedic parodies of his day was that, while no individual or profession was spared by the "discourse of these reprobates," everyone flocked to their plays. The multitude had easily learned to delight in their obscene pleasures that flaunted moral laws. Watching the mob collect around the performers, Cyprian complained about the actresses and the rise of celebrity worship. He found the obscenity of mere prostitutes surpassed by the public sensation of actresses' performances: "Nevertheless, those women whom their misfortune has introduced and degraded to this slavery, conceal their public wantonness, and find consolation for their disgrace in their concealment. Even they who have sold their modesty blush to appear to have done so." For this infamy he blamed a further wickedness in which an actor assumed the effeminacy of a woman, with limbs made limp so that he was neither man nor woman. The whole city was in a state of excited commotion over him and his "fabulous debaucheries."[58] The question for faithful Christians like Cyprian concerned the effects of such representations, particularly those of simulated lust. Cyprian feared that in the presence of such acting, audience members learned to lay aside their modesty and become more daring and licentious. A spectator learned to do what "he is becoming accustomed to see. . . . A method is sought to commit adultery with the eyes . . . whatever is not lawful is so beloved that what had even been lost sight of by the lapse of time is brought back again into the recollection of the eyes."[59]

A similar perspective on the enduring power of the images generated by the theater's less salubrious moments was captured by the "golden mouthed" preacher of the fourth century, St. John Chrysostom. As a youth he had plunged into the whirlpool of the world, which mainly meant the bawdy Roman theaters. When he visited one, he was struck by the visual impact of the performance on his memory. Seeking to reform the church, he had already exhorted people to eschew the great public sins of gambling, horse racing, and an indulgent use of wealth. He had questioned the value of pagan culture, seeing it as built on the sands of vanity and materialism. Now, however, he also warned of the consequences of certain theatrical images. Primarily he warned his congregation that when one saw a shameless woman in the theater, one who walked the stage

> with uncovered head and bold attitudes, dressed in garments adorned with gold, flaunting her soft sensuality, singing immoral songs, throwing her limbs about in the dance, and making shameless speeches, do you still dare to say that nothing human happens to you then? Long after the theater is closed and everyone is gone away, those images still float before your soul, their words, their conduct, their glances, their walk, their positions, their excitation, their unchaste limbs—and as for you, you go home covered with a thousand wounds! But not alone—the whore goes with you—although not openly and visibly . . . but in your heart, and in your conscience, and there within you she kindles the Babylonian furnace . . . in which the peace of your home, the purity of your heart, the happiness of your marriage will be burnt up![60]

For Chrysostom, conversing about theaters inflames the soul, whereas "he who converses about hell incurs no dangers, and renders [the soul] more sober." This is because, unlike the theater, hell "offers a wholesome theme for meditation."[61] In his sermon cited above and in his other famous excoriations of the theaters of the cosmopolitan Antioch, Chrysostom repudiated not only the theatrical arts but the rhetorical ones as well, as mere public spectacles without eternal merit.[62] By the end of his era, as Christianity became the official religion of Constantinople, pagan festivals and temples were closed, and the theater was forbidden on Sundays.[63]

Lactantius, tutor to Emperor Constantine's son Crispus, and another disciple of Tertullian, also challenged the encroachment of the stage on the pastimes of the Christian. Of chief concern were the young people who viewed the immodest gestures and dances of the imitative spectacles, because such youth were especially susceptible students of this school of lust. Rather than having their passions curbed and governed, they were being trained by these graphic representations to imitate vices and sin.[64]

By contrast, the Alexandrian School of Clement of the third century did not exhibit the radical distrust of culture exhibited by Tertullian and his disciples. Philosophy and the works of the heathen could be "handmaids" to Christianity. "Perhaps," mused Clement, "philosophy was given to the Greeks directly and primarily, till the Lord should call the Greeks. For this was a schoolmaster to bring the Hellenic mind, as the law to the Hebrews, to Christ."[65] Yet he too was suspicious of drama, particularly for its idolatry, its idle extravagance, and its lusts. "Art," he warned, "has another illusion with which to beguile; for it leads you on, though not to be in love with the statues and paintings, yet to honor and worship them."[66] Certain lifelike images and the drama could be praised, but not if it beguiled spectators by pretending to be the truth. Otherwise, it wasted time and money, was marked by disorder, and led to shameless performances and iniquity.

The antipathy between Christianity and the theater was reflected in the pronouncements of early church councils that forbade performers from sharing the sacraments or belonging to the community of faith, threatened to excommunicate Christians who attended the theater on holy days (an indication that a significant segment did just that), and raised barriers against the theater. The Council of Arles (314 A.D.) excommunicated church members who became stage actors or strolling players; the Council of Carthage forbade churchmen from being involved in the theater; a Council of Africa denounced plays on sacred days; and the Council of Rome (679) warned the English clergy not to permit revels or plays.[67] So, too, the Canons of *Concilum Trullanum* in 692 issued an edict against the theater as well as against bear and bull baiting, satyric masks, and mimes that regularly mocked Christian sacraments with obscene gestures. By 813, it had been widely established not only that actors should be banned from church membership but that clergy were also forbidden from attending secular theaters. Actors, who were mostly migratory entertainers at that time, were viewed as the devil's companions. The sophomoric reputations of the Goliards, traveling vagabonds more given to wine, women, and song (drugs, sex, and rock and roll), than to repentance, piety, and prayer aggravated the actor's expulsion to the fringes of the religious community. They earned this marginal status because they so frequently slipped from comedic modes of ridicule and mime into more indecent and irreverent performances.[68]

While short dramatic pieces called *tropes* entered the liturgy before 1000, a significant transformation of the theater from its earlier ribald and rowdy days of Greek and Roman excesses occurred in the twelfth century, nurtured by the visionary activist and Benedictine abbess, Hildegaard von Bingen.[69] In her convent of nuns she baptized the drama through her liturgical play, *Ordo Virtutum,* a musical medieval drama that situated the Soul as a character torn between a desire for holiness and the temptations of worldly pleasures, symbolized by the devil. The moral ritual follows her fall into misery and damnation through the prodigal's return to the shining beauty of God's virtues. Her innovative spectacle taught both theology and morality, vivifying the doctrines of the church for an illiterate people. In 1215, Pope Innocent III at the fourth Lateran Council, emphasizing the authority of the leadership of the clergy over all social institutions, stressed education for these same members, seeking to reach them through the pictorial and oral arts. One specific mission was to spread the stories of the scripture and the church through novel approaches in order to attract uneducated and superstitious audiences.

Another significant sign of a thaw in the church's attitude toward the theater appeared in the Middle Ages with the emergence of narrative enactments of Bible stories. These peripatetic presentations legitimized the medium and mode by their content—they told of recognizable biblical characters. Their popular religion popped up in literature and drama. By the fourteenth century Geoffrey Chaucer combined colorful tales of adultery and flatulence with orthodox morality: his motley band of pilgrims told these stories to one another as they rode to Canterbury Cathedral to seek forgiveness for their sins.[70] Pope Innocent III even permitted plays to be performed outside the church buildings, causing fairgrounds and town market centers to become open-air secular theaters. An ensuing golden era of church drama occurred from about 1350 to 1575, with local clerics and middle-class craftsmen producing their own cycles of religious drama. These vernacular plays were performed in large public squares: the York mystery cycles drafted hundreds of people to act in forty-eight short plays about the main events in the history of salvation. These biblical stories enacted by amateurs could stage and communicate the lessons of the Church in compelling ways.

Easter week reenactments and processions celebrated the Paschal Mystery and illustrated the doctrines for the masses, just as the mystery (or craft association), miracle, and morality plays dramatized the dogma and stories of the scriptures, often calling forth enthusiastic if rowdy participants, particularly with the comic tales of Noah and his shrewish wife. The mystery plays focused on the biblical themes of Creation and the life, death, and resurrection of Jesus Christ; the miracle plays honored the lives of martyrs and saints; and morality plays, the most irrepressible and full of broad, burlesque comedy, explored the seven deadly sins, with struggles for the human soul. In this last genre, the Devil often appeared as comic relief with his buffoon companion, Vice.[71] These plays were replete with nagging wives and lazy fools, straight out of the Book of Proverbs. Religion, recreation, and commerce converged in these dramas where worship, sermons, and moral instruction were mingled with art and some playfulness.

Performed by various guilds, the great Cycle plays told the story of God's ways with humanity from the Creation to Judgment Day and effectively translated the Latin Mass into the vernacular. Each guild owned its own tenuously appropriate biblical story at that time, with bakers retelling the sacred narrative of the Last Supper, winemakers reenacting the wedding at Cana, goldsmiths portraying the adoration of the Magi, and butchers enacting the crucifixion (with their ready access to blood for special effects). The trade guilds would join in building pageant wagons. Thus, in order to teach her parishioners the stories and themes of the Bible, the church was midwife to the rebirth and cleansing of the drama, appropriating its attractions to teach and to indoctrinate. Many early films followed these patterns set down by historical church drama, especially from the later morality plays. Silent film producer Paul Bern explained during a lecture at the University of Southern California on March 6, 1929 that "various photoplay characters, so that they might be easily understood by the simple audiences which saw them, were named Envy, Sin, Lust, Weakness, Love (something like some of the pictures of today)."[72]

Up to the late sixteenth century, the bishops of the Reformed English Church had little to say against the theater.[73] With the emergence of the Jacobean and Caroline theater, grappling with moral and religious issues was trumped in favor of exploitative plays, full of sensationalism, pathos, and titillation, as in the works of John Webster, John Ford, Frances Beaumont, and John Fletcher. Such shocking new styles had political repercussions, especially for the Protestant governing authorities. While the onset of the plague had temporarily closed the English theaters in 1636, the overwhelmingly Puritan Parliament followed suit and suppressed all stage plays in 1642. As they perceived English drama as the acme of all evil, another round of antitheatrical polemics poured from pens and pulpits, condemning theater going as smelling of brimstone.[74] After the Restoration, certain abuses of the theater's tentative new freedoms elicited some justifiable protest and calls for reform. The popular bawdy comedies of *l'amour*, with their naughty winking and nudging about adultery, overstepped the bounds of tolerance for Anglican clerics.[75] Fifty years later, William Law's 1726 publication of *The Absolute Unlawfulness of the Stage-Entertainment Fully Demonstrated* followed up on these arguments with reasonable but rigorously ascetic arguments. Mostly, Law believed that because the theater represented the world, it was necessarily worldly. And as worldliness was clearly anti-Christian, the theater was anti-Christian.[76] However, others in the seventeenth and eighteenth centuries, like Jansenist Blaise Pascal, advised temperate wisdom and caution, and gradually opposition abated.[77] There did emerge, in fact, a Jesuit theater of the Renaissance that provided a strong didactic purpose, namely to inform and to edify the congregations with lessons of doctrine, faith, and conduct.[78]

A credible defense of theater came from John Dennis, who struck an antiascetic pose, insisting on the usefulness of public diversions and the goodness of pleasure for the Christian life. Dennis wrote that: "Even St. Chrysostom read Aristophanes, and St. Paul read Epimenides and Menander."[79] In the early twentieth century, the argument that the pleasures of art could be salubrious for body and soul would ultimately prevail in the church. In his classic work on *Art and Scholasticism,* Jacques Maritain observed: "No man can live without pleasure. Therefore, a man deprived of the pleasures of the spirit goes over to the pleasures of the flesh."[80] However, for many the inspiration of the spirit was aligned with higher culture and art: the emphasis upon the body and the bawdy, the low culture, had fully surrendered to the flesh.

By the mid-1920s, a debate pitting high and low culture against one another would extend to the movies, complicating the issue for many church leaders. The sacred was aligned with the more sophisticated fine arts. Religious educator Augustine H. Smith situated drama, "the fourth of the fine arts," and dance within the church tradition of the Agape feasts and also, curiously enough, among "the flagellants and carolers in their combined song and action during the pre-Reformation days."[81] For Smith, high art, rather than comic productions, would save humanity. Serious drama could effectively convey religious truth.

Early in the century in which film grew to be the great popular art form, it was generally granted that dramatic art could be a signpost to the pleasures of the spirit, pointing toward a contemplation of eternal things. Thus, certain works of stage and cinema could also be considered good because they led to spiritual pleasure and/or rest and relaxation.[82] Religious defenders of the moving picture, however, did seek to separate the wheat and the chaff of drama, keeping film free from the taint of its theatrical roots. Where the popular stage was viewed as deleterious to public morals, moving pictures had a countering salubrious effect. In an effort to distance film from theater, Charles Johnson Post, editor of the *Christian Herald,* used a revisionist history to explain the origins of the former. Post located the origins of cinematic storytelling in the Bible and religious books, followed by the chronicling of events in newspapers, and finally in entertainment. While the motion picture came first as a news service, recording the "boardwalk at Atlantic City on Easter, the Durbar in India, the Spanish War, and various other news events," it rapidly became "identified with the theaters in which it was exhibited." Unfortunately, argued Post, the church ignored its value, and coupled "up their denunciation of the theater with the denunciation of the motion picture as another device of the Evil One."

> So there has been a double hostility that confronted those who realize the tremendous importance of the motion picture in all kinds of propaganda and idea-stimulating fields—the vague hostility of some church elements to anything new or savoring of theatricalism so that they let a great opportunity slip from them, and on the other hand, the eager, swinish commercialism of a tawdry-minded theatrical mushroom who "knew just what the public wants."[83]

For many church leaders, the popular stage would continue to reek of sensationalism, immorality, and the evil of modernity, as in the plays of

Ibsen. Ironically, it would provide a plumb line against which the moving picture in the early twentieth century would look virtuous. As moving pictures grew out of the legitimate theater in the first decades of the twentieth century, many religious leaders like the itinerant evangelist Billy Sunday would continue to condemn the latter, but bless the former. The kinetic visual fruit of the screen was more acceptable to the church than was its ancient root, the stage.

As we have seen, underlying the Christian film industry is an ambivalent, even schizophrenic, relation of faith to art and culture. We have traced the trajectories of Roman Catholic and Protestant perspectives on two of the most salient factors underlying an understanding of Christian responses to film, namely, the narrative drama of the theater and the aesthetics of the image. As we will see, the church's posture toward moving pictures in the early twentieth century corresponded to the historical church's positions on these two facets of the art of film itself. It is upon these foundations that we will now explore the immediate artistic precursors that contributed to the craft of Christian filmmaking in the silent American film era.

Cultural Precursors

> *The Church*
> *In which I had grown up, abominated*
> *The pleasures of the senses, abhorred pictures,*
> *Honouring but the incorporeal word.*
> Johann Christoph Friedrich von Schiller

In 1735 William Hogarth sketched a host of quirky caricatures in his *The Rake's Progress* as instructive moral pictures. The series depicted the downward moral trajectory of a young heir taking possession of his inheritance, being surrounded by artists and sycophants, wasting money in taverns and gaming houses, and ending up in prison and a madhouse. By way of *via negativa,* this illustrative tale communicated its sermon very convincingly. Other dramatic parables and moral instructions were drawn from sermons and translated into visual lessons. In William Sidney Mount's *The Card Players,* two gamblers, with a jug between them, enjoy the dubious pleasures of gambling and dissipation in a grungy setting. Yet, as art commentator John Kasson points out, Mount's illustrated sermon, full of its own comedy and irony, suggests that religious exhortations were insufficient bulwarks against such temptations, as among the debris where the two players are sitting is a crumpled page that reads: "Sermons by Rev. L. D.," the preaching discarded in favor of cards and idleness. Nevertheless, the picture communicated moral instruction, expressing its wisdom in a visual vernacular that the common man and woman could see, and possibly, but rarely, heed.

The Victorian artistic tradition showed the negative consequences of wayward behavior. In 1857, Queen Victoria had, quite ostentatiously and intentionally, hung the painting *The Two Ways of Life* in Prince Albert's study as an "Allegory on Dissipation, Repentance and Industry." Film scholar Ronald Holloway describes this visual sermon as a lascivious portrait in which a bevy of seminaked girls lounge in erotic poses on one side of the picture, "while a Madonna sheltering a half-dressed convert to religion is in the middle, and people busily engaged in various trades take up the other side." The contrast summoned up earlier visual juxtapositions of heaven and hell in the paintings of a Bosch or Cranach.[84] Art simultaneously entertained and instructed. By the end of the century, such "stories in paintings" easily became models for "sermons-in-motion." One exemplary parallel is found in *femme fatale* actress Theda Bara's 1918 film, *The Forbidden Love;* it is a clear extension of Ford Maddox Brown's earlier painting, "Take Your Son, Sir," showing what happens when a boy is led astray. While a wholesome film actress like Mary Pickford would model the conservative (but spunky) mores of respectable Victorian society, Theda Bara's films would show the moral consequences of an immoral life. Holloway compared the representations of the two actresses as the lamb versus the spider, or as "puppies, kittens and bunnies versus skulls, snakes and skeletons."[85]

A variety of popular art forms inspired, educated, and entertained religious audiences up to the late nineteenth century and served as precursors of a nontheatrical religious film movement. Such diverse practices as landscape painting and the stereopticon provided audiences with experiences that would prepare them for a sanctuary cinema.

Landscape Painting and Visual Sermons

Within the Victorian moral milieu but with a more transcendent vision of God, a nineteenth-century group of artists known as the Hudson River School found an almost divine vocation in continuing the tradition of religious murals and moral paintings. Hudson River artists such as Jasper Cropsey, Asher B. Durand, Frederic E. Church, and Thomas Cole contributed a strong sense of Christian symbolism and romantic allegory within exquisite landscape paintings.[86] Both the moral caricaturists and these painters were cultural precursors of the Christian filmmakers of the next century, planting Christian symbols and icons that pointed to heaven in crowning vistas of wilderness and gardens. These realms of static art were also linked with early moving pictures through narrative patterns of sequencing, of scenes connected to tell a story. Silent religious films would flow out of this vigorous tradition of moral and religious art, especially as the Hudson painters contributed to Protestant moving panoramas that invited spectators into a narrative world of space and time and visual preaching.[87]

These Knights of the Brush, as art critic James F. Cooper has called the Hudson River School, sought to recapture in their art what the painter Thomas Cole humbly saw as the creative and aesthetic power of the Almighty.[88] Cole's expansive painting, *The Voyage of Life,* followed man through his natural environment to reflect his view of life from childhood through youth and manhood to old age and hushed the spectator with its aesthetic piety and moral lessons.[89] Like brilliantly hued icons, Cole's paintings pointed to another world's beauty, a world of holiness. Viewers would gaze at the sacredness of the land, its beauty, and its promise intimately connected with America's covenant with God.[90] For these artists, paintings of geographical and botanical beauty pointed back to Beauty's maker like golden echoes. For a painter like Jasper Cropsey, "the voice of God came to me through every motionless leaf . . . on every blade of grass . . . in every breath of air . . . in all these things I could see the beauties of holiness and the greatness of the Lord."[91] His exquisite paintings whisper that the heavens declared the glory of God and the earth uttered His words—they were sermons from the psalms of nature.

What has been called the quintessential painting of the Hudson River School, Cropsey's *Autumn on the Hudson River* (1860), articulates two sermons, one that celebrated God's glorious blessings upon the landscape of America and one that poignantly lamented the coming loss of this Eden. In the most important American art journal in its day, the *Crayon* (one that frequently explored the nexus of art and religion), Cropsey wrote of nature pointing to transcendence: "Of all the gifts of the Creator . . . few are more beautiful, and less heeded than the sky [which] encircles us like a halo from above."[92] Pointing to God in clear, unequivocal

Protestant style, Cropsey and Frederic Church in 1850 contributed to a novel exhibition of *Bunyan's Pilgrim's Progress,* a series of moving panoramic landscape paintings.[93] Like Cole's earlier allegorical painting of *The Voyage of Life,* time was added to space, when sixty scenes (about thirty feet wide each) from John Bunyan's popular Puritan allegory unrolled as a pilgrimage through "strange, unearthly, and wondrous" landscapes from the Slough of Despond up to the beautiful Land of Beulah and the gates of the Celestial City. The sequence allowed for continuous viewing as a spectacular travelogue, often with appropriate music accompanying the presentation as well as "impromptu sermons" from clergymen like the Reverend Henry Ward Beecher as the painting "rolled."[94] Such a visual narrative panorama formed a link from the visual narratives of the medieval tapestries to the early stories of silent film, not much different from what an early storyboard of a photoplay version of *Pilgrim's Progress* would have looked like. Such representation forms anticipated cinema, providing striking antecedents of aesthetic and operational norms, with one critic accusing the chronologically ambitious and kinetic series of tableaux of trespassing the limitations of its art, as it "ostensibly strove for the illusion of spatial and temporal transitions."[95] The *Moving Panorama of Bunyan's Pilgrim's Progress* was even reproduced in a "revised edition," a precursor to numerous remakes that Hollywood would imitate. In fact, the Hochstetter-Pierson Company released the silent film version of *Pilgrim's Progress or the Life of John Bunyan* in 1912, frequently presenting it with a stirring lecture.

The artists of the Hudson River School emphasized the transcendent, sublime images of God's glory, hidden in creation, planting seeds for the faithful to enjoy the visual gardens of God's handiwork, even if at second hand. Underlying the school was an aesthetic tradition of Protestant Christianity that began with Jonathan Edwards and Horace Bushnell, and culminated in the theories of John Ruskin and Abraham Kuyper.[96] In this aesthetic tradition, physical reality itself offered a path to redemption in the "Reality of the Unseen." The heavens and earth were pregnant with the signs of God, if only one had eyes to see. Jonathan Edwards practiced a typological correspondence in which he detailed the relations of the natural and spiritual worlds. In his work on the "Images of Divine Things," he believed that through an encounter with God we learn to love beauty, and that the proper definition of true worship was "our joy in beauty."[97] Here was a great awakening through the senses that saw the mysteries and glories of God the Creator and Redeemer.

Through their own landscape paintings, the Hudson River artists opened up vistas for word-oriented Protestants to learn to see stories in pictures. Inspiring images of God's creation drew in Protestants who tended to be skeptical of all images, opening their imaginations to see how the visual could communicate truths of God's world. As such, these painters helped Protestants wary of images to be more open to them and prepared a visual path to religious cinema. Two important transitional figures of a second generation of spiritually perceptive artists were Albert Bierstadt and Thomas Moran, both of whose careers overlapped the arrival of films. In particular, the German-born Bierstadt was overwhelmed by the divine majesty of the American West. In his magnificent landscape painting of *Yosemite Valley,* Bierstadt telescoped the glory of God, shining through golden hues among the jagged peaks and serene valley. His paintings, with their experiments with light upon nature, their detailed panoramic views, and their spectacular atmospheric effects, provided a spiritually exalting experience, and romanticized as well as sanctified the American West.[98] In Bierstadt's *The Rocky Mountains,* one senses that the mantle of Cropsey was handed onto this painter, who believed artists could "raise to a divine use the objects of material creation" when they proceeded from a "religious heart."[99]

While one may view such images cynically as encompassing undercurrents of progress and Manifest Destiny, or as an invitation to domesticate or ravage the wilderness, these paintings reflected not only praise of God's creation, but a mourning and a jeremiad against the encroaching despoiling of the pristine land. With religious hearts they maintained that vistas of the American wilderness were surely inhabited by God, and also lamented the coming industrial corruption. Corresponding to the visual sermons of these painters were the evangelical commitment and inspired writings of conservationist John Muir, whose own Evangelical theology inspired him to try to rescue nature from development by those who would ravage the land. Scholar Dennis Williams describes how Muir's natural theology was embedded in his journals, speaking about how the great fresh unblighted nature reveals God's own character, His majesty, beauty, and awesome power.[100] What Muir preached on God's forestry and the *Mountains of California* (1894), the cinematography of early westerns was about to capture. Silent Westerns films would not only show the grandeur of God's creation, but also preach a biblical morality grounded in Natural Law.

Spectators of the early cinema marveled at the mere sight of nature in motion, of leaves blowing on trees or waves crashing on the shore. What might have been viewed as a mechanistic world was now reanimated; Nature breathed with divine life. One of the more telling intertitles of seeing God's world anew occurs in the silent film, *The Mollycoddle* (1920), when an effete, pampered easterner (Douglas Fairbanks) first encounters the fresh, invigorating, vast grandeur of the mountains and canyons of a masculine West. He exclaims with unabashed enthusiasm: "Yay God!" So, too, the eastern, urban spectator could look on the screen images of the Grand Canyon or Niagara Falls and praise the wonders of God in His created world.[101] The intimate and fecund connection between art and religion was transplanted from the Hudson River School to many of those who would paint with cameras.

Artwork came to take on an inspirational quality, setting the stage for the visual to again play a key role in communicating the sacred. In his superb study *Protestants and Pictures,* David Morgan traces the mass mediation and commodification of religious images for Protestants in the nineteenth and early twentieth centuries. These images, originally used for the didactic purposes of illustrating biblical texts and themes, particularly for children and immigrants, gradually assumed a more devotional utility, fostering a sense of piety in readers. Engraved and lithographic images ranged from the millennial prophecies of the two-horned Beast of Revelation to the pictorial prophetic charts of the Millerites and the diffused depictions of the "Heads of Christ."[102] Morgan argues convincingly, that an aggressive deployment of technologically produced visual images helped to establish a Protestant culture of visual piety. Through school primers with illustrated texts and "Perry Pictures" of scriptural scenes, children were taught their lessons visually.[103] The Sunday School Board of the Southern Baptist Convention issued a series of Sunday school literature picture cards called the "Kind Word Series" in 1891, which sought to communicate the Gospel message to boys and girls. These *Picture Lesson Cards* reached a circulation of 170,000 in a twelve-year period from 1903 to 1915.[104] Later film boosters pointed back to such visual religious instructional materials as well as to the spiritual oeuvre of James Jacques Joseph Tissot's historical paintings and his pictures of the Bible Lands and its peoples as building blocks for the use of motion pictures in churches.[105]

Morgan's thesis underscores how the Protestant Church began to look benignly on pictorial representations of Bible texts and spiritual lessons.

Another critic, John Davis, showed how one could, through nineteenth-century American art and culture, encounter a "Landscape of Belief" in images of the Holy Land.[106] In 1920, Christian educator Frederica Beard lauded the role that pictures, such as views of the Holy Land, could play in religious education because "a picture is the mean between the thing and the word."[107] Images in religious moving pictures as well as in biblical landscape paintings could supernaturally make the absent present; God could dwell on the screen, or at least one could see where God had walked.

Finding an *aura* of holiness ensconced within the image, the classic Protestant tendency toward iconoclasm gave way to an aesthetic of sympathetic identification and even to a cult of the artist. Protestants could interpret the religious image, like Bernhard Plockhorst's *Christ and the Rich Young Ruler* or Heinrich Hoffman's *Christ in Gethsemane,* as a method of soul culture, a means of inculcating character in the young, the immigrant, and in an entire society. Such practical goals were, in their own unwitting way, a liberal Protestant capitulation to a culture of secularization that would ultimately subsume the motion picture. Films would soon be recommended for the same reasons religious images were, so that they could teach immigrants the American way and train children in moral behaviors. In his own inimitable manner, caustic critic H. L. Menchen recognized this trend when he wrote about the methods of a Methodist clergyman brought into court for corrupting minors.

> This holy man, believing that the Jews, unless they consented to be baptized, would all go to Hell, had opened a mission in what was then still called the Ghetto, and sought to save them. The adults, of course, refused to have anything to do with him, but he managed, after a while, to lure a number of *kosher* small boys into his den, chiefly by showing them magic-lantern pictures of the Buffalo Bill country and the Holy Land.[108]

The satirist understood the persuasive appeal of the Western landscapes and the biblical locations to visually convey what the clergyman felt to be the power of the holy, or at least the power of a technological trick to lure in young converts. That the Hudson River and its Western natural counterpart also offered romantic and utopian allure for the restless at heart would not detract from their appeal as sermonic illustrations. And as scholar Anne Hollander described the continuities from painting to film, these pictorial images would come alive and *move* in silent imaginations.[109] "It is possible," observed French Roman Catholic film critic André Bazin, "that the cinema was the only language capable . . . of giving [the Western landscape] the true aesthetic dimension, and its full religious significance."[110]

According to historian Paula Marantz Cohen, Hudson River artist Thomas Cole opened up the natural majesty of the Western landscape as a Garden of Eden to Europe's Fallen World. Likewise, in a kind of "painterly montage" in his monumental canvases, fellow artist Albert Bierstadt lifted up the individual to a sublime but almost invisible place in God's spectacular creation. Critic Lee Mitchell described Bierstadt's American paintings as alive with "cinematic effect," begging for plots and characters to enliven them.[111] In light of the potential kinetic art of the Hudson River painters, Protestants required a dramatic narrative counterpart for these spiritual images to provide a cinematic aesthetic. The Protestant middle class was brought into the cult of silent moving pictures in large measure by the inclusion of religious themes and symbols through a genre of western films.[112] While other genres, particularly the *Passion Play* attractions and the Victorian melodrama,[113] mapped out middle-class religious concerns through various iconographic signposts (i.e., Bible stories, inclusion of clergy, concern for the poor, cameo appearances by Jesus Christ Himself), key western narratives in novels and films functioned in unabashedly explicit ways to proclaim Protestant perspectives. In Broncho Billy films, scripts showed individual sinners being convicted and converted by reading the Bible. Certain artistic and literary precursors had prepared the soil of the Protestant soul to become a fertile ground for cultivating habits of film attendance, especially when nineteenth-century religious western novels were translated into silent, religious western films with minor changes.[114] In his historical study of religion in film, Gerald Forshey argued that Hollywood's religious film genre had its origin in popular culture: "Religious spectaculars grew out of two popular artistic traditions—the spectacular stage melodrama and the popular quasi-religious novels of the nineteenth century."[115] In the nineteenth century, the protocinematic evangelical novels paralleled the artistry of the Hudson River painters, each medium eliciting positive responses from Protestant audiences. Protestants were thus primed to welcome an emerging technology that could wed image and moral narratives.

Catoptric Art

Questions and suspicions continued to haunt the church when it came to communicating to and through the eye. Were children of the light dabbling unnecessarily in shadows? Or were they helping light to shine out of the darkness that men and women might *see?* As we have seen, this ambivalence persisted throughout church history, and the early days of Christian film accentuated the tension. Alongside the cultural precursors opening up the possibility of visually communicating the faith, technological advances were to complicate this condition, setting the stage for the debates of a sanctuary cinema.

In 1646, a Jesuit priest described an innovation, presumably his own, called the "magic lantern," a prototype of the modern film projector, for which he found mischievous uses. With this magic toy, Father Athanasius Kircher projected dancing shadows of phantasmogorphic images onto sheets of cloth.[116] In an era of alchemy, where science and magic were one and the same, the good Father's projected images astonished audiences, who stood amazed as they gazed at eerie shadows dancing on the curtains and walls.[117] Likewise, a devout audience of fellow monks was fascinated and amused by his amazing program, enthralled until Kircher projected an image of the devil and his cohorts onto a cloud of smoke. Then suddenly, this marvel of the magic lantern was seen as the work of the devil; this eerie, supernatural "happening" so terrified and outraged his fellow monks that they rushed to exorcise both the room and Kircher himself. In a desperate attempt to defend himself, Kircher did what any good medieval or contemporary scholar would do: he published a paper. Under the impending threat of exorcism or clerical torture for this "catoptric (or reflecting) art," Kircher published *Ars magna lucis et umbrae* (*The Great Art of Light and Shadow*), a scholarly work that attempted to demystify the magic lantern's basic apparatus and means of making images through technical explanations and elaborate illustrations. Since his magic lantern show arose out of a science of optics and reflections, rather than magic and demonic activity, he tried to demonstrate how light and mirrors worked. He argued that the magic lantern projection had not conjured up demons but demonstrated divinely ordained, wondrous principles found within God's own created, orderly universe. Kircher's scientific explanations apparently appeased his religious community, but still Kircher put his magic lantern away lest some grand inquisitor should show a more robust curiosity in his dabbling in shadows.

By the eighteenth century miracle plays were often presented in magic lantern shows, as folk religion employed the newest available media to translate doctrine and legends into the vernacular.[118] Missionaries experimented with visual media to teach illiterate peoples around the world. In the early 1920s, Professor W. F. Russell of the University of Iowa found patron saints for religious education through film. Russell particularly praised Johann Amos Comenius, a seventeenth-century Moravian educator, as the "father of picture-books" who constantly preached "the doctrine of teaching through the eye." Comenius and his fellow pedagogue Pestalozzi were extolled as the "Fathers of Visual Education," and as clerics who would have welcomed movies into their vocations.[119] Comenius repeatedly cited Hebrew *Proverb* 20: 12 ("The hearing ear and the seeing eye, the Lord hath made even both of them") to emphasize the importance of sensory experience in learning: "The sense of hearing should always be conjoined with that of sight." As such he would incorporate pictorial representation on the walls of the classroom so as to impress instruction upon the minds of his pupils.[120]

In the late eighteenth century, phantasmagoric shows (magic lantern performances) were presented in a former Capuchin convent through the showmanship of Etienne Gaspar Robertson.[121] Robertson's magic was secularized as it transformed a convent chapel into a place of entertainment, a transformation characterized as *"a church functioning as an exhibition site."*[122] Robertson's shows sought to demystify the supernatural via technology, propagandizing the idea that enlightened reason was superior to faith; he used experimental artifice to exploit a delight in the supernatural and uncanny, and to simultaneously debunk it. The tricks of the eyes, these *trompe l'oeil* pleasures, were easily explained. American imitators advertised their own Optical Illusion shows with the same self-assured enlightenment: "This Spectrology professes to expose the practices of artful impostors and exorcists, and to open the eyes of those who still foster an absurd belief in ghosts or disembodied spirits."[123] Ironically, within about a century cinematographers out of Los Angeles would be claiming to have photographed materialized spirits, with copies of the films sent to the London Psychic Society.[124]

However apocryphal parts of these stories of the early light shows may be, images did find use (and abuse) within the church. Kircher's experiment was a forerunner of the motion picture industry that emerged over three and half centuries later. In the meantime, several subsequent image machines aimed at engendering and strengthening faith through the appreciation of God's creation. Technological development unleashed new marvels. Dioramas (Louis Jacques Mande's engineering marvel which manipulated the illusion of natural light—as though streaming through stained glass windows to transform sunrise to noon to twilight), eidophusikons (a miniature theater/peep show that provided "various imitations of natural phenomena"), panoramas (Robert Barker's 360 degree circular painting of famous religious and historical events), and stereopticons (exhibitions of photographic slides), all shaped nature for the consumption of a society that delighted in marveling thereby at the wonders of God's earth and heavens.[125] The heavens declared the glory of God and the earth expressed His handiwork, even more with a little help from human invention. And by opening its doors to the display of these marvels through optical illusion, the church of the nineteenth century embraced a celebratory exhibition of visual art.

In 1863 chemist John Fallon selected choice views of landscapes gathered from his travels around the world, transferred these views into photographic slides, and astounded both audiences and congregations with his stereopticon, "the scientific wonder of the age." Under the auspices of Central Congregational Sunday School in Massachusetts, Fallon hit the itinerant circuit as a traveling evangelist for modernity and faith. Congregations were, as one observer put it, "borne away on the enchanted carpet of the Arabian tale" shown through Fallon's slides, even in normally staid and refined Victorian churches.[126] Exhibitions of photographic slides met with much success in both educational and religious contexts, with lanternslides enabling exhibitors to give illustrated lectures and sermons and thus lure larger audiences into their sanctuaries.[127] Fallon's work and the entrepreneurial labors of traveling lecturer-moving picture showmen Burton Holmes and Lyman H. Howe provided high-class photographic work with beautiful hand tinting of God's own country. Yale University historian Charles Musser punctuates the point that evangelical Protestants embraced motion pictures with positive programs. "Indeed, although the Methodists categorically banned amusements in any shape or form for its members, they became one of cinema's strongest proponents. Their film programs entertained rather than amused."[128]

Following Fallon's success in Boston-area churches, prominent lecturer John Stoddard used the stereopticon to provide scenes of bucolic landscapes to enchanted evangelical Protestant and other proponents of genteel society.[129] Stoddard then offered programs of scripture scenes and travel lectures that wove elaborately illustrated images into a continuous narrative for first-rate entertainment and instruction. Around 1881, Stoddard experimented with a visual account of a recent passion-play performance from Oberammergau, Germany, and found himself established as one of the most prominent lecturers on that subject.[130] Religious leaders praised such showmen for vivifying both God's creation and biblical stories. In her history of the intersection of religion and entertainment between 1884 and 1914, Kathryn Oberdeck points to the contemporary support of British publicist and evangelist W. T. Stead who, in 1890, highlighted the need for the church to establish a "Magic Lantern Mission." Stead maintained, "Even down to our time, Voltaire's saying remains true that in Catholic countries the parish is the poor man's opera-house. It is also his Madame Tussaud's, his collection of statuary, and his school of architecture. In olden times it was also his theatre."[131] The church would soon be revived as the theater of the people if it were to capitalize on the opportunity of visual amusements.

Toward a Technological Sermon

In the late nineteenth century, illustrated travelogues and lectures enhanced with scriptural scenes were generally sponsored by one of two noteworthy cultural groups in American life: either by the refined and genteel cultural associations sharing an enlightened and progressive philosophy or by the evangelical religious groups primarily situated within church-based institutions. In addition, individual churches regularly sponsored cultural events, usually as an alternative to such corrupting amusements as melodramas and musicals currently showing at the local theaters or small-town opera houses. Ministers engaged in a more or less explicit crusade for the souls of the community and they considered the illustrated lecture to be one of the weapons in their arsenal and, therefore, frequently presented them. At the Orange Valley Congregational Church in Orange, New Jersey, the Reverend Lester Wells gave photographic lecture about conditions in Lower Jersey City.

Reformer Jacob Riis had seized upon projected photographs to communicate the needs of the poor to both state and church. The tough and realistic images exposed the impoverished and desperate conditions of the city's poor, providing a fiercely unforgettable sermon on the needs of the less fortunate.

A basic compatibility and common purpose developed between the cultural associations and religious groups sponsoring these illustrated lectures. One itinerant lecturer, Alexander Black, would alternatively deliver his picture plays at cultural affairs and at church-sponsored events. On the eve of the appearance of the first projected motion pictures in the mid-1890s these two groups were poised to become the most receptive audiences for screen images.[132] Of particular interest is the traveling exhibition career of Lyman Howe, who may have been the John the Baptist of visual entertainment among many morally and culturally conservative churches. Howe stood in the role of an adept forerunner of church film exhibitions (and a bit of a P. T. Barnum) as he introduced visual amusements into the Protestant communities of the American heartland. The conservative religious community, perhaps surprisingly, had a positive program embracing motion pictures.[133] This constructive openness to the cinema and to its potential as a means of communicating goodness was to summon men and women into the holy calling of making movies for other saints.

The production of popular religious stereopticon slides in the Victorian era sprang from artisans like Joseph Boggs Beale.[134] Typical literary lanternslide sets encompassed scenes from *Pilgrim's Progress, Quo Vadis,* and *Ben Hur.* During presentations of the latter, images of a chariot race elicited cheers, and images of Jesus giving Ben Hur water to drink awed and electrified congregations into a palpable hush. Beale, himself an avid churchgoer, found that the clergy was initially "prejudiced in introducing the lantern into their churches, thinking that some of the solemnity due on such an occasion would be lost."[135] Ministers were won over by the plethora of religious slides. Beale manufactured and painted over six hundred religious slides, including sets illustrating the Old Testament, the New Testament, and hymns. A story like David and Goliath engrossed younger male audiences with its dramatic and gory climax of the giant's beheading. It also attracted uncouth youth who were bored by traditional services but who appreciated a pictorially illustrated evening devotion.[136]

Beale emphasized the kinetic continuity of his slide shows. For example, slides illustrating the parable of the Good Samaritan tended to change faster (about every eight seconds) than normal lantern readings. The change in pace altered the show from providing a sense of a meditative documentary or a moment for visual reflection to an early cinema of attractions. Beale was also able to dramatize supernatural and apocalyptic images: angels, devils, burning bushes, seas parting, flood and fires and other disasters—astounding images described as possessing "truly Biblical proportions."[137]

In another field, hymn slides in particular seemed to fit into evangelist Charles Finney's call for "new men, new methods," in propagating the Gospel message. Hymns like music leader Ira Sankey's favorite "The Ninety and Nine" would flow into images of shepherds and wandering sheep. The pedagogical influence on middle-class Protestant culture from these Victorian slides of hymnody cannot be underestimated. Their emphases on salvation, heaven, evangelism, and personal decision making struck a deep chord in their religious audiences. Cultural historian Cheryl Boots points out that in 1879 magic lanterns were first adopted as a new idea in Sunday school entertainment and that this led to their incorporation into adult "congregational singing in a number of (Boston) churches. Where this innovation is made there is no reason why one who can sing won't sing. The objections of having no book, or of having left the book at home, or of eye-trying fine type, are annihilated."[138]

With slides of popular hymns projected on a screen, Beale anticipated the cinematic technology of crosscuts, dissolves, and superimpositions, as he communicated religious concepts through visual narratives. A particularly rousing example, *The Rock of Ages,* used Johannes Oertel's painting of a woman desperately clinging to a rock cross. Archivist and historian Terry Borton describes a condensed version of Beale's *Rock of Ages* in which two women (Faith and a companion) are tossed overboard in a terrible shipwreck. Lightning dramatically flashes over a rock upon which the women have thrown themselves. As a huge stone cross emerges from the rock, Faith pulls her companion from the rushing waters up toward the cross. The storm abates. A rainbow lights the sky and a vision of angels beckoning the women heavenward hovers above them. Finally, they rest safely in the arms of Jesus, a sure sign of Protestant salvation.

A 1902 Edison film of the same hymn, *The Rock of Ages,* now located in the Library of Congress, portrays a tame and limited version of Beale's lively slide presentation. In Edison's version, the picture opens with turbulent white water washing over a cross on a rocky crag against a stark black background. Out of the depths of the sea, a woman dressed in flowing garments seeks the support of the cross. She holds on to the cross and stretches forth her arms in trust. This was only a small technological change from the slides to the film, but it was a giant ascent into modernity that the churches were primed to make.[139] By 1911, film trade periodicals would announce that churches like Salem Congregational Church in Los Angeles were arousing interest by exhibiting illustrated hymns like *Rock of Ages* and by showing films like *Pilgrim's Progress* with the songs. (When film critic Louis Reeves Harrison reviewed this hour-and-a-half-long film of religious biography and allegory, he concluded that it was "too rich an offering for ordinary mortals." It would be more suitable for churches and schools, he thought, but not for motion picture theaters.[140]) The small step from the slides to the film would carry churches into a dynamic change that few anticipated. One who did foresee grand opportunities was the pastor of Salem Congregational Church, the Reverend B. H. Reutepohler, who issued his own call to arms in 1911: "In the past we have sent out our people to be amused by the devil. . . . I do not think that anything that will amuse and interest the people is necessarily bad; therefore I believe that the installation of moving pictures in the church will eventually tend to elevate the moral character of the entire community."[141]

In 1908, the same year that D. W. Griffith began making moral Victorian melodramas for Biograph Studios, Dr. Walter Hervey copyrighted a tidy pamphlet entitled *Picture = Work.*[142] His argument, which centered on the startling pedagogical impact of the visual arts on children, hearkened back to St. John of Damascus and the historical debates on images used in and by the Church. Hervey pointed out that great pictures and picture stories (drawn from the Bible) spoke to the very souls of children. Citing the Hebrew prophet Ezekiel and his own contemporary Dr. Parkhurst (who was involved in a public campaign against Tammany Hall corruption), Hervey showed how each used "picture-works" to preach graphically dramatic sermons. In Hervey's judgment, a picture helped lagging imaginations to "see more clearly, feel more humility, and act upon more faithfully the truth that is not or cannot be immediately present to our senses." He proposed that our understanding of the truth of God, for example, was "built out of our experience of mountains, flowers, thunderstorms, our mother's tenderness and our father's strength."[143]

Religious and educational agencies awakened to both the possibilities and the problems of screen presentation. Bold steps were being taken. For example, at the San Francisco Exposition, a projection room was operated by and for the Federation of Churches, indicating a lively interest by

Moving Pictures to Invade the Church?

Rev. W. G. Archer, Who Has Already Introduced Stereopٜtican Views and Illustrated Hymns, Thinks So

By 1908, significant press coverage predicted that religious moving pictures would follow illustrated hymns and stereopticon views into church work. *Moving Picture World* (June 27, 1908), 542. Editorial Cartoon: "Moving Pictures to Invade the Church?" Courtesy Library of Congress.

mainline ecclesiastical institutions in using film to show the glories of God's creation. By 1910 the churches had broadened considerably in their view of motion picture possibilities; then came the truly amazing announcement in 1913 that the Edison Company had arranged with the Presbyterian Board of Publications to supply films and projectors, with a subsequent heavy increase in projector sales to the churches of the Midwest in the following year.

Of course, clergy were not wholly ignorant of what religious moving pictures might do for them. As historian Arthur Edwin Krows pointed out, they already had provisions in many places for showing lanternslides illustrating Bible stories. Charles Kleine, a New York optical manufacturer who had substituted the calcium light for the old oil lamp in magic lantern projection and was selling his improved, duplex, dissolving stereopticons widely, had encouraged the idea.[144] His son, George Kleine, imported outstanding religious films, including the Italian *Quo Vadis*. The theatrical magnate zealously urged the integration of films into schools and churches, even issuing a catalogue in 1910 of suitable educational films, with over a thousand items listed and categorized by subjects licensed by the Motion Picture Patents Company.[145] While Kleine was opening the church field through the showman's angle, the aforementioned Lyman Howe was penetrating it by a different route. Coming out of Wilkes-Barre, Pennsylvania, Howe had begun his adult career by working for the railroad; in March 1890, he stepped from the post of baggage master to lecturer with traveling shows to order to introduce the lately invented phonograph. (George Bernard Shaw allegedly tried the same enterprise from a cart in London.) Howe transferred media and climbed the celluloid ladder to fame, gathering all suitable motion pictures to make a full evening's entertainment; he soon became a familiar attraction on the church and lyceum circuits. His privileged practice of operating Sunday performances earned him an unexpected status, as newspaper reporters began to refer to him as the Reverend Lyman Howe. He became, both wittingly and unwittingly, the entrepreneurial servant of pious art.[146]

By 1922, a fuller explication of art as the handmaiden of religion was articulated by Boston University Professor of Religious Art, Albert Edward Bailey. His work, *The Use of Art in Religious Education* explores the religious potential and functions of pictures for preaching and teaching. Bailey does not address the tasks of evangelism, but rather focuses upon the benefits of a social gospel and the prospect for the more unfortunate of becoming a better person. It is "man's religious task," he argues, to hasten the "universal reign of God." Bailey's work encompassed architecture, war posters, cartoons, photographs, and lanternslides. Visual art, he declares, is a "potent handmaid to faith. Religion still needs art. What God once joined together, man should not put asunder."[147]

Hervey, Bailey, and others were providing an apologetic framework for the acceptance of the moving picture by the church. Already, the use of static illustration in religious education was a discovery of fundamental importance to Sunday school workers and others who wished to enrich their teaching and preaching. This emphasis upon combining pictures with storytelling would provide fertile soil for the churches' acceptance of the new medium when they discovered the moving picture. Hervey recommended a list of pictures and "books from which pictures may be culled" that would serve as illustrative teaching material. Such publications as "The Photographs of the Holy Land" primed the church's fascination with the "actualities" that documented those special sacred lands and peoples on film.[148]

Numerous factors prepared churches for the possibility of moving pictures. The backdrop of the landscape paintings of the Hudson River School of artists established habits of viewing the spiritual in a public art form. The magic lantern, stereopticon, and hymn slides demonstrated how technology could be incorporated into church services and activities. All these precursors seemed to conspire to lay a foundation for building a sanctuary cinema.

Visual materials needed the thread of a narrative to become more directly instructional. "Of all the things that a teacher should know how to do," said Clark University President Stanley Hall, "the most important without any exception, is to be able to tell a story."[149] The development of narrative was a key factor in altering film from a mere novelty or mechanical curiosity into a major source of entertainment and instruction. Ministers could now stand before congregations explaining the silent images, narrating them in the context of a sermon or teaching. Thus the ability of movies to promulgate religious education by wrapping it in compelling images that told stories led to the church's early embrace of film. An early proponent of visual storytelling, the Reverend Chester S. Bucher, defended the film by referring to historical examples: "Jesus used a lost coin, a dead sparrow and a little child as object lessons. Beecher auctioned off a slave girl in a Plymouth pulpit. Wilberforce made them shudder when he held up the chains of Africans and dropped them with a clanking thud on the floor. Why should the churches disregard this great potential asset, especially since it was a clergyman, the Reverend Hannibal Goodwin, who was the inventor of the flexible film that made motion pictures possible?"[150] It was a question and challenge that churches would passionately address during the era of silent American film.

2

Sanctuary Cinema

> The Church that is not equipped to show motion pictures is as in-
> complete as a church without an organ.
>
> Rev. Leslie Willis Sprague[1]

In *Sullivan's Travels,* director Preston Sturges's 1941 satire on Hollywood filmmaking, a naive director of inane comedies wants to produce a socially significant drama. He takes to the road as a hobo, but is soon incarcerated in a chain gang. The oppressed prisoners are given a Sunday reprieve from their tortuous labors in a Black rural church. As they hobble into the sanctuary with leg chains clanging, the congregation is singing "Let My People Go." The director, John L. Sullivan, detained among the prisoners, sits in his pew as church lanterns are dimmed, a screen is lowered, and an old projector rattles. A Walt Disney Pluto cartoon is exhibited in the church, for the delight and true recreation of those whose lives are without joy or hope. The church becomes, for a brief holy moment, a sacred site of healing through comic film images.

The church's inaugural place in relation to silent moving pictures was as a site of exhibition. As the primary locus of social and spiritual community, the churches opened their basements and halls to the new medium in the late nineteenth century even as they had earlier appropriated the use of drama in morality and miracle plays and then the stereopticon and numerous lanternslide shows. Visions of moving pictures incorporated into preaching, teaching, worship, and the spiritual life of the community inspired church leaders to experiment with modes of adaptation. The use of moving pictures in churches gave rise to a debate regarding their role within these worshiping communities. The tendency of moving pictures to function solely as entertainment would have troubled its diffusion into the church had it not been for the emphasis on their potential for teaching and uplift. The positive historical uses of the icon and the theater for spiritual and moral instruction reminded religious leaders of the potential to adapt other means of communication for the work of the Lord. Although it would be years before churches regularly produced their own motion pictures, they began using them in church basements and halls for specific purposes almost as soon as the nascent film industry began making them.[2]

An auspicious event occurred in 1885 that enabled the religious use of the marvelous moving image. At that time, the Reverend Hannibal Goodwin was rector of a fashionable Episcopal church in Newark, New Jersey, the House of Prayer. An amateur chemist, Goodwin tinkered with a flexible, transparent film base that allowed successive photographic images to be coiled on one long strip. He wisely filed for a patent for his invention of celluloid film stock and to establish the Goodwin Camera and Film Company. Unfortunately, the rector later lost his business to George Eastman and only a lengthy legal suit restored his fame and part of the financial fruit of his labors; nevertheless, the motion picture bug had bitten the churchman. Goodwin was ultimately praised as the supreme missionary and educator, whose original motive was a spiritual one. In 1918, the Reverend W. H. Jackson, columnist for the early film periodical, *Moving Picture World,* commemorated Goodwin and his invention, noting that the moving picture was born a child of the church (although now in danger of neglect), and its original conception was to bequeath both education and entertainment to the Sunday school.[3] Goodwin's early biographer T. M. Dombey went further and noted that movements in the church to supplement sermons with screen illustrations of the Bible and to produce films from Genesis to Revelations would be ephemeral if "an organized movement of the Churches to give such exhibitions accompanied by teaching in Sunday School and to equip all manner of missionary forces" did not evolve from Goodwin's invention.[4]

During the first decades of film's development, various religious factions sought to utilize the new medium for sectarian purposes.[5] Having set up their own Cinematograph Department, the Salvation Army may well be the earliest on record to make use of film for religious purposes, coinciding with its own genesis as a movement at the end of the nineteenth century.[6] In 1899, in Australia, the son of the founder of the Salvation Army, Herbert Booth, used film as a means to propagate the faith and minister to the poor through storytelling. Claiming to be the first to use the moving pictures in the cause of Christianity, Booth argued that his Bioscope cinematograph was the "missing link" between the stage and the pulpit, adapting drama to religious use in a "safe, possible, and sanctified way."[7] In the Salvation Army pamphlet, *War Cry*, he joined the voices of medieval church artisans in challenging those who would reject the use of the dramatic arts: "These means are employed by the worldling; they form a source of attraction in the theatres and music halls. Why should they be usurped by the enemy of souls?"[8] For Booth, the novelty of film would help rescue people from pubs and music halls.

Booth and company exploited the "cinema of attractions," using images of such novelties as a hippopotamus to draw in a crowd. These early documentary films, known as "actualities," captured phenomena that were marvelous for their sheer quiddity and motion and this alone attracted spectators. But the Army went further to ensure an alert audience. Film historian John Hamilton described the Salvation Army as "motivated by a holy zeal to win converts by any legitimate means," which included the innovations of special effects like "fire, smoky vapors, boiling cauldrons, and the like to embellish sensational stories of early Christian martyrs, such as Polycarp at the stake."[9] One Australian paper in 1900 raved about how Commandant Booth had reenacted the lives of the holy martyrs, showing "the horrors of Nero's efforts to exterminate the followers of Christ, the tragedies of the dark catacombs, and the thrilling scenes that were enacted in the arena of the Coliseum."[10]

The Salvation Army was to transform the photoplay by offering a healthy evening's entertainment while avoiding the simpering sentimentalism frequently identified or confused with Victorian piety and religion. Rather, their photoplays would work as direct and masculine means of persuasion.[11] As Booth put it, "What photography has accomplished in the way of animated pictures has been adapted to the purposes of salvation."[12] This tradition continued until 1908 when the *Moving Picture World* marveled at how churches were taking the initiative to show such harrowing images of Nero's persecution of early Christians at church revivals. Six hundred children were terror-stricken when viewing a scene from the Edison film *Nero and the Burning of Rome* in which Christians were to be delivered to savage lions.[13] (When the *New York Dramatic Mirror* praised the feature *Quo Vadis*, it slyly noted that the audiences "spontaneously cheered for everything, including the spectacular thrill when the lions ate the Christians.")[14]

The appearance of two passion plays in 1897 and 1898, both given considerable publicity, aroused great interest in the church field. The visualization of the Bible story of Christ suggested an authentic and factual historical facsimile of sacred history. In 1898, Colonel Henry H. Hadley, a former New York journalist and corporate attorney turned evangelist, prophetically foresaw film's enormous proselytizing possibilities. Running a revival crusade in Ocean Grove and Atlantic City, New Jersey, he discovered the remarkable power of moving pictures. Armed with a print of the 1897 *Hollaman-Evaes' Passion Play,* Hadley, who had been preaching against the iniquities of hard liquor with a vigorous blend of damnation and salvation, attracted thousands of people to his camp meetings. "These pictures," Hadley prophesied, "are going to be a great force. It is the age of pictures. . . . These moving pictures are going to be the best teachers and the best preachers in the history of the world. Mark my words, there are two things coming: prohibition and motion pictures. We must make people think above the belt."[15] After sponsoring an exhibition at the Methodist convention ground at Asbury Park, New Jersey, Hadley took the film on the road for a highly remunerative tour. An early film critic, Martin Dworkin, praised such clergymen as Hadley for recognizing film's propaganda potential and showing a "prescient understanding" of how film could re-create the spirit of the people, "even as it altered their habits and occasions of communal living."[16] Instead of viewing the church as dwindling in the face of progress and modernity, one can see how it was responding with vim and vision, even becoming one of the leading purveyors of the new recreational culture.[17]

Edwin Krows, a historian of nontheatrical films, has argued that the first modest circuit of places for the exhibition of moving pictures "unsupported by jugglers and clog dances" was a chain of Houses of the Lord. In particular, an early exploiter of movies around 1900 was one Archie Shepard, who traveled through small communities in the Northeast and Midwest. He offered a lively family entertainment, using E. H. Amet's Magniscope projector developed for Chicago exchange man George Spoor of Essanay Studios. Shepard was forced to alter his presentations of films as vaudeville turns when he couldn't get into key theaters. When the only available alternatives for satisfactorily sized auditoria were in the churches, he obtained permission for his moral and inspirational pictorial turns. Shepard allegedly had a talent of ingratiating himself to clergy, as he would lend his pianist, a soloist, and some of his sanctified pictures to the church before he took up Sunday evenings to conduct his show. He was able to persuade the Cahn and Grant exhibition circuit in New England to permit him to perform in their houses on Sunday evenings, as no other options were available due to Sabbath and blue laws restrictions. By 1904, he could claim to be undoubtedly the "largest single exhibitor of motion pictures in the world."[18]

By June 22, 1900, the historic Tabernacle building—part church, part theater, and part Chautauqua lecture hall (a tradition founded in 1874 by Ohio inventor Lewis Miller and Methodist minister John Heyl Vincent for spiritual and intellectual renewal)—was already exhibiting motion pictures to the citizens of Long Beach, California.[19] There, Hollywood's roots grew out of the religious campaign of Horace Wilcot, "a God-fearing real estate speculator," who envisioned Hollywood as a model Christian community with "no saloons, no liquor stores, with free land offered to Protestant Churches locating within the city limits."[20] These Protestant churches were not only securing land in Hollywood, but they were primed to acquire the apparatus to attract the masses. All that was needed was a prophet and a model of operation.

The Cinematic Apologist

In a small community in New Britain, Connecticut, a progressive churchman was reflecting upon how to reach his neighbors for the Kingdom of God. Anticipating theologian Paul Tillich's similar formulation, the Reverend Herbert A. Jump believed that any cultural form, however secular in origin and intent, could potentially be made religious.[21] In a city of fifteen thousand wage earners, many of them of foreign birth, the Reverend Jump saw the motion picture as a potentially very serviceable adjunct to religious education. In contrast to strident reformers like Wilbur F. Crafts who in the tradition of Zwingli, believed that movies were "schools of vice and crime . . . offering trips to hell for [a] nickel," Jump envisioned the possibility of bringing the Kingdom of God to a needy world.[22] For Jump, it was without doubt a vital and unifying form of entertainment appealing to all ages, races, and cultural groups; it was one of the most democratic things in American life, in the same category as the voting booth and the electric car. Manufactured photoplays were even, like candy, "fresh every hour."[23] The Reverend Jump would become the St. John of Damascus for the motion pictures; however, his apologetic for the efficacy of icons in teaching the illiterate masses would be less theological and more pragmatic in keeping with the modern era. The celebrated religious icon was now kinetic.

In 1910, the former mayor of the city generously consented to endow a moving picture service in Jump's South Congregational Church in New Britain, Connecticut, for a test of thirteen Sunday evenings during that summer as an innovative way to draw the unchurched into a moral environment. Jump was so elated with the success of his experiment that he printed a detailed account in the following year to guide his fellow shepherds who might want to emulate him. Film historian Charles Musser notes the tremendous impact of this one farsighted minister in articulating the alternatives for the churches in their dealings of this novelty.

> In the late 1890s, while some priests and ministers railed against the sinfulness, actual and possible, of what was beginning to go on in the movie theaters, on screen and off, others hailed the manifestly immense power of the new medium as a blessing, and carried films of Bible reenactments, moral uplift, and instruction on missionary forays into areas remote from the cultural advantages of cities.

> While the intelligentsia—those worthies aware of their advanced education and superior literacy—except for a few educators largely disdained the new medium and all its works, there were clergymen who showed prescient understanding of what was recreating the spirit of the people, even as it altered their habits and occasions of communal living. In an early broadside—ignored by film historians and to this day inexcusably unknown—one minister of a Congregational church in Connecticut, Herbert A. Jump, proselytized for the incorporation of films into the liturgy, in order to confront the challenges to religion of the godless cities, and to make a new powerful "appeal to the unchurched."[24]

Jump's persuasive arguments provided a compelling apologetic for those who were uncertain about the value of motion pictures in church work and for those who didn't know how to use them. Jump's rhetorical skills displayed a "considerable sophistication about tactics of propaganda, shrewdly building on acceptance of the rhetorical and graphic arts by the faithful, won in recurring battles against the seductions of idolatry." His language assumed the authentic prophetic style in foretelling film's potential.

From 1910 onward, Congregationalists highlighted a vision for exploring the religious possibilities of moving pictures, such as showcasing actuality views of Palestine in 1924, through their official denominational periodical, *The Congregationalist*. Full page *The Congregationalist* "Motion Picture Number," CIX 13 (March 27, 1924). Cover Courtesy Library of Congress.

Jump was a sophisticated thinker who quickly recognized the cultural implications of film narratives, embracing film's utility as a social and educational tool in an industrialized urban society. As a result, Jump, like early *Moving Picture World* film reviewers Reverend W. H. Jackson and Stephen W. Bush, wielded significant influence in shaping Protestant ideas about film.[25] The seeds of that influence may be seen in his provocative little pamphlet that appeared in 1910, and that many film histories have overlooked, *The Religious Possibilities of the Motion Picture*.[26] For Jump there was great hope in the possibility of using the motion picture for the Kingdom of God. He believed that the feasibility of incorporating visual sermons into the sanctuaries was built into the very nature of human activity. He grounded his appeal in the communication strategies recommended by the Apostle Paul:

> We men and women who have ever shown interest in pictures, hanging them on the walls of our homes, seeking them in illustrated books and now in picture-postcards, should turn naturally to the motion picture sermon which puts the gospel in a pictorial form. Some of you who attend church love the doctrinal phraseology of St. Paul. There is many a hardheaded American workingman, however, who confesses freely that to him St. Paul is only a prosy old theologian. Paul, however, was not a prosy theologian to the men of his day. Why not? Because his illustrations for the gospel were taken from the life of his contemporaries—the racing habits of his day, for example, and the boxing matches. We ministers of today may not quite dare follow Paul in illustrating spiritual truth from the trotting park or a recent famous prize fight in a western city, but we have a right to use stories taken from life in the shop and factory and on the street as illustrations of the gospel to the men of today. Because the motion picture carefully selected will tell to the eye moral truths with vigor of illustration and an eloquence of impression that the most enthusiastic orator cannot command, it has a proper place in the equipment of any church trying to reach the masses.

In his pamphlet, Jump listed five ways in which the motion picture functions as a religious tool. First, he argued that it attracts as an entertaining storytelling device. Second, it aids in giving religious instruction in Sunday school. Third, it does "more for foreign and home missions than any agency yet utilized by our assiduous and ingenious missionary secretaries." Fourth, it also provides an agency for the religious and social education of the needy within the community. And finally, it helps the preacher by dramatizing his proclamation of moral truth.[27]

Among the Congregationalists of New England, the Hudson River painters had imprinted their vision of religion being communicated through visual culture. The *Congregationalist* periodical regularly showcased scenes from nature and from biblical locations on its magazine covers, both of which served as creative visual praise to the God of the Bible. Like paintings, motion pictures could open eyes encrusted with modernity and blinded from familiarity. Shaped by the Congregational (and transcendental) tendency to see God's handiwork in Walden Pond and the rest of the natural world, Jump recommended that religious leaders also view contemporary cultural interests, such as boxing, as illustrations of spiritual truths. Such an appeal to the people was cannily based in the Apostle Paul's own imagery in I Corinthians 9:26. It is not without its own irony that boxing was one of the most hotly contested subjects for censorship in the early days of the cinema, but Jump deftly appropriated the biblical imagery used by the Apostle Paul in his strategy of appropriating cultural practices as a means to effective religious communication.

Jump believed that the church should participate in all aspects of culture. He articulated the vision of a union between the church and moving pictures so effectively that his writings were reprinted in the *Motion Picture Story Magazine* and cited numerous times in early film periodicals.[28] By 1911, his writing was even lauded "as a classic in its peculiar field" (quite an accomplishment for so new a field). When he left his ministry to enter the lecture circuit, *The Moving Picture World* honored him as the "first Christian martyr for moving pictures."[29] Jump recognized that some dour Luddites might be prejudiced against his innovations and so he humorously preempted them: "To assert therefore that there are any religious possibilities in the motion picture strikes you as the acme of absurdity, as though one were to announce a sermon on The Spiritual Value of the Clog Dance." For detractors of the moving pictures, Jump placed their questions and concerns in a scriptural context. He tackled reports that motion picture stories were likely to represent crime, that they were too exciting, and that a film manufacturer exploited every phase of modern experience "as he scoured the universe to find novel subjects for his motion picture films." Jump argued that the biblical narrative was an ideal model for the moving picture scenario. Echoing Saint Bonaventura's insistence that images are better equipped to arouse devotion than can listening alone, Jump proposed that silent moving pictures offered a ripe opportunity for Christianity to speak to all people, regardless of national or linguistic tradition. Even those who cannot read can see and understand narrative images.

Beginning with Jesus' parable of the Good Samaritan in the *Gospel of Luke,* Jump identified several characteristics that the sacred story shared with the problematic medium of the motion picture. First, Jesus' story itself was taken from contemporary sources, and not from the Torah or the prophets, the Hebrew Bible of the day. It was, in that sense, a secular story. Second, it was an exciting robber adventure, its violence and rescue being particularly lively and thrilling for small boys (and adolescent men).

And third, it introduced morally shady characters—such as hypocritical religious leaders and highwaymen—and left them intact at the end of the narrative.

In fact, regarding the robbers themselves, Jump observed that "not only did the story give a most realistic description of precisely how they perpetrated the cowardly crime of violence, but it leaves them victorious in their wickedness, scurrying off with their booty, unrepentant of their sins, probably chuckling at the folly of the traveler." Jump went on to conclude:

> And yet, despite these three dubious characteristics of not being Scriptural to the people who heard it, of being exciting, and of having realistic and morally negative features in it, who dare assert that the story of the Good Samaritan has wrought harm in the world? Rather, has it not earned for itself recognition as being the central parable of all the Master's teachings? Has it not exhibited in complete and convincing fashion the very heart of the Gospel? Has it not urged more men into lives of ministry and helpfulness than any piece of literature of equal length, which the race has ever known?

Thus, for the Reverend Jump, the blueprint for effective evangelism and instruction through the medium of the moving picture existed right in the holy scriptures. He felt that only an interesting new title such as "The Adventures of the Highwaymen" was needed to make the parable photoplay marketable.

Simultaneously with Jump's leap into the foreground of a religion and film debate in 1910, one finds that the presence of motion pictures in church work was so widely recognized that the *Moving Picture World* maintained its own resident clergy, the Reverand W. H. Jackson, on its editorial staff to recommend new films suitable to churches. Likewise, through the same columns W. Stephen Bush, an itinerant lecturer from Philadelphia, volunteered repeatedly to guide clergymen in the incorporation of movies into their church work; he became a regular editorial writer for the *Moving Picture World* from 1908 to 1916. These two commentators, Bush and Jackson, eagerly cited numerous trials and triumphs of the new medium in churches, including enthusiastic demonstrations by ministers at Pasadena, California, Appleton, Wisconsin, and Brooklyn, New York—where films were shown twice a week in the Church of Our Lady. But the hero of the *Moving Picture World* was undoubtedly the

Reverend Jump. Jump's compelling apologetics both disarmed those prejudiced against the motion picture and charmed those who sought to make their sermons interesting.[30]

However, Jump's pamphlet may be seen as naively optimistic as well. When one of the more refined film manufacturers welcomed Mr. Jump into their camp, the producer promised the trusting minister: "The interests which you represent are the interests we wish to satisfy."[31] Religion and mammon allegedly served similar concerns for educating and uplifting people. At this particular time, spiritual and economic interests were uncomplicated and mutually beneficial; by the end of the decade those interests would diverge significantly. Nevertheless, Jump did challenge religious leaders to confront and include the moving picture as an effective means of evangelism, education, and entertainment. The effect of his eloquence in the moving picture's defense was far-reaching, as numerous churches clambered onto the moving picture bandwagon.[32] Citing Jump's contributions, the *Nickelodeon* noted that "the crowning possibility of the motion picture is its usefulness to the preacher as he proclaims moral truth."[33] Like the medieval rooster who woke the world with his crowing at the first light of day, the progressive preacher could now awaken and enlighten his congregation with the light of the motion picture.

Church as Exhibition Site

The call for a sanctuary cinema had a compelling logic: if the church was to reach the masses, it had to adapt all the available means of persuasion to draw them into its fold. An early moving picture journal, *Motography*, showcased various churches exhibiting the five reels of *The Life of Moses*, and extolled religious moving pictures that could be understood by everyone: "No speaker could create such an impression," the article opined, asking:

> Why should the church not adopt such excellent means of showing the lives and characters mentioned by the ministers at each service? The people who listen to the minister would be able to see pictured before their eyes the people and acts as described in the Bible.[34]

In 1895, the Reverend Robert Pierce, a Baptist minister from Rock Island, Illinois, wrote a book entitled *Pictorial Truth* that sought to justify a practice he called "Eye Preaching." Again, in the tradition of Bonaventura's insistence on the power of images to quicken worshipers to an imitation of piety, Pierce preached that: "Pictured truth is powerful, and if God has wisely used the eye as the channel through which his truth might be imparted, surely we may use this means of reaching the hearts of those to whom we preach."[35] The Reverend Robert Morris of First Baptist Church in Skowhegan, Maine, also opted for visual means when he replaced his sermon with the *Life of Moses*, accompanied by projected song slides for hymn singing. The *Motion Picture World* applauded such innovative forms of sacred communication, urging them upon others who would find them effective for preaching and teaching.[36]

Besides the interest among Baptists in incorporating visual modes of communicating Gospel truths, as early as 1910 Methodists were also asking, "Why should not the Church be as wise as the world and go in for moving-picture attractions?" In the *Literary Digest,* they suggested that churches needed to combine their resources and "send their preachers around giving shows somewhat after the early circuit method."[37] In Redlands, California, Congregational and Presbyterian churches did join in holding united Sunday evening services during the summer in the "Airdome," essentially an outdoor moving picture pavilion.[38] An era of sanctuary cinema, of the church as a central site of movie exhibition, was unfolding.

In the premiere 1907 issue of *Moving Picture World and View Photographer,* immediately following the title page and the editor's statement of purpose, a headline declared that churches had appropriated movies for their religious work.[39] In another trade journal, Boston was touted as having the first church with a roof garden and moving pictures.[40] In 1911, the Reverend Charles McClellen, pastor of Fairhill Baptist Church in Philadelphia, felt he could successfully compete with the saloon for the patronage of the working class by providing moving pictures and vaudeville on a roof garden above his church. At approximately the same time, the Fountain Park Congregational Church in St. Louis opened a motion picture showplace in a grove adjoining the church. The pastor promised there would be "no Wild West pictures or those depicting the James Boys, Nick Carter and others dealing with crime."[41] The *Moving Picture World* continued to be amazed by the extent of church participation in its industry. The demand from churches for religious pictures, it reported, had grown steadily, and one production firm alone was spending over $150,000 to produce a religious spectacular picture.[42] The nascent film industry discovered that it could not neglect the potential audiences within the religious community.

Historical figures like John Wesley, who had adapted the innovation of circuit preaching when he took to the field, and evangelist Dwight L. Moody were identified as precursors of itinerant evangelists carrying motion pictures. Wesley's habits of traversing the countryside to speak to the common man and woman were now imitated by traveling religious film exhibitors like Colonel Hadley. In 1911, Moody's heirs at the Moody Institute used motion pictures to lure indifferent passersby to a series of open-air meetings in South Evanston, Illinois.[43] Using film to capture the attention of such passersby and thus lure them into church was also the goal of the Reverend Potter Hitchcock of the Neighborhood Congregational Church of Pasadena, California. He believed that the destiny of motion pictures was to become the means of a moral and spiritual uplift, as well as entertainment, the most winning means of attracting the eyes and attention of youth. For Hitchcock, the challenge of teaching a child was most effectively managed by appealing to the "eye-gate as well as the ear-gate." Hitchcock also brought together Congregational and Presbyterian churches of Riverside to hold cooperative services in connection with moving picture entertainments. A confirmed champion of film, he reported how missionaries in foreign countries were now producing "invaluable moving pictures."[44]

Like local film exhibitors, progressive Protestant ministers could tailor the content of films to the interests of a local congregation.[45] Like to the Japanese *benshi* who provided running commentary on silent films, ministers would show films and talk at the same time, preaching alongside the moving images. Some would edit films they received from the distributor, doctoring them to fit their sermon topic or personal taste. There was a humorous story from Britain in 1898 about a chapel that was holding a bazaar and a cinematographer who offered to exhibit some films for charity. When the pastor discovered to his pious horror that one of the reels was entitled *Skirt Dance by Mdlle. X,* he protested and refused to have it shown. However, the enterprising showman found it would be inconvenient to leave it out; moreover as a color-tinted picture, it was one of his best. So he kept it in the program. When it was time to show it on the screen to the conservative audience, he announced that the prohibited dance was *Salome Dancing before Herod.* The film was received with enormous fanfare and appreciation and the pastor knew none the better. One old lady even commented, "Well, live and learn; I never knew until tonight that they took photographs in the time of Herod."[46] Rhetorical reframings could sanctify almost any image.

The most dramatic response to the religious potential of film, however, was that of the Reverend Harry Jones, pastor of the First Reformed Church on Long Island. Jones resigned his pastorate after seeing a film based on Bunyan's *Pilgrim's Progress,* and became a *cause célèbre* for the film industry.

> I realized that I was wasting my time, for I had before me living charac-
> ters whose actions as they unfolded their sublime story were far more
> potent than anything I could say in the pulpit. A religious subject, thus
> tactfully and reverently treated, in my opinion, will do more to advance
> the cause of religion and to uplift humanity than a thousand eloquent
> preachers ever can hope to accomplish by their oratory.[47]

When Jones provided an exhibition for the entire town, he wryly discovered the superiority of film over the spoken sermon. He observed an extraordinary phenomenon, namely, that in such a large gathering of churchgoers who had come to hear a pastor showing films, "none fell asleep." Jones left his ministry and went into business as an exhibitor of educational and religious films, frequently "drawing patrons from his late congregation."[48] What he left behind for his fellow clergy was a summons to exhibit films in their churches as an adjunct to ministry. Soon, as the Secretary of the Social Service Department of the Protestant Episcopal Church, Dean Charles Lathrop, put it, churches would see *"Every preacher a moving picture operator."*[49]

The Exhibition Venue

The greatest impact on church exhibition came in 1923–24 with the standardization of the nontheatrical Eastman Kodak 16mm film format and the advent of affordable Cine-Kodak cameras. Churches could now not only show movies but also make them. This do-it-yourself venture was also facilitated by the arrival of the Victor Animatograph and the DeVry Portable 16mm Motion Picture Projectors for Church Schools.[50] (Other recommended equipment for church exhibition included "rewind and splicing equipment, a pair of scissors and a bottle of film cement," which allowed clergy to be their own censors and editors.)[51] According to the

Graphoscope Company's advertisements, their projectors were more inspiring than stained glass windows, more effective than unlimited advertising, and "More Necessary than the Church Bell." Their ads appealed directly to the hope of Prohibitionists, namely, that the "installation of motion picture machines in churches will enable them not only to take the place of the saloon as a meeting place but to help build character, morals, and hope, just as much as the saloon was creating degradation, immorality and despair."[52] Churchman Orrin Cocks promoted the motion picture as the logical successor of the saloon. He argued fervently for the continued inclusion of motion pictures, with their emotional and inspiring effects in shaping positive civic behaviors, into the church, challenging religious leaders that motion pictures were the logical successor of the saloon. "Men have always insisted on play and some of their pleasure has been found in that passing social institution, the saloon, which has abounded in light, conversation, warmth and independence." Cocks suggested that saloons be transformed into community or parish houses, and that the church show movies so that all members of the family might be drawn in together.[53]

During this era leading up to Prohibition, holiness churches reasoned that movies were a legitimate alternative to the saloon. Alfred Hill argued, "If uplifting attractions are not provided, debasing ones will be. Will the church prove itself adequate if it is closed or cold except on Sundays and one or two evenings a week? The saloon is warm and doing business 108 hours a week."[54] However, according to an address delivered at the Methodist Tercentenary Convention in Columbus, Ohio, John Flinn indicated that saloons were on the wane and the motion picture theater had taken its place. "The sign 'Family Entrance' has been taken forever from the grogshop and swung over the moving picture theater entrance. It is a healthy sign." With a savvy understanding of what drew in the respectable middle-class audience, showman and theater exhibitor Samuel ("Roxy") Rothapfel argued, "Motion picture theaters are exceedingly prosperous in prohibition territory." Reverend Stelzle echoed this notion as undoubtedly true: "The motion picture house is the best saloon substitute in existence, "because it possesses "many of the virtues of the saloon and practically none of its vices." For example, one doesn't need to dress up to go to the movies and no one has a headache the next morning.[55]

The relations between theaters and churches in the early twenties were mixed. *Variety* happily reported that churches functioned as regular film houses (the Methodists took the Strand and the Presbyterians a film house across the street). The trade journal expressed surprise when one of its own exhibitors sold his interest in a string of motion picture houses after ten years to devote his life to being the rector of Christ Church, in Clayton, New York.[56] On the other hand, when the B. F. Keith management had generously and strategically loaned out one of their theaters for Lenten services, a Baptist minister launched a tirade against theaters as "gilded caves to lure children."[57]

Photoplay tried to do its bit to help organize churches and schools for the presentation of motion pictures, with Frederick James Smith exhorting every church in the land to "wake up to the great possibilities of motion pictures and get them harnessed and working as agencies for social uplift," and calling on businessmen to invest in the installation of projectors to improve their communities.[58] In 1919, *Variety* took notice of the growing trend of sanctuary cinemas. John McAleer, president of Screen Entertainment Distributors, closed a deal with Vitagraph and Universal studios for a selected run of suitable religious subjects. According to *Variety*, almost ten million churches and schools had been equipped with projection machines, which they prophesied would be a boon to the trade.[59]

Distribution companies, alert to potential profits from religious groups, appealed to churches both with films and with supplementary help. World Educational Film Company, for example, released *My Shepherd*, based on Psalm 23—a film with beautiful, vivid, and comforting imagery in the contemplative tradition of religious painting, along with a suggested service enclosed.[60] Such an employment of natural imagery as spiritual comfort and devotional guidance, initiated by the Hudson River School, would reach its apex with the *Hymnbook of the Screen* that provided early sacred musical movies, three minutes each, exalting the beauty of God's creation.[61] A later series known as *Hymnologues*, specifically designed for Roman Catholic audiences (e.g., *Ave Maria* and *The Angelus*), superimposed the words of well-known hymns over featured scenes of mountains, clouds, flowers, and seashores.[62] Creative framing would be constructed with scenes contained within the image of the cross, with the best films of the series being *The Lord Is My Shepherd, Nearer My God to Thee,* and *Rock of Ages.*[63] (Critic Paul Janes warned about showing inappropriate hymn films for services, distinguishing between worthy hymns and those that simply "jazzed up" the service. He reminded users that each hymn song should be assessed according to its theme, congregational response, and its effect to elicit adoration.)[64] Churches could be both picture galleries and worship centers.

In seeking to help pastors employ films, distribution companies offered specific instructions. For example, one two-reel film, *By Their Fruits*, illustrated in Hogarthian fashion the downward moral consequences of breaking the commandment "Thou Shalt Not Steal." The *Educational Screen* magazine recommended adapting the following liturgy.

> *A Suggested Service for This Film*
>
> *Opening Hymn*—Arise my Soul, Stretch Every Nerve
> *Reading of Psalm*—Psalm 119
> *Hymn*—My Soul Be on Thy Guard
> *Scripture Reading*—Proverbs 16: 1–25
> *Solo or Quartet*—Yield Not to Temptation
> *Sermon*—Leviticus 19:11—"Ye shall not steal."
> *The picture then follows.* (The Ten Commandments or other
>   suitable slide may be projected between reels.)
> *Prayer. Announcements. Offering.*
> Closing Hymn—*Take my Life and let it be Consecrated Lord
>   to Thee.*
> *Benediction.*[65]

The liturgy of most theatrical services followed such a pattern. For a service that he delivered at Mt. Vernon Methodist Church using MPPC producer Sigmund Lubin's filmed version of the Passion Play, the Reverend George Spooner described a scene in which the lights were dimmed, and the familiar flicker of the motion picture projector appeared with a ray of light shot to a screen lowered in front of the organ. At the close of the exhibition, the lights would go up, a hymn sung, and a benediction pronounced.[66]

The Reverend Carl Patton of the First Congregational Church in Los Angeles offered no apology for using Hollywood films in his church work because, "incidentally, my evening service is a delight and not a burden to me." Patton had debated Dean Charles Brown (who had delivered lectures at Yale Divinity School on the same issue) over whether to incorporate motion pictures in Sunday evening services. With a call to worship coming from a reading of the scriptures, prayers from St. Chrysostom and John Knox, and the singing of hymns from the screen with slides and films (and organ playing), Patton boasted an attendance of over one thousand five hundred people due to the draw of films: "I can lodge the great message in the hearts of that congregation as none of you preachers can do." He asserted that in singing Gospel songs and classic church hymns projected upon the screen, everyone in his congregation joined in looking at the words (even for solo presentations), helping them tremendously in listening with eyes and ears. The projected hymn insures that "there is no fishing of books out of the racks, no finding of the page. Everybody sings." Projected slides and films united the congregation, looking heavenward. Patton chose the pictures himself, selecting familiar films like *The Sky Pilot, The Miracle Man,* or *Faith Healer,* in order to extract a kernel of truth from the narrative that illustrated his sermon topic. An expert operator would show only one reel at a time, necessitated by the constraint of having only one projector, but the minister took the reel-changing break to speak. Because of Patton's pioneering work in church film use during the zenith of silent film, Will H. Hays cited the Congregational minister as a model churchman.[67]

Certain films stirred local pastors to public praise of them. The Reverend Thomas Gregory extolled the realistic virtues of Lois Weber's *Idle Wives* (1916), for being "true to nature" and showing men and women as they actually are in the world. For Gregory, while the film was not based on any particular biblical text, "it preaches a sermon greater than any that was ever heard in a pulpit."[68] Remarkably, the entrée of films into progressive church services disclosed how central the illustrated sermon had become to the liturgy.

Nevertheless, the religious community had not settled the question of whether the movies were a friend or foe, even as the 1920s came to an end. In 1928, *Christian Herald* writer Ron Pettey, comparing the use of film to the earlier use of colored picture cards that taught scriptural lessons from the Golden Text, felt that the new generation had a greater advantage "seeing the drama of the Bible in its lifelike figure move before him on a screen." He described a typical church venue as follows:

> [an] auditorium, its soft lights dimly reflected in the stained-glass windows, a comfortable seat, and a friendly welcome from the usher. The organ played softly in the background. Then a motion-picture machine flashed a prayer on a silver screen. The words were repeated by a man who stood beside the screen as those in the auditorium sat with bowed heads. A moment later we were in the Holy Land: places once dim and

far away became real as they were paraded before our eyes. For a full hour one could have heard the tick of a clock throughout the room; then the picture faded, the lights turned up and the minister spoke briefly from his pulpit of the Biblical significance of the scenes we had seen.[69]

Pettey pointed to the growing membership rolls of those churches that dared to enter the exhibition field and he asked, however, whether a pastor should go after the crowds in the commercial playhouses with their own attractions as an ally, or should he fight secular motion pictures as an enemy? Other questions needed answers as well, to Pettey's mind: Should a pastor merely recommend good pictures or should he show them? How should the minister who used pictures answer the critics who charged that such methods robbed the church of its dignity and turned it into a theater? And was it better "to carry a message to a thousand new faces than to preach to a dozen old saints?"

To answer his questions, Pettey assembled compelling evidence from prominent leaders. The Reverend Dr. Christian F. Reisner, pastor of the Chelsea Methodist Episcopal Church in New York City, had used motion pictures for eighteen years, since 1910. Other testimonials from converts who acknowledged the effect of Reisner's innovations, were presented.[70] In addition, Pettey cited a list of celebrity clergy who extolled the virtues of film with unabashed enthusiasm: Dr. Jason Noble Pierce, of the First Congregational Church (President Calvin Coolidge's church), testified that he employed films not only to help offset the harmful influence of questionable picture plays, but to make his church a real community center through visual evangelism. The Reverend Chester Marshall of First Methodist Church of Bridgeport, Connecticut, exhibited films on Sunday nights. (The trade periodicals praised the assertive leadership of Marshall, speaking for "forty-one thousand ministers of his faith" in promoting the use of motion pictures to widen the church's field of activities.)[71] The Reverend Dr. William Mitchell, pastor of Wesley Methodist Church of Worcester, Massachusetts, found that films functioned as direct messages to obdurate parishioners; those who were stubbornly slow to hear were quick to see.

Many other voices in the church agreed with Pettey's film advocates. The chairman of the Federal Council of Churches in Christ in America and leader of its Church and Drama Association, George Reid Andrews, acknowledged the value of ecclesiastical exhibitions of film and endeavored to assist the churches in their programs of picture showing, although he pointed to three basic persistent challenges: namely, the production, distribution, and exhibition of suitable pictures for the church.[72] The grand effort of the progressive FCC, established in 1908, was to use "modern movements" to promote Christian unity, and most modern of all was the moving picture.[73] Andrews pushed for the church to take its cue in religious education from the movies, adopting dramatic ideas for their sermons, for here was an effective means of inspiring both youth and adults.[74]

Edwin Gillette of Jacksonville, Florida, discovered uses for film in an urban setting to attract the many homeless young people of his neighborhood. Gillette sought out unchurched people by offering dramatic films like George Loane Tucker's *The Miracle Man* (top industry grosser of 1919) and *The Old Nest* (which he found perfect for evoking deep sentiments, particularly on Mother's Day). Gillette would often cut and edit the films he exhibited to fit his own sermonic purposes, even to the extent of omitting a reel or two.[75] Such aesthetic license was necessary not only due to constraints of time for viewing, but for content as well.

Other defenders of the Church Film movement cited the support of public figures like perennial presidential candidate William Jennings Bryan, who supported the use of the moving pictures as aids to both educational and religious instruction. Bryan touted the Bible as the apex of historical drama, revelatory of "real life and real life can not be improved upon." He recommended a film entitled *After Six Days* as "a wonderful picture," sympathetic and reverently handled, that could "impress Bible truths as they can not be impressed by reading only. The impressions that come through the picture are more distinct and more lasting than ideas presented in words, especially to children."[76] Called one of the most remarkable biblical pictures ever filmed, *After Six Days* was made abroad at an expense of more than $3 million and was allegedly financed by a European government bank. The *Christian Herald* also obtained exhibition rights, seeing the possibilities for visual religious education, which it found "far more forceful than the written or spoken word." Another influential booster of such movies was evangelist Billy Sunday, who also saw the Bible as the world's greatest picture source:

> It is an inexhaustible supply of tragedy, pathos, and drama and the time will come when the movies will present these stories reverently and faithfully. . . . God spoke through the Old Testament by means of pictures. That is the way Christ taught, because without a parable He spake not to any man. A parable was a picture.[77]

The Challenge of Exhibition

While likewise recommending the use of motion pictures in the pulpit, Dr. Mark Kelley of State Street Methodist Episcopal Church of Troy, New York, nevertheless faced numerous exhibition difficulties. These included the uncouthness of the apparatus of machines, booths, and screen, the inferiority of projection, the costs, the natural prejudice of some of his church people, and the perception that worship was being commercialized. Regardless, he boldly pushed film's use, adapting it as a vigorous and fresh method of presentation, not as a vehicle of showmanship, but as a handmaiden to preaching and worship. Critic William Mitchell noted that books on homiletics would dwell at length on the importance of introducing one's sermons with vivid and striking illustrations, so he asked, "Why not use film?" What could provide a more striking introduction, mused Mitchell, than a properly edited film with skillful transitions?[78] Slowly as film served to vivify threadbare sermons, and humbled itself to work as a servant to preaching and teaching, the church was gradually ordained and consecrated to serve as a site for holy exhibitions.[79]

In 1926 religious educator A. B. Hollis approved this new direction the church was taking, although claiming—in contrast to the trade journal *Variety*—a more modest figure of over fifteen thousand projectors being used in church schools. Nevertheless, concerned that the churches had surrendered the moving picture to Hollywood "bait, hook and sinker," Hollis urged a balanced perspective on the use of film in religious education. While it seemed that the film industry had taken possession of "every chamber of the mind over which lurks the faintest shadow of the label 'movie,'" the church could counter that it had been using the same medium in "evening services, in young people's meetings, Sunday schools, and various parish gatherings." Hollis's endorsement of movies included two caveats, however: first, the motion picture in the pulpit is "*not a substitute for a sermon*," only a short illustration of one. Second, he pointed out, the "Sunday evening service is not the principal place for the motion picture in church work. It is better served with youth, in benevolent work, and among the deprived, as the deaf, crippled and the shut-ins." As an adjunct to church work, it must be subordinate and not the main attraction, serving the needs of the church rather than becoming its center altar.[80] While filling his Sunday evening services with over a thousand people every week through the use of motion pictures, another clergyman, Dr. Frederick Fay of South Congregational Church of New Britain, Connecticut, echoed the necessity of preserving the proper atmosphere. At the same time, he acknowledged that since he had begun using films, collections had increased substantially.[81]

However, alongside the increased confidence in their potential that Pettey and others exemplified, the suspicion of movies persisted. A few critics presumed that film was as narcotic and addictive as alcohol, producing a sensational excitement of the nerves much like the "drink habit, in that the victim demands more and more of the same stimulation. Ordinary pleasures normal to childhood no longer have any power to please and children become small imitations of blasé adults who do not know what it means to be genuinely interested in anything unless it is some new and powerful sensation."[82] In 1926, outspoken female critics like Josephine Baldwin expressed their concern about the moral and religious effects of all films on children, who were becoming more "sophisticated and familiar with vice." She declared: "I have joined the Crusade for Clean Movies."[83] A similar wariness of films was expressed by Maine Bishop John Murray, who even raised questions regarding the showing of Catholic films in church recreation halls for fear that they would stimulate the "movie habit" among the faithful.[84]

The crusade for exhibiting clean and uplifting films was ecumenical. From the early days of the *International Journal of Religious Education,* an interdenominational monthly supported by numerous parachurch organizations, its editor Charles Banning sought to guide churches through the slough of motion picture use toward a more celestial screen. Over the years in which movies had evolved from a mechanical curiosity into popular entertainment, they had also evolved as a vital means of eliciting emotional responses in religious education, which Banning described as follows:

> Joy and pain, hope and fear, love and hate, gratitude and envy. Emotional responses are often registered by use of the "close-up." Visual education began with the cave man that carved his crude drawings on the walls of his cave. If a boy will use a part of his allowance to go to the movies to see Babe Ruth hit a home run, why could he not be interested through the same means in the romance of modern missions? If he enjoys seeing the Niagara and hearing the stories of the Indians in school, why is it not reasonable to suppose that if he were shown pictures of the

Jordan and the Sea of Galilee he would be led to a deeper interest in the Bible stories? We have an opportunity to appeal to the eye and add an emotional content and motion. The entertainment possibilities need hardly be mentioned. It has been so exploited and commercialized that it has become a millstone about the neck of any church, which attempts to put the projector to a better use.

Therefore the final test of films, observed Banning, was to see someone grip the minister's hand at the door and say: "That service touched me; I'll never be the same kind of a man again." Nevertheless, Banning argued that even if the cinema had been misused in the past, it could also be turned to good use. "If evil suggestions and wrong ideals and attitudes can be taught by use of the screen, is not the converse possible? Bible stories, missionary stories, pictures with a strong moral lesson, nature study, Church history, biography, and patriotism are all within the realm of the possible good from a wise use of films."[85] In the pious and learned spirit of Bonaventura, Banning called for his fellow Protestant film pioneers to maintain their vision, persevere, and keep the faith. The exhibition of good and decent films needed only the leadership of wise and noble religious exhibitors.

Theaters as Churches

In the early twentieth century, church auditoriums could recommend themselves as safe spaces in which to view moving pictures. In contrast to the often dank and unwholesome environs of earlier nickelodeons, the church offered a certifiably clean, supervised, and respectable site for the consumption of media. There was a general assurance that whatever was shown would be salubrious for eye and soul. Since the scriptures had warned not to place any unclean thing before the eye, churchgoers crowded with confidence into the sanctuary cinemas to see wonders from modern technological inventions that would enlighten and entertain them. Religious leaders felt that the churches had tamed this alloy of the icon and the theater and directed its use for good: there was nothing to fear. So some religious leaders turned their attention to invading secular theaters to transform them into makeshift churches. As the popularity of film exhibition grew in the churches, some borrowed or appropriated existing theaters for religious uses, thereby converting unholy ground into a sacred haven.

Portrayed as a Roman centurion, *The Moving Picture World* tried to caricature bigoted reformers as thwarting the opportunity for young people to see good films, like *Ben Hur, The Life of Moses,* and scenes from China, presumably all for educational and missionary purposes. Editorial Cartoon: "Fight for a Modern Sunday," *Moving Picture World* (February 5, 1916), 825. Courtesy Library of Congress.

The Reverend Harry Robbins described his pioneering venture into opening and maintaining a first-class moving picture theater as an ecclesiastical adjunct to his official ministry as "walking in where angels had feared to tread." Robbins sought to run a model movie house "good enough from an artistic standpoint to compete with other houses, and yet so clean and useful as to disarm the criticism of the most narrow church member."[86] In his view, light entered the temple of darkness and chased away the shadows of evil. Others had paved Robbins's way as entertainment crusaders invading moving picture theaters. A Congregational minister in the fast-growing town of four thousand, Gary, Indiana, leased the nickel moving picture theater for Sundays, and positioned himself on a program preceding a knockabout comedian.[87] A Methodist minister, the Reverend Dr. Bascom, believing secular shows could be reformed, befriended the owner of the Crystal Palace theater and secured it and its apparatus gratis, with only the cost of the lighting to be paid. Bascom's subsequent presentation of sacred moving pictures of Joseph and his brethren attracted such a crowd that two hundred persons were turned away.[88] For his part, the Reverend Zed Copp of Washington, D.C., secured the cooperation of various local movie theaters (the Royal, the Princess, the Scenic) and turned them into churches on Sundays, attracting a bedraggled and motley congregation—"the well-dressed and the ragged; the erect and the bent."[89] Along the same lines, when a fire destroyed a large church in Pittsburgh, the owner of the local moving picture theater loaned his building to the congregation.[90]

Many churches were now commandeering theater buildings as though conquering institutions of vice and civilizing them for moral purposes. When seeking a location to gather and counsel men who had been shut out of the saloons, one experimental congregation took over two small picture theaters as halfway centers.[91] The Reverend Bertram Brown, rector of Calvary Episcopal, took his congregation to the local picture house in Tarboro, North Carolina, and used the theater to draw in other citizens in order to minister to their souls' spiritual needs and to "soothe the yearnings of the human heart for clean, wholesome entertainment."[92] Secular theatre sites were sanctified by the regular presence of clergy; they could be converted to religious uses, as actually transpired in one emerging city in the South.

Norfolk, Virginia, was a midrange city of around 67,000 people in 1910, and uniquely marked as an entertainment "gateway to the south" and commercial market where religion and the moving pictures were conjoined in numerous ways. Annual Lenten noonday services, particular of liturgical churches like the Episcopal, were conducted at various theaters like the Granby and the American.[93] The local paper, the *Virginian-Pilot*, promoted the series by regularly reporting how capacity crowds attended the services in the new theaters.[94] Similarly, a visiting New York City evangelist, C. E. Heard, intrigued his theater audience with his timely sermon at Norfolk's grand American Theatre entitled "Biblical Exposition on 'The Fall of Babylon,'" delivered immediately after D. W. Griffith's *Intolerance* had played.[95] Seats were free and he promised to take no collections. Another evangelist, Irwin Richardson, appeared at the nearby Colonial movie picture theater, to speak on the Great War in relation to biblical predictions.[96] Richardson had secured the Colonial to lecture on the fulfillment of Bible prophecy, "because of its large seating capacity."[97] Judge Rutherford even took out large ads inviting people to the Colonial Theatre to hear his message: "Millions Now Living Will Never Die." The judge's sermon topic was connected to a local cult's prediction that the world would come to an end on December 17, 1919 because of planetary alignment. On December 18, Norfolk paper's front page headline read "End of the World Seems to Have Been Postponed," and a week later a column on the weather mockingly announced, "Sun Shines for First Time since World's End."[98] At the Olympic Theatre, another advertisement tweaked similar interest with "Evangelist Claims Empires Will End."[99]

Even in evangelistic meetings as early as 1908, there was remarkable cooperation between church and theater.[100] In that year, the proprietor of the Barton Theatre in Norfolk, Virginia, actually urged evangelist Mr. Asher to visit and conduct services in his theater, where prominent men and women of the city gathered to pray and worship God. In perhaps the apotheosis of all theater-conversions, Mr. Barton himself was subsequently and dramatically "saved" in his own theater. The press reported that

> this place of amusement, known to Norfolk citizens as a variety house, where questionable women sing and others perform and allow men to buy them drinks, was filled last night not by the usual type of citizens that patronize the place, but by some of the best and most prominent men in town. Up in the boxes ordinarily used as a place where drinks are served and women and men were gathered prominent citizens and the women who sat beside them knelt in prayer and joined in the singing of religious songs and hymns. It was a joyful sight to see every man and every woman kneel for ten minutes on the dirty floor of this same place and beg God's forgiveness for sin and promise to mend their lives.[101]

About forty men signed coupons declaring their intention of becoming church members that very night. Even James M. Barton, proprietor, had his hands uplifted, and he decided to get out of this business of "salooning."

Other Lenten devotions were conducted for businessmen at Norfolk's Granby Theatre, as clergy thought it "advisable to obtain a larger auditorium than that used heretofore and the management of the Granby theatre has generously offered the use of this building."[102] One obvious reason that theaters opened their auditoriums to churches during the Lenten season was economic. According to historian Thomas Doherty, when Roman Catholics celebrated Lent, box office revenues dropped off sharply.[103] Similarly, *Variety* worried that religious observance of the Jewish Passover, Lenten, and Good Friday services confused and altered moving picture exhibition schedules.[104]

As the churches began adopting theaters, they also began adopting theatrical methods to attract worshipers. Methods included using entrancing posters advertising religious services at some hall or theater, while others continued to lure non-churchgoers through illustrated sermons and dramatic sermon titles. The Reverend Frank Pratt found the Wonderland Theatre an apt site to advertise his provocative sermon: "Is There a Devil?"[105] The Reverend Zed Copp followed Jesus' call to go after "the people who are some times looked down on by churches and church people—the great army of down and outs."[106] In the local papers in Norfolk, not only were advertisements for the theaters aligned on the same page with church news, but the theaters also advertised the religious activities taking place at their sites. The Crosman Theatre, for example, announced that the Reverend Frank Pratt would speak Sunday nights on such themes as "The Way Our Bible Came to Us." They quoted his invitation to strangers to attend the theater for his entertaining Sunday school class, "a school in harmony with the modern spirit."[107] Competition between the institutional church and the new photoplay religion elicited sly comparisons when it came to sermon titles. The *Christian Herald* mockingly commented that Hollywood and the church should cooperate on sharing sermon and film titles. H. L. Lambdia recommended that sensational moving picture ad writers dress up sermon titles with such alluring phrases as "Dancing with the Devil." In Portland, Oregon, actual sermon titles like "Ruined by Rum" or "Pickled in Gin and Sin" were suggested to Hollywood executives, since they would appeal to both moving-going publics and church congregations.[108]

The Arcade Theatre promoted Salvation Army evangelists like Colonel John Dean, who traveled to Norfolk to lecture on crooked women and purity of living.[109] A citywide Baptist revival occurred in the sacred halls of the city's Majestic Theatre, where the union services "were marked by intense feeling and deep spiritual power." [110] However, after some success, Baptist pastors decided that more constituents could be reached by changing the place of meeting from the Majestic Theatre to the First Baptist Church. The Majestic then hosted the colored Baptist conference of Norfolk, which decided to "enter a simultaneous campaign for the uplift and betterment of its race in the amusement center." [111] With the persistent practice of segregation, black churches found it necessary to establish their own community centers for entertainment and social gatherings. *Film Progress* sought to promote what it saw as a need for better films in black theaters and to endorse Sunday evening motion picture services. [112] Throughout the decade, black churches continued to use and sanctify theater sites for religious services, educational centers, musical concerts, and old-fashioned revivals. [113] One theater in particular, the Attucks Theatre in Norfolk, became a focal point of entertainment and social and religious life for the town's black community. [114]

Apart from of periodic debates regarding Sabbath observance, churches were remarkably cozy with the theaters. Religious leaders debated whether the "Church or Devil [was] to Entertain Young of This Century" and chose the former. Speaking for the worldwide Sunday school movement, Luther Tesh observed that young people were going to seek entertainment: "If the people of God do not furnish that entertainment, the devil will." [115] Under the auspices of the Church Federation of Norfolk, Virginia, various sermons, services, and social actions were held in the local theaters. [116] The St. Vincent de Paul Conference adopted a novel system to provide for the poor by collecting and distributing clothes from the old Victory Theatre. In addition, they were to open up the theater for film exhibitions and distribute all the proceeds (after paying for necessary operation expenses) "for charitable purposes so that persons attending this show can feel that a part of their admission price paid will go towards relieving need and distress in Norfolk." [117] So too, the Rector's Guild of Emmanuel Church presented animated pictures enhanced by appropriate music to raise a goodly sum. [118]

Children, Immigrants, and Building Community

While Progressive reformers fretted mostly over the impact of moving pictures on impressionable children and immigrants, many church groups targeted these two audiences as mission fields to be reached through the same medium. With the support of the Baptist City Mission Society, Manhattan's Harlem Baptist Church had already claimed the distinction of being the "First Church in the World to Show Motion Pictures" in the autumn of 1903. The church had a tradition of presenting stereopticon lectures by high-class traveling showmen like Lyman H. Howe, but Pastor Adam Chambers's introduction of films met with some early opposition, particularly with regard to attracting poor children to the sanctuary. Some members of his congregation complained that he was not only blaspheming the name of religion but was drawing in "hundreds of little ragamuffins from the streets who would mess up the carpets and soil the chairs." Chambers appealed to his critics by emphasizing that when he was called before God as an accountable steward the Lord would not be concerned about how well the carpets and chairs were cared for, but would ask: "Where are the children?" Apparently his homily worked, as his congregation was in tears imploring him to carry out his vision with the ragged urchins of New York's East Side.[119] After his persuasive sermon on priorities, championing the value of helping urchins over maintaining decorum, Chambers found support for providing Tuesday night moving picture programs, averaging around four hundred to five hundred children at his penny shows. For Chambers, motion pictures were "bait" for the children, the "best 'bait' the church has ever found. My plan has always been to win the children first and through them the adults." Later, he would meet with young professional men who bragged that they had been known as "one of Adam Chambers' boys."[120]

Throughout the second decade of the twentieth century, churches aimed particularly at focusing on both children and immigrants and attempted to socialize them into mainstream American life through educational pictures. A Presbyterian church, the New York Labor Temple, brought together an interchurch world brotherhood for its diverse neighborhood of Italians, Irish, Slavs, and Jews in which the dominant feature was its use of motion picture exhibitions. The Reverend F. E. Wilber, in conjunction with the Reverend Charles Stelzle of the Presbyterian Board of Home Missions, found the film forums were the best way to deal with urban, immigrant populations. The church was praised for accomplishing a great deal of social good.[121] In certain progressive churches, usually Congregational, ministers sought to promote various aspects of the Social Gospel as well. For example, in 1912 in Appleton, Wisconsin, a Congregational church secured a copy of the suffragist film, *Votes for Women*, and sought to educate its congregation on key reform issues—as well as to get the gathered folk to pay five cents. For this initiative, *The Moving Picture World* cleverly coined a new phrase, the *nickeclesia*, literally the nickel church, as opposed to the nickel theater, the *nickelodeon*.[122]

The Church Motion-Picture Society organized by Cleveland Moffett followed Chambers's example and treated immigrant children of New York City to free movies during Christmas holidays at Fifth Avenue Presbyterian Church and the Church of the Ascension. The Reverend Moffett promoted his vision for using films "of a more elevating sort for the entertainment of the poor children swarming the streets of New York."[123] A key target audience was orphans, frequently invited to free entertainment. Down in Norfolk, Virginia, the Cumberland Street Methodist Church set aside every Thursday night for the gathering of the children and tired mothers of the community, where they could see pictures of a high moral tone and also enjoy good music.[124]

Yet, in contrast to such appeals to children, the head of the Pinkerton Detective Agency warned of the evil of criminal films upon young impressionable minds: "The motion picture is now, and will become more so, one of the greatest educational factors in modern life. The forbidding scenes of the underworld are the snakes in the grass that should be scotched and crusht for the general good."[125] Six years later, in 1920 the *Literary Digest* echoed these two alternatives: "The Motion Picture either can be made of assistance to the Church, as a vehicle for religious, educational and diversionary propaganda, or it may be left as an opposing weapon for satanic mischief."[126] One Cleveland censor, R. O. Bartholomew, canvassed over 5,800 children and 140 teachers, and collected over 1,500 essays by children on why they went to the movies. Examples ranged from a desire to learn about other lands to the thrill they got when "you go to a show you see men robbing houses and you learn to rob houses and people."[127] Very few of the children spoke of its positive moral influence. In order to promote positive propaganda about the uplifting effects of movies, the Reverend Moffett opted to join the British philanthropist, the Duke of Manchester, in planning the formation of a company to produce religious and educational pictures. With Vitagraph Studios supplying the films, their vision was to father a substantial strategy that would take children off the streets and offer spiritual and educational alternatives. An immediate challenge, however, was to convince "scared cats" worried about the desecration of the sacred edifice of the church about the importance of brightening the lives of children through moving pictures.[128] The worthiness of the project seemed obvious to leaders like Moffett, recognizing the films' appeal films to children. The *Chicago Post* cleverly articulated this attraction's appeal to kids:

> Remember when you were a small boy and sat in a hot, stuffy pew in a hot, stuffy church on a hot, stuffy Sunday morning while the preacher droned through an interminable sermon? Sometimes you caught flies in your hand or folded the church bulletin up into a flytrap. Or you helped pass away the time by drawing little faces in the O's on the title page of the hymnbook. When the preacher would arrive at the "fourthly," you knew the ordeal was half over. When he reached "fifthly, brethren," it was only fifteen minutes more till "one last word and I am done."
>
> The small boy of the coming generation will not have to resort to fly catching or to marking up the hymnbook to endure the service. The hours will pass on golden wings. For movies will replace the sermon. Instead of "fourthly," it will be a four-reel film. The centenary conservation committee of the Methodist Episcopal Church has come to the conclusion that movies are the thing, and expects soon to introduce film sermons into the Chicago churches.
>
> Of course there will be no train robberies or holdups, no harem queens, adventuresses or anything so lurid as all that. But the pictures won't be exactly tame, either. Missionaries in all parts of the world from Greenland's icy mountains to India's coral strand, are busy making views of life in those far lands where only man is vile. African pigmies, Eskimos, Arabs, headhunting Dyacks and Fiji Islanders will march out upon the silver screen. The various activities of the church—these, by the way, do not include fly-catching—will be shown."[129]

Many churches responded with the same kind of enthusiasm to what they viewed as a new educational and spiritual aid to religious work, especially among children. In 1921, in her early history of the nontheatrical church film, beginning with the groundbreaking work of Adam Chambers, "Church Motion Pictures—Its Development and Growth," Hilda Jackson sought to identify appropriate films for children. However, while optimistic about finding such films, she complained about the difficulty of "find[ing] the few grains of wheat in the bushel of chaff."[130] The Reverend Ernest Miller of the M. E. Church of Cuyahoga Falls, Ohio, identified *The Holy City* and *Pilgrim's Progress* as effective religious films, in contrast to superficial pictures like *The Soul Herder*. While his primary concern was to expand the viewing capacity of churches by providing spacious assembly rooms, he had to concede that producers often failed to get the religious viewpoint, emphasized insignificant details, exposed sectarian prejudice, and used religious characters for comic effect.[131]

By 1911, the YMCA in New York had set up a motion picture bureau to energize young men and was coordinating the distribution of religiously oriented films and building libraries of rental films to serve church and community organizations. The YMCA had enjoined Edison to help attract young men and women, commissioning films that would teach English, moral uplift, or bodybuilding. Later, when cooperating with its Industrial Committee of the International Committee, the YMCA tended to produce films with a more ecumenical spirit that emphasized "Americanization" projects with the immigrant working class. In conjunction with the National Board of Censorship, the YMCA also published a pamphlet on *Motion Pictures in Education* which explored how moving pictures could be used educationally, noting that both sermons and temptations to wrongdoing could be conveyed more vividly through motion pictures than through printed materials.[132]

Like the churches, the YMCA sought to reach out beyond their Sunday programs, especially in ministry to youth. Using a technology of recruitment, the YMCA showed movies at factories, schools, playgrounds, and churches, anywhere that people gathered.[133] The disruption of the family by modern industry challenged Progressive religious reform movements to reinvigorate the social realm. In response, the "uplift movement" hoped to promote a more modern and moral society through the educational use of film. Part of that strategy was the tactic of Americanizing immigrants who were flooding into Ellis Island and spreading around the country. The YMCA sought to defuse any class warfare by using the modern technology of film as a vivid, efficient tool of pedagogy; films were the best rhetorical means of public address for European immigrants.[134]

A Secretary of the YMCA would stand beside the screen and talk to the audience mesmerized by the film, indicating the fruit of civic obedience and virtue. One could see in the films how "bad men" suffered the consequences of their rebellion, disobedience, and bad citizenship while good people were rewarded. The exemplary visual contrast was an easy lesson to teach. A committee from the Young Men's Christian Association opined that moving pictures were for the mass of people "the greatest educational and refining influence that has arisen in this century," in that they exposed many to the inside of a beautiful home, to the proper courtesies practiced by gentlemen, and to foreign lands.[135] Such educational entertainment strategies were applauded by the Society for Visual Education based in Chicago. Under the editorial guidance of Nelson Greene, its monthly periodical aimed to develop teaching programs for progressive schools and religious institutions. In its inaugural issue in January 1920, it proposed a standard for visual education, noting that in all probability "the first hieroglyphics were merely entertainment."[136] Nothing was beyond the scope of visual education; topics included physics, optics, mechanics, agriculture, as well as the important American task of teaching English to foreigners.[137]

Social activist Jane Addams's description of the American motion picture show as "the house of dreams" inspired many to see in it a wholesome alternative, particularly for the immigrant class, to less salubrious activities like drinking, dancing, and cards. Likewise, church educator Henry Atkinson argued that it was only the abuse of popular amusements that made them dangerous and that it was the responsibility of the church to inculcate good principles and so transform the tastes of the people.[138] Films magnetically attracted immigrants and educated them on good citizenship as well as biblical stories.

In an early study on the science of the moving pictures in 1912, Frederick A. Talbot averred that religious institutions had "not been backward in realizing the value of animated pictures in preaching the gospel of faith." The institutions realized that any episode from the Creation to the Resurrection could be produced to familiarize young and old with Bible stories. Talbot related an anecdote that demonstrated the wonderful cogency of animated pictures. A Sunday school teacher was describing the Passage of the Red Sea to a group of children which included one who had seen a motion picture on the subject. As the teacher told the story of Moses, one piping voice exclaimed:

"Yes, teacher, I know that is right!"
"Why?" asked the somewhat startled teacher.
"Because I saw it!" as the child explained that the previous evening she had been to a picture theatre and had seen the Israelites crossing the Red Sea.[139]

Such experiences reaffirmed Bonaventura's recommendation that the uneducated and illiterate be given images that they might be able to read and remember the stories of the Bible. Such lively images also aroused their issued at the close of the school session. A staff of 10 registrars recently handled nearly 400 children in less than an hour. We now have 918 season tickets out in the neighborhood, and hold two programs each Friday —one at 3:30 and one at 7:30; the afternoon program shows to the younger children the same picture which is shown to the adults at night.

As soon as the registration cards are available, we throw our whole organization into the work of calling on the homes of children who go to no Sunday school.

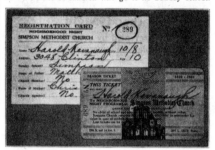

Children unless accompanied by parents are admitted by ticket only. The leads from the registration cards are followed up and bring many inactive members back into the church.

Names of such children are furnished to the teachers of Sunday school classes. We have been able to make 100 calls per week on these "prospects" with the result that scores have come into our Sunday school. The names of the fathers and mothers give us a fine line of "prospects" for our adult classes. Our men's class recently conducted two visitations among these men, securing a considerable number for the various activities of the church.

When the financial canvass was made for the year's budget of the church, these "outsiders" contributed almost $1,000 toward our annual expense. Many church letters have been found as we have called in the homes, and many others have been brought into the church through profession of faith, the first contacts being made through the "Neighborhood Night." We consider this registration plan absolutely essential to our organization.

The committee on film consists of the pastor, a member of the board of trustees, and the superintendent of one of the grade schools of the city. All films pass the inspection of this committee. Some of them we review, some of them are accepted on the judgment of film exchanges whose judgment we have learned to trust, and some of them are secured through trust-

This school has been increased almost 40 per cent in the course of one year through the use of pictures. The popular Friday night program has become so big that it has had to be divided into an afternoon and an evening session.

worthy advice from other users. By following suggestions in THE MOVING PICTURE AGE we get much help in the selection of film. The National Board of Review issues a booklet which lists many fine features. The following pictures have been used in our programs with splendid success:

Tom Sawyer	Famous Players-Lasky
The Warrens of Virginia	Famous Players-Lasky
Freckles	Famous Players-Lasky
Huck and Tom	Famous Players-Lasky
Mrs. Wiggs of the Cabbage Patch	Famous Players-Lasky
The Copperhead	Famous Players-Lasky
Sis Hopkins	Goldwyn
The Kingdom of Youth	Goldwyn
The Cinderella Man	Goldwyn
Jack and the Bean Stalk	Fox
Fan Fan	Fox
Treasure Island	Fox
Babes in the Woods	Fox
The Life of General Pershing	Fox
Smiles	Fox
Evangeline	Fox
From the Manger to the Cross	Vitagraph
The Fortune Hunter	Vitagraph
Anne of Green Gables	Realart
Erstwhile Susan	Realart

The following pictures have a fine appeal for an adult audience, but do not appeal to the children so strongly:

The Blue Bird	Famous Players-Lasky
Little Women	Famous Players-Lasky
His Majesty Bunker Bean	Famous Players-Lasky
Les Miserables	Fox
Tale of Two Cities	Fox
Puddenhead Wilson	Famous Players

We seldom use more than five reels because of the time involved. Occasionally we make up a program of miscellaneous films, educational, comedies and animated cartoons. Younger children enjoy these programs better than adults, because their minds will grasp a shorter and less involved tale more readily.

Young people between the ages of 18 and 24 have less interest in our general programs than either adults or children. We have found it necessary, on many occasions, to organize programs especially for this group which can be held separately. It is a good plan to have a committee from among the young people themselves select their own film under tactful leadership.

The Work of the Program Committee

A brief space of time elapses between reels as the machine is being reloaded. Unless careful provision is made, this break becomes demoralizing. Something has to be provided the instant the picture stops. We usually spend three minutes in "specialties," furnished by the audience. Occasionally guests are imported as entertainers, but we prefer to use our own talent. Sometimes it is the Sunday school orchestra, sometimes a child vocalist or reader, and sometimes a simple trick of magic which points a moral. The Chicago Magic Company, 72 West Adams Street, Chicago, publishes a little booklet by a young Baptist evangelist, which is of great help in such work.

We have made up several sets of slides illustrating hymns and patriotic songs. These songs thrown on the screen are enthusiastically sung by the audience. We also use the intermission in which to announce Sunday services and other features of the week's program, also as an opportunity to take the collection. We pay no one for participation in the program, and all funds collected go to pay for the film and publicity.

One of the essential elements in the program is "pep." Long waits are fatal. The violin must be tuned and ready to go when the picture stops. Singers are seated next the aisle to avoid delay. The pianist is regular, understanding every point in the program, and has

(Turn to page 15)

If children attended Sunday school, they would receive free tickets for the "Neighborhood Night" moving picture performance sponsored by the Church. The bribes worked wonders. *Moving Picture Age* (January 1921), 8. Courtesy Library of Congress.

interest, and drew in children to churches in droves. In 1913, the prolific and frequently self-promoting Methodist leader Christian Reisner published *Church Publicity* as a manual of modern advertising strategies to "compel youth to come in," and promoted the purchase of Motion Picture Plants for churches.[140] (The Motiograph machine manufactured by the Enterprise Optical Manufacturing Company of Chicago was the projector of choice to defeat the cheap theater that catered to the baser instincts of youth.) At his own Grace M. E. Church, Reisner attracted over sixteen thousand children who shouted with glee and the wildest enthusiasm at his motion pictures shows, even at such seemingly stodgy documentaries as *Stoddard's Travelogues*. Stoddard offered middle-class entertainments that transported viewers to the culture of distant countries, travelogues suitable for the whole family. Children were issued prized tickets in Sunday school enabling them (for one or two cents) to attend church-sponsored films the following Saturday night. Attendees were then quizzed on films like *Bell of Justice* to see what they had learned, for example, regarding kindness to animals.

More frequently the social event of showing films would follow the story related by the YMCA's Industrial Department Bureau of Motion Pictures and Exhibits (BMPE), the primary distributor of films for the YMCA, where on one Sunday morning several hundred immigrants from nine ethnic groups watched a silent melodrama about a moon shiner, the U.S. revenue officer, and a comely mountain lass. A secretary of the YMCA, representing a modern pastoral presence, spoke over the rush of images,

> reading the titles in very simple English, composing short sentences from the picture action: such as "the door opens," "the man comes out," "he looks around," "he hears a noise," he grabs the gun," "he shoots the man," "he breaks the law," "he is not a good citizen," "a good citizen will not break the law." Those men went home that afternoon with higher ideals of citizenship, and best of all, they had been helped to think in English.[141]

The moral education of young men was as important to churches as inculcating them with a sense of civic duty. During World War I, many churches in navy towns like Norfolk, Virginia, sought to attract military men through the use of the moving picture. The Cumberland Methodist Church made a concerted effort to lure sailors with their big screen show, providing moral uplift for the young impressionable men away from their own homes and churches. One movie in the series *Samson's Betrayal* was shown to a group of sailors attended to by the Methodist Church's volunteer staff of young single women ushers, who, "heavily laden with roses, presented a flower to each man in uniform."[142]

Everybody's Magazine featured a story on the Episcopal Reverend Harry Robbins as the "Parson who believed in pictures," who transformed Canaseraga, New York, a small town where kissing games and surreptitious spooning as the only forms of entertainment led to a high percentage of illegitimacy. Rejecting both the legion of bad junk films (artistically, dramatically, socially, and morally bad) and "goody-goody" pictures, Robbins coordinated with the local Roman Catholic priest to experiment by creating a community theater, the Kingston. Though initially opposed by the Presbyterian, Methodist, and Baptist clergy, he installed the equipment and ran the theater himself as a hobby, which proved to have a profit-yielding capacity he did not expect. He promised free tickets to children if they went to Sunday school, *any* Sunday school, including those of his opposition. (Two of the churches, however, closed soon after.) The local Board of Trade praised his work for stimulating community activity, except for complaints from the saloon in the hotel. And dozens testified to less visible results: mothers said their children were easier to manage and

> that Jenny had stopped hanging around with that fresh Smith boy, thank goodness! There were matrons to say (and they said it to me) that the housework didn't seem quite so hard since they could count on seeing, two evenings a week, Douglas Fairbanks or William Hart or some of the rest of them.[143]

Photoplay characterized Robbins as a courageous pioneer who endured the bitter opposition of other clergy, but had ventured into fresh and fertile territory.[144]

Like Robbins, Marion Simms, pastor of First Presbyterian Church of Vinton, Iowa, realized in 1915 that his work in his own rural community consisted mostly of keeping his flock "unspotted from the world" and that he spent comparatively "little time spasmodically in helping to snatch a 'brand from the burning' and save his soul." He also identified another missing ingredient in his work, namely, a ministry to the poor, the sick, and the needy outside the church. Seeking to follow

Christ's admonition to serve the meek and lowly, Simms led his congregation to construct (after their original building conveniently burned down in 1912) a community social center, that included a gymnasium and an auditorium equipped with a motion picture booth that was used on Sunday evenings. Simms acknowledged that two-reel films enabled him to preach a far more powerful and effective sermon in fifteen minutes than he could preach in "thirty minutes with words alone" and ensured that he would reach a far larger audience.[145] However, Simms's successor, the Reverend R. H. Rolofson, confessed to the difficulty of finding suitable films; he described himself as wrestling with that "peculiarly balky nightmare," "the snake in my grass," and cited the fictional text: "Verily, that parson who maketh pictures to preach in his synagogue will study and labour with a fervency that endeth not" (Hezekiah 23:23). He found the India missionary film, *Ram Das*, packed in crowds that no missionary service of his had ever done. A viewing of *The Widow's Mite* augmented the annual canvas for funds. For Mother's Day, he drew a "hushed, solemn, deeply touched, tear-stained audience" with *The Stream of Life*. He also used "A Favorite Hymns Program" with suitable scenes cast upon the screen for vibrant singing. He confessed to his audacity in prophesying that with the basic soundness of pictures as a "means of conveying thought," and with the inevitable adoption by the church of new methods for permeating the minds of men with Christian truth, "the church will become a major exhibitor of films."[146] Not only would it be a safe harbor for children and immigrants to see moving pictures, but the church would also emerge as a fully equipped community center.

Dr. Charles Stelzle sought to manage a program of educational, inspirational, and even humorous pictures to be shown in four hundred churches around the nation. "The plan is to have sixty centres," said Stelzle, "with a moving picture operator for each centre" who would carry his moving picture machine from city to city. Stetlze argued that certain communities needed such a service desperately:

> It has always been a problem to find some form of entertainment to take the place of dance halls after they have been closed up. I once asked one of the foremost evangelists in this country what people should do for recreation in such a case. He answered: "Let them play chess." Imagine a boy mechanic and a girl factory worker sitting down to a game of chess after a hard day's work.[147]

The moving pictures could seemingly become the recreation and supplementary education that people needed, and by supplying it, the churches would be able to become centers of community at home as well as make use of it in international missions abroad.

Missions, Pedagogy, and Moving Pictures

Riding the wave of student missionary movements of the early twentieth century, the Inter-Church World Movement (ICWM) defined a set of motion picture principles for the church in a 1913 pamphlet. The movement then formed a motion picture/stereopticon division headed by Dr. H. H. Casselman and sent out teams to shoot footage around the world to provide firsthand data on Christian missions.[148] Unfortunately, while the team was out shooting over five million feet of film in Japan, China, and India, the ICWM was liquidated and the expedition was stranded. Providentially, commercial interests picked up its stock footage and the Methodist Board of Foreign Missions bought its slides. Casselman went on to head up the Bureau of Visual Aids of the Evangelical and Reformed Church.

The missionary trend to incorporate moving pictures was remarkably ecumenical.[149] The *Presbyterian Banner* called on churches to adapt the motion picture in its outreach efforts, especially among children in foreign mission work.[150] George White of the American Baptist Home Mission Society found in movies the value of "Missionary Messages," a vital response to the needs of the mission field, in which situations were portrayed with emotional and spiritual impact through photoplays. Such messages aroused sympathies and stimulated many into action.[151] In 1916, motion picture educator Ernest Dench found that the eloquence emanating from the screen had an astonishing effect upon the "heathens" of Africa.[152]

In 1920, the Interchurch World Movement (IWM) based in Troy, New York, believed it had found a renaissance of international interest and activity in motion picture production. With visionary and eager enthusiasm, it organized a series of specialized films of home and foreign missions for exhibition in churches of all denominations. Behind the leadership of its president, William McDonald of Albany, the IWM formed as a cooperative venture of various Protestant denominations, from which were drafted prominent clergy and social workers. Coordinating their mission with Educational Films Corporation, IWM sent professional, fully equipped expeditions to North Africa and Asia to make mission films.

One group of filmmakers was sent to visually detail activities of foreign missions, showing American and indigenous workers and the conditions, manners, and customs of the visited countries; the other group was to edit a religiously oriented newsreel series, *World Outlook on the Screen,* for distribution to all commercial theaters.

IWM publicist Eva Chappell suggested a revised image of the traditional missionary coming through the films. "The missionary, as these pictures will show, is, of necessity, a versatile man; the camera is as likely to catch him extracting the teeth of a wriggling native, or climbing the rigging of an elephant, or killing a boa constrictor, or being stalked by a lion, as engaged in the performance of his more strictly ministerial duties." Also, Chappell promised that the films were to show the new life of women, as part of the presentation, "even though the word feminism and its equivalents have not penetrated" the native consciousness.[153] The pictures were "not of the 'preachy' variety, which dispel rather than encourage interest, but of the live, wide-awake sort which make regular patrons of those who have once seen them. Chappell's rhetoric is the equivalent of saying that the church has learned that pictures pay."[154] (Various other mission boards had already discovered how forceful documentary slides and films of camels in the African desert or of the child of the slums could be in raising interest and financial support.)[155]

The missionary impulse emanating out of the youthful and visionary International Student Missionary Movement (ISMM) aimed to keep pace with modern methods of evangelism. Free exhibitions in Japan and China were seen as effective approaches to helping unfortunate children and to making known the Gospel to all who visited the missions.[156] Missionary educator Harry Myers extolled the rhetorical virtues of using images as the primary means of communication in a foreign culture. For Myers, a moving picture was

better than 10,000 words! Can you see the old Chinese philosopher with skull cap, pig tail, gray chin whiskers, long flowing robes, standing before a little group and speaking these startling words? Perhaps he had been explaining some simple fact and suddenly turned away from mere words to a picture. Jesus' pictures, his parables, were remembered more than any abstract teachings. "I will lift up my eyes unto the hills"; "The Lord is my shepherd, I shall not want"; "I am the vine, ye are the branches." The Bible abounds in pictures like these. The power of the Bible, at least in part, is because it is so easily quoted. Its ideas stick![157]

Recognizing the value of such word pictures, the church also sought to make "parable films," films that demonstrated rather than preached their messages. For example, *As Ye Sow,* an early 1915 World Films production of the Reverend John Snyder's Cape Cod Drama, taught the lesson that "if ye sin it will reap punishment." When the villain reaped his just desserts in the end, the lesson was clearly shown. Snyder claimed that his play was not a modern novelty, but harkened back to early days in England when the church was the only author of plays and melodramas and wrote them with a religious purpose. In the spirit of some Puritans, Snyder emphasized that "comedy is the only drama that is not essentially religious."[158]

Visual parables were not only instrumental in conveying stories in foreign settings; they were also crucial in enhancing teaching in all situations. Congregationalist minister John Stapleton identified the primary pedagogy of Jesus as speaking in parables, a form of communication particularly effective in attracting and moving the masses. Film was the modern equivalent means of communicating stories to the multitude. For Stapleton, however, the use of the film in religious services was fraught with difficulties; he believed that the simple attempt to produce Bible scenes and characters with authenticity challenged filmmakers. He pointed to a much-advertised *Life of Christ* picture in which one of the soldiers of Pilate could be seen throwing away a cigarette. As a teaching lesson, this was unacceptable, he complained. "To present a sacred scene you must have people who feel the sacredness of the scene." He argued:

> The church of Christ has never been commissioned merely to entertain people. There is a type of film, however, which is free from all these objections. I refer to the industrial films . . . one put out by one of our great electric supply corporations. It depicts the discovery of power by man. Then portray Christ in the moments of his manifest authority—healing the demoniac, stilling the waves, raising Lazarus, cowing the mob—you have presented an introduction for a fifteen-minute parable that gives you the tense attention of any audience."[159]

Such use of film as parable resonated with the Reverend Thomas Opie, who connected Shakespeare's ability to see "sermons in stones" with the churches' call to see "sermons in pictures."[160] As the rector of the Episcopal Church in Burlington, North Carolina, Opie had initiated a Sunday evening movie about biblical characters in lieu of a service and would show movies upon which his next Sunday's sermon would elaborate. He confessed, however, that Bible pictures were not "quite so attractive and successful as modern dramas which are based on Biblical and religious concepts."[161] Beulah Amidon also described the need for "new guises for old truths," quoting the Harmon Foundation's mission: "Old eternal truths occasionally require new habiliments—a refurbishing and sometimes entirely new clothing."[162] Likewise, the Religious Motion Picture Foundation incorporated in 1925 sought to refurbish Protestant church services with motion pictures both aesthetically pleasing and reverential. It echoed the hope that spiritual and religious subject matter would add vital interest to church services "if properly conceived and executed according to the highest literary, dramatic and photographic standards." The new clothing of old truths would not only be fresh, but also fashionable. But the modern look of competing Hollywood films proved too fashionable for those involved in international evangelism. *Christian Century* magazine saw in the Hollywood film exports the toxic "spread of a universal language," which presented problems for missionaries, as people from other cultures would look at these films as representative of a "Christian civilization" and believe a false Gospel.[163]

While many missionary films maintained their staid and solid Victorian appearance, Maine Baptist pastor H. F. Huse found that lasting impressions were made with his congregation when he exhibited a missionary picture entitled *Gospel Work among the Monos,* dramatizing how the Mono Indians came to walk the "Jesus Road."[164] The Forward Movement of the Missionary Society of the Methodist Church in Canada boasted the "finest set of missionary motion pictures in the world."[165] For their Methodist missionary, the Reverend H. B. Mansell, when it was not "feasible to bring Mahomet to the mountain, it is often quite a simple thing to bring the mountain to Mahomet."[166] The mediated world was to be made into one universal community.

Community Centers through Moving Pictures

In the early twentieth century, the churches' recognition of the need for play and recreation coincided with progressive religious movements seeking to reduce the workweek, establish child labor laws, halt the exploitation of the underprivileged and dispossessed, and promote social justice. One of the forces driving churches to provide recreation through community centers was the social and labor unrest following World War I.

CLEVELAND MOFFETT'S IDEAL CHURCH

Cleveland Moffett's "ideal" Church came under attack for its modernist tendencies, for higher criticism theology as well as in his use of church movies, indicating the iconoclastic controversy was far from over. Horton, T. C. *The King's Business* (May 1919), 396. Courtesy Biola University.

Many wanted the church to appeal to outsiders and minister to the social needs of the larger community, and, of course, a primary means for accomplishing such fruitful action was through moving pictures. The *Education Film Magazine* editorialized in 1919, "The church must for its own good and for that of its adherents capitalize [on] the pull and the popularity of the movies. If it does not, movies under other auspices will gradually tend to make the church a dying and eventually a dead limb on the community tree." Confident of their opinion, the editors promoted a slogan that offered churches the proverbial two ways: "*Show movies, survive, and flourish. Ignore movies, decay, and perish.*"[167]

The promotion of the recreational aspects of moving pictures by the more progressive churches raised an outcry from the conservative ones. Parochial dances, oyster stews, movie shows, card parties, and bowling alleys had become part and parcel of the church as community center, along with libraries, gymnasiums, and clubrooms: this development troubled many. While Methodist Alexander Gross recognized the economic and social advantages of using motion pictures in churches, he challenged the optimistic view of their utopian potential. What community centers gained in promoting an ethical and moral community resulted in the loss of religious significance: the social mission was supplanting the evangelistic spiritual mandate. Gross defined the problem as a contrast between faith and ethics. He encouraged the use of motion pictures to illustrate the customs, domestic life, and business activities of foreign countries, because this would increase interest in foreign evangelistic work of the church and aid in its missionary education.

If Christianity were merely a great code of moral or purely ethical religion, then the motion picture could easily play a prominent part in the Sunday services of a church, as, he noted, has been advocated in the press by certain "modernists" such as the Reverend Herbert Jump. On the other hand, he hypothesized, if Christianity does actually transcend morals and ethics, even while including them, and has "its purpose in the salvation of men through Jesus Christ, the living Son of the living God, then moving pictures can have no part in the sacred worship of God by the congregation." Gross argued that such an act of "throwing on the screen in a darkened building a photoplay of the good Samaritan after reading that master parable of the Master, then sing a few songs, have a pastor make a few remarks and a prayer fitting the occasion, and expect the congregation to be spiritually edified" would be crude. No doubt it would be an entertainment with a moral uplift, but for him the essentials of worship would be conspicuously absent. Few would leave the building "filled with the Holy Ghost and fire." Gross concluded, "We are taught not to try to make images of God. . . . Christian principles, if made by photoplays, would lose their religious significance, because of the quality of entertainment inseparably connected with movies. Keep the movies away from the services of worship."[168]

This theological warning from Gross was echoed in conservative religious periodicals, often in creative ways. Editorial cartoons in The *King's Business* satirized the church losing its spiritual focus to become an amusement center. Illustrations of churches as alternate bowling alleys, dance studios, wrestling match sites, and other amusements mocked what was seen as the waywardness of certain progressive churches, particularly that of the innovator minister, the Reverend Cleveland Moffett.

Other less reactionary Christians were not fully convinced of what the distinguished author Charles Sheldon saw in the movies. Was it an appeal to hedonism, to the pleasures of the eye. With the old debates regarding the alluring idolatry of graven images reverberating in his rhetoric, Sheldon complained that the church suffered by comparison to the "thrilling moving picture shows," because it didn't "appeal to our senses." He asked whether the modern minister had to compete with the motion picture show or if he could convincingly demonstrate a need for "a taste for the plain Bread of Life?"[169] One of Sheldon's early novels, *The Martyrdom of Philip Strong,* had been adapted by the Edison Studio in 1915 and released by Paramount (the feature was called a "good Edison, but a poor Paramount"). In the film a Wanderer appears at the door of a prestigious minister and represents himself as "Brother Man." The minister becomes so obsessed with his earthly ministry that he leaves his prosperous pulpit to work with the poor in the slum, in the process losing congregation, wife, and child. The yarn was possibly also an allegory about those who would use films in church to draw in the outcasts. It was criticized by *Variety* as having a moral that "the reward will be paid in Heaven" after much earthly hardship and suffering.[170] Nevertheless, in spite of what some saw as intransigence, the movies continued to move churches toward becoming social centers.

University Place, the college town suburb of the University of Nebraska near Lincoln, did not permit commercial motion pictures in the early twenties. The First Methodist Episcopal Church, realizing the lack of suitable activity for young people, coordinated a film exhibition program (financially profitable at that) in the spring of 1923.[171] This program was but one rolling stone in the avalanche of church film centers, as books from the Religious Education Association were pointing to the use of films in worship and education.[172]

In another argument for the introduction of film exhibition, many thought that if churches did not promote film exhibition, the only alternative was that the "million-dollar" church buildings would be closed six days a week. Church leaders argued that the use of motion pictures kept church doors open and enabled the church to be the real social center of the community. Reverend Reisner, pastor of Grace Methodist Episcopal Church, had illustrated his sermons with films way back in 1910 to packed crowds, tripling the attendance at his Louisville church; he conceded that some might come only to be entertained, not uplifted. But, he noted, Christian history is full of stories of "those who come to scoff and remained to pray."[173] In any event, he pointed out that church films enabled him to have a tremendous social as well as religious impact, particularly in promoting "Neighborhood Nights" as a means of building an encompassing religious community.[174]

Similar Church Night programs appeared for the uplift of the community across the country. For one pastor of Wolcott, New York, S. G. Houghton, the Church Night was a wake-up call for the church to "grasp the mighty weapon of destruction in the hands of the devil and make it a mighty lever, lifting our communities heavenward and towards God!"[175] The First Methodist Church of Kalamazoo, Michigan, inaugurated Community Night on Fridays using a Powers projector in the church auditorium. Their method of financing included collecting nickels from each child or ten cents from each adult (children who attended Sunday school were admitted free). Their primary purpose was to serve the community, and they boasted that "Many parents permit their children to go to movies only at the Methodist Church."[176] The Judson Memorial Baptist Church sponsored Thursday evening movies under the inviting designation of "Happy Hour" times. Families paid one cent for the entertainment of a movie show sponsored by the church and New York University, such as *Quo Vadis* or *Silas Marner.*

Film critic Homer Croy observed that during the previous five years motion pictures had been used in a desultory way, but now in 1920 something consequential was being accomplished, namely, the coordinated building of community centers, of places where people could gather for worship and for social interaction. With thousands of churches using motion pictures in some form and new converts being added daily, Croy observed that several governing church bodies had begun to standardize exhibition practices. At the beginning of such ventures, attendance was usually small. In one experiment, however, a subsequent Monday showing doubled the audience to over one thousand. "Now," boasted Croy, "there is not a seat in the auditorium from where the screen can be seen that is not filled. As the writer was standing in the hall waiting to speak to the pastor he overheard one woman say, 'I liked it as well as any movie I have been to in a long time.'" The show attracted droves of new people to Croy's church community center, many of whom were children from "over the boundary line" who couldn't afford to attend movies.

They came pouring in from all sides, their bright eyes shining, and so successful was the experiment that a children's matinee is now a regular feature of the Church work. As a result two shows are put on Monday, one in the afternoon and one in the evening. There are now strange faces at the church that were never seen there before. The church is now coming in contact with just the people it has been seeking for years to reach.[177]

Croy's church discovered that the pictures more than paid for themselves; in fact, they became a financial asset through voluntary collections. What made the church a community center rather than a competing commercial institution to the theater in Croy's mind was that it did not charge an admission fee. It welcomed those in the neighborhood who could not go elsewhere. Croy identified another exemplar of the Community Church movement in St. Timothy's parish in Chicago. The rector, the Reverend Cyrus Andrews, had started using films for Sunday school instruction and found that Sunday school had immediately became the most popular thing around the church, with "Jew and Gentile coming in," until Andrews had to open up the gymnasium. In an attempt to assimilate the diverse audience Andrews selected generic moral subjects, which he believed offered greater latitude than religious stories from the Bible as the latter aroused more criticism from easily offended parishioners. Andrews's goal was that the audience would leave as "better citizens and better Christians for having seen the films." The films essentially promoted a basic patriotism, "respect for one's neighbors, the folly of Bolshevism, or some present-day principle." Croy pointed out that most experiments with motion pictures in churches had been confined to Sunday school activities, but reiterated that sermons synchronized with motion pictures "will be used to illustrate doctrinal precepts brought out by the speaker." Croy's own most successful experiment was his "Community Night'" when the church hosted the entire community with motion picture exhibitions. It replaced the "old-fashioned oyster supper or strawberry festival," with crowds coming to movies with the same eagerness as they displayed toward the strawberries of old. "The film entertainment has the added advantage that it can present Christian ideas to the people at the same time, and carry on its real work while the people are making merry."[178]

The Reverend Dow Beene, pastor of First Congregational Church, Chappaqua, New York, also defended his church's practice of providing motion picture entertainment for the whole community. While some kids attending the films would hoodwink the collection plates by substituting buttons for pennies, nevertheless the program "made practically every child in the village a personal friend to the pastor and added to the membership of the Sunday school without 'stealing sheep.'"[179] By now numerous books and articles advised churches how to effectively use the motion picture in the pulpit, and many churches experimented with these "Neighborhood Nights." The Reverend S. W. Stackhouse went so far as to petition local barbershops, bakeries, and fish markets for funds to show pictures and bring the community together at his First Baptist Church of Hempstead, Long Island.[180]

The Reverend D. T. Robertson found that films also fit his evangelistic needs. "There was a time when an organ, piano, or a violin were barred from the church as of the devil, and yet these have proved a blessing instead of a curse." One prayer meeting group found their use of the film *The Envious Prince* to be a particular blessing in effectively dealing with the evils of envy. Other churches found success attracting new audiences with such features as George Arliss in *The Man Who Played God*.[181]

Another of the Social Gospel advocates, Washington Gladden, contributed the introduction to author Henry Atkinson's *The Church and People's Play*. The book, extending Gladden's concern for the dispossessed and the oppressed, recommended that the church minister to them by appealing to all their needs and interests, including entertainment and recreation. Assuming the mantle of social responsibility, Atkinson believed that motion picture shows had done more to redeem the theater than any other thing, simply because they "presented the best in drama and literature in a pleasing form and at a price that is within reach of all people."[182] Atkinson represented the liberal Congregationalists in favor of social ministries; Christian Reisner was an American Baptist and George Esdras Bevan a sound Presbyterian; all weighed in on the same side of the debate. Reisner emphasized the need to combat the trend for other institutions to supplant the church as a social center; the church was to be the primary source of understanding life and of learning one's morality, not the theater. He argued that one way to fight against potential rivals was to steal their weapons and furnish free motion pictures to children on Saturday afternoons.[183] Also in support of the church's role as a community center, Bevan, minister of the Greystone Presbyterian Church in Elizabeth, New Jersey, published *Motion Pictures: The Experience of One Church*. This book espouses the use of cinematic propaganda for attracting "delinquent church members, indifferent Christians and people who have forgotten the church, forgotten prayer and forgotten God."[184]

Like Bevan, Pastor Roy Smith of the Simpson Methodist Church in Minneapolis, Minnesota, a contributing editor of the *Moving Picture Age,* published a book of articles from that periodical on getting his church into the picture business and using film for community, educational, and religious purposes. In his *Moving Pictures in the Church,* Smith discussed how his church used moving pictures, including its handling of Neighborhood Night.[185] Responding to the criticism that the church was never open except on Sunday, Smith experimented with motion pictures to "tempt 30,000 Lonesome, Homesick, and Tempted young People of Chicago into Goodness." With a DeVry "C 90" portable projector, he opened the church for a Sunday afternoon open house of communal time. Mondays became "Neighborhood night for children of foreign parents." Fridays were for "Friendly Friday Night Movies." Attending Saturday and Sunday school gave the children blue and yellow tickets to use at these two shows. For Neighborhood Nights, where the purpose was primarily entertainment, Smith preferred the "Edgar" Comedies of Goldwyn ("above reproach") and the drawing room comedies of Mr. and Mrs. Drew. (The children preferred Larry Semon and Charlie Chaplin for their rowdier slapstick.)[186] Smith explained his simple strategy: "Pictures help build up the people, who in turn build up the church. We used pictures exactly as we would use music, for their educational and entertaining value." Smith, described as a "self-made, self-reliant type of minister, progressive and aggressive," was also a former cartoon lecturer and used movies as regularly as he did music and coal, coming to regard them "almost as indispensable."[187]

Smith encountered minor opposition from some parishioners and more from the managers of commercial houses in the neighborhood. Exhibitors complained that the church, in taking advantage of unfair competition, was drawing audiences away on the theaters' best night, Friday.[188] Smith retorted that theaters were already competing with the church on Sunday nights.[189] His response to his own people was that the purpose of the picture business was to render community service and to inculcate in the community what he called a "picture conscience."[190]

As a social center, a key component of the church's service to the community was the provision of religious and moral education. The era of the

1920s was ripe for the development of innovative pedagogical techniques, primarily visual, for use in both schools and churches. While *Christian Herald* magazine was advertising Bible verses with matching pictures, Sunday school leaders were seeing that the younger generation, including newspaper boys, being drawn to the church. For this reason, the Reverend Adam Chambers, pastor of Harlem Baptist Church, would generally show comic movies: "The pictures are the bait, without them we could not get the audience. This meeting is our fishing pond, from which we gather into our clubs and Sunday school." Boys on the street, who learned hymns at what they called the "Harlem Baptist Movies," were transformed into "wonderful missionaries" and "advertising agents" for the film services.[191] At the same time, church outreach activities included the instruction of young women as well as young men. Calvary Baptist Sunday School in Washington, D.C., led by the resourceful and energetic Miss Jessie Burrall, inaugurated a pilot educational program in 1917 with a class of six girls. When the test class grew to two hundred, they relocated to a movie theater across the street (with the free use of the theater's pipe organ and moving picture resources), and then grew to eight hundred girls a week.[192]

The Social Gospel function of moving pictures was widely recognized. The Reverend Charles Banning honored the work of churches where children learned Bible stories visually and where they were taught to read (via silent film intertitles as well as books). Vacation Bible schools showed educational, industrial, and scenic films to expose poorer children to the world outside their neighborhoods. Of particular salience for the Social Gospel was a film entitled *Cotton* which showed Vacation school children the hard labor that was "largely done by Negroes—which allowed a study of starting Negro churches, and ministering to the needs of the Negro today."[193] Then, so as not to tax their young charges, comic reels were shown. Animated cartoons from John Bray studios (e.g., *Bobby Bumps*) were praised as ideal. With educational shorts and the objectionable parts of other films eliminated, Neighborhood Nights drew people to the church, provided wholesome entertainment, and encouraged family attendance.

The minister of the Baptist Temple in Rochester, New York, Dr. Clinton Wunder, stubbornly took an interest in motion pictures as an agency of religious education. His interaction with Hollywood screen stars, directors, and producers convinced him that movies could be converted into becoming a "preacher." Actress Leatrice Joy had told him, "To me pictures are what the pulpit is to you. A mission is involved in following either career. You preach faith, hope, and charity. We feel we are bringing home to our spectators the lessons of right living and right thinking in an abstract sense."[194] Along the same lines, several progressive churches utilized motion pictures for intellectual enrichment, as an alternative to the string quartets and dramatic book talks of the Sunday Night Chautauqua Church Service.[195] In England a remarkable exemplar of Christian action, Thomas Tiplady, Superintendent of the Lambeth Mission of the Methodists, went further by establishing what he called the *Cinema Church*. In the tradition of John Wesley's appeal to the common working class, Tiplady opened a Mission and provided cinema entertainment for the slums as far back as 1909. Bringing what he saw as refreshment of spirit to laborers, the minister attributed a great deal of his Mission's "remarkable moral and social improvement of the last twenty-five years to the influence of the cinema." In 1928, believing that many working patrons were being cunningly turned toward communism, Tiplady obtained a cinema license, joined the Cinematograph Exhibitors' Association, and renamed his church "the Ideal." He conducted a daily cinema for several years, keeping, as the Home Secretary stated in 1932, "boys out of mischief." His cinema services received coins from many lands in the collection plate, as well as buttons, sweets, and notes saying "I.O.U. a kiss." It was truly important for Tidlady that the Bible stories and the moving pictures created a sense of community and Christian fellowship, even if marked by occasional scuffles among the ruffians.[196]

Tiplady's notion of opening a seven-day church was imitated at the Wesley Methodist Episcopal Church in Worchester, Massachusetts, by Dr. William Mitchell. Mitchell presented two reasons for the installation of daily motion pictures in his church: first, because they appealed to children and youth (especially favored were the animated cartoons of Felix the Cat and the *Our Gang* comedies), and second because the church could enlighten the public on standards against a tide of serious moral decay. In a few instances, the church's Sunday club that projected the films for Family Night Showings "beat local exhibitors to the showing of certain films. . . . Opposition and interference with the various exchanges from which the films were secured immediately began to develop."[197] Thus, in the teens and twenties, many churches reflected the progressive concerns of the Social Gospel in reaching out to communities, and a very significant aspect of that outreach was the use of motion pictures to advance a sense of community, both in tending to marginalized groups and in attracting new converts to the church itself.

Church-Theater Tensions

On May 5, 1916, evangelist Billy Sunday's arrival in Kansas City for a seven-week revival meeting immediately impacted local theaters. "His opening sermon drew an audience of 37,000, while the theaters reported a slump in attendance."[198] A similar slide occurred in Boston where Billy Sunday drew 54,000 to the Tabernacle on his first day, and *Variety*, the vanguard periodical of the entertainment industry, lamented that he was to be in town for ten weeks.[199] Religious performance now competed with entertainment for audiences secular. Even one Pentecostal spectacle caused concern exhibitors; in the mid-Atlantic region, icy baptismal services vied with the theaters for spectators. In 1925, thousands attended Pentecostal meetings, with attendance at the theaters lagging significantly. As one nonsympathetic writer for *Variety* observed, "A cardinal principle of the Holy Rollers or Pentecostals is opposition to all forms of amusements. Probably that's the reason for their staging of such freaky and eccentric performances in the name of Worship."[200]

In Connecticut, a religious revival broke out in a newly constructed tabernacle sponsored by the Federation of Protestant Churches of New England. George Wood Anderson, an evangelist of the Billy Sunday type, attracted thousands, which according to *Variety*, "seriously nicks the theatre attendance in this town." Drawing up to three thousand per night in South Norwalk, evangelist Anderson commanded considerable daily space in the newspapers and was blamed for the precipitous drop in business for the theaters, where record low grosses were recorded.[201]

However, competition with entertaining evangelists was only part of exhibitors' problems. Religious holidays, especially the Lenten season, caused slumps in theater business and furthermore the various religious observances of moviegoers often confused exhibitors. The Keith office first decided to delay matinees on Good Friday until after the services were over, but as it was also the beginning of Passover, complications arose as to when they could open.[202] The Binghamton theaters cannily adapted other tactics during Lent, opening their theaters for services and providing passes to ministers to show how clean and wholesome their films were.[203]

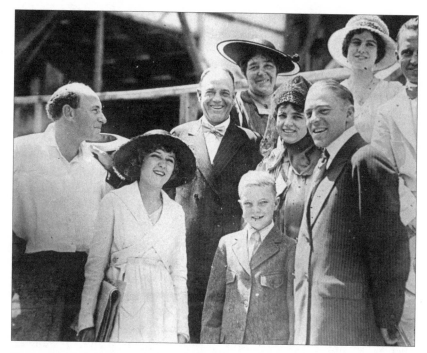

Due to his personal association with Hollywood personalities like Cecil B. DeMille (left) and Mary Pickford, evangelist Billy Sunday frequently endorsed the film industry as an alternative to the saloon and the theatre. Courtesy Culver Pictures.

Secular exhibitors in other religiously sensitive areas designed marketing campaigns that cited familiar biblical texts, with producers colluding in framing their appeals in religious language and images. Advertisements in conservative periodicals like *The Saturday Evening Post* exploited scriptural knowledge to help the religious showmen. *The Post,* for example, included one particular ad to exhibitors: "Esau Sold His Birthright for a Mess of Pottage—Don't Be an Esau, Friend Exhibitor, and Sacrifice Your Theatre for a Mess of Pictureplay Pot Boilers."[204] Another advertisement wrenched a New Testament Gospel passage from its theological context and adapted it for the movie business: "And the rains descended, and the floods came, and beat upon the house, and it moved not, for it was founded upon a rock." For that exhibitor, the ad claimed, the shifting sand was any studio base other than the studio House of Selig. The rock of financial responsibility, artistic worth, and dependable service was to be found with Selig films, which was a "safe shelter from money getters."[205]

Along with the use of religious rhetoric, secular producers garnered support for their products from various ecclesiastical movers and shakers. They continually quoted the religious leaders in the pages of periodicals like *Moving Picture World,* with exhibitors following their own constituency. Fundamentalist revivalist Billy Sunday's name and influence, for example, was appropriated in recommending certain films; his endorsements promulgated a view of film as an effective means for uplift and edification.[206] For the gigantic Klaw and Erlanger production of *Ben Hur* at the Colonial Theatre in Norfolk, Virginia, the papers quoted what "the Reverend Billy Sunday Says." "Ben Hur with its galloping horse in the chariot race, typical of life of man, its slaves, its lepers, and its beautiful 'light' that irradiates the world, is like a plow digging deep into men's thoughts and stirring their consciences. I should like nothing better than to talk to 50,000 men and women just after they had seen "Ben Hur."[207] In another full page ad, Billy Sunday recommended D. W. Griffith's *The Two Orphans* and launched into a sermon on "orphans of spiritual neglect" and on the role of movies. "The power of the moving picture should be used to inculcate warnings and lessons that the world needs," and here is a "sermon of the highest value. Would that every story carried on the screen might have a lesson as powerful, and as useful, a motive as praiseworthy."[208]

While grateful for ecclesiastical blessings removing any objections to movies, exhibitors in the early 1920s did not welcome what they viewed as the modest but trespassing financial competition of the sanctuary cinemas. With the church's success, however, came political and practical problems. As early as 1911, the film industry was alerted to the encroachment of the church into the entertainment business. From Brooklyn to San Francisco, churches competed with picture shows by showing their own films.[209] The *Nickelodeon* trade periodical warned, for example, that the First Congregational Church of Toledo, Ohio, was entering into competition with the theaters and moving picture shows for "the patronage of some of the pleasure seekers." They quoted the pastor Dr. Wallace, who said, "If the people must have pictures and shows, we will give them one at the Old First Church."[210] Juvenile Judge Ben Lindsay laid down the gauntlet in this contest between the movie industry and the churches, boldly advocating films for churches as rivals for the theaters:

"The time is not far distant when churches will be turned into moving picture shows."[211]

The *Film Daily* quoted the president of the nontheatrical American Motion Picture Corporation, John Edgerton, announcing that plans were being drawn up for the churches to enter the picture business on a competitive scale.[212] Edgerton explained that some theater exhibitors and exchange managers were "frightened at the recent growth in number and patronage of community motion picture shows in schools, churches, YMCAs and other local institutions."[213] *Variety* fanned the flames by headlining the plan of a Bronx Catholic church to get into the exhibition business,[214] but then sought to allay exhibitors' anxieties by also reporting on its front page that the City Council of Burlington, Vermont, required churches showing films to purchase a city license.[215] *The Moving Picture World* reported that in Nebraska and Iowa churches were demanding a high standard of picture and were paying distributors more than the local theaters were.[216]

In several other cases open conflicts erupted between churches and local theaters. Wilshire Presbyterian Church in Los Angeles showed *Pollyanna* while at the theater across the street a Lon Chaney feature was being exhibited.[217] Likewise in Kansas theater owners retaliated against church exhibitions by showing films on Sunday.[218] In Kansas City exhibitors reacted to the controversy by vigorously fighting the release of commercial films to churches rather than to legitimate picture theaters.[219] Militant moral reformer Canon William Sheafe Chase castigated Hollywood czar Will Hays for not assisting churches in getting amusement films shown in parish halls or church halls because of the commercial power of the Motion Picture Theater Owners' Association. Chase accused Hays of favoritism to the theatrical industry, where "the exhibitor must be protected!"[220]

In Hagerstown, Maryland, Baltimore and Washington exhibitors viewed church shows at St. John's Lutheran Church as encroaching upon their business.[221] The successful showings at a Baptist church in Utica, New York, raised eyebrows among local theater owners. Numerous other exhibitors protested the invasion into the moving picture business by pastors who hosted Sunday film showings.[222] Inspectors in Pennsylvania stopped film shows in the First Presbyterian, Lutheran, "Italian Catholic," and YMCA because of what they saw as violations of the "Panic Law," since these exhibitors did not have licensing permits.[223] Methodist churches in Memphis did such capacity business on Sundays with free will admissions underwriting their moral pictures that neighborhood theaters, obliged to close, protested.

Variety complained that these occupants of the pulpit were "laughing in their boots" at the theatrical mangers of the town.[224] A Methodist Episcopal Church in Massachusetts, for example, gave a program of popular movies every Thursday and Friday nights free.[225] Taking advantage of Cecil B. DeMille's successful promotions, a Baptist church in Boston cleverly competed with Paramount's *Ten Commandments* by showing the Italian Artclass Picture Corporation's inferior feature *After Six Days*.[226] *Variety* interpreted such riding on the coattails of *The Ten Commandments*' advanced advertising as deceptive, since the church advertising mentioned that it would show a film on Moses and the commandments.[227]

Other churches and theaters found a satisfactory compromise: when a Presbyterian church in Pierre, South Dakota, could not contain the crowds to its Sunday evening films, it rented a nearby downtown theater to accommodate its fifteen hundred spectators.[228] In the same way, when a Presbyterian church in Omaha, Nebraska, outgrew its sanctuary, it rented a theater that seated five thousand. In a curious switch, when the Easton Pennsylvania Presbyterian Church played to between 700–1200 people with a program of sermonettes, lectures, moving pictures, and music, the most vociferous opposition came not from local exhibitors, but from other ministers. In this internal ecclesiastical rivalry, other denominational churches instructed their parishioners not to go to the Presbyterian Church; however, the ironic outcome of their denunciation was unintentional advertising that increased church attendance for the Presbyterian picture shows.[229]

Variety reported an open breach between exhibitors and churches when theater owners finally protested the showing of films by professional reformers and their church allies under the auspices of the religious institutions. *Variety* noted that this practice had grown to large proportions in smaller cities and towns. Competition had reached such heights that many exhibitors insisted that either churches must stop the picture exhibitions or exhibitors would have to close their doors. The conflict escalated to the point that local exhibitors were carrying their fight directly to the public via newspapers. Some exhibitors sent an appeal to Will H. Hays, the reigning titular head of the Motion Picture Producers and Distributors of America: "In New England the church exhibitor situation has become quite an issue, but the exhibitor, because of the church influence

Another Picture Presentation of Columbus Features

The Big Screen, as Seen from the Stands

Back View of Screen, Showing Reinforcements

In Columbus, Ohio, at the 1919 Methodist Centenary, a gigantic open air screen measured 136 by 146 feet and projected moving pictures (boasting actors "vaster than twenty Goliaths.") for thousands of Methodist pastors and lay workers. "Photograph of Giant Screen" Johnson, Julian. "Let There Be Light!" *Photoplay Magazine* 16 (1919), 46–47 "Making a tremendous impression on film exhibition among religious visitors, the Centenary leaders promoted a reinforced giant screen, looming like a giant pagan idol, as a vision of the future modern church." "Another Picture Presentation of Columbus Features," *Centenary Bulletin* (July 3, 1919), 3. Courtesy Library of Congress.

in the community is getting little or no sympathy or co-operation."[230] Trade magazines found unexpected allies among atheists in their attack on Sunday church movies, but they cautiously avoided aligning themselves too closely with such socially undesirable collaborators.[231] In 1926 Hays observed what he interpreted as a positive trend, with many cases of direct cooperation between local churches helping to choose programs at motion picture theaters; however, this may have simply been official public relations puffery by Hays' organization.[232]

An early internecine battle regarding Sunday evening films occurred in New Bedford between Henry Williams of the Baptist Church and the Reverend Frank Ramsdell of the North Congregational Church. Williams complained that too many Baptists were sneaking to the Congregational Church to watch films. Responding to his fellow cleric, Ramsdell quipped: "'Human nature is human nature. I found it difficult to make non-members stay away."[233] Congregationalists promoted such technological innovation in their services more than most other denominations. The *Advance,* official publication of the Congregational Church, even offered a prize for articles on the use of the screen in the church.[234] More such competition emerged in the plans of the Wilkins Avenue Southern Methodist Episcopal Congregation in Baltimore, Maryland, to include not only a complete gymnasium but also facilities for showing moving pictures. The Reverend H. P. Baker did also promise, however, not to permit any "wild-fire movies" but to show only Bible and educational films. A hot debate over whether churches should be inclusive in inviting other churches to share in their film exhibitions led to a consensus around the Topeka Kansas Ministerial Union's recommendation that churches let their conscience be the guide.[235]

Of course, it was inevitable that the Church Film movement would be satirized. *Vanity Fair* took on the modern churches, depicting an after-dinner symposium among "big business men" who hired a Presbyterian to add a little ginger, pep, and punch to Sunday services.

And every Sunday he has some new up-to-date subject, not theology you know, but something that will hold and interest the people. Last Sunday, for example, he preached on the Holy Land (he was there for the Standard Oil people six or seven years ago) and he showed it all so vividly (we've fixed him a moving picture machine where the font used to be).[236]

The Methodist Centenary and the Eight-Story Screen

In July 1919 the *Christian Advocate* boldly announced that "The moving picture has been converted into a missionary advocate."[237] The event that marked the zenith of a church-film alliance was the 1919 Methodist Episcopal Centenary in Columbus, Ohio.[238] Glory, laud, and honor were poured upon the leaders of the movement from all corners of the film world. Dr. Earl Taylor, the "most fiery and uncompromising champion of the Motion Picture in all Christendom" and editor of *World Outlook,* was identified as the chief of the celebration.[239] Taylor and other leaders at the watershed Summer Camp Meeting Conference constructed an open-air moving picture screen that was 136 feet high and 146 feet wide, with a seating capacity for over four million.[240] When Taylor was told it would be impossible to build a lantern that could project such a huge, "eight-story" picture of at least one hundred square feet, he was undeterred.[241] A high-powered, long distance super-lantern was indeed set up to project the pictures.[242]

One of the more remarkable surprises of the celebration was the presence of Hollywood dignitaries like Adolph Zukor and Kentucky Methodist D. W. Griffith who agreed to address the seventy-five thousand attendees.[243] Griffith was key in expressing the alliance between film and the church: "Motion pictures," he declared, "can link the people of the world in understanding because the films speak a common language—the language of the eye."[244] With director A. P. Hamberg, Griffith actually began shooting *The Wayfarer,* the master pageant of the exposition, at the Centenary.[245]

Various periodicals praised the religious world's fair that featured films so prominently. *Variety* announced with fanfare that the Methodists had appropriated $300,000 for financing an ambitious motion picture enterprise in which not only would the denomination be filming authentic scenes in Palestine, with ten biblical pictures being made for $30,000 each, but it also would be showcasing the use of the motion picture in religious work.[246] The Methodist photographic department was primarily responsible for developing the program, particularly by providing cinematographic records of life at many foreign mission fields. It sent out skilled photographers with Methodist missionaries to all parts of the world to supply motion pictures.[247] An African booth exhibited Roosevelt and Rainey motion pictures, showing episodes from "lion hunts, Kaffir dances, the Uganda railway and African mission scenes."[248] S. R. Vinton had shot film in China, Japan, and Korea that was used as the nucleus of a foreign picture exhibition. Of particular note at the Centenary was a film used in the India Building taken by the Reverend L. E. Linzell entitled *From Krishna to Christ.* Actually it was the product of a native Indian filmmaker.[249]

The principal hall in which pictures were shown could seat between twelve to fifteen hundred people, with seven other halls devoted to special mission fields. For example, special screening rooms exhibited oriental scenes from Japan, Korea, and Burma taken by S. R. Vinton. In conjunction with Griffith, Reisner and a dozen Methodist laymen devised "ways and means to raise a fund of $120,000,000 for the purchase of entertainment devices to be placed in the churches of this denomination." The churches numbered over sixty-four million in the United States. The grand vision was to enable a mature Methodist Church to become "one of the most important film producing and distributing concerns in the world." It would then have more churches in America "where screens will be maintained, than there are motion picture theatres at the present time."[250]

The *Bulletin of Better Films* reported that the motion picture held primary place at the most "forward" Columbus conference of this "greatest Protestant religious body." Throngs were being entertained "three times a day in three different places" and the films effected the conversion of "a steady stream of Methodist bishops, clergymen, and churchmen who had never darkened the door of a commercial theater." Seeing the power of the picture in conveying ethical and religious teaching, the Methodists felt their hearts strangely warmed, and one machine company received well over $100,000 in orders for motion picture machines.[251] Motion picture projector companies were quick to note the trend, with three commercial machine companies advertising in the prestigious Methodist periodical *Christian Advocate* in September 1919 alone.[252]

With the help of members of the National Association of Motion Picture Producers, the Centenary operated an almost continuous program of pictures. Pageants and films were staged continuously on the big screen located on the Fair Grounds racetrack and in the Coliseum and in the Motion Picture Auditorium in the Asbury Building. The films showcased included *The Wayfarer*,[253] *The City Beautiful, The Children's Crusade, The Parade of the Nations, The Spirit of John Wesley, Daddy Long Legs, Nearer My God to Thee, Hit-the-Trail Holiday, The Sign of the Cross,* and the classic *From the Manger to the Cross*.[254] One particular film inspired from the Methodist Centenary was *God and the Man,* Robert Buchanan's story about a man and his daughter influenced by the preaching of John Wesley: the Ideal Film Rending Company showed the struggles of the early settlers in America, shipwreck, fire, and storms, and conveyed the spiritual message that the God of Love replaces the God of Vengeance.[255]

Besides the religious pictures, several exotic Ditmar animal pictures, Educational Film Corporation travel and scenic pictures, and Burton Holmes travelogues, some of the most popular films shown on the sidelines of the festivities were comedies, notably again those of Sidney Drew (e.g., *The Amateur Liars*). *Pathe Weekly,* covering a Children's Rally and curious performances of Folk Teams, planned to distribute the photographed local events nationally.[256] The only fly in the ointment seemed to be protesters who filed indignant complaints because scalpers had sold tickets that belonged to faithful Methodist season ticket holders.[257]

The Program at the Columbus Centenary was praised for furnishing entertainment and for demonstrating the potential for film and church working together. The extraordinary event was seen as breaking a deadlock that had developed between churches and producers; the churches perceived increasing difficulty in locating appropriate religious films to show their constituencies and argued that it was useless to install motion picture equipment because there were no suitable films available while the producers had argued that the church field was not profitable enough for them because there were so few equipped churches. Here at the Centenary, however, the opportunity for churches to use films for "wholesome recreation, for clean amusement and for missionary education and for definite religious instruction" was excitedly demonstrated.[258]

On the evening of July 4, the largest moving picture crowd of four million viewed a movie screen six times the size of the average screen, with the pictures being "remarkably clear and sharp. The blinking of a man's eyes shown in a close up was plainly discernable two blocks away."[259] Success of the venture thus met one of Taylor's goals that everyone could view the films. Along with Reisner and Marshall, now pastor of St. James Methodist Church in New York, Taylor had explained that

> the use of motion pictures at the celebration grew out of a desire to give a demonstration to the churches of the possibilities of motion pictures along two lines: First as providing material that would make the church a social and recreational center in the community; second, as furnishing by all means the best method of missionary education.[260]

His demonstration was an astounding success. The international effects of the centenary were phenomenal. Interviewed on "What I Saw at the Methodist Centenary," the Reverend Arthur Simmons from Great Britain communicated to *Moving Picture World* that the grand screen was a moving picture "billboard" advertisement for the church to use in its missions. The screen was enthusiastically welcomed as a handmaid to the church. "I predict the day will come," gushed Simmons, "when the movies will invade this church, as every other church in the land. Sunday-schools will meet to hear the stories of the Bible illustrated on the screen."[261]

In the United States the Methodists were unanimous in heralding this new medium for winning souls to the Christian faith. Taylor had envisioned that a modern church could not only reach out in evangelism but also become a social and recreational center in the community and around the world through the use of motion pictures. After the celebration, the editors of *National Geographic Magazine* urged missionaries to carry cameras, as they had access to original material that the casual traveler could never see. Every missionary "ought to carry the best camera that can be had and ought to use it as often as he does his Bible." The primary reason for this proposal stemmed from lessons gained by noting the attractions at the Centenary celebration, namely, that "one human-interest picture is worth a score of missionary addresses and that pictures reach influential persons who never attend missionary meetings of the old type."[262] Within the year, The *New York Times* would note how this denomination was exporting the Gospel in its missionary ventures in Africa, China, India, and Malaysia through the sanctified medium of the motion picture, all inspired by that majestic celebration in little old Columbus.[263] Certain missionary films such as Father Dufays's *From Dakar to Goa* and *The Blood on the Sand* (about martyred missionaries in Central Africa) and the film of the Reverend Bernard J. Hubbard's trip from the "torrid Saharan desert to the icy solitudes of Alaska" even enjoyed some success in public movie theaters, proving to some that "the missionary cinematographist is in a position to film documentary pictures of human life quite out of the reach of other operators."[264]

The ripples of the event overlapped into the film community. *Photoplay* publicized how the event triggered the formation of the Better Photoplay League, whose platform would insure clean minds as much as clean communities.[265] In contrast, The *Moving Picture World* reflected on the impact of the Centenary a year later, when the 1920 General Conference of the Methodist Church closed its quadrennial session at Des Moines "without changing the traditional attitude of the church on the theatre, dancing, and card-playing." While progressives had urged a modification of this enduring standard, the General Conference kept it by a vote of 3 to 1. However, the same periodical reported with some glee that while remaining adamantly opposed to the wickedness of the stage, the church again endorsed moving pictures and "asked that arrangements be made to circulate films from general headquarters of the church and form special supply houses to be established in different parts of the country." The field director for the Society for Visual Education, Edna Moody Howard, then went to Des Moines to help the Methodists outline methods for using "movie textbooks" in the local religious schools.[266]

In another article entitled "Let There Be Light!" Julian Johnson, editor of *Photoplay,* hyperbolically compared Taylor to the Almighty, as the one who opened the windows of the world for the church. He credited this Methodist entrepreneur with inventing the panorama slide and with developing the sanctuary motion picture that helped the church to become a "real community center, showing the people, once more, *how to live.*"[267] Taylor's consummate objective not "to promote sectarianism, to win members, or to establish a hidebound orthodoxy and promulgate the tenets of a creed," but simply to use films to uplift the community appealed to the secular Johnson. Promoting religion was less important for members of the motion picture trades than promoting movies. The desire of the film producers was honestly mercenary, simply to find a noncommercial ally in using and promoting their commercial products, and it looked as though they had found their own success through Taylor's grand experiment.

Across the nation churches expanded their ministries by exhibiting films and seeking new audiences through the fresh material of moving pictures. All such activity culminated in the Methodist Centenary of 1919. However, within the year, major religious organizations would gather to produce their own films. Many recognized the need to develop their own scripts. As a Hebrew prophet had once warned, how could you trust the Philistines to make weapons for you when you soon might be going into battle against them? It was time for the church to construct divine shows.

In the voluptuous imagery of Roman Catholic artist, Peter Paul Rubens, *The Brazen Serpent* becomes a wilder and more dramatically potent graven image, suggesting dangers beyond its Divinely ordained healing powers. Courtesy National Gallery of Art, United Kingdom

Jasper Francis Cropsey's *The Millennial Age* (1854) beautifully conveyed the spiritual truths of the Hudson River School, of God's crucial presence underlying a sculpted lion laying down with the lamb, even as the sun set on the distant mountains. Oil on canvas, 38 x 54 inches. Courtesy The Newington-Cropsey Foundation, Hastings-on-Hudson, New York

The patron saint of moving pictures
and apologist of divine images, St. John
of Damascus, almost single-handedly
defended the church's use of icons
against the iconoclastic heresy of the
eighth century. Courtesy of
Monteaux Photographs

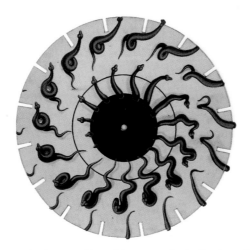

Joseph Plateau's Phenakistoscope (spindle viewer),
one of the early (1832) optical toys that predated
the moving pictures, could mesmerize viewers by
making bronze serpents spin and squirm. Courtesy Monteaux Photographs

Joseph Boggs Beale's series of magic lantern slides enhanced Augustus Toplady's 1776 Calvinist hymn, *Rock of Ages*, prefiguring the Edison Studio's silent film on the same theme. Courtesy of The Borton Collection

THOU
SHALT
NOT
STEAL

THE
GUIDE POST

SUNDAY
SCHOOL

THE DEVIL'S RECRUITING STATION

THE PUCK PRESS

L. M. GLACKENS

FROM THE SUNDAY-SCHOOL TO THE——

YOUNG AMERICA AND THE

L. M. Glackens' illustration of Young America and the Moving Picture Show not only portrayed the alleged hazards of moving pictures, but also indicated that good influences upon youth could be found up the "Road of Decent Moving Pictures." Glackens, L. M. "Young America and the Moving Picture Show" *Puck* (September 11, 1910). Courtesy Library of Congress

HEAVEN,
ACCORDING TO
THE
MOVING PIC-
TURE MAN

Films for
to day
THE
SAFE
CRACKERS

— MOVING-PICTURE SHOW IS BUT A STEP.

"WHERE DID YOU LEARN TO BREAK A SAFE?" BOY-"AT DE MOVING PIC-TURE SHOW"

MOVING-PICTURE SHOW.

Tinted versions of films like Pathe's *La Vie de N. S. Jesus Christ* (Maurice Andre Maitre, 1914) helped to confirm St. John of Damascus's vision of icons conveying the splendor (and spectacle) of the Incarnation. Courtesy of Fort Lee Film Commission

3

Divine Shows

Satan has a new enemy.

K. S. Hover[1]

In its first several decades, Hollywood attracted religious audiences by producing significant appropriate product such as the moral melodramas of director D. W. Griffith and the conversion westerns like Essanay's *"Broncho" Billy*. Films like the secular Kalem Studio's *From the Manger to the Cross* and *David and Goliath* were exhibited in numerous religious settings.[2] The Savior Himself appeared in the productions of Griffith (*The Avenging Conscience* and *Intolerance*) and Thomas Ince (*Civilization*). Three hundred clergymen attended a showing of Ince's spectacle at the Tremont Theatre in Boston and advertised its religious power, some seriously suggesting that the antiwar film could convert the world to "Christian-sanity."[3] Western star William S. Hart, primed to enact justice on his adulterous wife in *The Disciple*, was averted from personal vengeance by a vision of the three crosses on Golgotha. Like the unmistakably luminous image of the cross in Jasper Cropsey's *The Millennial Age* (1854), the emblazoned image of the old rugged cross on Calvary stood as the apotheosis of grace in Hart's religious western film. Mary Pickford in *Sparrows* would see the Good Shepherd dissolving out of the side of a barn and taking a dead child into a pastoral heaven. In *Shadows*, Lon Chaney's Chinaman converted to Christianity after he witnessed the forgiving spirit of a maligned minister. King Vidor's *Sky Pilot* would bring salvation and masculine friendship to the Canadian town of Swan's Creek. Such religious presentations from Hollywood fueled Christian visionaries' belief in the religious possibilities of the motion picture. Clergy believed it was not enough to exhibit these films; they felt called to produce their own cultural and spiritual art.

With an optimistic and poetic spokesperson like Vachel Lindsay, many waxed eloquent on a vision of film as a new language of "American hieroglyphics," a universal Esperanto connecting viewers around the world to the aesthetic tradition of the Hudson River artists as well as with the transcendental legacy of Emerson and Whitman. In fact, in his Gospel of Beauty, poet-evangelist Lindsay showcased the inspiring and intimate links between magnificent forests and "groves of giant redwoods" and a category he labeled "Photoplays of Religious Splendors." Praising the glories of the spectacular cinema, he entreated the "most sceptical reader of [his] book to assume that miracles in a Biblical sense have occurred," as nature was its witness.[4] For Lindsay, and for a host of clergy, the same religious truths promulgated by the Hudson River painters, namely, the notion of God's presence in His creation, were to be located in moving picture scenes of the American mountains and valleys. The moving picture camera was an honest and unsullied eyewitness to the glories of God in the handiwork of His creation; its record revealed the possible redemption of the world. The Reverend James Ecob, echoing Calvin, reminded preachers that the natural world was the scene, or theater, of divine action, and the story of creation was a living series of moving pictures "or cartoons, vast in outline, deep in color and suggestion, moving in panoramic majesty."[5] One precedent for interpreting signs of God's activity in natural phenomena came through the typological imagination of Puritan preacher Jonathan Edwards, for whom even craggy mountains and thunder clouds offered shadows of God's majesty and evoked such "mild attributes" as His goodness, grace, and love.[6] Ecob suggested that intimations of a Protestant faith could be seen not only in the thunderclouds and flowers, but also through the arts of painting and moving images. The images of Creation were replete with God's fingerprints.

Photo-Drama of Creation

Religious cinematic innovation burst upon the theatrical milieu in 1913, when the International Bible Students Association (IBSA) produced an eight-hour *Photo-Drama of Creation*, released as three separate features.[7] The "nonsectarian and interdenominational" biblical extravaganza was presented free to local community theaters (often cosponsored by anony-

While biblical events and characters, such as Moses and the Brazen Serpent, were portrayed in classic illustrative poses, the *Photo-Drama of Creation* emphasized the allegorical and anagogical meanings of the texts. *The Scenario* (34). Courtesy Atlantis Photo.

mous donors), promoted as pure philanthropy, and shown free in all principal cities.[8] Amazed that this independent film was enjoying such a wide release, *Moving Picture World* decided it was worthy of review; their movie critics found it especially commendable that no charge was made for admission in such a mercenary business as film production.[9] Even *Billboard* and The *New York Times* were impressed with the scope of the film's exhibition circuit.[10] Working under a British charter, the IBSA aimed at exemplifying a new breed of filmmakers, supported by voluntary contributions, with a staff of accompanying lecturers operating out of London and Brooklyn. Its object was "through various means, to encourage Bible study, and in the moving picture exhibitions it hopes to be especially helpful in this regard."[11]

The *Photo-Drama of Creation*'s eight-hour panorama of hand-painted, "colored lantern slides, tinted moving pictures and synchronized phonographic lectures supplemented by appropriate musical selections taken from the classics," thrilled viewers.[12] Hoping that witnessing biblical events would "stimulate interest in the Book of Books" among those who had been indifferent to religious matters, the ISBA sought to draw new converts through a story of creation, beginning "with the earth being without form and void, the ages of the nebulae; then to the creation of the animals, the coming of man, the story of the Garden of Eden," and finally the great procession of events which brought humanity up to "the year of grace, 1914."[13] Where the Hudson River painters had suggested the sublime presence of God, the *Photo-Drama of Creation* spelled out God's actions with broad strokes and unabashed zeal. Dealing mostly with the transgressions of human nature through the ages, images of thorns and thistles replaced gardens of glorious beauty. The artistry of a painter's brush switched to cinema as prophetic hammer.

In his insightful study, historian Richard Alan Nelson assessed the *Photo-Drama* as a bit of "clerical filmmaking." Sponsored by the controversial cult pastor, the Reverend Charles Taze Russell, the project flashed forth as one of the most dynamic and innovative attempts to propagandize for God. Russell believed that the Lord had sanctioned visual communication through His use of "parables and in the symbols of Revelation, which are word pictures." He declared, "Pictures, in my opinion, next to the power of the tongue, are the most powerful things in the world."[14] Russell's apologetic pointed back to St. John's treatises on the defense of iconography as a means toward veneration of the true God behind His creation, wherein the Holy Scriptures and the holy icon are "mutually revelatory."[15]

The ISBA's original plan was to provide free entertainment—a decision grounded in their vision of alternative religious education, specifically in using the movies to tell stories and truths of the Old and New Testaments:

> Time was when the little Bible student of the Sunday School classes pictured in his mind's eye the happenings as recorded in the Good Book from the many colored lithographs that went to illustrate a text. But the day of the modern has arrived—a day when it is not quite necessary for the rest of the picture to be drawn by the descriptive ability of the Sunday school teacher.[16]

Technologically, the photoplays utilized voices emanating from a phonograph attachment that kept exact time with the action and provided both a lecture and a service of song. Such innovation as seeing and hearing Nebuchadnezzar read his doom on the walls in letters of fire was lauded as "nothing short of magic," with "no greater miracle than this wrought by Divine intelligence working on the brain of man." New exhibitors waxed eloquent on how the ISBA had adapted the modern motion picture to religious purposes by extending the typical thrills of the motion picture beyond "the doings of border outlaws."

> The stories of Joseph cast into the pit, of Absalom hanging by the hair in the branches of a tree, have their counterparts in modern life. Several of the large moving picture concerns, indeed, have prepared impressive photo-dramas dealing with the life and works of the great Teacher of men, who called as His disciples the lowly fishermen by the Sea of Galilee.

Actuality films shot in the Holy Land, inside Jerusalem and on the Mount of Olives, appealed to the visual piety of many church congregations. In the view of philosophy professor Herbert Martin, they also lent a measure of realism to religion, yielding renewed reverence and credence to faith. The invention of the cinematograph provided a means to display actual places and things and to infuse its subjects with an aura of scientific and modern authority. In 1910 Albert Schweitzer published *The Quest of the Historical Jesus,* paralleling films that explored the historical loci of Jesus' ministry. Both sought to re-create the historical reality of the person of Jesus. In "actuality" films, the visual demonstration of biblical events, no matter how artificially produced, lent authenticity to ancient narratives. Churches could subscribe to visual Bible stories, an iconic salvation history in the movies of Bible land travelogues, testimonies, prophecies, parables, and moral and cultural instruction. Under the spell of progressive modernism, the evidence of real and recognized locations convinced audiences of the validity of the stories themselves. The *Photo-Drama* thus advertised its authenticity, its actuality, and its appeal, boasting that it had all the necessary accessories in place for a spiritually moving experience:

> Nature has not changed the face of the land of Palestine much for so many centuries and houses, customs, and dress are much as they were before the Christian era. Men of many nations have participated in the acts of the great photo-drama, showing to those of this present day how the people of old lived, acted and died, as they played their parts in the great scenes of the ages.

The IBSA producer of the *Photo-Drama* extolled the benefits of moving pictures, even over books, as an unconventional but effective means of teaching biblical content. Phrases of the King James version of the Bible that were deemed obscure or required laborious instruction to be understood could be translated into clear visual images, directly shot in the Holy Land. For example, the film helped to illustrate Jesus' odd saying that

> it was easier for a camel to enter the needle's eye than for a rich man to enter the Kingdom of Heaven. Many who have applied the text all too literally have rejoiced in the belief that their wealthy neighbors could no more attain everlasting bliss than the tall humped camel could force his way into the eye of the cambric needle in mother's sewing basket. The moving picture shows the camel actually at one of the small doors in the gate of the walls of Jerusalem, the Needle's Eye. It is possible for the camel, by getting down on all fours, to get through, but in order to succeed he must first be divested of all his burden. The camel driver removes everything and after he has managed to get the Ship of the Desert safely through he drags the packs and cloths and saddles after him and reloads the beast. It is difficult for the creature to enter the Needle's Eye, but he does.[17]

The obscure word was "interpreted" and visualized. The film suggested that the salvation of wealthy men was possible by showing how the struggling camel negotiated his way through the difficult point of entry. Other graphic and "grewsome" scenes of early church history were also deemed appropriate for inclusion in order to quicken the hearts of spectators and instruct them in holy history. Still and moving pictures were combined to elicit such responses; one such stereopticon image was Gerome's picture *After the Exhibition* which depicted the lions being driven from the sands of the arena after an act of fiendish cruelty.

The final reel began with Daniel and concluded with the death and resurrection of Jesus. As with the earlier releases, no admission fees were charged; neither were there any direct or indirect solicitations of money. Producers provided phonograph recordings ("canned oratory") of beautiful renderings of hymns and sermons that emphasized the wonders of Creation and Salvation history. Reflecting the fundamentalist struggle against the mounting Darwinism of the era, the dramatic lecturer on the recording tells his audience to observe that "our blessings are not the result of evolution, but because we are living in God's due time for lifting the veil. The drama claims that we are living near the time when the Messianic kingdom will be established, and that the wonderful blessings of our day are but a prelude to the still greater blessings."[18] The optimism of postmillennial theology, which corresponded to the progressive mood of the era's social reformers, emphasized the improvement of both the individual and society, even to the point of creating a heaven on earth. Thus, according to one anonymous critic who saw the film's potential to save souls,

> the pictures' claim to harmonize science, history and the Scriptures is done in a very plausible manner. . . . There was nothing in the pictures of the teachings of any sect or denomination, but the phonograph lectures adapted the pictures to the teachings of Pastor Russell and "Millennial Dawn." Not only will the race be brought to human perfection, but incidentally man will have obtained the needed experience in respect to good and evil. Meantime, also, the earth will be gradually coming to a state of perfection—Paradise restored worldwide.[19]

Furthermore, one teacher of the IBSA movement believed that stereopticon slides would acquaint teachers from every nation with a new world order, effectively propagating millennialism worldwide. Peace would inevitably reign on earth *because* these films provided the world with *universal speech.*[20]

D. W. Griffith picked up this same phrase the next year as he filmed *Birth of a Nation.* Admonishing his young actress Lillian Gish for her playful mischief on the set, Griffith solemnly intoned that the moving picture was ordained as the "first tiny steps in a new glorious medium that had been predicted in the Bible and called the Universal Language. That when it could be brought to its full power, it would bring about the millennium."[21] Griffith's utterance of the phrase "universal language" was opportunely and curiously connected to the *Photo-Drama.* He appeared to believe in the impending arrival of a postmillennial paradise, perhaps borrowed from the Reverend Russell's eschatology.[22]

Little about the *Photo-Drama* was praiseworthy, however. One astute critic from the *Moving Picture Educator* leveled several accusations against the film. First, he was disappointed that half to two-thirds of the presentation was composed of antiquated stereopticon views, "many of them of ancient vintage, crude and coarse." Second, he disliked the arrogance of the Reverend Russell, who shamelessly described himself in the film as "so great a teacher." To the contrary, he saw flagrant biblical errors, as in the story of Moses and Pharaoh. He thought Russell's version of the "Flight from Egypt" was staged like a parade "with Pharaoh in the viewing stand and Moses leading with a measured tread like a drum-major." The reviewer was most disappointed, however, by the way that Pastor Russell's dishonest "point of view" bent, twisted, and distorted the scriptures into political propaganda. For example, the image of Samson pulling down the great pillars was entitled "How Samson predicted the fall of Socialism." Finally, Russell's hobbyhorse of the millennium was duly mocked. According to the *Moving Picture Educator,* Russell "beggars the glorious future by showing a picture of a nice suburban house; with pretty floral surroundings, an automobile at the gate; and entitles the scene *Paradise.* Evidently many who live under such conditions are in Paradise already and need not wait for the millennium."[23]

Providing free entertainment proved to be expensive, and the ISBA had to change its exhibition requirements in 1914 to urge local exhibitors for contributions.[24] But the venture was still not self-sustaining. By 1917, the Mena Film Company sought to purchase exhibition rights for the production by selling stock subscriptions, thus hoping to subsidize its dramatic vision of enabling spectators to see God's glory. Incorporated under the laws of New Jersey for $250,000, the official primary object of the Mena Film Company was to supervise the selection and editing of scenarios and to produce motion pictures that would illustrate, elucidate, and popularize the various features of the Divine Plan of the Ages. Mena promised that motion picture stars in their films would be able to depict vividly the "events of fifty or one thousand years hence: the Resurrection of the dead, to the amazement and delight of the living."[25] Profit making was, at least on paper, secondary and incidental. However, the *Watch Tower* reported that Mena's purchase of the *Photo-Drama* was cancelled due to objections from the "brethren."[26] Overall, Mena's projects garnered only limited profits and the company did not survive.

Nevertheless, the universal appeal of the Bible stories, coupled with free admission for this "public benefaction," marked the fusion of film and sacred history, even in a cultic version, as a noteworthy model for religious film production. The *New York Times* proclaimed this "Gospel by Film Drama" a triumphant success.[27] It considered it "the most astounding feature of [Russell's] Work . . . the acme of beauty and charm, and correspondingly entertaining and instructive."[28] By incorporating a force of advance "field men" who traveled twenty circuits about the world exhibiting the three-part film, the *Photo-Drama* was shown in eighty cities and towns daily. However, like Mel Gibson's twenty-first century *Passion of the Christ,* it was still a Bible story; another film genre was needed to expand the horizon of religious filmmaking.[29]

The Stream of Life

In the October 1921 issue of *Pictorial Review,* Percy Waxman reiterated a question that had been frequently posed in the previous decade: "Motion Pictures in Churches, Why Not?"[30] The question harkened back to the controversies of the Reformation, with the haunting spirit of Zwingli's abhorrence of imagery being challenged by the light of practical theology. In a study of nineteen churches with a combined seating capacity of over sixteen thousand, Waxman tellingly noted that only 1,817 persons were attending these churches on a given Sunday night. "The photoplay is not the *reason* for the empty church seats; it is a *result,*" he argued. When one does not incorporate film into church services, the result will be empty pews. For Waxman, where a picture flickers on the screen in churches, there can be no "dim religious light," as Milton called it. For any who might be agitated by innovations, Waxman cited both conservative Methodists and the Pope as endorsing and sanctioning its use for religious instruction. Calling in an even greater authority, he pointed out that the Savior's own visual style in parables was "rich in pictorial values." Waxman then delivered a set of "movie commandments," such as not expecting films to provide what the minister must provide, or using films as mere entertainment. His goal for film included much more than illustrating a sermon. An effective use of films could promote a sense of community, what Waxman described as a more democratic feeling pervading the ranks of the congregation and obliterating class distinctions even found in churches.[31] To augment such a promising trend, he indicated, one must find better films—films that would attract, uplift, and inspire congregations.

This need to find suitable entertaining moving pictures in the church was underlined by The *Christian Herald* when it contrasted two photographs: one of a motion picture theater and the other of a church, two minutes' walk away on the same street. The photos were taken on a Sunday evening in September 1922 and vividly demonstrated that the bustling crowds preferred the entertainment to the uplift.[32] A related editorial blared:

"WHAT CAN WE DO ABOUT IT?"

By then, churches had been exhibiting films for almost twenty years; some religious entrepreneurs, disillusioned by what they perceived as the lack of appropriate product coming from film production companies, finally decided to make their own films as a way to draw in the crowds and satisfy their thirst for a good elixir. In 1914, the Duke of Manchester, the Reverend Cleveland Moffett, and scenario writer Katherine Eggleston had agreed to form a company to produce religious and educational pictures, but they had to fight "scared-cats" who advocated a "moss-back policy which shuts up the great, idle, expansive pile of stones [the church building] half of the time," worried lest the "sacred edifice be desecrated." Miss Eggleston explained, "If all the churches and the schools of this country were in the market for good pictures, it wouldn't be a year before the output of the various producing companies would show an improvement in subjects."[33]

A general demand for good pictures was not forthcoming, but one very notable religious feature eventually sprang forth, namely, *The Stream of Life* (1919). The scenario for this first Christian "blockbuster" was written and produced by the Reverend Dr. James K. Shields, an Episcopal clergyman in the artistic tradition of fellow rector and celluloid inventor Hannibal Goodwin. While Shields extolled the preeminence of the sense of sight as the primary channel for carrying the Gospel message, he simultaneously warned of the moral hazards of filmmaking. "Unfortunately," he wrote, "greed has seized upon the motion picture machine and has monopolized its use, to such an extent that the Church has allowed itself to become prejudiced against an instrument which holds the greatest possibilities of spreading abroad the fundamental principles and teaching of the Gospel." For Shields, the cinema was comparable in potential religious use to the organ, "the greatest of all musical instruments— once looked upon by church folks as the *devil's own*—that never came to its best until it entered the sanctuary to thrill and inspire the people with its divine melody in its interpretation of spiritual aspiration." He argued that anyone hearing the organ and the cinematograph working together in perfect harmony will feel that they are "as naturally wed one to the other as the bird's song is to the springtime. And they will yet be working together for the glory of God."[34]

The Editorial Forum ❀

DR. CHARLES M. SHELDON
Editor-in-Chief

RAE D. HENKLE
Managing Editor

DR. GEORGE H. SANDISON
Editor Emeritus

Two Pictures

These two photographs were taken at eight o'clock on the evening of Sunday, September 24, in New York City. One is a motion picture theater. The other is a well-known church, doors open for the evening service, on the same street and only a two minutes' walk away. WHAT CAN WE DO ABOUT IT?

Rediscovering Simon Patten's observation of two distinct places only two minutes away from one another on a Sunday evening, *The Christian Herald* dramatically pointed out that audiences were attending the movies and not the churches. Two Pictures *The Christian Herald* (October 14, 1922), 720. Courtesy Library of Congress.

The production of *The Stream of Life,* supported by prominent New Jersey businessmen who organized the Plymouth Film Corporation, was based on Shields's pamphlet, *Philip Maynard,* and on a series of national circuit lectures given by the author.[35] Under the auspices of his own Plimpton Epic Pictures, Horace Plimpton directed *The Stream of Life* at his studio in Sherwood Park, Yonkers.

At a private screening at the Rialto Theater, New York, on October 20, 1919, an audience of ministers viewed *The Stream of Life.* Critic Frances Agnew extolled the exceptional film as illustrating the far-reaching possibilities of the motion picture and collected favorable comments from the ministers and from business leaders in attendance.[36] Most notable was her conclusion that the impressive film would "convert many still out of the fold to the cause of the moving picture." She felt that it would appeal to a "better class of patrons," one known as the "spiritual class" of people, that would elevate the quality of audiences at theaters. Another reviewer alerted exhibitors that the film's strong religious appeal would "stir up greater interest among church goers." To succeed commercially with this picture, theater owners were recommended to get the cooperation of ministers, providing them with private invitations, securing their endorsements (and their mailing lists), and posting the clerical endorsements in the lobby. It seemed to exhibitors that the film, would be more effective in drawing in new audiences than the preaching of a sermon: religious leaders saw it differently; it did preach a sermon.

The Stream of Life is the tale of a farmboy who becomes a bank CEO and drifts from his biblical foundations to a sophisticated club life. The boy, Philip Maynard, has been reared in a country home, surrounded by the best and most wholesome simplicity and religious influences. He is lured as a young man to the siren call of the city. To the city he goes, with the Little Bible inscribed by his mother. The film introduces the standard melodramatic elements of a Victorian home of refinement and culture: his wife, a beautiful little daughter named Marjorie, and a pious but delightful old Mother who "brings embarrassing reminders of the omission of grace at meals, family prayers and neglect of the dust covered Bible." When the little daughter dies, the pain of loss compounds Philip's rebellion and unbelief. His business prospers, but his soul plunges deep into despair. His grieving wife seeks surcease of her sorrow in social club life, until one day she passes the open door of a vine-covered chapel. As she kneels at the altar to pray, a choir sings directly to her of God's comfort.

Comforted, Marjorie arises with the assurance that death is only a transition, and rushes home to relate her experience to Philip. However, he thinks religion is only for women, and that God and faith have no place in the life of a strong man. Philip remains inconsolable until one rainy night when he goes to the chapel with an umbrella and raincoat to fetch his wife home and overhears her testimony of faith. He is convicted of his own waywardness, but still stubbornly resists the whispers of God's Spirit by seeking relief at his club. However, when he returns home Philip opens the old family Bible and reads from the book of *Revelation,* "Behold I stand at the door and knock . . ." Then suddenly, Christ stands before him. He falls to his knees and cries, "I believe."

In summing up the climax of the film, the Reverend Chester Marshall pointed to the significant social consequences of Philip's conversion. After his life is utterly transformed by faith, Philip gives lavishly to orphanages and other philanthropies. When his bank partner invests in a foolish loan, money is embezzled and the bank fails. Faced with his depositors, Philip devotes his vast fortune to repaying them. Having lost all, he moves to a humble cottage, visits the embezzler in prison, and continues his good works and keeps an unwavering faith in his living Redeemer: "Thus, at last," wrote Marshall, "we see his life ebbing out with the tide to be lost in the great ocean of the God-life from whence it came," the stream of life doing its redemptive work. Marshall pointed to the film's simplicity as an analogy between "a human life and a stream, starting as a mere rill up in the hills, broadening out and deepening into the brook and then the great, strong river current that is borne out into the sea."[37]

Highlighting the power of the visual, Marshall argued that when Jesus wanted to bring to this world a full understanding of His love and mercy, when He wanted to present His Father in His truest form,

He took His brush and in such vivid colors as were never mixed by artist, painted the picture known as the Prodigal Son. There is the picture of God at His best and of man in his greatest need. The picture method was the way to make it remembered. True, this was a word picture—the only kind He could well employ. Only once, so far as our record goes, did He ever write—but when He did write He stooped down and wrote in the sand. The very picturesque nature of His method made an indelible impression upon His spectators.

Those offended by the film were reminded of Jesus' methods of using pictures and parables for dramatic effect. Praise poured on Shields's film, which offered numerous poignant allusions for the person brought up in a religious home: "the devout old grandmother, the hymn singing and prayer, grace at table, the simple prayer meeting. The church audience will find everything it seeks." According to critic Gladys Bollman, many at the premiere screening wept. A glimpse of the little prayer meeting was the touch that unlocked the viewer's heart to "the comfort of religion," especially with the emotional tug of appropriate hymns played by the organist. Bollman identified the differences between this picture and others: "First, the point of view is frankly religious. Secondly, the finely conceived characters make convincing scenes that the weak-fibered persons of most picture plays can never portray. There is a point of view genuinely expressing reverence, tenderness, and respect for the best, neglecting neither goodness nor the good things of life. Action is substituted for pretty padding. It is sincere, and therefore simple and unified. More than all, it says something—and says it in a way to be remembered."[38]

Variety praised the Methodist inauguration of the ninety-minute long-film as "a unique method of preaching a sermon, "drawing "home a lesson proving religion is a necessity of everyone's daily life, despite one's state of affluence."[39] Marshall explained that just as Jesus had used the picture method in the parable of the Prodigal Son, he could point to this "one picture which perhaps more than any other demonstrates the power of motion pictures in evangelistic use"—the seven-reel *Stream of Life*.[40] Also resonating with the audience were both the film's use of subtitles quoting such luminaries as Longfellow, Tennyson, and Oliver Wendell Holmes, and its evocative musical score fitted with many old familiar hymns. Numerous reviews mentioned the subtitles, and praised the role of the familiar poetry of Tennyson, whose "To the Brook" was quoted throughout. His "Crossing the Bar" quietly ended the film.[41]

Working with Marshall, Reisner once again solidified his radical reputation as an innovator. Asking whether the Gospel could be preached through the moving picture, he did acknowledge that there were undoubtedly "multitudes, and among them the best people of the world, who . . . say emphatically, 'No! It belongs to the devil.'" However, this was not Reisner's opinion, and the film substantiated his view when it was shown in a prominent New York City theater at noon every day for a week.[42] Joining the Methodist Centenary group, exhibitor Lee Shubert experimented with this picture. During Easter week, he donated his

Casino Theatre on Broadway for free exhibitions. Every day people were invited in to see a noontime showing of the film and they came: audiences of over two thousand, comprised of every creed and nationality, packed the theater, "Jews, Catholics, Protestants, and the unchurched." Shield's central purpose in *The Stream of Life* was to visualize the need of "every man and woman to have faith in God in order to endure the crisis that of necessity comes into every human life." An evangelistic strategy was planned: after each showing, a brief two-minute homily would be delivered with "an opportunity given to those who wanted to renew their loyalty to God and to be remembered in the prayer to follow, to indicate their desire and intention by an uplifted hand." Its effectiveness at inspiring such a faith was described by a reviewer as follows:

> As the last scene faded out, the lights were turned on and a minister stepped quickly to the platform and with uplifted hand said: "Just a minute, boys, before you go. In the last hour and a half you fellows have had to take stock of your spiritual possessions, and a lot of you are short and you know it. How many of you feel that you would like to have some one pray for you before you leave the house?" Instantly, without a moment's hesitation, eight hundred men raised their hands.

According to Shields, an amazing statistic of "nine-tenths of those present daily held up their hands." Hundreds of spectators who had not been in a church for years were spellbound as a "vital, throbbing, Christian message" was projected to them; there was "scarcely a dry eye in the house." As part of his evangelical strategy, Shields formed exhibition teams to place copies of the Gospel in each man's hand and provide lists and addresses of New York churches for follow-up ministry. Shields claimed that "a score of noted preachers in as many churches would not have produced a total effect commensurate with that secured by the showing of this picture. If a similar method were to be adopted next Easter week in cities all over the land it would afford a tremendous contribution to Christianity."[43]

For writer-producer Shields, this mass conversion scene demonstrated the efficacy of moving pictures as a means of preaching powerfully. His specific objective was to reach the multitudes that didn't "yet attend the House of God." He explained that in addition to preaching evangelists and singing evangelists, the church would one day commission "motion picture evangelists, men and women who will, with the same divine consecration, pour the heart of the Gospel into simple stories and great dramas for the screen that will draw and grip the hearts of thousands and millions that the preaching and singing evangelists can never reach because of their physical limitations."[44] Although financial problems, prejudice against such modern contraptions, the lack of secondary exhibition and distribution channels, and objections from the theatrical exchanges loomed for those who envisioned such an opportunity, Shields was undaunted. He believed that the number of churches catching the vision of the possibilities in motion pictures was increasing rapidly. In addition, he envisioned that both the production and distribution of gospel pictures would eventually become a distinct department of Christian service and activity. "When the Church wakes up to its real opportunity, our congregations will not be slipping away to the Sunday night theater and picture house, but will be looking forward with pleasure and inviting their friends to join them in a beautiful and uplifting service in their home church."[45]

However, in advocating pictures for church services, Shields emphasized that the moving pictures must be scripted from the church's point of view. "Second-hand pictures will not answer, and by second-hand we mean those pictures that have run their course through the regular theaters and then, after they are no longer a financial asset, they have been expurgated by cutting out immoral or suggestive parts." Shields was not above using some splendid weekday reels for the purpose of entertainment, but the Sunday evening picture must be a "Gospel picture; it must radiate an influence and carry a message of divine truth and drive it home. It must be prepared in the same spirit with which a minister prepares his sermon—to do good and not to make money, must dominate the heart of the writer." Eschew dry and uninteresting scenarios, Shields recommended, as "mediocrity will not be forgiven in the church any more than in a theater. Arouse the memory of the best and the sweetest things in life. Purge all [that is] melodramatic and unreal. Portray those things that can happen and do happen; presented in modern dress and experience[d] with the widest range of wholesome humor, deep pathos, and true love. The church picture, from the standpoint of artistry and execution, must be the equal of any to be seen in the picture palace downtown."[46]

The progressive theme of an applied Social Gospel also promoted a simple moral lesson of returning to old-fashioned social and religious ceremonies; it drew upon such classic tropes as the little country schoolhouse, the Church in the Valley by the Wildwood, the quiet nook in the river where the fish bite, and the swimming hole. The cradle-to-grave narrative concerning the moral trajectory of a businessman whose success estranged him from his religious upbringing resonated with the respectable middle-class audience. When Philip and his wife found solace in a restored religious faith, they devoted the rest of their lives to helping others in true Social Gospel style. *The Stream of Life* curiously combined elements of an emerging fundamentalism and of adherence to one's faith tradition with the progressive reform actions of helping those less fortunate. It also advanced a disciplined model of the muscular Christian man who would be softened by the transformation of faith. This cinematic model fit what Clifford Putney identified in the origins of the YMCA as a virile "muscular Christianity" that appealed to the emerging men of business. Shields successfully sponsored his "drama of moral regeneration and faith restored" as a means to evangelize and undergird his support for Prohibition.

According to the Reverend Carl Nau, what attracted people was the film's "undenied entrance to the soul through the eye," which he equated with Jesus' use of parables: "With Him it was the 'candlestick' in the Temple, 'the flowers,' 'the nets,' 'the vine,' 'the sheep,' 'the seed,' 'the child,' etc. All these were things 'seen and handled,' but under His realities." Likewise, the Reverend Chester Marshall argued that the picture represented both the best of Americanism and the best of religion, the two becoming inextricably interwoven, creating an electric atmosphere. "Laughter and tears are intermingled and every emotion of good is stirred and deepened into a resolution to make life count for God and humanity."[47] Other testimonials came from clergy like Frank Field of Holmes Memorial Methodist Church in Detroit, Michigan, who used *The Stream of Life* several times in evangelistic meetings, followed by a series of four sermons on successive evenings.[48] Looking back at Shields's work, critic and historian Arthur Krows noted that

> None but James Shields, himself, can have a fair conception of the patient scheming, the wheedling, the haggling, the counting of pennies, the incessant pounding towards a goal but dimly seen, which the film entailed. But the minister, especially the clergyman much engaged in social service, is of necessity a trained promoter. He hobnobs with wealthy persons, who, in the leisure of their retirement, are disposed to bargain with God by yielding a percentage for the conduct of his work.[49]

Marshall hoped that through Shields's promotional work a sufficient number of additional churches that had hitherto not considered movie

THE·CHRISTIAN·HERALD

AN·ILLUSTRATED·NEWS·WEEKLY·FOR·THE·HOME·
·GRAHAM PATTERSON, PUBLISHER·

The portable projection machine for motion pictures opens up heretofore undeveloped fields for the exhibition of clean, wholesome films. The Sunday School room, the lodge room, the home, the public school, are all potential exhibition halls. The photograph above shows the machine and a Christian Herald film being projected from it in one of the rooms of the Bible House.

Motion Picture Madness

The Church Has Neglected a Great Opportunity to Use the Screen as It Used the Printing Press in Its Period of Evolution

By CHARLES JOHNSON POST

WHEN the men—and the girls, too—who cast their first vote last year were still squirming in their first year a new magic lantern show was advertised in New York City. And the pictures made by this new magic lantern, or stereopticon, moved! It was a most astonishing thing. There were the waves at Atlantic City breaking in long crests so that it seemed as if the front seats must be showered in spray. There was the Empire State express on its way to Chicago and roaring its way right out of the picture into the audience until the unsophisticated of those days scrouged against their neighbor in an effort to get off the track. There was a fire-engine going to a fire! Elephants at work in Burmah piling teak! A Chinese street! A bazaar in Algiers! Marvelous!

And the people moved, the steamers churned the waters of foreign ports, the sampans paddled—and all the world moved closer and walked among as as human and real as if we had journeyed on the magic carpet of Arabian Nights. For the magic carpet had been invented, but it transports to us all the distant worlds and makes them visible and living close at hand.

Then what happened? The cold keen business minds that know everything about business and money-making laughed.

"The motion picture," they said solemnly as they buttoned up their pockets and put a dime in the missions box, "the motion picture is a toy—nothing but a toy."

So the motion picture had to struggle on as best it could and with the lesser minds. Theater managers who first ran them as a novelty and who knew what the public wanted at any hour of the day or night began to drop them.

"The novelty has worn off," they said, "and since we know what the public wants we'll run them to get rid of our audiences and make room for the new crowd."

That is those who ran cheap vaudeville theaters. Other theaters wouldn't have them at any price. For they knew "just what the public wants."

Then some one tried to tell a story on the screen—to make a fiction idea visible. Another man hired a vacant store and a few wooden chairs left over from a political campaign and opened the first motion-picture theater in the world. These men didn't know enough to know what the public wants—not

TODAY an estimate places the motion-picture attendance at something like twenty million people a week; the whole population of the United States in a little over a month! Fifteen years ago it was no industry at all; and today it is one of the leading industries in the nation with an income of something like *eight hundred millions of dollars a year*—or over fifteen million dollars a week. Yet today the motion-picture industry is in a desperate condition as it staggers under expenses and suspicions and a disorganization and recklessness that beggar imagination. Think of a business terrorized and terrified by its own incapacity and yet into which one-fifth of the entire population of the United States is willing to pay tribute each week!

There are two elements in this situation. One, the element that took up motion pictures in its early days and that has remained in control long enough virtually to characterize it—and that is for that matter practically in control today. At least they are in virtual control of what is known as the motion-picture theater field; they are not interested in the non-theatrical field.

The second element is the motion picture itself; it is the greatest invention for conveying human thought and for visualizing that has been invented; the motion picture—in its capacity for story-telling—fills a deep, vital human need. Just as every tribe has had, from days unknown, the tribal story-teller or the Arab story-teller sitting in the market place telling his tales, so there is the motion picture telling its stories all over the world in every language and in the one language of vision that all understand. It makes every one an eye-witness of any event, and it gives every one a front seat. It is reality itself multiplied indefinitely and for each beholder. It is no toy; it is a social instrument of enormous service in every field of human thought, in every art, and in every

then. Now they know all about it, and freely admit it.

channel whereby it is desired to spread ideas and give them quick, firm, visible root.

It is hardly necessary to consider the first element. These producers give the public what they think the public want—and since they risk their money in it, and in large quantity, we can credit them with sincerity. They have little imagination of an esthetic kind, their background in general lacking in any other motive than that of getting the money from anything they can get the money for. They are shrewd, they yield to pressure, when they can see or feel pressure—though to have a production "roasted" by the pulpit for licentiousness or immorality of subject or presentation means nothing more than good advertising and an added argument for their film salesman as "sure-fire stuff, hot stuff." A sort of craft fellowship has bound them together so that they never troubled to purify their own ranks—if it ever occurred to them that they needed purifying at all. And the man that they chose as chief and head of their craft laid his foundations of artistic success as a manager of prize-fighters—a fact of frank pride.

THE whole business of motion-picture production was in a state of evolution without check or balance of competition—except the competition within its own ranks. Its cultural consciousness in the literary field possibly rose as high as the dime novel but probably stopped at the half-dime series—or the factory-bride-of-the-mill-owner of the Bowery drama, or of the celebrated Laura Jean Libbey. To them adventure meant violence; romance meant degradation; and the unsavory divorce scandals the normal of well-clothed circles. It is tragic, this period of motion-picture development, for all this came from the background of dull, sordid, unimaginative lives for generations—the dull drab of ghetto, the poverty of clothing sweatshops or the reek of furs; and the men, unfamiliar with the wonderful imaginative creations and art of civilization were lifted by accident and the floods of money that poured in upon them to be the exponents of the greatest social instrument of the world.

They could not understand their own success. Here and there art and literature began forcing their way in against minds that were contemptuous of all but gross receipts. And not infrequently art and literature simply rephrased the old trash and moved

THE CHRISTIAN HERALD, July 1, 1922   Page 465

The Christian Herald exhibited its newest films through a portable projection machine, equated its revolutionary use for Christian communication with the printing press. "Motion Picture Madness" *The Christian Herald* (July 1, 1922), 465. Courtesy Library of Congress.

exhibition, would catch the movie bug and become equipped for projection so that producers could get their investment back in a reasonable time; Marshall also hoped that other pictures of the right kind would be forthcoming. They would, but without the success of Shields's pioneering feature.[50] Shields followed his own film with a docudrama scenario for *The Life of John Wesley,* incorporating the circuit-riding Wesley's words, "I look upon the world as my parish," as a validation of his own missionary work through films. Shields's production company, Plymouth Pictures, continued to distribute his films to churches through the diligent labors of his son, Wendell Shields, but no one was able to duplicate the phenomenal success of *The Stream of Life.*[51]

The Christian Herald Phenomenon

By 1923, "motion picture madness" had not only taken over the nation, it had infected many within the church as well. With an estimated 20 million patrons attending a movie at least once a week, and theaters collecting over $15 million a week, the movies now dominated the entertainment activities of the jazz-age generation. Examining this cultural trend, *Christian Herald* writer Charles Johnson Post believed that the church had neglected a great opportunity to incorporate the movies as it had incorporated the printing press in an earlier day.[52] Even though by 1921 more than two thousand churches throughout the country allegedly operated their own projection machines, Post's vision encompassed all churches. He reminded his readers that motion pictures could potentially function as an instrument for propaganda, for inculcating truth and virtue to young people.[53]

Economically, the theater by this point had developed a reputation as a rival of the church. Charles M. Sheldon (author of *In His Steps*) tabulated the box receipts for movies as $600 million in 1926, as compared to $500 million in tithing to Protestant churches, giving the entertainment industry the edge and showing that the average American was paying more for amusement than for his organized religious life. This proved to Sheldon that America was "Amusement mad." Sheldon, the foremost advocate of bringing Christ into the marketplace of ideas and images, served as the vanguard of a movement to engage the Christian faith and culture. In various issues of the *Christian Herald,* he inserted his ubiquitous thematic inquiry, "What Would Jesus Do?" into numerous professions.

In one particular theatrical script on December 1920, he devised a conference on the theme, "What Would Jesus Do with the Drama?" This Meeting of the Minds included the Manager (exhibitor), the Actor, the Dramatist (playwright), the Public, and Jesus in a roundtable discussion about the propriety and spiritual calling of the theater (and indirectly the moving picture). After various instances of the parties scapegoating and blaming one another, Jesus stepped in and proposed that the Dramatic Art was a noble and useful art that had been degraded and perverted by being commercialized and catering to vulgar demands. He indicted them all for misusing such a noble Art: the Manager for debasing his business and making it a commercial entity; the Dramatist for compromising his high calling by giving in to the popular cry for mere amusement; the Actor for losing sight of his genius to represent the noble rather than the petty; and the Public for encouraging low and vulgar plays by frequenting them. The main need of the theater once it was freed from its mercenary purpose, Jesus argued, was "the need of a different personality in the people who dedicate their lives to the Drama. These should be consecrated to their high calling, the same as ministers or missionaries." Jesus concluded that: "If those who manage and write plays and act in them, were my disciples, think of the millions, more than 16,000,000 every day in the picture houses alone, who would be influenced by great truths and impressed by thoughts that would make a better world."[54] For Sheldon and many others, the debased theater could be redeemed, but only by transforming it from its perverse uses for religious and moral communication.[55]

Before preparing for production, Sheldon outlined his plain and practical plans for exhibition at Sunday evening services, on how to use pictures. He included the purchase of first-class equipment, the secured approval of the Church Board, a selection of pictures with great care and relevance for vitality of message, the use of familiar devotional hymns (with a special emphasis that special quartet music be avoided), the taking of a silver offering between films to pay for film rentals, and the limitation of the minister's sermon to only ten minutes at the close of the film on the theme of the film. Finally, he asserted, after "a few words of invitation, the call for definite decisions should be made, *no matter what the picture has been,* and the net drawn, the pastor remaining after the people have quietly gone out, to meet any who decide to begin the Christian life." For Sheldon, both exhibition and production must continually focus on the end in view. A church was not in the entertainment business, but one might use the same means of the professional theater "as a means the Master Himself might use it—simply as a means to the great end of reaching and saving the people."[56]

The movie madness of the time itself invited investigation. Dean Charles N. Lathrop of the Social Service Committee of the Federal Council of Churches of Christ in America conducted a survey entitled "The Motion Picture Problem . . . What kind of social control is going on?"[57] Many clergy thought it was urgent that churches become involved in counterpropaganda as they spread the fiction that Hollywood was avoiding religious questions and themes in its productions. Critic Charles Post found it unconscionable that a certain tradition in the motion picture field had been established that "bars religious pictures. Think of such a tradition, of such a principle in an industry to which twenty million people a week pay tribute!" Post pointed out that statistically there were over forty million registered members of various churches in the United States and suggested that with and for an audience that large, the film industry might imagine that a picture with a religious theme would be "worthwhile even considered purely as a business move. On the contrary a religious picture—one with a religious theme is taboo."[58] Post ignored the fact that Hollywood had, in fact, actually produced films with religious themes. His task was not to praise Hollywood, but to separate his readers from its fold and deliver them to a new "religious" market. Post conveniently disregarded the existence of religious films like *The Miracle Man, Shadows,* and *Hell's Hinges* to lay the foundation for his own agenda of Christian filmmaking.

Seeds of anti-Semitism were sown and sprouted during this time. In his attempt to promote the church's counterindustry, Post lambasted the moral bankruptcy of an immigrant-dominated Hollywood. He blamed Hollywood's Jewish producers for shaping the questionable character of the motion pictures from its earliest days. Post believed these "producers give the public what they think the public want—and since they risk their money in it, and in large quantity, we can credit them with sincerity." However, he accused them of having little aesthetic imagination, and of reducing their motive to the merely mercenary. His racist stereotyping portrayed the producers as a shrewd conspiracy yielding to social pressure only when it threatened their profits. Post did recognize the marketing ploy that having a production "roasted" by the pulpit "for licentiousness or immorality of subject or presentation means nothing more than good advertising and an added argument for their film salesmen as 'sure-fire stuff, hot stuff.' A sort of craft fellowship has bound them together so that they never troubled to purify their own rank."[59] Post interpreted the aesthetic mission of the Jewish producers as meaning that "adventure meant violence; romance meant degradation; and the unsavory divorce scandals were the normal standard of well-clothed circles." He was convinced of their moral poverty, stemming from a tragic "background of dull, sordid, unimaginative lives for generations from the ghettoes and poverty, lifted by accident and floods of money to be the exponents of the greatest social instruments of the world."[60]

In similar vein, the vitriolic pronouncements of Edward Packerd in his "New England Essays" sought to build a Christian film industry on the sandy foundation of anti-Semitism:

> I look for an era when the Christian Church will get onto her job and great pioneers arise who will organize a motion picture, press and advertising business equal to the Jewish movie machine, put up motion picture movie mission theatres all over the world and solve the exhibition problems of churches in establishing the supremacy of character building, civilization-advancing, religious-evangelism movies, pictures that will lead humanity farther than a skirt, a bag of money, and a bundle of stunts— that will lead the human race to God and to sound life standards.

The weeds of anti-Semitism would spread in the next decade, but its insidious roots had already taken hold among these Hollywood detractors. However, Post did praise the motion picture as the

> *greatest invention for conveying human thought and for visualizing that has been invented; the motion picture—in its capacity for story telling— fills a deep, vital human need. Just as every tribe has had, from days unknown, the tribal story teller or the Arab story-teller sitting in the market place telling his tales, so there is the motion picture telling its stories all over the world in every language and in the one language of vision that all understand.* [Emphasis in original] It makes every one an eyewitness of any event, and it gives everyone a front seat. It is reality itself multiplied indefinitely and for each beholder. It is no toy; it is a social instrument of enormous service in every field of human thought, in every art, and in every channel whereby it is desired to spread ideas and give them quick, firm, visible root.

To Post, the motion picture was a new evolutionary form of printing, a visual newspaper for the world, for it spoke "a common tongue, the language of the eyes." Recognizing the notoriety of the theater, he dismissed its connection to the movies themselves. He himself rooted the genesis, or evolution, of film not in the theater but in the printing press that had been quickly seized upon by the forceful members of the Reformation. For Post, the church was in a position to be the fulcrum suggested by Archimedes, and the motion picture was the lever that could move the world.

Canon William Sheafe Chase, "the Little Giant," rector at Christ Episcopal Church in Brooklyn, and director of the Lord's Day Alliance, was a leading champion and regulator of motion pictures.[61] Having devoted a lifetime to denouncing vice (catalogued alphabetically from Billiards to Theatre) and lobbying for purity, since February 1914 he had been particularly involved in regularly showing religious pictures to the younger generation from the immigrant class. However, he challenged Frank Dyer, former president of the General Film Company, in a *Motion Picture Magazine*'s three-part "Great Debate: Shall Pictures Be Censored?"[62] Dyer, of course, argued in the negative, extolling the virtues of an industry that brought fresh recreation to the masses. Chase thought such a stance was naïve, as a more intentional role was needed to guide young people in their amusements. However, by 1920, in spite of his active participation in bringing uplifting films to the masses, Chase believed that the church was the only power that could redeem the motion picture; he subsequently advised the church to create a fund of $20 million for the manufacture of religious films and pictures teaching "Christian morality and patriotism," and to establish free film libraries.[63] He pointed to the remarkable example that had been set by the YMCA when it furnished religious motion pictures to army training camps: back in 1915, the Federal Council of Churches had commissioned Edward McConoughey to report on "Motion Pictures in Religious Education Work," with the result that the YMCA Motion Picture Bureau saw an opportunity to distribute films that would educate immigrants on the Christian faith and Americanization. Canon Chase cited the leadership of George Zehrung as an exemplary model in training ministers on the use of films as the basis for object lessons or as modern parables and outlined his own views in his *Catechism on Motion Pictures*.[64]

Leaders of the *Christian Herald* magazine had a similar vision of church leadership in film production. However, they suggested that the motion picture must first be carefully studied in the nontheatrical and church field. They launched their own ethnographic study, garnering firsthand accounts of the troubles or successes church leaders had experienced in using motion pictures. The study's authors then proposed to lay a sound foundation in not only "cleaning out the trash" of Hollywood, but in acting as a clearinghouse for better pictures and better services to "the forty millions of church members." They believed they were equipped to assist in the channels of supply and distribution and "even to inaugurate an appropriate service of supply and distribution if that should prove necessary or desirable." The editors of the *Christian Herald* believed they were mandated to assist in the deadlock between censorship on the one hand and the failure to organize or serve the higher and cleaner and more progressive elements of America. They were positioned to lead in appropriating the tremendous value of the motion picture, "a value beyond all estimation for missionary endeavor, religious work, education and the field of wholesome amusement in which every community is struggling."[65] Capitalizing on a nationwide conservative sentiment against the amusement film industry, the *Herald* rallied support for its venture into production and distribution.[66] It felt the groundswell and enthusiasm were already firmly established. The editors offered two examples out of hundreds of illustrations to show

> how the film has been made to serve the cause of the Kingdom. What motion pictures can do for the churches of the country is no longer an academic question. Too many churches, working under heart-breaking handicaps, have proved the value of the film. Take, for instance, the experience of a young home missionary in the Blue Ridge Mountains who traveled by horse or mule into the hills and delivered his message at the crossroads to forty or fifty people. Some one provided him with an inexpensive automobile and portable motion-picture equipment that he mounted on the rear of his car. His services now are attended by 400 to 500 people, who travel for miles over the mountains to reach them. Or Dr. Charles M. Sheldon's old church, the Central Congregational, in Topeka, Kansas, under the pastorship of Dr. Rahill. On Easter Sunday last year 120 persons were admitted to fellowship in the church, all of whom said they were first attracted to the church by the motion-picture services held every Sunday evening, and at which the pastor builds his sermon around the story shown on the screen.[67]

Thus, the most comprehensive movement toward a church-film association occurred in the boardrooms and pages of The *Christian Herald*

Magazine, where a four-point proposal for a picture bureau was articulated. The first point attacked Hollywood Czar Will H. Hays and the contemporary Hollywood film industry. When harassed by the public for its transgressions and industry scandals, the Motion Pictures Producers and Directors Association drafted the squeaky clean former Republican Postmaster and Presbyterian elder Hays to be its titular chief, governing and guiding the moral content of movies. Asked if films were better after Hays had taken over as President of the MPPDA, the editors' answer was a resounding "no!" in response to all the unabated lurid ads and titles for sex films.[68] The editors of the *Christian Herald* further argued against what they saw as the spurious claims of Hays that he was working for American families. In spite of his support from the Federal Council of Churches, they saw him as a mere puppet of producers and exhibitors. *Variety* acknowledged that some viewed the theater as having been evacuated by the church and that "the Canaanite has moved in and is in possession."[69] Editor Rae Henkle believed that the amusement industry had marginalized "advocates of clean film as bigots"[70] and held Hays responsible for much of the slide away from purity.

On their second point of attack, the *Christian Herald* editors reignited the issue of Sunday showings, a fervent and incendiary issue for Christians during the first several decades of moving pictures. Prohibition against Sunday films did not apply to church showings. Yet, as "religious exemptions," churches unwittingly became a wedge to allow various educational and then entertaining films to be shown on the Lord's Day.[71] The primary fear was that moviegoing was becoming a commercial "entering *wedge*," opening the way for a variety of antibiblical activities.[72] The critics suspected that the real purpose of the movement in favor of Sunday showings was not to provide people with uplift and entertainment, but rather to provide money-grubbing businessmen with a chance to "pillage" on the Sabbath. "They have six days in which to make money, and if they can't make enough on those days they ought to go out of business."[73] No doubt, some moving picture exhibitors viewed sacred film subjects as "a crafty device to evade Sunday blue laws" and as a wedge to squeeze in all manner of Sunday showings.[74]

In their third point, *Herald* editors built their case with positive articles and testimonials from church leaders who had used films successfully and had also undertaken thorough research to determine the feasibility of their practice. Numerous articles promoted the use of motion pictures by churches even before the ecumenical periodical invested in vertical inte-

Joseph arriving in captivity in Egypt   *(From the Holy Bible in Moving Pictures)*

Shooting in Palestine, *The Christian Herald* presented biblical stories, such as Joseph's arrival in captivity in Egypt, as their first major venture into film production and distribution. *The Christian Herald* (September 20, 1922). Courtesy Library of Congress.

gration of film production, distribution, and exhibition. Methodist Church dignitaries considered whether to accept film advertisements in their church papers, though the *Christian Herald* did so without hesitation.[75] (Their decision to accept film advertisements was a harbinger of the Methodist Church's action at the 1923 General Conference to drop its official ban on theaters and amusements.)[76] Tributes and declarations of support poured in to bolster the *Christian Herald*'s efforts to establish a church-film association. An influential club woman and President of the Institute of Government, Haviland Haines Lund, contributed her voice in addressing the church's dilemma between the Scylla of Hollywood corruption and the Charybdis of religious inaction: "Manifestly, we must do something to control this great educational engine called the motion picture."[77] Russell Conwell, humanitarian and founder of Temple University, joined the throng of endorsing agents, as did many notable dignitaries.[78]

As the fourth tactical attack, the leaders of the magazine finally aimed to produce and promote the films themselves. To make churches completely independent of any output by the theatrical motion picture interests they would supply a cornucopia of film product. These films were to be written only by "consecrated Christian men, acted by Christian men and women," and produced under the most talented and inspired direction with all the technical excellence of Hollywood. Confidence at the *Herald* brimmed over with the hyperbolic report that over nine million churches were already equipped with complete projection machines and film libraries that held not only biblical pictures but also wholesome comedies and dramas, the entire Burton Holmes travelogue series, pictures of mission lands and mission activities, stories of Sunday school work, educational reels, and films on innumerable other subjects. Full-page advertisements announced the timely arrival of the Church-Film Association project to produce and distribute films.

A plan seeking to reproduce the entire Holy Bible for the screen within two years was conceived; these films could be "displayed and taught at Sunday school, church services, revival meetings, prayer meetings, or on other occasions when a congregation assembles to study the Gospel."[79] The debate over the importance of the visual as a primary means of communication harkened back to the iconoclast controversy and revived issues of visual learning. Believing that nearly 80 percent of what is learned comes through the eye, the Reverend Richard Braunstein underscored the *Christian Herald*'s strategy to show Bible stories: "Naturally, it is not hard to grasp a subject when it is illustrated."[80] Referring to a silent filmed version of the Life of Christ, a writer for the *Literary Digest* noted, "When the people actually saw Jesus sink to his knees under the weight of the cross, there were involuntary exclamations of horror as the Roman soldiers goaded him on with the points of their spears."[81] Thus convinced of the potential of movies to vivify biblical stories, to combat cultural contamination, and to exploit the effectiveness of the "projector method" for teaching youth, the *Christian Herald* would release clean wholesome pictures untainted by Philistine or Hollywood tendencies.[82]

The campaign to generate support for the *Christian Herald*'s production of films began with deliberate discussions regarding how pastors used movies and what benefits the films offered. Supporters built upon the enthusiastic testimonies of ministers like the Reverend Myron Collins of First Methodist of Burlingame, Kansas, who had returned from the Methodist Centenary full of vim, vigor, and idealism.[83] But such testimonies also clamored for more films developed by Christian sources. Thus the *Christian Herald* sought to produce and promote the films themselves.

In September 1922, in response to what it saw as widespread demand and support, the magazine announced the incorporation of the "CHRISTIAN HERALD MOTION PICTURE BUREAU to Provide Clean Pictures for Clean People in Morally Healthful Surroundings."[84] Giant advertisements, showing a contract for fifty-two subject reels, promoted "The Holy Bible in Moving Pictures Pictured in Palestine" and promised a library of Old Testament pictures, a large variety of biblical subjects, and "excellently and reverently made" travel pictures—many from mission lands—produced by the celebrated Burton Holmes.[85] CHMPB also guaranteed Robertson-Cole dramas, comedies, scenics, and the not-to-be-missed U.S. Naval Academy athletic instruction pictures.[86] One pastor, the Reverend Edgar Swan Wiers, enthusiastically recommended the Burton Holmes films of the Holy Land and Italian Old Testament films for use in the Sunday school.[87]

According to Rae Henkle, the managing editor, each of these films from the CHMPB would be inspected and stamped with a guarantee from the *Christian Herald,* with the assurance that "it conforms to the highest standards of morals and good taste. There are Bible stories, travel reels, comedies and dramas with clean, wholesome stories for entertainment, natural history subjects, camping, hunting and fishing pictures, exploration, and everything else that would go to make a diversified entertainment for a mid-week evening or to provide the illustration for a Sunday evening lecture."[88] Henkle argued that the motion picture industry had made a colossal mistake in refusing to have business relations with the religious and educational institutions of the country.[89]

> The church and the school, next to the home, have more to do with molding the lives of children and young people than any other factors in our national life. On them rest American culture. On them rests the moral growth of the generation. The almost universal attendance at motion picture theaters makes the film an extremely important influence that must be taken from commercial hands and placed under the control of devoted and consecrated men who will use it for the highest purposes.[90]

The *Christian Herald* also took over exclusive national distribution of all the biblical moving pictures produced by Sacred Films, Inc. It had culled suggestions from all over the United States that the magazine was the most logical institution to inaugurate such a service and had garnered numerous pledges of support. The practical problems of making, booking, and distributing pictures on a nationwide scale were mere logistical challenges to the *Christian Herald*. As large theatrical distributors had branch offices in key cities, so too would the Christian Herald Motion-Picture Bureau (CHMPB), headquartered in the Bible House, New York City. Investing heavily, CHMPB organized twenty-six branches to be operated in association with the National Non-Theatrical Motion-Pictures Inc. that had profitably supplied films to schools, colleges, manufacturers, and others outside the religious field. CHMPB joined in with numerous catalogues of approved films and the availability of "portable projection machines on easy payment plan."[91]

By 1922, after its own thorough inquiry, the *Christian Herald* had ironed out whatever difficulties it thought it might encounter and organized the Herald Non-Theatrical Pictures, under the leadership of Albert Beatty, a businessman particularly sympathetic to the problems that faced ministers and educators. Beatty had kept up morale during World War I when he headed the entertainment organization of the American Expeditionary Forces; he had also directed the Chautauqua system in the Midwest, which brought him into "intimate touch" with churches and schools. And so he was drafted to preside.

At last, with evangelistic fanfare and pomp, the *Christian Herald* had announced the release of their films. Distribution and exhibition plans

THE·CHRISTIAN·HERALD
AN·ILLUSTRATED·NEWS·WEEKLY·FOR·THE·HOME·
· GRAHAM PATTERSON, PUBLISHER ·

"The Bible and the Constitution are the foundations of our country and they are going to guide the policies of this newspaper." The young editor in "When Right Meets Might," the new photoplay on law enforcement, announces his program to the members of his staff

"Give Us Clean Pictures!"

And the Christian Herald Is Answering the Call that Comes from Home and Abroad for Good Motion Pictures

By RAE D. HENKLE

A T a meeting of a Chamber of Commerce in California a few weeks ago the guest of honor and the principal speaker was a prominent Chinese business man.

"I want to ask you," he said with all the seriousness of which he was capable, "to be careful of the kind of pictures you send to our country. If you can't send any better illustrations of domestic life in America than those you have been sending, keep them in the United States. Provided you want China to think well of you and Christian civilization."

This Chinese gentleman touched on a matter that has been emphasized by missionaries from all countries for considerably over a year. They tell us—these men who have given their lives to the work of the Master and who have spent hundreds of millions of dollars in their various missionary activities—that films of the worst sort of standard—immoral, and apparently uncensored, have poured into their countries from America and are rapidly undermining their missionary efforts.

The other day we had a letter from Japan, pleading that Americans give them pictures that illustrate the best side of American life, not the worst side—pictures that would portray and interpret the great truths of the Bible.

"Help us missionaries," it asked. "Our people go to the cheap motion-picture place and see films that could not be exhibited in any screen in America, and from these films many, many thousand obtain their conception of Christianity and a Christian civilization. Give us good pictures that would in some measure counteract the effect of the pernicious, immoral picture. Our people can not understand your language, but they can understand your pictures."

And what is true of religious teaching, and moral, clean entertainment in the missionary field is of course equally applicable to the young minds in America. Fathers and mothers and religious workers everywhere

have been appealing to us to undertake this motion-picture problem.

I SN'T that a call to be heard and answered? And it could be duplicated hundreds of times in every one of the foreign mission fields. The devil is using

the greatest power in the world today, the most tremendous force yet found, for the transmission of thought. The motion picture and its influence can be either good or bad. We have let it be bad! Let us use it to tell of the glories of God. Christian people, wake up!

It is less than a year since the Christian Herald published the first of a series of articles relating directly to the question of motion pictures in religious and educational work, and indicating that in response is urgent and widespread requests it would interest itself in this field of service. This announcement followed months of consistent inquiry, investigation, survey and discussion. But from all of this consideration, as it developed, there came only a small measure of appreciation of what such an undertaking involved.

There have been nine months of correlating idealism and practicability, for ideals will remain visions unless some way is found to apply them to the problems of every-day life.

The Christian Herald believes now this way has been found. Under its auspices and with its support there was organized the first of this year Herald Non-Theatrical Pictures as a medium through which its motion-picture activities could find expression. That organization has been functioning as a practical undertaking. It has been in contact through correspondence and personal conference with several thousand churches, clergymen, school teachers and associations of persons who are interested in religious and social welfare work and education. It has ironed out difficulties, solved perplexing questions, eliminated weaknesses and developed strength. The prospects for its future are happy because they are founded on service, and service, when all is said, is and always has been the keynote of the Christian Herald.

J UST at this point one of those rare persons, the ideal man for the job at hand, became available in the person of Albert M. Beatty, who has been brought

A graphic example of the effects of the bootleggers' poison, from "When Right Meets Might." Davenport (right) is killed by wood alcohol and Woods (left) is blinded as a result of a drink from the flask Davenport holds in his hand

THE CHRISTIAN HERALD, June 23, 1923   Page 495

Christian missionary work was blended with American virtues as in the Christian Herald's *When Right Meets Might*, a "clean picture" warning against liquor and commending the Bible and Constitution. Henkle, Rae D. "Give Us Clean Pictures." *The Christian Herald* (June 23, 1923), 495. Courtesy Library of Congress.

had been set. However, most of the pictures that the *Christian Herald* released seemed more concerned with Prohibition and good citizenship than with Christian doctrine. The most acclaimed feature to be released was a photoplay, *When Right Meets Might,* produced by Charles Hall, founder and leader of the Men's Bible Class of the Temple Baptist Church in Los Angeles and an aggressive teetotaler. Seeking to emphasize personal piety and civic righteousness, the story focused on law enforcement and the effects of alcohol upon criminals. Driven by Hall's intractable position on Prohibition, the film chronicles the effects of "bootleggers' poison" on a corporate leader who is killed and on his friend who is blinded when they illegally and unwittingly imbibe wood alcohol. Echoing the attitude of author Sheldon's novel, *What Would Jesus Do?* a young editor investigates the scandal and vigorously announces to his staff his mission of standing up for what is right: "The Bible and the Constitution are the foundations of our country and they are going to guide the policies of this newspaper." Hall's film was hailed as the pinnacle of religious art, useful for every church board and temperance society. Essentially a didactic piece of propaganda for enforcing the Eighteenth Amendment, the five-reel photoplay was still praised as dynamic, dramatic, technically correct, and extraordinarily well acted, with the *Christian Herald*'s appeal that "Every church and every schoolhouse in the United States should show this picture in the next twelve months."[92] It did not happen.

Most of the *Christian Herald*'s subsequent films were less ambitious and less dramatic than *When Right Meets Might* and the group's fervor for filmmaking waned considerably in light of that film's meager impact. Ultimately the CHMPB failed to pave the way for a compelling religious cinema movement. Several factors contributed to the CHMPB's decline as a viable, vertically integrated production house. Its first problem centered on the limitations of its output, consisting only of biblical and missionary films. When it was eventually taken over by United Cinema Company of New York City, it handed over fourteen episodes of Old Testament history, a five-reel photoplay of the life of Jesus, and twelve reels of missionary work in China and India.[93] The producers recognized that their religious films could not compete with the snappy Hollywood entertainment of a Mary Pickford, Harold Lloyd, or Douglas Fairbanks feature. They conceded that, in comparison with such celebrity-driven features, even "constructive" Hollywood pictures like *The Courtship of Myles Standish* and *The Shepherd King* were financial failures. The editors of the *Christian Herald* resigned themselves to the belief that only "destructive," or merely entertaining, pictures would flourish.[94] A second factor concerned the basic economics of film production. It was much more expensive than they had imagined; they had not, to use biblical language, counted the cost before "building the tower."

A third factor in the decline of the passion to produce movies stemmed from the evolution of a new medium, radio, which attracted the attention of both the *Christian Herald* and religious film pioneer Dr. John Roach Straton. Suddenly, preaching seemed better suited to the oral medium of radio than the visual medium of the silent film.[95] The magazine ultimately acquiesced in Hollywood's dominance of film production, settling for the practical tasks of writing reviews of Hollywood films and selling advertising space for its film products. For example, the *Christian Herald* promoted D. W. Griffith's *Way Down East* as "carrying the unqualified endorsement of more than three hundred ministers." The magazine also wrote a laudatory review of the Wm. Fox production of *The Fool*, about a young minister who tried to live as Christ, with the world mocking him as the titular Fool.[96] The *Christian Herald* itself had tried to produce biblically-based films, but discovered that it had been a naïve fool in the midst of a burgeoning entertainment industry.

The *Christian Herald* mission constituted the most comprehensive film production effort by any religious organization of the silent era. The muted denouement of this noble experiment did not even make front-page copy. The earlier vibrant vision to produce films slowly slipped into *errata* sections of the periodical. By the next decade, the *Christian Herald* emerged as the Protestant equivalent of the *Churchman* and other Roman Catholic periodicals, as a champion of the good and enemy of the bad, but in the film world of the brazen serpent it completely relinquished its creative production potential. It traded its birthright to supply the churches with fresh Christian film narratives for a bowl of critical opinion. In an effort to shape better pictures, it chose to critique movies rather than create them.

Suitable Sectarian Films

When sectarian companies other than the *Christian Herald* began to shoot films, they also offered biblical films that reaffirmed and reinterpreted Bible stories. One particular company followed the Hebrew tradition of Midrash interpretation, of filling in the gaps and ellipses left by the sacred narratives. In 1922, Sacred Films released two-reelers of *The Creation, Cain and Abel,* and *The Deluge,* all offering vivid illustrations of familiar biblical narratives.[97] Over five thousand extras and eight thousand animals were used in the Palestine production of the King David story. The producers unabashedly acknowledged that they were not adhering to biblical accuracy when they scripted a love scene to take place after the battle of David and Goliath.[98]

The craze for biblical pictures continued with the Geographic Film Company of Cincinnati announcing a series of fifty biblical films in the Holy Land and Palestine.[99] Exhibitors found it possible to crowd a Chicago house with a biblical film such as *Immortality,* from the Company Societa Italiana, showing the life of the Savior. Along with its vivid and accurate historical details—showcasing everything from pyramids to the Jordan River to the "rocky heights of Calvary"—it reproduced famous paintings: Da Vinci's *The Last Supper,* Rembrandt's *The Descent from the Cross,* and Mantegna's *Crucifixion. Immortality* was viewed as a truly educational picture conveying the dignity and reverence appropriate to its sacred subject.[100] Columbia University also exhibited a series of remarkable Italian films produced by Armando Vay that built upon scholarly research of biblical sites and archeological findings, shot on location in Egypt, Palestine, and Babylon.[101] Vay's remarkable productions cost over $3 million, utilized ten directors and fifteen cameramen, and employed more than ten million actors. Sacred films flickered on the screens of churches and Sunday schools with the fanfare, glamor, and pictorial quality usually associated with Hollywood.[102] Authentic locations of Abraham's homeland of Ur enhanced the trustworthy quality of the films that simultaneously incorporated Hollywood narrative techniques and effects.[103] By 1926, ads in the *International Journal of Religious Education* were promoting the "Whole Bible in Pictures."[104]

However, religious educators realized how delicate an operation it was to produce biblical films. Critic Catherine Ely envisioned how the religious word made celluloid could appeal directly to the masses such as the 106 churches in the greater New York area, but conceded that filming biblical stories was one of the most precarious ventures that a motion picture producer could undertake.[105] Nevertheless, because the American audience was viewed as innately religious, she felt that a visual Bible was essential to enable spectators to draw out the spiritual meanings of the

Book.[106] Furthermore, Bible films were popular, even with children. Religious films used in churches also provided ways to teach children about common fears and about art. For example, H. S. Brown of Chicago used *The Call of Samuel* story to allay a child's fears about a storm. Both George Frederick Watt's painting *Hope* and Alfred Tennyson's poem that inspired the painting *The Beggar Maid* were said to reveal the inspiration behind great art in films of the same titles.[107] In 1922, Charles Sheldon promoted the production of a fifty-two reel film entitled *The Holy Bible in Motion Pictures*.[108] Various advertisements for pictures of the "Bible Land and Its People" corresponded with a vibrant interest in studying the context of biblical texts (and for collecting visual souvenirs of biblical scenes called Perry Pictures).[109] Simultaneously, moving pictures of the Holy Land quickened a desire for firsthand touring experiences. Actuality films prompted a desire to experience authentic locations.[110] Various other educators and religious workers cooperated to film scenes in Palestine so that churches would be "supplied with a regular change of bill for its weekly movie film service."[111] Part of that bill could be exotic travelogues from missionary societies.

Out of Watertown, Massachusetts, came a letter from Edward Packard announcing that Christian Pictures, Inc. could supply the kinds of pictures that Protestant evangelical churches wanted.[112] He envisioned a two-hour all-pictorial Gospel that would appeal to businessmen. Along with hymn and Bible text slides, his proposition included a fifteen-minute Church Review newsreel of Christian humanitarian world happenings and the motion picture, *The Bad Mr. Goode,* a life history of the well-known Bowery mission worker, John Goode, whose fifty years of wickedness were rescued by ten years of faith.

While ministers clamored for films made primarily for religious use, some enterprising clerics even made their own films. The diffusion of 16mm cameras enabled numerous Protestant ministers to incorporate homemade 16mm films into their Sunday night services, even as Roman Catholic priests scripted films for their own religious instruction. Not only could churches purchase films through local branch exchanges, but they could also shoot their own homegrown films. As a result of producing and exhibiting their own films, attendance at churches like St. John's Episcopal in Larchmont, New York, increased more than 300 percent. "Local actuality" films highlighted familiar people and places in smaller towns, singling out individuals who were well known in the community.[113] The Better Films Committees were advised to attend to the exemplary story of the Reverend H. W. Stockton, minister and amateur filmmaker. Arriving in Newport Beach, California, he took his own pictures of the "locals" and lured the seashore resort inhabitants into church to see themselves on the screen. Combining these home movies with educational films, he built up his own congregation at the Community Methodist Church. Not only would he film a spectacular fire put on by the oil refinery, but he would also shoot the meetings of other churches and comic film bits of boys and their dogs, archiving local history. He also shot "every baby in town, just as soon as he heard of its arrival."[114] The Thanhouser production company showcased religious leaders like Cardinal Farley by building a film around the dedication of St. Joseph's Parochial School in New Rochelle, New York, and publicizing the worthy community work of its parish in a dramatic film that embodied the Pauline truth *But the Greatest of These Is Charity*.[115] The Reverend S. R. Bratcher innovated amateur church filmmaking by capturing local citizens on film in order to draw them into his church in Waverly, Tennessee. For example, he shot film of the "cradle-roll department" and announced, "Tonight is baby night." When the evening exhibition was crowded beyond expectation, he asked, "Do you wonder why all the mothers, old and young are there?" For Bratcher, the motion picture, properly used, was not an interloper, but a legitimate tool for the work of the church, especially in uplifting, educating, and entertaining poor and underprivileged parishioners.[116] One could easily see that better films were needed to fill the slate on Sunday evenings, even if the congregation was the star attraction in church basements.

The International Church Film Corporation

In 1918, the International Church Film Corporation (ICFC), headed by the notorious Methodist minister, the Reverend Paul Smith, entered upon a program of manufacturing sacred and ecclesiastical motion pictures for use in Protestant churches. Smith had stirred controversy when he filmed the infamous *Finger of Justice*, ostensibly about the white slavery market in San Francisco and the corrupt collaboration of the city council.[117] *The Christian Advocate* viewed this film, distributed under the title *The Finger of Fate*, as an "instrument of preaching incomparable in its power to reach millions who never entered a church."[118] "Crusader" Smith was also credited with leading the fight that "put San Francisco's picturesque but iniquitous Barbary Coast out of existence" through his film.[119] Throughout the film, Smith drafted a number of Methodist ministers in the cast to create a spiritual melodrama, preaching the need for mercy to Magdalene and justice for her exploiters.[120] Writer for the *Congregationalist*, Elisha King, toasted Smith as an active director who knew how to make the kind of films the church needed.[121]

Smith boasted that he had devised one of the most extensive and elaborate systems of its kind for making relevant religious films.[122] The ICFC advertised their advance plans of quarterly productions of four parables (with the parable of the Good Samaritan being used to fight race prejudice), four missionary histories (Livingston and Stanley), two episodes from the life of Peter, and three episodes of Esther and Mordecai on slate for the first quarter of 1919. Having discovered a market for church films (such as the filming of the canonization ceremonies of St. Joan of Arc by a papal cinema institute), the ICFC planned to shoot a series of travelogues, clean comedies, and Bible stories.[123] The entire purpose of the ICFC program was to be uplift, which meant in part that "no players are to be starred or featured in the productions." The cast was not even to be named, so that they would be "obscured by the message the motion pictures carry."[124] One of its films, *Miracle Money* (1920), made by the Interchurch Movement for the ICFC, showed the native life of China as influenced by missionaries.[125] By 1921 the ICFC had completed eight new biblical pictures that paralleled the historical and contemporary dramas of Cecil B. DeMille. In *The Temple Builders,* a biblical tale of David and Solomon is juxtaposed with the modern story of a father who wants to build a college. Like the King of Israel, however, he is thwarted in building such a "temple."[126] Smith had re-created a veritable Holy Land film set along the Palisades overlooking the Hudson. He regularly had clergy write and comment upon all scenarios, such as *The Child Samuel, The Ninety and Nine,* and other literary and educational reels.[127]

As the premier interdenominational production unit, the ICFC sponsored filmmaking expeditions to Africa and the Far East, also under the supervision of Casselman. It also released interchurch missionary subjects taken in the inner sacred city of Peking.[128] It then picked up the creative services of a New York businessman, John E. Edgerton, to work with the Reverend Paul Smith.[129] For the ICFC, Edgerton and Smith next sketched an animated historical chart of the Methodist Episcopal Home Missions.

In the three-reel film, *The Expanding Years,* Smith drew a picture of the missionary church helping "scores of southern Negroes" as they emigrated north, ministering to immigrants through films, and bringing "dying churches to life."[130] Working with the Reverend Charles Wesley Blanpied, Smith premiered his film at the 1920 Des Moines General Conference to rave reviews. The Methodist Book Concern commissioned a second film entitled *Along the Years from Yesterday* that retold the apostle Paul's journeys with reference to his letters from prison. Another documentary that premiered at the same conference chronicled an immigrant family's history in America from their arrival to their partaking of the Sacrament of the Lord's Supper in a Methodist church. A fourth motion picture from the Methodist Book Concern brought to life the lonely circuit riding of John Welsey and Robert Williams.[131] Despite these successes, however, and despite a rousing financial campaign that raised over $800,000 (mostly by selling stock) in the early twenties, the ICFC itself only ended up with five reels of scenic shots that were used to illustrate the Psalms and an animated subject made by F. A. Dahme, entitled *How the Brooklyn Bridge Is Made.*[132]

As President of the International Church Film Corporation, Smith continued to operate from New York City, coordinating fifteen branch national offices to handle the distribution of the films to churches. He also organized Sunday programs that consisted of a one- or two-reel picturization of material for denominational Sunday school lessons. Basing many of his films on Bible stories, with missionary and ethical subjects as occasional variations, Smith boasted, "The once despised movie is an instrument of righteousness, a medium for the spreading of Christian ideals. It knows no language and needs none for a field ripe for harvest."[133] Smith productions of what he called his "statistical films," blandly entitled *Expanding Years* and *Methodism in Action,* provided basic information of activities sponsored by the Methodist Church.

However, without a fully developed plan of production and distribution, the vision of the ICFC perished. With its sudden demise, Paul Smith moved into the Masonic Temple Building in New York City and conspired to find an alternative way to distribute films for churches. Rather than rent them, his refurbished Church Film Company (CFC) would supply free films. Working with clergymen like Shields, Smith persuaded Methodist pillar and wealthy woolen manufacturer, John E. Edgerton of Tennessee, to underwrite his new enterprise of the CFC. Edgerton had been president of the National Association of Manufacturers and felt that the company's name was too narrow. So, with the influence of his investment, the CFC easily became the American Motion Picture Corporation (AMPC), to serve the broader field of all nontheatricals. Its fundamental goal, once suggested by Edison, was to provide nontheatrical exhibitors with both unit programs and musical cues for atmospheric accompaniment. Edgerton was quixotic and naïve in his enthusiasm for the project; he was quoted in 1923 as saying that the AMPC planned for the church to enter the motion picture business on a competitive basis with the theaters, which he felt were making films of dubious moral quality. Following the discovery that over ten thousand YMCA buildings and church auditoriums existed in America, Edgerton boasted that the AMPC would turn these into motion picture theaters and then produce suitable films for them. In public Smith downplayed Edgerton's sophomoric zeal, while keeping his benefactor's "glowing utterances for his backers and subscribers." Branch offices were set up in dozens of major cities, from Boston out to St. Louis and Minneapolis, almost all of them east of the Mississippi River. Thirty program units were assembled, with films allegedly contracted with Ernest and Nell Shipman and Charlie Chaplin, as well as Helen Keller's *Deliverance*. With diligence, workers at the AMPC also developed special lyceum course plans for the thirty-six reels of Holley's Holy Land series.

The fatal flaw in this admirable scheme was Dr. Smith's suspiciously creative financial plan. Smith's proposed enterprise was tailored as

a stock-selling proposition, although the larger aim was benevolent enough. Numerous small investors, including it is said, many church widows and orphans, were attracted by a project headed by a crusading minister, backed by substantial businessmen, and having the intention of offsetting the alleged depraving influences of the theatrical screen, and so confidently purchased shares in American Motion Picture Corporation. But surely there was no deliberate deceit. Certainly neither Smith, nor any of his moneyed associates, anticipated the eventual disaster.[134]

The disaster unfolded in the Fosters Community Pictures Library, located within the same Masonic Temple Building that the AMPC occupied. Smith bartered for their library of four to five thousand reels, ultimately issuing stock notes as payment (while simultaneously placing several Foster family members on the AMPC payroll for organizational and editor-

Unshackle the Motion Picture

An Answer to the Great Question of Screen Freedom

By HAVILAND HAINES LUND

The sacrifice of Isaac, as depicted in "Abraham and Isaac," which is distributed by Herald Non-Theatrical Pictures

GOOD people and thoughtful [throughout the country have for the past several years evinced grave concern over conditions existing in the motion picture world. Practically every club and welfare association has its better film committee; several organizations exist solely for the purpose of improving the screen. On all sides we hear the clamor for better films. The members of these committees have passed innumerable resolutions for the betterment of the situation. The agitation finally reached such proportions that the motion picture industry was threatened with the choice of censorship in forty-eight states, federal censorship, or the improvement of the film from within the industry itself.

Much of the confusion in the motion picture industry is inevitable. Within a short period of fifteen or sixteen years this new industry has become the fourth largest in the world. The development of such a huge business enterprise in an unknown field must necessarily be attended with the waste and blunders of experiment. The automobile industry, for instance, passed through something like this before it found itself, but there are certain elements in the motion picture situation which do not lend themselves to charitable explanation.

A few years ago it became evident that there was quietly operating within the industry something less innocent than business blunders attending a pioneer project. Over three years ago the situation became so acute that the Federal Trade Commission began an investigation and on May 4, 1923, the Commission began bearings before an examiner on the charge that the Famous Players-Laskey Corporation, six and six individuals were in a trust and engaged in a conspiracy to dominate the business. The facts developed during the session, through examination and cross examination, are quite out of the knowledge of the bulk of American citizens and are significant in the consideration of the motion pictures as a factor in our nation's life.

THERE is entire agreement on the part of every one involved in the investigation that the motion picture is the most important instrument of education before the public today. Thomas Edison, Hon. John F. Tigert, United States Commissioner of Education, and Colonel Alvin Owsley, Commander of the American Legion, in their testimony before the Federal Trade Commission said that in their opinion the motion picture is of greater educational value than the pulpit and press combined. The mere physical fact that we receive more impressions per minute from the eye than we do from the ear should be remembered. The psychology of the two hours spent at the movies is significant. We go to be amused and are in a receptive mood; we sit in a darkened room, restful and relaxed. The motion picture has the opportunity to get one hundred per cent effect.

We are familiar with the arguments against unclean films, but I doubt if that angle of the problem is the most vicious. There is a natural reaction against obscene films, making that phase easier to remedy.

A recent article published in a popular magazine made clear that the greatest difficulty in the present situation is the stupidity rather than the cupidity of the producer in control today.

Men high in the industry tell me that whoever controls the news weeklies of the screen controls the most powerful political engine in the country. It is this angle of the motion picture industry that most needs watching today. The industry is thoroughly frightened. Our result is to give us better films, but when the excitement incident to the Federal Trade Commission's investigation dies out, and when the few who know the facts have forgotten, and the million-dollar publicity engine created by the producers has accomplished its purpose, what about the political power incident to the control of the motion pictures by any one group of men? Those who know most about the power behind the motion pictures believe that our tion pictures believe that our political integrity is dependent upon maintaining competition in the motion picture field.

Inasmuch as the motion picture industry is one of the most complex and intricate in existence, the tinkering of the amateur is fraught with grave consequences. For instance, forty-eight state censorship would wreck the industry. Friends of censorship admit the weakness of this demand and those who know the fallacy of federal control and the dangers inherent in the centralization of such great power as a federal censorship would carry, consider that we stand between Scylla and Charybdis.

MANIFESTLY, we must do something to control this great educational engine called the motion picture and as manifestly this control must be directed along lines which permit of a profitable conduct of the business. We sometimes forget that there is a natural law which operates to regulate a situation of this kind when it is not artificially interfered with. We had reached the point when this natural law was about to operate advantageously to the nation. People were up in arms in all directions against the industry as conducted.

The men responsible in the industry for that which they resent recognized the handwriting on the wall. They realized that control would be taken from them and that the competition essential to the development of the right kind of picture would soon become possible. They decided to develop censorship within the industry and gave us several samples of such industry-controlled censorship. We have had the National Board of Review and the Motion Picture Producers' Association.

According to Mr. William A. Brady, President of the Motion Picture Producers' Association, this last-named organization was given an opportunity never before extended to a business enterprise. Secretary

Lane, while in the Cabinet, called a meeting of the Committees on Education of the House and Senate to confer with the motion picture magnates as to the development of proper Americanization films. A resolution very helpful to the producers was passed. It gave them enormous publicity; it conveyed the idea that there was Congressional support instead of Congressional sympathy. The producers pledged themselves to certain procedure and according to the annual report prepared and signed by Mr. Brady they admit that they failed completely to carry out their promises.

Then, when public pressure became stronger, when the Federal Trade Commission's investigation loomed and the champions of censorship clamored from all directions, the industry sought to engender the necessary confidence in its own power to clean its own house and called in Mr. Will H. Hays, formerly chairman of the National Republican Committee, to straighten out the situation. Mr. Hays's association represents some of the principal motion picture companies, but by no means all of them.

Is it not strange that during the very months when the Federal Trade Commission is holding its hearings in fifteen cities of the United States to determine whether Famous Players-Laskey constitutes a trust inimicable to the best interests of the motion picture world, that men and women of such fine character as those acting on the Hays's committees should not be reluctant to hold up the hands of a concern under investigation until the Government shall have completed its findings? As a result of the motion picture investigation by the Federal Trade Commission we learn that the crux of the situation lies in the control of theaters.

WHAT, then, is the answer to the question? The Federal Trade Commission says that it is through ownership of theaters and a system known as "block leasing." This "block leasing" system is a vital point in the question of film control. United with the theater control it effectually shuts the field to all but the favored few. No film can be a success unless it can be exhibited in the first-run theaters in the principal cities. Motion picture exhibitors in other towns must exhibit the successful, well advertised films that have enjoyed exhibition in these theaters or lose money. To obtain these well advertised films they are compelled to take the entire list of films put out by the firm owning the key city theaters whether they be good, bad or indifferent. Hence, a great deal of cheap, indifferent film is booked upon one or two first-rate pictures.

Before this theater control was effected the independent producer felt no pinch. If he could raise money to make the picture and was well, but dating from the control of the theaters in the key cities, the independent producer has been unable to market his production at a profit, if he has been able to market it at all. One independent producer in his testimony said that he exhibited one picture for a Broadway run that netted the theater $30,000 while his share came to $400.

The government investigation made by the Federal Trade Commission should be the basis of a complete reorganization of the industry and it can accomplish this providing the people in the film committees, above referred to, will avail themselves of the information which the government has placed at their disposal. The thing most necessary for film freedom is at least one American motion picture unit to be made up of both the theatrical and non-theatrical motion picture producers and distributors. There should be one theatrical and one non-theatrical neutral distributing agency and some basis for co-operation should be evolved whereby members of this group can meet the existing competition.

What is the first point to be taken toward motion picture freedom? First, free the theater; second, demand neutral distribution; third, oppose block leasing; forth, refuse to serve on motion picture committees financed by the industry; fifth, invest your money in an all-American unit of motion pictures. Let patriotic service be your first concern and profit second. Profit is inevitable when service is acceptable and the amount invested adequate. The motion picture screen of the United States with its colossal educational and political potentiality must be free if we are to continue to enjoy free government.

Distributed by Herald Non-Theatrical Pictures, Sacred Films offered their authentic reconstructions of biblical locations, with archeologists conferring on how Sarah dressed her hair or how Abraham prepared Isaac for sacrifice. *The Christian Herald* (April 7, 1923), 277. Courtesy Library of Congress.

155

ial services). In late 1926, historian Arthur Krows remembered a great hush descending over the tenants of the building, succeeded by the dreadful whisper that the AMPC was bankrupt. The collapse of the corporation brought Pat Powers, notorious corporate bully of the motion picture industry, who usually participated in "dissolution proceedings of any considerable film receivership," arriving with his own agenda. Taking off the gloves, Powers put the library back in the Fosters' hands and Smith discretely escaped to California. There he died in the Barbary Coast, in the same place where he had first used his film, *The Finger of Justice*, in a stunt to clean up San Francisco and attract fallen women to his church.[135] Thus, another noble experiment fizzled out and its participants disappeared into the shadows.

Incorporating Sacred Films

Independent entrepreneur and Episcopal Reverend Harwood Huntington ventured west to make a series of what he called "nonsectarian" quality films on the Old Testament. By 1921, he had established Sacred Films Incorporated in downtown Burbank, California, where Edgar J. Banks, noted archeologist and Semitic historian, joined him. The adventurer Banks, who had climbed Mt. Ararat and excavated Babylonian ruins, wrote an article on "Educational Bible Films" for the *Educational Screen Magazine* in 1922 in which he castigated "fly-by-night" religious filmmakers as carpetbaggers:[136]

> Several organizations have been founded to film the Bible. Some have had as their sole purpose the selling of stock. Others have been crushed by the enormous expense of such a gigantic undertaking. Still others have reproduced spectacular films to which have been attached the name of some Bible character, but with almost nothing Biblical in it. There is one company that has survived, and is far on the way toward success. I refer to Sacred Films Incorporated in Burbank, California. The purpose of the organization is to bring the Bible back to the great masses of people. It has no other purpose.[137]

Banks argued that the better filmmakers were turning to history, geography, and even to his beloved field of oriental archeology to make unique educational films. Sacred Films Incorporated, one of the better groups in his opinion, was producing fifteen one-reel films on such topics as the Creation, the Sacrifice of Isaac, Noah and the Ark, and Jacob and Esau. These splendidly pantomimed dramas revealed a creative Midrash of the biblical texts, drawing out background stories (e.g., Abraham rejecting the god of the Ur-Chaldeans). By the early 1930s, narration by Wilfred Lucas would be added to these films to explain the Hebraic contexts for church audiences. However, much of the supplementary commentary aimed at a cultural elitism, quoting Shakespeare in the story of Cain and Abel and promoting theistic evolution in the post-Scopes trial era. For example, Lucas solemnly intoned that the two brothers were "not so quick witted as we are," suggesting a progressive and optimistic view of humanity that had learned to control the consuming fire of jealousy.

The Weiss Brothers, producers otherwise noted for cheap dramas and westerns, funded these exemplary revisionist films. They proudly boasted that the entire staff was college educated. According to Banks, the purpose of these sophisticated, intellectual films was to elevate the motion picture world rather than to reap great financial returns. "It is not a stock selling proposition; it has no stock for sale. It advertises no 'stars' and yet it employs them." Banks recounted how Huntington, the president of Sacred Films and a clergyman, and he had been fellow students at Harvard, and came together to answer such questions as "How did Sarah dress her hair?" Their chief concern when making the films was the absolute accuracy of historical details, as in reconstructing the walls of the Babylonian city of Ur and the engraved statue of the great horned Moon-god Sin, who desired human sacrifice.[138] Biblical archeologist Banks had been asked to consult on such cultural issues of Bible times, particularly for the films on Abraham. In his research, Banks claimed that he culled images of the moon god that had survived on gems and seals of Abraham's time.

> Upon his head were the horns of the crescent moon. His face was concealed with a long black beard; his garment of gold was richly embroidered; his feet were bare, and at the end of a staff in his hand, he held his symbol of the crescent moon. The altar before him was richly decorated with horrible demons; upon it was sacrificed fruits and grains and pigeons and sheep and goats and even the first-born of the children.

Such "historic" details were the delight of producers and sponsors.[139] As mentioned above, Banks had left his lecture work to be associated with the work of Sacred Films Incorporated. He wrote numerous letters to pastors from his Burbank headquarters recommending the films; in an early form of market research, he claimed to know the preferences of his audience quite well and so tailored the films for them:

> The pictures are especially adapted to a church audience. They are in no way sectarian or preachy. They are highly inspirational, and remarkable in homiletic value. Their moral and religious lessons, with which the Old Testament is filled, are taught as they could be in no other manner. The objectionable features, so common to many motion pictures, have been entirely eliminated.[140]

The nonsectarian movement to visualize the Bible inspired another transient entrepreneur in Los Angeles. A former Shakespeare actor, Frederic Vroom, had become, in his own publicity rhetoric, "a photo-play actor, with more than 300 appearances in presentations of the largest concerns to his credit." Vroom, a dreamer of great dreams, however naïve, believed that as a literary masterpiece the Bible would become universally popular as the result of the production of biblical photoplays. He became the director-general of a new enterprise of biblical films which planned to depict two-reel biblical subjects for exhibition.

Vroom's company intended to make its subjects strictly nondenominational so that they could be shown in any church without objections from any member.[141] He ardently believed that his biblical films would elevate the motion picture industry as a whole, and that when secular producers found that such historical narratives appealed to a large percentage of the public they would change the tone of the offerings they were now making.[142] Vroom's company, the Excelsis Film Corporation, was capitalized at $500,000 and sought to sponsor projects like Ralph Connors' *Sky Pilot*, Sheldon's *Crucifixion of Philip Strong* and *His Brother's Keeper*, and also *Three Short-Sighted Fools*, an up-to-date cine-dramatization of Christ's parable of the men who were invited to the wedding feast but refused.[143]

Competing with Vroom in filming the Bible was Dick Ferris, promoter of circuses, shows, and spectacles. His ballyhoo promotion of a picturized Bible "from cover to cover!" promised to show all the prophets, saints, and sinners with "six Christs—of various ages" and "asses and other animals trained to do their duties according to the Book." Surprisingly, he gained financial support from the publishers of the *Los Angeles Times* and the *Chicago Daily News,* Harry Chandler and Victor Lawson, respectively, and also squeezed $5 million of capital from John D. Rockefeller. His nonsectarian films were to be released to churches, providing visual biblical libraries.[144] Both Ferris and the finances however, evaporated into the mists of movie making tomfoolery.

While Paramount filmmaker Cecil B. DeMille found a large audience for his ostentatious biblical spectaculars, only a few religious silent film production companies attempted to keep up equivalent work through the 1920s.[145] Both the Reverend John E. Holley's Holy Land Pictures and Russell H. Conwell's Temple Producing Company were established in 1922. Holley and his cameraman, Mr. Krippendorf, claimed to have photographed "every spot mentioned in the Bible," but eventually lost money because there was not yet a sufficient market to support their enterprise.[146] Conwell, who had founded Temple University and garnered fame for his "Acres of Diamonds" speech on finding the wealth of the world in your own backyard, produced another celebrated story of self-sacrifice, *Johnny Ring and the Captain's Sword,* which also lost money.

Yet these two filmmakers dreamed small dreams compared to financier James A. McGill, who controlled a chain of theaters in the northwest. His Historical Film Corporation ambitiously sought to film the whole Bible in its entirety.[147] Starting in 1919 in southern California with the Book of Genesis, the Historical Film Corporation completed fifty-two reels, culminating in the Ascension of Christ. According to the claims of Raymond Wells, a dramatic director in charge of the Los Angeles area film shooting, "the ancient holy city of Jerusalem, the Babylonian halls of Belshazzar, the ark on Ararat, Solomon's temple—all are to be erected in heroic replica according to the best conception of archaeologists employed as expert guides."[148] McGill himself balked at the idea of starting the Genesis production with the Chaos behind Creation, as a "motion picture camera has no business in the midst of whirling nebulae and cosmic conflagration," so he decided to start with Adam and Eve and end with Paul's ministry.[149] *Variety* reported that Raymond Wells was following a tradition of biblical films in casting his first character, Romayne King, as Adam. King was to be the "only male in the picture for several reels."[150]

But by the end of the twenties, productions of biblical films for churches had waned considerably, as producers found more profit in other genres of religious film. The Pathe Exchange supplied twenty-one-reel pictures of the Holy Land, such as the serene *Sea of Galilee,* but they were quietly consigned to showings in church basements.[151] Biblical travelogues had also lost much of their fascination as actual locations even with personal stories intertwined, as in *The Habousch Travelogue—The Shepherd Boy of Galilee*.[152] The making and selling of religious films depended upon the investment of independent filmmakers and denominational committees. Better films would have to come from outside religious circles.

Protestant Production

Now that the church had mastered film exhibition, production and distribution became prime objectives. Ministers and church committees frequently organized their own distribution channels and also selected the pictures to be shown. For example, six Protestant organizations in Elgin, Illinois, including Grace and Epworth Methodist Episcopal churches, coordinated a church film circuit for the use of films with film exchange men. Their efforts resulted in tremendous growth for their congregations.[153] In his more aggressive distribution campaign, the Reverend Harry Robbins advertised that he had secured New England rights to all the great sociological photoplays and the best motion pictures on the life of the Lord for exhibition in the regions' large churches. Where necessary, he would also supply the machine, a fireproof booth, and an operator. *Photoplay Magazine* honored Robbins for injecting new life into the whole community of Canasaraga, New York, by using films in church.[154]

What stood out as unique in the field of distribution, however, were the road shows put on by itinerant evangelists. Individual distribution frequently followed the model of the Reverend C. H. Schreiber, who ministered in central Washington State, among many remote communities without electric lights. Seeing the opportunities for evangelism through motion pictures, Schreiber bought a Ford car and equipped it with a generator to run his portable projector. With his "Lizzie," he was armed to "bear light and truth" throughout the Great Northwest, pulling alongside weather-beaten schoolhouses, revving up the generator with his car engine, and entertaining the settlers with "reg'lar movie shows." Likewise, the Reverend Aiton rendered a similar service in Montana, exploiting the "magic of the electric current and projector" to proclaim the Gospel message through the land.[155]

Making films became as important as showing them, in part because the church believed that Hollywood was out of touch with its values and needs. Thus, an ecclesiastical mission evolved among many lay church leaders to make and market the films themselves. As we have seen, the 1910s had marked the earliest excursions of the church into the production of religious films, with most producers aiming to establish their credibility (and markets) in sacred history and geography. Beginning as a rental company, the Church and School Social Service Corporation, headed by the Reverend William Carter, announced in 1914 that they were negotiating to make their own religious and educational films, and in particular to send cameramen to the Holy Land.[156] Lewis J. Selznick, vice president of the World Film Corporation, joined the campaign, especially to expand exhibition opportunities; he noted that the only two fields not developed by the motion picture industry were the educational and religious, and these were almost sure to prove "the most permanent and profitable."[157]

In 1916, the Young Men's Christian Association contracted with George Zehring and A. L. Fredrick to produce several supplementary educational films for use in the field—films especially geared for Sunday evening services.[158] As with Carter's Corporation, or Bureau, the independent producers consulted missionaries, ministers, and teachers to ascertain the best material. In the next year, 1917, the Bible Film Company was formed with the purpose of producing a religious spectacle.[159] An outgrowth of the National Bible Play Society, the Bible Film Company coordinated the vision of a board of clergymen and laymen of various churches in the Las Vegas area, already becoming known for its pep and progressiveness.[160] The board purchased the Montezuma Hot Springs resort of almost a thousand acres to establish its studio site for producing Bible stories and pageants. Yet like other later Las Vegas gambles, the project came to nothing.

Other religious entrepreneurs of various denominational lines entered into the business of film production with sporadic success. *Reel and Slide Magazine* hailed the six-reel production of *The Problems of Pin-Hole Parish,* by Presbyterian minister the Reverend Charles Bradt, dubbing it the "First Missionary Photoplay Produced by Religious Body."[161] Done in conjunction with the Church Missionary Institute of Chicago, centered upon one church's battle for righteousness; its showing was generally accompanied by a sermon, usually on Sunday nights. The film shows a freshly ordained pastor and his wife arriving at their new parish in Pin-Hole. The wife of the pastor is interested in missions, while her husband and his church practice an antimissionary agenda. The intertitles explain that she believes in "books," while he is particularly concerned with his "salary." With winsome subtlety, the pastor's wife tries to implant the "idea of the Great Commission" into her husband's "pin-hole" head and heart. However, when another church deacon borrows one of the books on missions, the idea escapes from the book and infects him. Subsequently, the contagious idea works "wonderful transformations" among the church members and finally in the dense husband and pastor, who then zealously promotes foreign missions.[162]

Presbyterians engaged in effective distribution as well, with the New Era Movement of the Presbyterian Church using motion pictures in its campaign to communicate the role of the Christian faith in the world.[163] Also known as Paragon Film Bureau, New Era Films produced films made expressly for the nontheatrical circuit including its two stupendous features, *Satan's Scheme* and *The Great Miracle*.[164] New Era classified its films under three distinct categories: Religious Pictures such as *Satan's Scheme*, *The Problem of Pinhole Parish*, and *Little Jimmy's Prayer*; Screen Sermonettes that preached the Gospel in capsule form, and Moral Features such as *The Story the Keg Told Me* and *The Turn of the Road*. Bertram Willoughby, Religious Director and Vice President of New Era Films, claimed that numerous churches had increased their attendance (promising growth from 50 to 1,200 in one short program!) by using their "Church Movies" and screen sermonettes. To counter the effect of bad films, Willoughby warned that the church could not afford to merely sit back and carp, but would need to "see the possibility of the motion picture for righteousness and use this great invention for the Glory of God and Salvation of Men."[165] Along the same lines, the Reverend George Esdras Bevans of Greystone Presbyterian Church in Elizabeth, New Jersey, wrote a pamphlet entitled *Motion Pictures: The Experience of One Church* for the Presbyterian Board of Home Missions.[166] Other Presbyterians seeking worthy movies from New Era Films were mostly served by the distribution system of the International Church Film Service.[167] Critics like J. Ray Johnson noted that the ICFC supplied a tremendous distribution service. Their slogan of "Fewer and Better Pictures" heralded a release of pictures of "more soul and less slam, more art and less splendor."[168] The New Era Movement of the Presbyterian Church produced three practical ministry films: *You and the Task*, *The City and the Task*, and *Miracle Money*, all shown at the 1921 Philadelphia General Assembly.

The difficulty of securing nontheatrical films was exacerbated by competing jealousy with exchanges and by the lack of financial profits for distributors. However, *Church Management* identified two trends indicating progress occurring in the mid-1920s. First, a standard width reel was more widely accepted; second, the development of several services provided a more complete set of films for church use. One key service from New York City was the Neighborhood Motion Picture Service. Its strength lay in coordinating its offerings with the visual instruction services of colleges and universities as well as churches. Another service based in New York, the Motion Picture Bureau of the International Committee of the YMCA, expanded its operations into the Midwest in Chicago by 1927, with extensive educational listings put at the service of community interests. The DeVry Corporation brought together a large library of prints to serve its patrons, and in 1925 it founded a summer school led by A. P. Hollis, to provide, with no tuition charge, teachers and ministers with more technical education to use films effectively. Most impressively, the summer school staff of instructors included directors of Visual Instruction from places like the University of Texas, Austin, and the University of Oklahoma.[169] By now, *The Educational Screen*'s booklet of *1001 Films* classified over three thousand films suitable for rental in schools and churches.[170] Finally, as we will see, the dominant organization of distribution to evolve during this time was the Religious Motion Picture Foundation. The foundation's channels included Presbyterian, Congregational, Episcopal, Lutheran, Methodist, and Reform churches, as well as Friends' meeting houses. It followed its rentals with printed questionnaires in an attempt to ascertain the response of the congregations; many pastors reported that their churches had increased by as much as 50 percent.[171]

Methodist progress with film production and distribution paralleled the success of the Presbyterians with New Era Films. After the phenomenal triumph of the Methodist Centenary in 1919, the denomination built a significant network for production and distribution by the early twenties. The Methodist Committee on Conservation and Advance had published its white list of the 1,001 Best Films as compiled by the *Moving Picture Age* and supplied, mostly without cost, all necessary cuts for films they furnished.[172] The achievements of the Methodist Church Board inspired others like the Presbyterians, Baptists, Lutherans, and Congregationalists with a similar vision of filmmaking. Dolph Eastman, editor and publisher of the *Educational Film Magazine,* saw the trend as a sign that the Church as an institution had thrown off "the dark and dusty cloak of tradition and has come forth into the world of men and women, the world of everyday thought and action, prepared to serve the insistent needs of mankind."[173] This progressive model of casting tradition aside in favor of innovative ministry marked a swell of optimism for religious and educational filmmaking.

In *Variety*'s opinion, the film that marked a surge in religious filmmaking was George Loane Tucker's 1919 *The Miracle Man,* which demonstrated the triumph of faith over materialism.[174] (It allegedly prompted people to go to faith healers, whether they were members of the Evangelical Church or not.) *Variety*'s editors were very impressed that "more noticeably out of town [i.e., New York City], the tendency has grown for the clergymen themselves to show pictures in their own parish houses." Rural clergy were seen as becoming picture producers and exhibitors of significant account, at least as far as rental lists could demonstrate. *Variety* praised Protestants for being less "embarrassed" about showing pictures, which they followed up with a dance and a dish of ice cream.[175]

The Ideal Film Lending Company produced its own Methodist hagiography in *God and the Man,* a six-reel feature photoplay from a Robert Buchanan novel dealing with the founding of the Methodist Church by John Wesley. The scenario, situated in the eighteenth century, portrayed the struggles of the early settlers in America who "replaced the God of Vengeance with the God of Love." The script offered shipwrecks, fires, severe storms, snowbound passengers, and the final deliverance of the pioneer Methodists.[176] Another Methodist production, *Out of the Christian College,* showed how American ideals rested upon Christian education and concluded with President Woodrow Wilson endorsing the Christian education movement.[177] In the film, the Christian Education Movement joined with the International Church Film Corporation to attack the "Prussianized and pagan" educational system of Germany that had overrun the larger universities.[178]

Among the Lutherans, amateur filmmaker and pastor the Reverend O Hagedorn of Milwaukee, Wisconsin, produced church films like *Little Jimmy's Prayer* and *After the Fall.* Hagedorn viewed all technological inventions, such as the steamship, the piano, and the moving picture as "instruments of service to the Gospel." Hagedorn advocated for adding details of imaginative action to bring biblical stories to life, as he had done with *After the Fall,* his Midrash adaptation of the story of Cain and Abel. For the Lutheran filmmaker with a creative sense of hermeneutics, historical biblical pictures did not need to worry about "absolute historical truth in the details," stressing only the need for dramatic presentation of real stories that "stir the emotions and teach needed lessons."[179]

With the financial assistance of laity like Theodore Lamprecht, the Lutheran Church chose to import and distribute through its own Lutheran Film Division a road show of an eight-reel German biography of Martin Luther, simply titled *Martin Luther: His Life and Times* (1923). Chronicling the trajectory of Luther's reforms, the film mapped out the Reformation's spiritual, economic, and cultural crises of faith even as it commented on the use of symbols ("crutches to uphold a doddering faith") and images (with Master Raphael painting the Pope). The film, which was accompanied by its own musical score, drew rave reviews from enthusiastic critics like the Reverend Frank Jensen of the *Educational Screen Magazine*.[180] "This is in all probability the most extended film experience in the Lutheran Church," observed critic O. H. Pannkoke a year after its release.[181] The *American Lutheran* periodical reported that the continental classic went on tour about September 1, 1925, and drew stupendous praise from various parts of the country, playing to crowded houses in Newport News, Virginia, and Providence, Rhode Island.[182]

The film was an illustrated history lesson with intertitle commentary preceding vivid tableau events, from the martyrdom of John Hus through to the protestations of the reformer at the Diet of Worms. As such, *Martin Luther* established a generic paradigm for hagiographic films, films in which saints were presented as spiritual and moral models. Luther, in somewhat naïve fashion, was portrayed anachronistically strumming "A Mighty Fortress Is Our God," as a footnote to the narrative action. In his review of this film, Jensen opined, "Art inculcates valuable lessons in a visual form." The success of *Martin Luther* induced other Lutherans to sponsor a second German film on the life of Christ, entitled *I.N.R.I.* It was distributed in America in 1926 as *Crown of Thorns*, despite earlier protests of German writer Dr. H. Petri, who found in his analysis of the cinematic portrayal of Christ that "such efforts to depict the life of Jesus must always fail, as the movies cannot convey religious conviction or edify the soul."[183]

In bold front-page headlines, *Variety* announced in 1921 that the Methodist Episcopal Church was going into the motion picture business, taking over a four-story factory structure in Chicago to manufacture religious and missionary films such as the five-reel film, *The Open Door*.[184] The Presbyterian Board of National Ministries likewise initiated denominational filmmaking in 1924, hiring the Reverend Robert Wightman, a Presbyterian film-minister from Elizabeth, New Jersey. Such decisive moves prompted the militant Reverend Chester Marshall, reviewer for *Educational Screen Magazine,* to express his optimism in 1925, prophesying that

> in some not far distant day every state board of education and every church denomination will own their own libraries of film, equal in artistic value and merit to the best product of the entertainment field, but produced by educators and church men for their respective fields.[185]

Acting as the Executive Secretary of the Religious Film Association (RFA), William Rogers coauthored *Visual Aids in the Church* with Yale University professor, Paul Vieth. They argued that 1919 had been the peak year for the churches' use of stereopticon slides for educational and missionary purposes, due to affluence within the church. The two historians pointed out that by the middle of the 1920s denominations had committed themselves to visual ministries. The Presbyterians made films to raise money for their colleges; Northern Baptists documented their work among Native Americans; and Methodists produced films especially designed for their mission boards.[186] Special Denominational Films of Religious and Educational Value emanated from the Board of Education of the Methodist Episcopal Church, who also distributed their own synopses.[187]

In an editorial in 1934, *The Christian Advocate* lamented that too many preachers now spent their time agitating against indecent films, cursing their darkness when they could be lighting candles of worthwhile virtue by helping to financially underwrite uplifting films. For example, as Methodists looked at the tremendous success of the biographical feature film on Martin Luther, they recognized that one unlit candle still awaiting financial backing was the dramatic story of John Wesley. In extolling the virtues of the feature film, *The Story of Louis Pasteur,* a Methodist editorial complained that if Pastuer could be picturized, why not Wesley? "There should be money enough in the stewardship of Methodists to produce a picture that would compare in power and beauty with Pasteur, "where Jews and Catholics as well as Methodists and Presbyterians stand in queue."[188] So too, the clamor to produce a feature film on *Pilgrim's Progress* on the two-hundred-fiftieth anniversary of John Bunyan, proclaimed that such a religious spectacle would be the

Even while lauding the innovative techniques of John Wesley's circuit evangelism adapted to church work, *The Moving Picture World* satirized film exhibitions in church as being motivated by commercial aspects, as seen in H. F.
Hoffman's cartoon. "The Sermon/The Business Meeting" *The Moving Picture
World* 7:4 (July 23, 1910), 202. Courtesy Library of Congress.

kind of moving tale full of unexpected turns, that lends itself to the kalei-
doscopic art of the screen. The characters are simple and vital, the stereo-
types who can always be depended upon to be "dopey" or "sneezy" or
"bashful," the kind of folk whom the director can be sure will always be
true to type. The Valley of Humiliation and Vanity Fair would lend themselves to the talents of the masterminds of stage setting. And the popular
appeal is unquestioned. Best of all, *The Pilgrim's Progress* has a happy
ending, to be a box office success.[189]

The key to success rested on box office profits. Money still underlay every
moving picture promoting God. It behooved the church community to
economize in the production, distribution, and exhibition of religious
films; most of all, they had to seek out better films and find ways to make
money.

Several practices helped churches to adjust to financial pressures. Educational specialists Don Carlos Ellis and Laura Thornborough observed
the positive economic benefits of churches establishing their own film libraries. In conjunction with the Better Pictures movement, they also
identified suitable biblically oriented films which churches could purchase
to upgrade their film programs. A treasury of relevant films, like the

"beautiful" Old Testament series, adapted Bible stories such as *The Eternal Light* and *Behold the Man,* and modern parabolic photoplays like *The Stream of Life* and *The Burning Question* could then be exchanged or shared with other churches.[190] Secondly, the technical development of the 16mm projector introduced by Victor Animatograph Corporation in 1923 enabled churches to offer cheaper film programs. Unfortunately, churches that had invested in silent 35mm projectors found that no new worthwhile films were being released in that format.

With the advent of affordable 16mm production and exhibition, prophetic voices envisioned a renaissance in the Church Film movement, proclaiming that motion pictures in the church were there to stay. The Reverend Elisha King of the Community Church in Miami Beach, Florida, crowed about attaining too much success and making "so much money out of the enterprise that we don't dare tell the people how much we have in our motion picture fund."[191] Although King defended his experiment of showing pictures and concomitantly promoting a spirit of worship by pointing to the profusion of "serious" requests for prayers at the close of picture programs, unfortunately profit making and commercialism had already contaminated the process.[192] While others perceived a danger in compromising with the devil and mammon, King chose to see his work as pouring new wine into new wine bottles as a profitable ministry.[193] Churches had entered the business of making movies.

Production challenges throughout the twenties included identifying objectives (deciding whether to produce biblical films or short fictional films to hold the attention of the younger generation), securing "scarce" outside capital to finance features, and building a church film circuit.[194] *Variety* itself was not certain what the status of acceptance of these church films actually was. It reported contradictory data, pointing to a Baptist church in Topeka, Kansas, that had abandoned religious subjects as they were limited in scope and variety and did not draw in crowds; in contrast to this "dark" Baptist church (which had turned out its projection lights), a neighborhood rival, the Reverend Charles Sheldon's Congregational Church, was playing to large audiences on Sundays.[195] A few months later, *Variety* reported that an unusual amount of production activity had appeared in the genre of religious films: "The demand for the church films is on the increase, film men declare, with the films being used as features for benefits, with one day showings booked." Notably a prominent new organization was formed with the intention of making films for church use only, the Religious Motion Picture Foundation, Inc., headed by the ecumenical William E. Harmon.[196]

The Harmon Foundation

From the Church Department of the *Educational Screen,* Chester Marshall administered an informal questionnaire from October 1924 through January 1925, surveying hundreds of clergy, newspaper writers, educators, film producers, and exhibitors under the heading of "What Shall We Do with the Movies?" He tabulated and reported the answers to nineteen questions, dealing with subjects like film preferences—where educational pictures received the largest number of votes—and perspectives on social, economic, and moral effects. For their social effects, films were viewed as the poor man's club that stimulated thought, widened horizons, disseminated knowledge, brought the farthest corners of the earth to neighborhood theaters, and inculcated an appreciation for beauty.[197] Marshall investigated whether the moral quality of the film was improving or declining, whether the film's effects had raised or lowered community standards, and finally what kinds of films were being patronized in communities. One exhibitor bragged to him: "I have owned and operated seventeen theaters and have never run a picture I would not be willing my mother should see."[198] In answer to the question whether Sunday shows should be run for profit, respondents were three to one against commercial Sunday shows. In response to whether children under ten should attend movies at all the overwhelming response was yes for educational purposes and for carefully selected films. On whether there should be restrictions on children, three out of four favored supervision of children's viewing. Marshall also asked questions about the legal control of films. Sixty percent endorsed some form of legal control over films, but were emphatically uncomfortable with national censorship. Finally, his research indicated a readiness for the church to move further into production, as the *Christian Herald,* the NCWC, and others had been doing at this point.

Marshall called attention to Mrs. Alonzo Richardson, chair of Atlanta's Better Film Committee, as a significant leader who affirmed the production of the right kind of pictures. For Richardson, the technology involved in motion pictures was simply a demonstration of "God's laws harnessed. It is time we hitched them up to the church and school and let them do their full share of God's blessed work for humanity."[199] Overwhelmingly, public and religious educators like Richardson supported the filming of good books, as well as incorporating more films into educational curricula. Educators who answered Marshall's questionnaire strongly corroborated the value of films, going so far as to assert that their pedagogical benefits had been "scientifically demonstrated beyond the shadow of a doubt."[200] All voiced a desire to see films used more generally in the church, but sensed a reluctance among religious organizations to fully utilize them. Educators attributed this reluctance to several causes: the expense of equipment, the great dearth of suitable films, fear of criticism, inertia, and stubborn conservatism. Baptist pastor H. F. Huse, awaiting the day when churchpeople would provide the financial resources to "secure spiritually minded directors with spiritually minded actors to produce an adequate supply of pictures in every way suited to the use of the church," argued that the church should establish a more aggressive agency to make this open-handedness happen.[201]

However, there were obstacles to large-scale production, one of which was the lack of coordinated and substantial sponsorship. Individual efforts such as that of James Shields and the Christian Herald Film Bureau had sparked hope, but they failed to build an economic base that would sustain an ongoing production and distribution schedule. The central question had already been posed before the 1920s: "Why not a Christian film foundation?" To meet this challenge, the *Educational Film Magazine* in 1919 recommended recruiting potential donors and patrons of the art such as Henry Ford, George Eastman, Coleman Dupont, or "any of the Rockefellers."[202] However, none of these was forthcoming.

Enter the Harmon Foundation and its innovative mogul. In 1922 William Elmer Harmon, an aggressive suburban real estate tycoon and merchandising entrepreneur from Ohio, formally established the prestigious Harmon Foundation and brought a strong ecclesiastical cast to the nontheatrical field.[203] The Harmon Foundation's initial mission had focused on building playgrounds and providing educational loans for needy students. Incorporated under New York state law two years later, the Harmon Foundation organized the Religious Motion Picture Foundation (RMPF) to produce and distribute religious films with an initial grant of $50,000. The RMPF became the last major attempt of big business to enter the nontheatrical field during the silent film era. The sixty-three-year-old Harmon (whose wife was an ardent Episcopalian) had been impressed with a vision expressed by their friend, Bishop William Lawrence of the Protestant Episcopal Church in Boston. The bishop was pondering how to stimulate churchgoing in a conversation with Professor Samuel McCune Lindsay of Columbia, when they broached the subject of films as a promising means of quickening the interest of an uninspired public.

In the forward to a 1927 pamphlet, Harmon argued that the Protestant church everywhere found it increasingly difficult to keep up church attendance and active interest in religious matters not because people were irreligious or dead to spiritual impulses, but because

> old eternal truths occasionally require new habiliments—a refurbishing and sometimes entirely new clothing. What stained glass windows once accomplished as an appeal to the emotions through the eye, and what music later added to the richness and dignity of devotional worship, could "through faithfully depicted inspirational and beautiful motion pictures on Biblical and religious texts" bring about today a renaissance of Christian devotion in the service of the Master.[204]

Beginning in 1925, the newly and shakily formed RMPF hired Presbyterian George Reid Andrews (who eloquently articulated its mission) as the Vice President and General Manager. Andrews had also been a former Chairman of the Committee on Educational and Religious Drama of the Federal Council of Churches.[205] As president of the philanthropic foundation, Harmon drafted Andrews to assist the churches in adapting the motion picture medium to their need.[206] However, the great coup was securing the contractual services of director Major Herbert M. Dawley, who had once caused dinosaurs to walk the streets of London in *The Lost World*.[207] "Anyone familiar with the ordinary 'movie lot,'" wrote Dawley, "would have been amazed at the atmosphere pervading the barn that was our studio. Even the little ragamuffins that we collected in the streets were filled with awe, and responded to the figure of Christ in a natural and touching way."[208]

Andrews first sought to determine whether the RMPF should invest in films for use in church services.[209] Recognizing the expense of producing films, Andrews introduced the RMPF as the correct body to enable a vertical integration within the church for movie making, distribution, and exhibition.[210]

At the same time, Andrews hedged defining the term "religious" in the RMPF: "The true artist does not waste much time in phrase-making; he is content to paint. We shall seek to give expression to these universal religious experiences of men insofar as we can discover them and thus let the action reveal the inner spirit. We shall seek to employ the test of the Great Teacher, 'by their fruits shall ye know them.'" So in both the spoken and silent drama, the "word must become flesh if there is to be drama at all. Whether we will or not, we cannot spend our time in fruitless theological argument; we shall be forced to think vitally and concretely about religion. By means of the dramatic method we hope to give newness and freshness to the things of the spirit."[211] Essentially, his broad philosophy of religion could be summarized as that which cultivates the affections and makes for the best wholesome relations among human beings; RMPF's films were to stress the nondenominational and universal aspects of religious faith. Andrews identified the RMPF's tasks as supplying suitable pictures for church use and studying how to produce, distribute, and exhibit films within churches.[212] The RMPF ran an experiment in which it chose eleven film subjects out of the nine hundred submitted. These films were then tested in ten country churches in upstate New York, with no advertising other than word of mouth allowed. According to Harmon, the ten-week experiment of using pictures in churches resulted in an "average increase in church attendance of about forty per cent."[213]

The Harmon Foundation was seen by many as the one organization sufficiently and tactically equipped to rescue the Christian film industry. The apex of the Christian film industry's production had occurred in the early 1920s; after several intermittent successes, Christian filmmaking had declined precipitously. Exhibition continued unabated, but the demand for better films outpaced supply. While some church leaders still optimistically expected the motion picture industry to adjust to the Church's viewpoint, only needing encouragement to create suitable and usable pictures for the Church, others saw an urgent need to declare independence, and believed that such independence could come from the RMPF.[214] In 1925, even *Variety* pointed to the particular uniqueness of Harmon's specialized organization for religious motion pictures. Citing various film men, *Variety* claimed that the demand for church films was on the increase, with the benefit of films being booked for one-day showings.[215]

Andrews theorized that teaching religion through motion pictures depended upon certain proven assumptions that people and children like motion pictures and that those pictures "directly affect attitudes and therefore character development."[216] In cooperation with the Federal Council of Churches and Will H. Hays of the Motion Picture Producers and Distributors of America (MPPDA), the Harmon Foundation there-fore aimed to produce such nontheatrical and noncommercial pictures. Harmon and Andrews were encouraged by the participation of Hays, even as the czar of the movies was under attack by Protestants for lack-ing moral muscle.[217] In conjunction with the MPPDA and the Federal Council of Churches, an experiment was conducted to develop motion pictures based on biblical themes according to church demand, with Hays pledging support to the Foundation.[218]

Thus, the Harmon Foundation's first year, beginning in June 1925, was to be devoted to a study of filmmaking and the production of a few demon-stration pictures.[219] The RMPF prepared this group of demo films espe-cially for church services. While high-class professional actors and direc-tors were employed, nonprofessionals made up the cast. An unknown actor named Jean Del Val portrayed the Savior in one film, along with some students from the theological seminary at Madison, New Jersey, "who fell very naturally into the spirit of the work," playing biblical characters.

The RMPF completed four films excelling in their Palestinian setting, but only partially successful in their dramatic impact. Avoiding any doc-trinal statements, the films used terse intertitles that consisted mostly of familiar Bible quotations. From a studio in Chatham, New Jersey, four episodic films on the life of Christ emerged by the end of 1926: *Jesus Confounds His Critics* (on the woman caught in adultery), *The Unwelcome Guest* (on Jesus visiting the house of Simon, the Pharisee), *Forgive Us Our Debts,* and *The Rich Young Ruler.*[220] Three clergymen, Dr. Daniel Russell of Rutgers Presbyterian Church, Dean Howard Robbins of the Cathedral of St. John the Divine in New York, and Dr. S. Parkes Cadman in Brooklyn, were recruited to introduce RMPF movies as sermon illus-trations.[221] In the early 1930s, H. Paul Janes suggested a method for "in-terpretative teaching" through a film like *The Unwelcome Guest.* With a reading of the appropriate Scripture of *Luke* 7: 36–50, the teacher would introduce terms like Pharisee (with synonyms like Hypocrite, Bigoted Re-ligious Leader, Self-Righteous Aristocrat, and Lawyer) and Hospitality and then lead a discussion on how the film demonstrated the meaning of such terms—a method similar to the Roman Catholics' use of the moving picture in catechism.[222]

The visual sermon, *Forgive Us Our Debts,* showed an unjust Persian servant who does not forgive even after he has been forgiven. It ended with grisly emphasis, as the guilty party is "hung by the wrists and lashed se-verely on the bared back until great welts appear." Because of limited funds, the RMPF employed professional actors only for leading roles in *Forgive Us Our Debts,* hired amateur but enthusiastic volunteers for the mob scenes, and shot it in a little studio loft at Chatham, New Jersey. When it was presented at Cadman's Brooklyn Church on All Hallow's Eve in 1926, *New York Times* writer and critic P. W. Wilson used the film to launch his own exegetical commentary.[223] Wilson's use of *Forgive Us Our Debts* met Harmon's philanthropic goal of blazing a trail to combat public lethargy, enrich worship, and drive home the basic truths of the Bible.[224]

Wilson's critical engagement was a partial fulfillment of Harmon's vision. Harmon hoped to contribute to augmenting church attendance, believing that "beautiful and reverential motion pictures built on spiritual and religious subject matter, would add vital interest to church services, if properly conceived and executed according to the highest literary, dramatic and photographic standards." The Harmon Foundation's research indicated that the Bible provided models of dramatic methods that could be used to illustrate religious doctrine. The motion picture's role, therefore, was to enrich the spoken word with visual tropes and narratives.[225] As their propaganda noted, "Nearly all of our great preachers, Beecher, Moody, Spurgeon and others were masters of the word picture."[226] Likewise, William Hansen reminded his readers that in the Middle Ages,

> great artists and craftsmen decorated the windows of churches throughout Europe with graphic representations of Biblical stories. These windows served the dual purpose of decoration and instruction. This was pleasing artistically and at the same time served to familiarize the people with figures and events of the Old and New Testament. Moving pictures can serve the same purpose of the 20th century that stained glass served in the 16th century and the Foundation is attempting to present movies of that sort.[227]

The novelty of showing religious films to attract audiences declined significantly during the early 1930s. However, church interest in technical innovations, particularly in the advent of the 16mm sound camera and projector, bred a generation of independent amateur filmmakers that resulted in the emergence of fresh changes in pedagogical emphases. Part of this upsurge in independent filmmaking was the fruit of the Harmon Foundation's novel effort to bring the arts back to the people.[228] The Harmon Foundation's Directory included titles of a thirteen-reel pictorial study of Jesus' life and ministry in Holy Land settings, the four original episodic films in the life of Christ, studies of great leaders like David Livingston and Martin Luther, adventures in understanding the American Indian, the "our neighbor" reviews of missionary activity in several foreign lands, entitled the *Spirit of Christ at Work* in China, Brazil, India, Africa, Porto Rico [*sic*], as well as "well-rounded, unbiased" films on comparative religion.

Harmon himself, retired from the real estate business at the age of sixty, devoted himself to finding a place for motion pictures in religious education. "I am certain," he reiterated in an interview with critic Gilbert Simons, "that we can draw people into the churches and, by means of these pictures, open the minds of the congregation to the sermon." He averred that in some churches, attendance had doubled and even quadrupled, even without advertising. The clergy, already faced with a "growing public lethargy," needed to embrace this means of "driving home the basic truths of the Bible."[229]

Harmon's very intelligent and conscientious personal assistant, Mary Beattie Brady, oversaw much of the work of the Harmon Foundation in the decades of the 1920s and 1930s.[230] She first produced religious films, then researched and promoted the Foundation's work, releasing, for example, the results of her study that opposition to the impersonation of Christ in movies had decreased.[231] Brady was the chief advocate and champion of religious film during these decades of difficulty, and she doggedly promoted supplementary ways in which films could aid preaching, teaching, and worship. During her reign at the Harmon Foundation, she instituted technical training for future filmmakers. This opportunity provided by Harmon literally involved calling on lovers of film to express their vision through cinema, and resulted in a modest revival of religious visual education in the late 1930s and beyond.[232] The availability at last of augmented training, affordable equipment, and new Kodak film stock introduced new markets in the temple.

Brady's research, underwritten by the RMPF, was the fundamental key to its success. Brady enlisted denominations in a "Crusade of Discovery." She proposed that churches use films no longer than fifteen or thirty minutes; silent films should be accompanied by musical accompaniment or even with phonograph records if no organist were present. She also felt that hymns illustrated with pictures were very effective in inspiring congregations.[233] Film, she believed, should generally be used just after the second hymn or just before the sermon. She addressed issues of the location of the screen and projector, and considered the psychological aspects of creating a suitable atmosphere for worship and instruction. She believed that semidarkness would enhance feelings of reverence, neutralize distractions, and suppress inhibitions, as a fully lighted sanctuary would not do. Thus one would be liberated to worship emotionally. However, in spite of claims that "supernatural powers" were possible through a new camera for pictures in churches, the films themselves remained functionally didactic and pedestrian.[234] Emotional liberation seldom came through the Foundation's church films.

It was also Brady who recognized the nature of the laggard responses of churches to the vital opportunities of film, and discerned several reasons for their hesitation. First, there was the dearth of films themselves. Second, there was still some suspicion of film as "cheap" showy entertainment, particularly as some clergy tried to let films "do the whole job of teaching or preaching."[235] In the 1920s, a number of scandals had arisen in Hollywood, such as the politically charged accusation against Fatty Arbuckle for the alleged rape and manslaughter of a Hollywood extra. As a result many churchpeople in the late 1920s revisited their opinion of films, viewing them as "paths to the devil's playground." At the same time, Brady blamed producers for treating religious communities as one vast, nondiscriminating market upon which it could unload irrelevant product. "Failure usually has been the rule," Brady wrote, "because the project was presented but did not meet a recognized need, and any demand created was largely an artificial one." In the past, according to Brady, motion pictures had been used to a very large degree "as bait to get people to come to church for service for one purpose or another. Sometimes a minister or leader with a genius for showmanship and an understanding of the value of the motion pictures has worked wonders with the ill-assorted material at his disposal, but at large the general experience was distinctly of a makeshift nature."[236] Brady, a canny critic of religious film programs, questioned how films were used in churches while simultaneously promoting the production of "amateur movie photography."

As growing costs during the Depression frustrated many churches in pursuing such a course of action, Brady recommended that denominations affiliate in producing movies to economize. Likewise, Beulah Amidon, responding to the cost of distribution worked out through the Neighborhood Motion Picture Service at a rental fee of $7.50 per reel, argued that one should pay for religious motion pictures as one did for good music or stained glass windows. "The films are not produced for profit, but neither is the RMPF a charitable organization."[237] The Reverend A. M. Hanson advertised his own successful financial formula in an experiment in his church in Minnesota; he invested about $12 a night on film rental and collected over $15 per night through offerings.[238]

In the era of sound, Brady would be among the vanguard in initiating various film projects at Yale Divinity School, Emory University, Boston University School of Religious Studies, and at smaller private religious colleges like Ohio Wesleyan University.[239] These projects shone as bright beacons for religious production in the transition to sound films. However, in 1942 the Harmon Foundation turned its work over to the RMPF (an organization conceived in 1925 and stitched together with members from the publication houses of a number of Protestant church groups).[240] According to its own self-critique in 1949, the RMPF fell short of its goal of carrying on the work of the Harmon Foundation and of coordinating a broad coalition of denominations and independent religious producers. Where films had first been produced for use in formal church worship and later had incorporated documentaries of foreign lands specifically designed for mission study, a frustrated RMPF blamed churches for being "too slow to take up visual programs" and said of church productions to date that "the work was discouraging."[241] This disappointing realization of the lack of church use of film nudged the Harmon Foundation in its last days toward sponsoring other cultural and artistic ventures, particularly with regard to international arts and black artists.[242]

4

Better Films

Motion pictures which flourished by clinging to Satan have discarded him for Mother Church.

Alva Johnston

As nontheatrical church production waned and Hollywood's productivity waxed, the church turned toward critiquing rather than creating film products. In response to the growing suspicion that Hollywood was the source of a creeping secularization, some church leaders joined together to resist what they saw as a deluge of modernity and immorality gushing out of the film industry. However, as a result of this conservatives were marginalized, accused of adhering to the spirit of the Iconoclasts, of being out of touch with the advanced, modern age, or of trying to keep "the life of a busy world in tune with the words of the Bible, an essentially pastoral book."[1] To a lesser degree, lacking the access and resources to produce their own sound films, mainstream churches now turned to judging Hollywood's output. What they found was displeasing. Although in 1922 the industry had appointed a moral overseer, Will H. Hays, after the Hollywood scandals of the previous year church leaders suspected that their own religious mongoose was fraternizing with cobras.

Criticism extended beyond Hays, however. Addressing another issue of film propaganda, the *International Journal of Religious Education* pointed to the contributions of the National Film Estimate Service that reviewed and recommended hundreds of films each year. The increasingly political, as opposed to aesthetic or religious, nature of the recommendations was exposed in certain pacifist reviews. They accused early 1930s newsreels of fostering distrust among nations and other films of being instruments of propaganda for militarism. Such criticisms of the media spread. More than one thousand Princeton University students and faculty protested the Hearst Metro-Tone newsreels as vicious propaganda. The Garden Theatre management in Princeton actually had to discontinue the newsreels.[2] Religious educators were likewise urged to obtain better, more politically and religiously correct, films. Film was being converted into a battleground of ideologies rather than an uplifting playground. The now vigilant, even vigilante, church abandoned its productions, and many of its exhibitions, in favor of debating the cultural blights of the industry.

Independent Film Distribution

Religious groups recognized that they needed to find reliable distribution networks for original moving picture products. For example, as a quasi-religious social organization, the Young Men's Christian Association wanted its own dependable distribution circuit in order to exhibit films as recreation in its training camps. It subsequently established the YMCA Motion Picture Bureau as a free lending library. The YMCA issued a forty-two-page booklet devoted to its use of film, with suggestions about manufacturers and organizations useful for religious purposes.[3] Key sources for religious motion pictures included the American Motion Picture Corporation, the Children's Bureau, the Community Motion Picture Bureau of New York, the New Era Films, International Church Film Corporation, and others.[4] Sacred Film Productions of the Paragon Film Bureau, which released Sacred Songs on film and suggested ways to use the song films, and Plymouth Pictures, stood out as exemplary supply centers.[5]

Plymouth Pictures incorporated in 1919 to promote James K. Shields's productions and became the Pilgrim Photoplay and Book Exchange. Shields created notable work for the church with three "virile pictures, each with a heart thrilling sermon visualized." As we have seen, *The Stream of Life* preached the spiritual message of strength and peace of a home that finally finds God. *A Maker of Men* summoned men to the high calling of God in ministry. *Lest We Forget* used the "poignant facts of the now outlawed beer saloon with its train of heartaches and crime and shows that out of which we have come. See Uncle Sam and righteously indignant citizens nail up the stupid old saloon, the entire congregation unites in one resolve: 'It must not come back!'"[6]

RELIGION-AND-SOCIAL-SERVICE

A SCENE FROM THE FILM VERSION OF THE PARABLE OF "THE GOOD SAMARITAN."

BIBLE STORIES ON THE SCREEN

One of the most enduring Bible Story screenplays, inspired by Herbert Jump's recommendation, was the parable of *The Good Samaritan. Literary Digest* "Bible Stories on the Screen" (November 13, 1920), 36. Courtesy Library of Congress.

Plymouth Pictures's choice feature promoting pacifism was Shields's post–World War I *Hell and the Way Out,* decrying the horrific ravages of war.[7] The Chicago-based Pilgrim Photoplay Exchange also distributed *The Lord's Prayer,* with a suggested service of scriptures and hymns, and twenty-five other single-reel films with biblical themes like *The Good Samaritan* and *Light of the World.*[8] Another Chicago company, the Film Library of Associated Churches, produced a six-reel *Life of Our Savoir;* a "chaste" comedy called *The Butterfly Net* (showing how to catch a wife), and a family melodrama, *Do Children Count?* reaffirming God's providence. Its most ambitious release was *The Protestant Prince,* about a nineteenth-century religious struggle between Roman Catholics and Protestants, which closes with the Prince, in the true spirit of Christian love, generously forgiving the papists.[9]

For those seeking reliable distributors of church films, Christian reviewer Elisha King identified the American Motion Picture Corporation (AMPC) as one of the best. AMPC handled such works as *The Voice of the Land* that mapped the historic geography of the Holy Land and furnished various one-reel sermon illustrators (e.g., *Picture Parables, Immortality, Church and Community*), "just long enough to illustrate a sermon but not to take its place."[10] AMPC, however, quickly sold out to the Community Motion Picture Service. The World Educational Film Company distributed religious documentary films like *Liberated Jerusalem* and *At the Wailing Wall,* a Burton Holmes Travelogue emphasizing the sorrows of the Jewish people where the Mosque of Omar had replaced Solomon's Temple.[11] They added explicit missionary slants to travelogues on Japan and India, along with the internationally effective Indian film, *Ram Das.*[12] The Ford Motor Company found it could offer its industrial films and nature studies for church education exhibition, even if they were subliminal commercials.[13] John Bray, son of a Methodist minister, formed the famous animation house of the Bray Studios. Their Better Babies series and the popular Bobby Bumps cartoons played well for Sunday school and children's programs.[14]

The peak of production and distribution of films for churches around 1925 was such that the *Congregationalist* periodical rejoiced that it had "found so much more material at the disposal of churches this year that we cannot possibly compress all the information into one article."[15] Their contributor, Elisha King, praised everything from James Shields's films to the Sacred Films. The first bulletin of the Pilgrim Photoplay Exchange listed numerous biblical subjects, as well as furnishing motion picture hymns like *Onward Christian Soldiers* and *How Firm a Foundation.*

Marketing to the nontheatrical field only, the Pictorial Clubs, Inc., established branches by 1926 in Boston, Philadelphia, and Omaha and adopted the slogan "the Organization the Non-Theatrical World Has Been Waiting to See."[16] They allegedly engaged an unknown animator, Walt Disney, for seven animated cartoons made especially for the Clubs.[17] Pictorial Clubs's first two-reel Bible picture was Henry Christeen Warnack's *As We Forgive,* based on Paul's epistle to Philemon and updated with a modern parallel.[18] It was followed up by the *Come Back Club* about a young man who drifts into a city mission, *Blood Will Tell,* and the Bruce Barton 1925 revisionist story of Jesus as an American capitalist, *The Man Nobody Knows: A Discovery of Jesus Christ.*[19] This six-reel feature shot in Palestine sought to present Jesus without "dramatization." However, Barton's intertitles shaped Jesus in his own masculine, corporate American image.[20] Other Pictorial Club films included the four-reel *Wagging Tongues* (showing the restoration of a criminal back into society by a devoted minister), *The Four Seasons* (extolling the wonders of God's creative and preserving powers manifest in nature), and *Give Us This Day Our Daily Bread* (entreating Americans in their bounty to give to the needy in the Holy Land).²¹ As well as producing and distributing their own pictures, they promoted such "wonderful" works as *All Hail the Power* based on Psalm 19, *The Prodigal Son,* and a reedited version of George Kleine's intriguingly titled *The Story the Keg Told Me.*²² Pictorial Clubs also distributed Sidney Olcotts's *From the Manger to the Cross,* coordinated with personal tours by Henderson Bland, the English actor portraying the Savior. Bland appeared at churches like Grace Methodist Episcopal to share production gossip with over fifteen hundred people on how "women stepped forward and kissed my robe."²³

Orrin Cocks of the National Committee of Better Films printed a pamphlet on sources of information on films for churches in 1920, in which he catalogued the primary producers of religious and ethical films, as well as magazines that addressed related issues. Included in the list were exchanges like Atlas Educational, Educational Film Corp of America, and Bray Studios. Cocks's own National Committee became the clearing house for all their films.²⁴ Pathe exported the respectable series *A Pilgrimage to Palestine,* faintly praised as "not dramatized, but good sermon material."²⁵ As one advertisement asked: "If you can't go to Palestine, why not bring Palestine to you?"²⁶ Likewise, critic W. Stephen Bush posed the same issue to the churches: "How are we to understand the East, so thoroughly different from us in its thoughts and its manners, its habits, its social conditions, its ways of viewing life (if we don't have movies on the Holy Land)?"²⁷ Bush asked more difficult questions as to the reverence of sacred pictures. While rejecting sectarian films, Bush advanced his argument that the motion picture remained the churches' greatest ally for religious propaganda.²⁸ The impression that film had become a strong ally of religion was generally accepted by the middle of the decade. Film not only revived Sunday evening services and illustrated mission work, but also solved economic problems for previously struggling churches.²⁹

Better Picture Movements

A movement to promote suitable films embraced the idea of selecting Hollywood films appropriate for in church use. As Secretary of the National Committee for Better Films, Cocks advertised his vision for promoting uplift through moving pictures, spelling out his systematic plan for selecting fine pictures and his "Motion Picture Principles for the Church."[30] By 1914, Gardiner Wood, the editor of *Ladies World,* campaigned for "better pictures." It was to be a stirring battle cry in drafting devotees for a campaign for progressive uplift.[31] The endorsement of the National Board of Review in 1915 sparked the formation of local better film groups, mostly populated by concerned, reform-minded women. When E. Milliken, nationally known Baptist churchman and governor of Maine from 1917 to 1921, was appointed secretary of the Motion Picture Producers and Distributors of America, he assured church leaders of the advent of Better Films.[32]

Soon, the new Better Films movement was issuing its own *Bulletin* with news items, published addresses, and film lists for church use.[33] Herbert Sherwood and the editors of the *Bulletin* cultivated a quarterly "Garden of American Motion Pictures," compiling a list of wholesome and healthy nourishment for church audiences. Of course, this did not mean that evil was to be banished from church viewings. "I am not certain that all drinking, gambling, dancing, criminal and low moral scenes should be eliminated. Are You? You remember the son in the far country, the greedy builder of barns, the wailing and gnashing of teeth, the woman taken in adultery, and the unjust judge."[34]

By the early 1920s, the Better Film Movement evolved into *Film Progress,* a more modern moniker for progressive reform. *Film Progress* fought against imposed censorship, citing John Ruskin's adage that while "innocence is good, character is better," adding that the church had better not shirk its responsibility. In 1921 *Variety* reminded the clergy of the origins of sin in a news item highlighting a short Douglas Fairbanks propaganda film entitled *The Non-Sense of Censorship* that sought to thwart any movement toward censorship and to agitate against blue laws. In the film an actor is intently reading "The Rules of Censorship," which explain: "The Motion Picture is about 15 years old. Sin is somewhat older than that, yet the censors would have us believe that it was not Satan but Thomas Alva Edison who invented 'The Fall of Man.'"[35] *Variety* noted that if such censorship were applied, it would destroy Shakespeare, Dickens, and the Bible itself.

The plans of Better Pictures emphasized ethical subjects over religious ones.[36] *Film Progress* charted the benefits for children educated with suitable films at popular matinees, suggesting a definite moral and social amelioration. When the city fathers of Emporia, Kansas, expressed their disapproval of the cigarette-smoking actresses in *Carmen* and the bare knees of Pavlova, the First Presbyterian Church decided to adopt better pictures as a regular part of its Sunday evening service. Its progressive pastor, Dr. J. M. Todd, purchased the most advanced projector and screen obtainable. He firmly believed that he could not preach to people unless they attended the church, and that by adopting modern methods he could attract a crowd by showing highly selective films with a strong moral and religious allure.[37]

The movement to show better pictures encouraged ministers to identify and publicize what they foresaw as boons to their churches and communities. As local parishes discovered, moving pictures provided an opportunity for social action and for gathering disparate groups of people. They also believed that church film exhibition inevitably raised the standards of motion pictures in the local movie houses, as competition would breed improvement. What was most significant for Better Pictures, however, was that these pictures could be combined with good lectures, involving the entire family in educational entertainment.[38] While wondering if rural churches could expediently operate a community picture show, W. O. Benthin of the United Church in Parkdale, Oregon, successfully experimented with a film lecture program, forming the Forum Entertainment Bureau. He declared, "We educate as well as entertain. In place of cheap and often questionable comics of most theaters we offer several reels of scientific and educational weeklies."[39]

The primary question remained: Where could one find the right films? The most helpful solution for meeting film supply needs was to be found in the White Lists published by the Methodist Committee on Conservation and Advance. The Committee sent out a selected list of the best 1,001 films available for church and school use to more than two thousand Methodist pastors.[40] The Methodist Episcopal Church went so far as to officially recognize the possibilities of motion pictures by creating its own Department of Films and Slides, made up of a group of clerics and lay people who compiled the remarkably inclusive White Lists. They catalogued films by Lutherans and Roman Catholics (e.g., *Jimmies' Prayer, The Fall, The Blasphemer*) according to their distinctive, but nonsectarian, propaganda. There were other sources for film lists as well, such as the Church Film Company of New England. Mr. Charles Cox, a Christian businessman from Boston, formed the Church Cinema Club as a film service especially designed for churches. It spoke their language regarding the suitability of films for differentiated church needs.[41] Nevertheless, the best source for appropriate pictures was to be found in the publications of the National Committee for Better Films. Its Department of Films, of National Board of Review and Photoplay Guide, and *Film Progress* published special reviews of pictures for church use selected by ministers who used pictures. They regularly identified exceptional photoplays and additional materials that had special applications, such as films for Lenten use.

To assist the churches in garnering films from all sources, the aforementioned National Board of Review's National Committee for Better Films gathered, catalogued, and successfully released a twenty-page booklet on *The Best Motion Pictures for Church and Semi-Religious Entertainments,* which included over nine hundred dramatic, missionary, travel, and instructional pictures for use.[42] Entitled "Selected Pictures" (formerly "A Garden of American Pictures") the booklet included, for example, *The Chosen Prince,* an eight-reel photodrama of the lives of David and Jonathan, released by the United Projector and Film Company.[43] *Visual Education* vigorously promoted certain films to be used in connection with preaching: *The Power Within, Fires of Faith,* and *After Six Days* were showered with praise.[44] The Committee on Visual Education of the International Council of Religious Education also recommended "Films for Church Use" in a column appearing regularly in the *International Journal of Religious Education.*[45] The journal had launched its own recommendations of films, culling reviews from the National Film Estimate Service's listings in *Educational Screen* magazine since September 1926.[46] The latter periodical provided Film Council Recommendations for such films as Metro's *The Rag Man* with Jackie Coogan and Griffith's *Isn't Life Wonderful* as wholesome entertainment for church use.[47]

Last, and perhaps least, was the film supply series of the *Educational Screen* out of Chicago. The *Educational Screen* positioned itself, under the supervision of editors like the Reverend Frank Jensen, as the main arbiter and guide of churches seeking to use motion pictures. Not only did it promote the publication of copies of the Methodist *1000 and One: The Blue Book of Non-Theatrical Films,* but it also provided reviews through a special column entitled "Film Estimates," and pointed to a diverse body of free films.[48] The *Educational Screen* publicized the contract of the Claiborne Avenue Presbyterian Church for fifty-two Ford Educational Weeklies to enhance the Reverend Dr. A. H. Zeimer's weekly sermons as a sterling example of their contribution to nontheatrical exhibition.[49] Sadly, however, in spite of the apparent cornucopia of visual materials offered by the *Educational Screen,* one branch manager of a nontheatrical exchange secretly confided in 1924 that the new two-hundred-page *Catalogue of Films Carefully Selected for Schools, Church, and Community* contained mostly junk.[50] The Methodist Church produced a White List of acceptable movie actors and actresses as well, indicating which ones were acceptable for church viewings.[51]

The prospect of better films raised the specter of the effect of all films. Was visual material actually a spur to education or merely a sedative? Were movies killing the imagination, as the *Christian Science Monitor* claimed?[52] Responding to these questions, the journal *Visual Education* marshaled numerous testimonies to film's efficacy in teaching everything from biology to how to get the world to sing, provided they were the right films.[53] Cultural critic Catherine Ely responded to Chinese businessmen decrying the immoral exports of Hollywood with a call for better, more humanizing films. These international emissaries had complained that "If you can't send any better illustrations of domestic life in America than those you have been sending, keep them in the United States, provided you want China to think well of you and Christian civilization." In response, Ely argued that better movies would countermand such deleterious international effects.[54] In England, the *Manchester Guardian* reported that a Church Pictorial Movement had been conducted around "circuits of villages by motor-lorry" and shows were given, which, without being in the least "goody or churchy are free from the lurid suggestion or the silly 'knock-about business' of too many of those with which the towns are familiar."[55] Better pictures "do good." However, the most salient issue in supplying better films around the country and world depended upon finding suitable films.

Suitable Secular Films

The primary secular films included in the Better Film movement were those unequivocally identified with safe subjects, usually centering on the Bible. According to church leaders, the most suitable films were those that furthered the cause of church evangelism and religious instruction, which meant Bible films. Before religious groups had picked up the mantle to produce visual documents of biblical history and geography, production companies associated with the Motion Picture Patent Company (MPPC) experimented with religious filmmaking. According to the Reverend

Christian Reisner, MPPC leader Thomas Edison began early on to picturize Bible scenes and characters. In 1918, the Edison Company redoubled its efforts to create an attractive, entertaining group of desirable pictures for churches called the "Conquest Pictures."[56] Young home missionaries, who had traveled the Blue Ridge Mountains by horse and mule, now delivered the Gospel with portable motion picture equipment.[57]

Various other early MPPC studios catered to religious markets, George Kleine's *The Lord's Prayer—Illustrated* (1910) being produced especially for churches. Kleine had induced the French Gaumont Studio to generate numerous religious and historical subjects for him to distribute, but his ingenious project for the Lord's Prayer elicited the greatest praise. This rapturous work of art was well fitted for church work and would "uplift cinematography and win for this class of amusement praise and recommendation from the pulpit."[58] Clergy praised such prayer scenes in pictures as inducing a perceptible hush over audiences. One photoplay even confessed in an epilogue, "This may not be a good picture, but if it makes any one write home, or better, go home to the old folks before it is too late, then it will have proved itself a good picture."[59] Kleine was also credited with distributing the first multiple-reel feature film for the church, the 1913 Italian production of *Quo Vadis,* and simultaneously published an educational catalogue (revised and compressed in a 1915 reissue) that recommended such inspirational religious spectacles as *Ben Hur* and *Cabiria* for many congregations. Great Britain, Germany, France, and Italy also reported distinguished productions and commendable reception of Bible films during the early 1900s.[60]

Kalem Studios provided Bible study pictures from five reels shot in Palestine and Egypt extracted from their widely popular 1912 production of *From the Manger to the Cross, or Jesus of Nazareth.* Kalem's producer-director, Sidney Olcott (having lost a court case of literary copyright infringement on his 1907 static, one-reel production of *Ben Hur*) boasted that his film story of *From the Manger to the Cross* met with no clerical opposition (in either New York *or* the Midwest), was presented with dignity, reverence, and faithful adherence to the biblical story, and led to a "revival of sacred history."[61] Corresponding to Albert Schweitzer's quest for an authentic historical Jesus, the Kalem executives announced that "wherever possible each scene is to be enacted in the exact location as pointed out by leading authorities."[62] Film critic W. Stephen Bush called it a cinematic Gospel and exclaimed that because of this sublime work, it will be easier than before to go forth and teach all nations."[63]

The key source of primary material for early religious films was the Oberammergau Passion Play performed in the Bavarian Alps; its dramatic presentation had been played since 1634 and inspired films like Sidney Olcott's *From the Manger to the Cross* (1912). Olcott's film, based on a script by his leading lady, Gene Gauntier, enjoyed a greater sense of credibility on account of its authentic locations in Palestine and Egypt.[64] Bush praised its realism, although it may have been a little dull, as indeed were many of the uplifting films competing with the melodramas of their day that employed Griffith's dynamic editing. Éclair's two-reel religious dramatization of Christ's ministry as translated by St. Bernard of Clairvoux [*sic*] developed out of the song "The Holy City" (aka *Jerusalem*), and was lauded for its "careful research and even more painstaking execution." Its director appealed to churchpeople by pointing to ancient times when "the greatest art was that of the Biblical story. These pictures were sold by the artists and today they are the greatest heirlooms of the world of art, as well as religion."[65] The producers aligned themselves with classic religious artists like the Hudson River painters, who worked commercially. The producers claimed that they, like their predecessors, breathed into their work a religious feeling of deep reverence.

An additional aspect of the producers' self-proclaimed credibility rested in the grounding of their films in sacred geography. The Holy Land functioned as a key site of piety for Protestant and Roman Catholic audiences. To see the roads and paths where Jesus walked was to be transported into His presence. However, some promoters pushed spurious copies of Palestine over the more expensive original presentations. For one theatrical agent, nickel shows of religious dramas shot on the Bowery were just as religious as those from Oberammergau. Talent Booking Agent George Tyler accused his competitive Austrian promoters of being guilty of the "rottenest graft." "Imagine my feeling," wrote the American capitalist agent whose own reputation was dubious, "when I found the representative of Christ selling his autograph for two marks or as much as he could get."[66]

Pathe's seven-reel, colored edition of the preeminent *The Life of Our Savior* appeared in April 1914. This "lovely" subject, produced in Jerusalem and first shown publicly in America at the Manhattan Opera House, New York, elicited a rapturous review from the Reverend Boudinot Stockton in the *Moving Picture World*. The columnist waxed eloquently about its religious possibilities for "missionary work, for inciting devotion, for rousing dormant and sleeping religious impulses and sensibilities." According to Stockton, the film could be used by a good evangelist or parochial missioner with telling and incalculable effect, such that "even without the personal urging of an evangelist . . . [it could bring] some erring souls to repentance." For the critic, *The Life of the Savior* was undoubtedly one of the most distinct steps forward in the production of religious pictures.[67] Another reviewer, W. Stephen Bush, opined that the film captured the "best traditions of Christian art," reminiscent of iconic works of earlier Christian painters, full of sweetness and beauty.[68] Another film, the Thanhouser Film Corporation's tableau production of *The Star of Bethlehem,* was also enthusiastically received by among church leaders.[69] Not only did it provide an asymptote of biblical aesthetic authenticity ("all the manger scenes are exact reproductions of famous paintings"), but it also attracted enormous rental business from the churches. Bert Adler of Thanhouser Marketing acknowledged that "it was used in many churches during the recent Christmas holidays with marked success; in some, it replaced the customary cantata."[70] A joint fund-raising operation of the Collinwood Congregational Church and the Virginia Theatre utilized the film as a means to draw in those interested in both culture and religion.[71] The manager at the Lyric Motion Picture Theatre in Ft. Atkinson, Wisconsin, arranged for a special showing for clergy, all of whom recommended it to their respective congregations.[72]

According to the editors of *Nickelodeon,* the only shortcoming in the Bible was that it was not sufficiently illustrated. So J. Stuart Blackton, executive of the Vitagraph Studio, engaged the services of the Reverend Madison Peters as a producer of biblical pictures. In 1909 *The Life of Moses* marked the first "epoch in the productions of its maker."[73] Filmmakers appealed to religious congregations by promoting a combination of biblical accuracy, authentic interpretation, and public piety. One *Moving Picture World* review noted that the graphic reproduction of biblical events closely corresponded to the conception that had been "inculcated in the minds of people who have attended church and Sunday school."[74] Such biblical stories, attired in stained glass attitudes, were easily marketed to evangelists and ministers as visual reinforcement to their preaching. A subsequent daring eight-reel Vitagraph feature adapted from Hall Caine's novel, *The Christian,* was seen as a triumph of the "whole art of visualization over that of literature."[75] The Reverend John Snyder produced his melodramatic Cape Cod Drama, *As Ye Sow,* for World Film

Pictures in 1915, but it did not garner the attention that other films had achieved.[76]

Pathe presented *Christus* and twenty one-reel subjects in their *Pilgrimage to Palestine* (1925), starting with *Bethlehem* and *Nazareth*.[77] The Shubert exhibition circuit took Pathe's film, *The Life of Our Saviour* (curiously advertised as produced by "neither progressive America[n] or the advanced religious thought of Protestant Europe but rather the conservative Greek Oriental Church of Rumania") and rented it during the 1914 Easter season.[78] Biblical films could even be marketed according to a variety of genres. The Reverend Dr. William Carter found tragic and comic elements in various photoplay scenarios drawn from the Bible:

> What could be more dramatic than Elijah on Mr. Carmel with the 450 of the prophets of Baal, waiting for God's answer by fire to show the true from the false? What could be more thrilling than Jezebel being thrown from a window to the dogs below for her wicked and licentious folly? What could be funnier than Balaam's ass turning to tell his master to "go fast," or Eutychus falling asleep when Paul preached too long a sermon, and falling out of a three-story window, thereby breaking up the sermon and the congregation at the same time?[79]

Others commentators were not so kind about religious pictures made by secular organizations. The *Los Angeles Examiner* lambasted *The Life of Our Saviour* as an "atrocious vulgarity," commenting that its angels were represented by girls "who would be appropriate to an Amazon march in a burlesque" and that Heaven itself was "pictured[with the tawdry stage women posing as triumphant angels blowing trumpets of praise." To the *Los Angeles Examiner,* the Delsartean gestures and theatrical poses made this the most "inexpressibly shocking and repellent" picture.[80] Writing in the *New Republic* about DeMille's *King of Kings,* critic Gilbert Seldes complained that all the great scenes were mere static reproductions of famous paintings. Everything was treated "as painting composition—and nothing as cinema, as moving pictures." A movie should move.[81]

In contrast, critic W. Stephen Bush affirmed his faith in an imminent and profitable market for films of a purely general religious character and approved of film exchanges becoming part of the working force of most churches. The one necessary criterion for Bush was that the films be nonsectarian; otherwise "the Catholic portion of an audience would feel offended at any special glorification of Protestantism, and the Protestants have an equal right to resent an obtrusive flattery of Catholic ideas. The Jews again would have a right to feel aggrieved over a film comparing their religion unfavorably with that of the Christians."[82] When an industry film was too sectarian, like the Roman Catholic story of a monk in *The Broken Vows* (1911), Bush argued for a more balanced and ecumenical representation of religion. According to Bush, "common sense and common tact would seem to forbid the preaching of sectarian morals on the screen of a moving picture house."[83]

Several churches seriously questioned the target audiences of Better Pictures, with some religious groups even faulting films dealing with the Bible. About to release the fifty-two reel pictures of the Bible land made under the auspices of the Reverend Dr. J. E. Russell, Fred Warren of the America Releasing Corporation convened a meeting to discuss the series' reception. One well-known rabbi, Dr. Silverman, objected to the project on the basis that whatever subject was selected from the Bible, the theology of one sect or another would be favored, which this would offend dissenters. Supported by dignitaries like Reisner and the Catholic Actors Guild, Warren countered that these were not staged scenes but merely travelogue subjects, depicting matters of historical interest: scenes of camels, gardens, or Hebrew customs were simply scenes of camels, gardens, and Hebrew customs.[84]

Such concerns underlay two competing conceptions of the use of Better Pictures by churches. On the one hand, some advocated the use of generic feature motion pictures not produced directly for church use, but identified and recommended as appropriate products by the Hollywood industry. On the other hand, some argued that the church should revive the production of overtly religious motion pictures especially scripted and prepared for the church. Carl Milliken differentiated these two views by contrasting the commercial man who invests in Hollywood's pictures and the "churchman who would like to see the motion picture devoted exclusively to the services of religion."[85] Within the Hollywood industry, religious melodramatic stories dotted the cinematic landscape of the twenties and found a particularly sentimental resonance with church—audiencessuggesting a subterranean tension between popular images of the commercial pursuit of jazz-age pleasures and the haunting spiritual tales of religious and moral judgment that would follow such futile pursuits. From this group of Hollywood products, ministers like Frederic Fay from South Congregational Church in New Britain, Connecticut, used popular films like First National's *Idle Tongues,* Griffith's *Isn't Life Wonderful,* and Vitagraph Studio's version of Harold Bell Wright's *The Mine with the Iron Door* to his great satisfaction in teaching moral truth.[86] Also from Hollywood, obvious religious blockbusters like Fred Niblo's *Ben Hur* and Cecil B. DeMille's *Ten Commandments* and *King of Kings* overshadowed numerous other religious releases such as *Dante's Inferno,* D. W. Griffith's *The Greatest Question,* Michael Curtiz's *Noah's Ark,* and other tales which explicitly pointed to the wages of sin and the blessings of goodness, which usually included romantic as well as material success.

Cecil B. DeMille's classic *King of Kings* (1927) appealed to almost everyone.[87] Financed by New York philanthropist Jeremiah Milbank's Cinema Corporation of America, it enjoyed worldwide distribution. The blockbuster film illustrated familiar Bible stories, incorporated numerous hymns in its presentation, and washed away many fears of religious films. Its impact proved monumental, even evoking viewer responses, as many testified that they saw the face of H. B. Warner (DeMille's actor playing Jesus) whenever they prayed.

A thirteen-reel series entitled *I Am the Way,* made by the Harmon Foundation from reedited and unused portions of DeMille's film, composed a category known as "Religion and Life" that proved to be the top rental for churches.[88] *Christian Herald* writer Gretta Palmer identified *King of Kings* as Hollywood's most far-reaching success, noting that thousands of 16-millimeter versions (in Chinese, Turkish, Arabic, Hebrew, and Hindustani) had been distributed to missionaries around the globe. "In our Southern mountains, the Paulist Fathers have shown *King of Kings* to audiences who have seen no other picture. Three missionaries in India still replace their old prints every three years." Palmer cited Alexander Wolcott's classic review predicting that "It is my guess that *The King of Kings* will girdle the globe and that the multitude will still be flocking to see it in 1947," and concluded that he was right.[89]

Artistically it did not matter that DeMille's theology was a bit fuzzy, a sort of nebulous liberal Protestant humanism: "Whether one believes that Jesus was a divine being who descended into humanity or a human being who rose to divinity," he said, "it is not after all tremendously important in view of the fact that His ideals apply to us all."[90] *The King of Kings,* like a Shroud of Hollywood, allowed viewers to project whatever theological significance they wished upon the silent images. Nevertheless, missionary bodies felt that such biblical films needed to be exhibited overseas in order to counteract what they felt were the corrupting effects of Hollywood's other movies. Dr. Charles Gilkey, pastor of Hyde Park Baptist Church in Chicago, told attendees at the scholarly Fourth National Motion Picture Conference meeting in February 1926 that on his recent visit to the orient, he had "learned that the motion pictures in the orient were misrepresenting American ideals, thus prejudicing foreign people against our country." (At the same conference Judge Lindsey of Denver said that there were more incentives to misdirected passion and immorality in the *Song of Solomon* than in all the motion pictures ever produced. "And more girls have been led astray on their way home from Sunday school than in 4,000,000 cinema palaces.")[91] Based on questionnaires to several hundred students in India, however, one study did argue that Hollywood's films had a relatively small influence on Hindus who lived in villages, away from larger urban centers.[92]

Hollywood industries invaded the religious world with campaigns to promote their own products. Paramount Studios threw the gauntlet of motion picture quality back at the churches, announcing, "The Screen Will Be What YOU Make It."[93] At the same time, director Cecil B. DeMille chastised the church for its lack of global vision in using film as a universal language, presumably thinking that he could make still more money from *King of Kings*.

> Pictures are the greatest factor in the world for uniting the races and the nations. Pictures speak an international language that everybody can understand. Say a Japanese jingo goes in to see an American picture. He sees a mother with a poor sick baby. An American doctor is trying to help her. His heart warms to that picture, and he says, 'After all these Americans are not half bad!' You church people are always talking about the international mind. The pictures are the strongest medium to produce that international mind."[94]

Films dealing with American religious history also attracted church exhibitors. One special conflation of religion and patriotism occurred in Yale University's research and development of the aforementioned dramatic religious history of America in its *Chronicles of America,* especially in episodes with a distinct spiritual message dealing with the Pilgrims and the Puritans.[95] Because Producer Macalarney saw little merit in making only one or two pictures, he decided to produce a series of thirty-six subjects on his *Chronicles of America,* of which only fifteen (or forty-eight reels) were realized. His scheduled budget kept to about $12.50 a foot of film, but he found himself in the inevitable position of being torn between vexations from within and unscrupulous preying harpies from without. MacAlarney undertook the challenge coordinating basic history requirements with the content of the films, with Yale's Department of Education pressuring him into developing reports on how to use the films. In the Lynd studies of Middletown, the series had such poor attendance that exhibitors swore "Never again!" for such educational films.[96] Various field studies in local high and middle schools resulted in the 1929 publication of *Motion Pictures in History Teaching* by Daniel Knowlton and Warren Tilton.[97] Other academics also proved to be busybodies in the production of such an acclaimed series, and not only in terms of historical accuracy. As the shooting was delayed while experts debated costumes or cabin equipment, decorative moldings out of period, or the wrong regimental buttons, other problems were more vexing. The casting director was required to get his cast approved by professors untrained in film. In an effort to allow for outdoor shooting, MacAlarney tried to rebuild the famous Jamestown settlement, but raw and frigid weather frustrated his creativity as one of the players, "pretending to be an Indian and half-naked, developed pneumonia and died." Joining with the Film Guild, with an independent photographing unit headed by Fred Waller, the Chronicles contracted Frank Tuttle, former head of the Dramatic Society at Yale (and subsequently assistant editor at *Vanity Fair*) to direct the episodes. Although Tuttle tried to make the films theatrical, the end result resembled so many slow, pedantic history lessons. An official who reviewed the films later conceded, "We are, of course, the first to recognize that their entertainment appeal is low—actually has been since the beginning, when action was purposely held to a minimum."[98]

As far as content choices, however, church exhibitors ignored the Yale University Press series of historical films, noted for being dull failures, and opted for Hollywood films. In their study of Middletown, the Lynds observed that among the Protestant middle class "Harold Lloyd comedies draw the largest crowds."[99] Certain "recommended" films, like William Fox's *Evangeline* or Griffith's *Broken Blossoms,* could be praised as jewels without price. The recommendations reflected a triumph of subjective spirituality. In Griffith's sentimental melodrama, for example, congregations were directed to understand that "under a yellow man's heathen skin may repose a white man's Christian soul." For educational film critics like Dolph Eastman, such works of art evocatively conveyed what he viewed as *spirituality* "in the sobering spirit of love and faith and loyalty and self-forgetfulness; but [*Evangeline*] goes even beyond this—it vivifies and vitalizes a creative work of art."[100]

The educators, professionals, and critics worked hard to infiltrate church markets, or at least to influence congregations to believe that film-makers and churches shared a similar vision, particularly in helping the poor. After promoting Shields's film, *The Stream of Life*, critic Gladys Bollman reviewed what she labeled as "sociological lecture" films. One film in particular, *Who's Your Brother*, produced by Curtiss Pictures, dealt with ministry to the poor in the city's slums. However, Bollman lavished most of her praise on the striking Mayflower Films secular produc-tion, *The Miracle Man*. Bollman pointed out that both these two films were "for (and possibly by) social workers and churchgoers," but the lat-ter appealed to a greater audience in the habitual moviegoer.[101]

In the *Moving Picture World*, Benjamin Prager, president of Mayflower Photoplay Corporation, echoed Bollman's sentiment. He first noted that any strong prejudice harbored by producers against pictures dealing with or touching upon religious themes "is rapidly disappearing under the weight of accumulating proof of public response to entertainment of this type." The public reception in the early 1920s to photoplays dealing with religious subjects (e.g., *The Miracle Man*, *Earthbound*, and *The Right of Way*) seemed unquestionably warm and positive. To substantiate his as-sertion, Prager listed a host of productions such as George Loane Tucker's *I Believe*, Winston Churchill's *The Dwelling Place of Light*, William Christy Cabanne's *The Stealers*, William Allen White's *In the Heart of a Fool*, the Vitagraph productions of *The White Sister* and *The Rosary*, and scores of pictures of similar character, all which centered on religious themes. (By religious picture, Prager meant one that derived its drama from "some broad principle of religion to which all systems subscribe, such as belief in the Divine Power, piety and morality," and not from "palpable ef-forts at preachment nor the dramatization of a sectarian creed.")

Prager saw a twofold purpose in this trend of religion in film that would ameliorate the art of the photoplay. First, it would remind the clergy that screen entertainment offered a significant means of moral teaching. Second, it would instruct producers who believed that all pic-tures should be mere entertainment and feared that any picture with a re-ligious thought was solely a sermon. Prager believed that

> For a long time, producers—with a few exceptions—have been utterly unable to reconcile religion with entertainment. They have held to the

belief that a religious play can have but a very limited appeal. Billy Sunday dispenses religion. Yet is his audience confined to Methodists? No, people of all sects and creeds jostle and elbow their way into an auditorium to hear him. He mixes religion with entertainment without distorting values. He preaches to you and makes you like it. Whether or not you believe in his doctrines you are impressed by what he says.

Prager argued that watching skillfully handled religious pictures could have the same effect as hearing a dynamic Billy Sunday sermon; for Prager, one photoplay that combined this religious recreative power with uplift, artistry, and financial success was George Loane Tucker's *The Miracle Man*. For Prager, it revealed the power of faith, the basis of all religion, and in its revelation enthralled a nation and gave it a deeper understanding of the spiritual forces that govern life. The film itself reaped a bumper crop of conspicuously religious themes, sparking a vogue that Prager hoped would endure. Prager argued that if the motion picture industry was to progress as an institution, religious pictures, not mere vapid sentiment and airy romances, nor mere pageantry and magnificent spectacles, must be made. The industry was vitally in need of substantial, nutritious fare if it wished to grow. With quixotic optimism, he concluded,

> By turning our attention to stories of a religious mould, we will of necessity improve standards of production, for sacred themes cannot be entrusted to the care of hacks and slip-shod workmen who would but degrade them with mawkish sentiment and stifle with convention. We will develop a new order of motion picture genius who will measure up to the task of bringing to the screen inspired dramatizations of life's most poignant theme—religion.[102]

In the early twenties, the fanfare surrounding several professional theatrical religious pictures encouraged church leaders seeking quality films. Several films were produced in conjunction with Hollywood studios, while independent investors underwrote others. A 1924 remake of the 1911 film, *The Ninety and Nine*, concerned a drunken son, a pitiful representative product of Harvard University, who got a job on a sheep farm where he sobered up, then was rediscovered by and reunited with his Victorian patriarch. It was praised as a powerful religious picture whose theme resembled the parable of the lost lamb.[103] Director Hall Caine's controversial *The Christian* advertised itself explicitly in its title.[104] In a similar attempt to restore respect for the name of the Deity, the Catholic Art Association, in conjunction with the newly organized Religious Film Association (RFA), produced a nonsectarian moral film, *The Blasphemer* (1921), and promoted it in a nationwide campaign.[105] This drama portrayed a self-made financier who bragged that he was master of his fate at a celebration dinner; such defiance ultimately led to the loss of everything he had, which in turn finally led him to repent and return to his childhood faith. Viewed as a well-crafted and engrossing spiritual drama, *The Blasphemer* sought to vividly dramatize the Second Commandment "Thou Shalt Not Take the Name of the Lord Thy God in Vain," explicitly attacking the pride and greed of wealthy American businessmen.[106] Like previous defenders of the religious icon as a visual sermon, such images had the potential not only to teach those who couldn't read, but also to arouse sluggish emotions and lead people to follow a moral path.

As we have seen, however, several key obstacles still blocked the progress of movies in the church. First and foremost was the lack of religious and biblical subjects. By 1917, *Motion Picture World* had published a list of only forty-five Bible stories produced in film.[107] Two years later, an ample supply was released to churches, parish houses, settlements, missions, and similar institutions; what was desperately needed was a system of film libraries for churches. Two production companies, Pathe brothers, who had pioneered the Life of Christ reels, and the Kalem Company, whose *From the Manger to the Cross* stood as the biblical standard, were viewed as key suppliers.[108] Famous Players-Lasky saw the handwriting on a Methodist wall and jumped into the market with its educational department, Community Screen Productions/Community Motion Picture Bureau, which served as a national clearing house and guide for ministers, Sunday school superintendents, and social workers. Screen Entertainment Distributors announced that they would offer films suitable for church entertainment. Charles Stanley Jones identified over a hundred suitable films for church use, highlighting *The Shepherd King*, taken from the stage play and photographed in the Holy Land.[109]

Concerned churchman B. F. Wahlstad also tackled the problem of a shortage of material for church pictures, explaining that the problem was that no adequate channels of distribution could be found. Many churches were chagrined and disheartened by the lack of help and direction. Acknowledging as well the entirely unsatisfactory revenue secured from religious productions, religious educator James Kelly suggested distributing one "locked-reel" to churches a week, especially as the demand exceeded the supply. He envisioned a film corporation created for the express purpose of furnishing films for churches—a corporation that would have "its own scenario writers, its own studios and its own distribution agencies all over the country, transporting new reels every week."[110] An additional obstacle included the inadequate apparatus operated by the churches, arguably the largest users of nontheatrical film. Church film users labored "under the disadvantage of having poor lanterns and indifferent screens; they have no license to sell tickets, as a rule; they wish a full set of reels for one night only; the console of the organ is rarely placed so as to give an organist a chance to adapt the music to the scene."[111]

A final obstacle focused on the simmering criticism emanating from religious leaders like Dr. Charles F. Aked, who saw a decay of the American church tied inextricably to the uncritical exhibition of sensational moving pictures used to attract people to religious services. The films shown were not religious at all.[112] The Reverend Roy Smith rejected films with thrills and pleaded for a supply of strictly biblical material from producers like the International Church Film Corporation, Vitagraph, and the Educational Film Company.[113] Smith requested films that appealed to the conscience—pictures that would form the basis for a "sermonette." Pictures could not, he argued, be relied upon to deliver the message or compel personal decisions from guests in the church; rather, they built "atmosphere" and furnished illustrative material. Smith defended a constructive use of movies in his *Sentence Sermons,* a publication of five hundred humorous and philosophical illustrations. In it, he explained that

> *The Movies Are Not—*
> To blame for all the failures of youth.
> As racy as the advertising would lead you to believe.
> The solitary candidates for censorship.
> Going to improve so long as the public is satisfied.
> Worried about an excess of good scenarios.
> Apt to lose popularity because of too much real artistry.
> Failing because of the lack of frank criticism.[114]

According to Smith, church leaders who knew the right pictures to use would counterbalance such misleading and erroneous assumptions. The old iconoclastic controversy had evolved into a moving picture debate over the content of decent and worthy films.

On the subject of whether there were suitable films, the *Congregationalist* offered remarkably balanced views. More in line with John Calvin and Martin Luther, Congregational pastor Caleb Justice acknowledged that not all films recommended by distributors were fit for church use. Using an allegory from John Bunyan's *Pilgrim's Progress* in which various armies assaulted the gates of the City of Mansoul, Justice warned viewers about what he saw as the most vulnerable of all the senses, namely, the Eye Gate; all manner of vile sights could come through the eye. With a Reformed affirmation of the Word of God as superior to images, Justice explained, "No matter how illustrative of religious truth a motion picture may be, it seldom can take the place of the oral sermon." For Justice, pictures could be an integral part of the message, but the sermon must dominate the picture. Justice pointed to a suspect film, *Father Tom,* as a mischievous example. In this feature, a genial kindly clergyman succumbs to the temptation to race his horse for the good of the church. Justice argued that a picture such as this was not redeemed just because it portrayed a few scenes from the Bible or quoted God. So, too, he raised a wry eyebrow at *The Woman God Changed.* In this photoplay of a very questionable conversion story, a society belle vindictively killed her prodigal husband and was then wrecked on a desert island with her lover, whom she married "à la mode de la Nature." Finally, after five reels of a sensuous and worldly life, she decided, in the last half reel, to repent and start anew. Justice averred: "You cannot convert a bad feature by a sanctimonious flash." For Justice, there were appropriate and inappropriate images for religious use.

Justice did recommend director Robert J. Flaherty's staged documentary film, *Nanook of the North* as a powerful visual sermon on how to endure hardships as a good soldier of Jesus Christ, allegorizing the physical difficulties of life in a hostile environment translated in terms of the Kingdom of God.[115] He also lauded *The Turn in the Road.* Inspired by Basil King's book, *Conquest of Fear,* the film portrays a young widower who suffered Joblike comforters who told him that his wife's death was the will of God and that he must submit to that will. Believing such a God to be horrible and vindictive, he chose to become a wanderer. In platitudinous biblical fashion, a little child led him and showed him the way back to life, reciting a Sunday school lesson in which light comes in through the shutters to scatter the darkness away. The film highlights how God becomes the widower's refuge and strength, a very present help in trouble. (Throughout this silent film, hymns were sung, such as "Jesus,

Savior, pilot me over life's tempestuous sea" and "Abide with me," ending with "All Hail the Power of Jesus' Name," all of which made for a full religious service, except for the offering plate.)

In the same issue of the *Congregationalist,* Elisha King touted films from the American Motion Picture Corporation.[116] William Foster, a Christian layman overseeing the nontheatrical American Motion Picture Corporation, claimed that films like *Eyes That Are Opened* actually reclaimed drunkards, quickened consciences, convicted sinners of sin, standardized Christian social theory and practice, and presented crystallized arguments for the social Gospel.[117] According to Foster, the film accomplished a work worthy of God Himself. Writer Oscar Mehus, with more modest praise, approved a list of wholesome entertainment that included Yale University's historical film series, *Nanook of the North,* and *Human Wreckage,* a gripping story against the "dope evil" that proved more effective than any sermon.[118]

In 1924, at South New Britain, Connecticut, the Reverend G. W. C. Hill preached a series of Lenten sermons on "Where the Trail Begins." Using film clips from *The Miracle Man, Message from Mars, Tol'able David,* and *The Maker of Men,* Hill marshaled sermons on a cure for selfishness, the triumph of aspiration, the triumph of truth, and voluntary sacrifice.[119] But other films could provoke controversial splits among church congregations. *Inside of the Cup* exposed hypocrisy in high religious places and thus stirred strong passions for and against it.[120]

In light of a growing unease about movies in general in the mid-twenties, a 1927 issue of the *Congregationalist* decided it was time to revisit old concerns about the moving pictures. The periodical devoted itself completely to reevaluating motion pictures in the church, investigating particular films and the state of the church in using films. Returning to the forefront after a long silence, the Reverend Herbert Jump reissued a challenge to his fellow religious leaders. He had been coordinating religious services with university students in Ann Arbor, Michigan, and found it inconceivable that films were still not utilized to their fullness in ecclesiastical settings. He inquired, "If it is orthodox for a sermon to enter the head through two side doors, the ears, what objection is there to its entering the head by two front doors, the eyes?"[121]

As we have seen, by the mid-1920s, even though some church leaders persisted in believing that churches could produce their own celluloid sermons and that Hollywood had responded to their demands for better religious films, the Sanctuary Cinema movement had peaked. Throughout the previous decade the vision had been cast and appropriated by churches of all denominations; yet religious institutions had fallen short in conceiving and underwriting their own creative products. Various bureaus and exchanges had been set up and Protestant denominations and the Roman Catholic Church sponsored films for in-house use, and even the one last noble attempt at the end of the era, the prestigious Harmon Foundation experiment with a vertically integrated project, had withered and wilted. Then unexpectedly, for those marketing the snake oil of the brazen serpent, a groundbreaking technological invention burst upon the scene. Warner Bros. Studio introduced sound. The era of silent film was over. No longer could churches afford to make movies or often to even exhibit them. During the next decades, churches would instead channel their resources into radio ministries and express their aesthetic vision in architecture as they built new edifices for worship. For over two decades, moving pictures would wane in churches as a positive option for religious communication; in Hollywood, however, moving pictures would be transformed into a rival religion.

Conclusion
Film as Religion

If Christ went to the "movies"—He would approve.

Rev. Percy Stickney Grant[1]

By the late 1920s Hollywood executives were well aware of the religious milieu in which they sold their products; nevertheless they remained generally ignorant or dismissive of the theological and moral concerns of the Roman Catholic and Protestant constituency. In an apocryphal story told by biographer Bob Thomas about Columbia Studio's legendary Cohn brothers, the two producers debated the prospect of making a religious film. Harry challenged his brother Jack, claiming that he knew nothing about religion:

"What the hell do you know about the Bible, Jack? I'll bet you fifty bucks you don't even know the Lord's Prayer," said Harry.

"Oh, yes I do," boasted Jack.

"Well then, let's hear it," prodded his brother.

Jack started: "Now I lay me down to sleep . . ."

"Okay, okay," conceded Harry. "You win," and handed over the fifty bucks.[2]

From the late 1920s to about 1944, when Bing Crosby merrily sang in *Going My Way,* major Hollywood studios avoided overtly religious themes, with the well-publicized exception of Cecil B. DeMille. During this time religion was generally not taken seriously when Hollywood did incorporate it. When critic Herbert Corey lambasted films in the mid-twenties, he mockingly characterized the male actors as "apple dumplings," the girls as pretty, curvy "movines," and the average writer-director as "a 90-year-old moron who had been missing his sleep." The movies' only redeeming quality, he quipped, was that "the audiences all laugh at the holiest movie moments."[3] On June 13, 1934, the Production Code Administration set regulatory guidelines governing the production of all movies and warned filmmakers not to show any disrespect to religion or ridicule the clergy. Religion was off limits. Humorist Alva Johnston derided any code that forbade satirizing clergy as "an absurd invasion of the rights of churchmen who are as much entitled as any others to the moral tonic and wholesome discipline of satire." Johnston mocked another prescription requiring that constituted authorities and the rule of law must always triumph over law-breakers in the movies, "a rule which would require the director to throw the sympathy with the lions as against the Christians in *Ben Hur*."[4]

Laughter at the holy moments was both symptomatic and symbolic of the church's ultimate lack of success with movies at the end of the silent film era. As we have seen, the potential for the religious use and possibilities of the motion picture and the realization of the dream of a vibrant church market were inadequately achieved. Questions raised by the ambivalent relationship of Christianity to the icon-image and to the theater continued to frame the churches' posture toward film. Inquiries such as "What is a graven image?" "How can an icon provide a book for the illiterate?" or Tertullian's "What has Jerusalem to do with Athens?" helped to shape the responses of religious artists and critics in appropriating media for social, ecclesiastical, and spiritual uses. The church had hoped that experiments with the magic lantern, lanternslides, and stereopticons would help the Lord's servants promote the new media of the moving picture. However, the dramatic narratives of both evangelical novels and religious paintings that served as models for what a Christian film could become, led instead to an endless debate on whether this modern instrument of visual communication supported or subverted the mission of the church.

The church's ambivalent relation to the moving picture reflected the uncertain and schizophrenic connection the church had to modernity itself. With the enlightened emergence of science, technology, urbanization, and industrialization, the spirit of modernity reigned over the realms of the motion picture industry. In investigating the interactions between modernity and melodrama, film scholar Ben Singer identified modernity as a mode of social life marked by democratic instincts, secularity, and late capitalism with a litany of socioeconomic conditions, particularly the explosion of forms of mass communication and mass entertainments such as modern cinema, characterized by its individualism and sensory stimulation.[5] Other scholars have explained that modernity was best understood as "inherently cinematic" and have proposed cultural links to industry and technology beyond the traditional precursors of theater and novel.[6] For religious audiences, these two classic connections helped to make sense of cinema's acceptability and usefulness within the confines of the church. Modernity, no doubt, brought a change in religious experience and perspective, opening up new landscapes in which one lived and moved in the realm of technology, akin to riding the railroad. Like the railroad, cinema was a window to the world, shaping the way that spectators saw life as it moved along the tracks or through the projector.[7] Some have argued that modernity became hegemonic through technological innovations like the *motion* picture.

Modernity, in theological terms, entailed what conservatives viewed as a slipping trend toward secularity, higher criticism with its overemphasis on human rationality, and doctrinal and moral license. Modernist ministers like Harry Emerson Fosdick of the Riverside Church in New York City questioned and challenged doctrines such as original sin, the Virgin birth, and the Resurrection, while conservatives like Gresham Machen adamantly averred the "fundamental" tenets of the faith. The acceptance and subsequent rejection of films by various Christian groups parallel their ambivalent, even cyclical, relationships to iconography and theater. The conservative church's embrace of secular—or, for some, pagan—cultural conditions led to a spiritual wrestling with a perceived entanglement with the world. However, while many conservative churches opted to adapt defensive positions vis-à-vis Hollywood films, they adopted the cinematic apparatus for their own missions. Among both liberal and evangelical groups, films functioned as a handmaiden to their preaching and teaching.

For churches the root problem with modernity was the problem of secularity, in its multiple manifestations. Secularity connoted the twin vices of sexual immorality and excessive violence. These were the warts of the Hollywood body of films in the late 1920s. Film itself remained a neutral medium, much as rhetoric had for St. Augustine, and Christians could accept the technology without the secular content.

Cinema, like other potential idolatries and cults of modernity, promised utopian states to its adherents, and even churchmen boasted that it could help usher in the millennium. Likewise, for rhapsodic religious poet Vachel Lindsay, film would help "Americanize" the world through its visual "hieroglyphics."[8] Pioneer filmmaker D. W. Griffith saw in silent cinema the imminent epiphany of a "universal language," uniting its global spectators even as it enabled filmmakers to create narratives that could end intolerance. Herbert Martin, professor of philosophy at the University of Iowa, echoed Griffith's sentiment, writing: "The dispersion of tongues at Babel, with its consequent and cumulative alienations, has been annulled in the one language of the cinema, known and read by all men."[9] Martin pointed out that the line of divine visual language had gone out unto the whole earth, and, as the psalmist sang, "There is no place where it is not heard," from the Congo to Cambridge. Film historian Miriam Hansen sees in this and other early utopian visions a conflation of the Babylonian motif with the totalizing tower of Babel, a conflation that highlights the tension between "cinema's role as a universalizing, ideological idiom and its redemptive possibilities as an inclusive, heterogeneous, and at times unpredictable horizon of experience."[10] As the utopian vision held, film could be viewed as a savior; it could unite the world. And if it had such influence, was the church not right to try and develop its potential?

Pioneering leaders like the Reverend Herbert Jump, scriptwriter James Shields, and the editors of the *Christian Herald* envisioned immense opportunities in exploiting the motion picture; yet the vision was neither sustained nor sufficiently funded during the early years of the silent film period. At the end of the period, the transitional Harmon Foundation had tested whether church ventures into film production were feasible. Dismayed at the disappointing prospects, it surrendered to the inevitable economic constraints and eventually handed over the reins to other interested groups. After this, some church leaders allowed the production of appropriate films to slide back to the Hollywood professionals in their movie studios, even though they proclaimed the continued importance of church films to counter the effects of the Hollywood product. Chester Marshall, for example, praised DeMille's *Ten Commandments* as the "finest and most deeply spiritual motion picture ever filmed . . . [where] God has rarely been more real to us than he was for the space of one afternoon."[11] If the professionals could communicate spiritual truth so effectively, why should the church get involved? This question was especially pertinent if the church produced merely pious, moral films. George Bernard Shaw had quipped, "The movie play has supplanted the old-fashioned tract and Sunday-school prize: it is reeking with morality but dares not touch virtue." Likewise, an article in *Church Management* put the issue in a similarly jaded perspective: "Pious pictures are something like pious books. Everybody recommends them to their children, but no one likes to read them."[12]

In this book, several themes have emerged as critical to an understanding of the genesis of the Christian film industry. The multifaceted historical relations between the image-icon, the theater, and the church laid the foundations for the debates about cinema as a means of effective religious communication, while the spiritual art of the Hudson River painters and the economic phenomenon of the evangelical novel at the end of the nineteenth century provided narrative paradigms for a religious cinema. Finally, and most importantly, church bodies took an active role in exhibiting, producing, and utilizing films for their own religious goals, to their ultimate disappointment.

Paradoxically, the theatrical image possessed the potential of aiding the work of the church, but carried equal potential as a rival. Historically the church had alternately characterized the invention and expansion of the arts as interloper, competitor, and handmaiden. Many visionaries have believed that the teachings of the church could be renewed if it became culturally relevant and adapted new technologies.[13] For some religious leaders of the early twentieth century, film could still assume a prophetic mantle, or at least expose social ills and injustice. The *Christian Herald* went so far as to compare film to the prophet Elijah, who "found out" King Ahab and demonstrated that the wicked king could not keep his sin a secret. The *Christian Herald* pointed to the revelatory role of a particular film in exposing evil, as in a smoke-abatement campaign in St. Louis:

> Householders have denied that their chimneys were pouring out black smoke until confronted with moving pictures of their chimneys in continuous action. Sin hates publicity; and it would be well, before yielding to any sin, to think of the moving pictures of the recording angel which are continually taken of our deeds and words and even of our thoughts and feelings.[14]

In such cases of film use, the church's vision of preaching the Gospel or helping the needy through film proved worthy, even if in other cases, the church witnessed the abandonment of God and the selling of His image to the image makers in the marketplace of film culture, where congregants were reconstituted as consumers.[15] Over the course of the church's early forays into film, the church assimilated this cultural innovation as a tactic for accomplishing noble aims, refusing to become marginalized by the milieu of social and technological progress. Churches did not hide from progress, but rather investigated, tinkered with, embraced, and adopted film technology. In this visionary spirit, many church leaders sought to engage the changing cultural apparatus and to implement its emerging technologies for their own ends. Yet the church chose not to invest sufficiently in the material culture in which it found itself embedded. This was one of the most salient causes for film's ultimate failure to establish a religious foothold. While pressing its cause in exhibition, even to a point of worrying exhibitors, the church's persistent hesitation to invest financially in film production and distribution kept it on the periphery of success.

The New Cinematic Religion

The cultural diffusion of films within churches accelerated a transfer of spiritual authority from a Protestant biblical base to what Robert Bellah has labeled a "civil religion," a fervent belief in patriotism and a God-ordained manifest destiny. God wants all men and women to be American heroes and heroines.[16] The reward of virtue and punishment of vice were the ethical foundations of a faith that believed in a manifest destiny of the American dream—a dream in which one could be captain of one's fate, the blueprint for the classical Hollywood narrative paradigm. This civil religion expressed in and through the technology of film replaced traditional orthodoxy; it performed the alchemist's goals of manufacturing golden dreams and achieving a sort of immortality, even if simulated and illusory, and came to replace the traditional Protestantism in cultural hegemony. In 1922, the president of Occidental College, Dr. Remsen Dubois Bird, noted the failure of America's three foundational institutions, namely, the church, the home, and the school, to contribute to society. Then he drew a contrast, shocking for his day: where the church had been marked by petty bickering, the cinema now provided a "binding force" for families and educated children better than did many schools. The movies were not merely handmaidens for uplift, but had now become a savoir for society.[17] The sassy, cheeky servants of culture had become the masters; or, as Cardinal Newman warned with regards to the arts as handmaidens, these special attendants of religion were "very apt to forget their place."[18]

The damage had been incremental. Not only had the technology been sanctified by its inclusion in the churches, creating a wedge that opened up Sunday showings, but the "religious content" of the cinematic images had also been slowly altered. These images were no longer simply perceived as religious but, as sociologist Emile Durkheim observed about religion itself, these images were equally and "eminently social." In his view, the former gods of formal religion had grown "old or dying" and made way for new public, popular gods.[19] The images of the new gods were not merely private, dispassionate, and contemplative, but they also contributed significantly to and were influential in the making of meaning in everyday life. The new idols advised courses of action from fashion to racial ethics and instructed the ways one should act through mimesis, setting models of romance and of social habits like smoking and drinking. Walt Whitman's sweet, poetic portrait of a child's education took on a new, darker significance:

> There was a child went forth every day,
> And the first object he'd looked upon, that object he became
> And that object became part of him for the day or a certain part of
> the day
> Or for many years or stretching cycles of years.

Children were now gazing upon cinema. It was assumed that youth could be educated through the visual media of moving pictures, both in the religious as well as the moral dimension. By 1933, Ohio State University professor W. W. Charters, Chair of the Payne Fund Studies on *Motion Pictures and Youth*, reported that a research group of psychologists and educators from universities like Chicago and Yale had produced data on numerous effects of films upon youth, but could not determine a scale of relative influence against other agencies such as the home, school, or church.[20] They did confirm that children remembered 90 percent of what they saw on the day following a viewing, and that the memory endured for months, echoing Pope Gregory's observation that people remember what they see more readily than what they hear. The young children, the research confirmed, were also emotionally "possessed by the drama."[21] However, religion communicated through the movies had an ephemeral effect. Ohio State University professor of education, Henry James For-man, likewise affirmed that the drama of moving pictures could be of enormous service to education, but was apt to dissipate. His summary of the Payne Fund studies on educational research and film, while a bit skewed, found that even the powerful influence of films like *Ben Hur* or *King of Kings* did not endure for long. He quoted one boy who had seen *Ben Hur* three times. At first, the boy wanted to live an "unselfish, self-sacrificing life," but he found that this ambition lasted only a couple of weeks, adding: "I have gradually lapsed back into normal again."[22] The impact of moving pictures on youth had yet to be fully determined; how-ever, in the public imagination, the effects were decisive: the movies would shape the malleable minds of children in the mold of the secular world.

The same emerging dominance of the secular appeared to have conta-minated the progressive wing of the American church as well. A self-de-scribed "broad-minded churchman," the Reverend Dr. Percy Stickney Grant believed that visual images would supplant "pen and word pic-tures." His faith in the value of the photoplay altered the traditional con-ception of Christ himself into a white, middle-class American Jesus. Grant argued that if Christ went to the movies, "He would approve," for "Christ approves of anything that makes for the happiness of mankind; anything that lifts the minds of His people to a higher plane, to anything that refreshes and interests them after a day's hard grind."[23] For Grant and other liberals, movies were the new gospel pouring out a therapeutic tonic that would "clear out the cobwebs of the mind . . . and the un-healthful fantasies of the brain." Where Jesus once taught in parables, now the pictures themselves became the modern parables of an optimistic and progressive generation. In contrast to Jesus' preaching a need for di-vine help, American movies in particular emphasized self-help and indi-vidualism.

Historian David Bordwell and others demonstrated that the myth of the independent protagonist overcoming obstacles by sheer personal grit or talent or pluck became the norm within the classic Hollywood narra-tive paradigm during this era.[24] This growing trend toward secularization was accelerated by Cecil B. DeMille, whose religious productions such as *The Ten Commandments* (1923) and *The King of Kings* (1927), were renowned for including sex, suds, and spectacle under the cloak of sanc-tity.[25] To the multitude that cried out, "We would see Jesus," DeMille's *King of Kings* ostensibly obliged, but with its own embellishments of the sacred narratives which were recast in secular terms.[26] The popular media borrowed the rhetoric and appeal of the church, and by so doing weaseled their way into the inner sanctum and then desecrated it. As media critic Quentin Schultze observed in his *Christianity and the Mass Media in America*, the "very media that would usher in the Kingdom of God on earth became the domain of mammon."[27]

When American religious leaders sought to claim a place for religious expression beyond the confines of the pulpit and pews, they frequently envisioned the film screen as offering such a public place, even if it were a simulated site.[28] What Pandora's Box this worship on unholy ground opened was investigated by quirky independent commentators like C. H. Jack Linn, who saw the movies as the "devil's incubator" and judged that they had transferred religious and moral authority from the pulpit to the screen. The great influence wielded by the moving picture aroused a spirit of inquisition among certain preachers.[29] These prophetic fundamentalist critics tried to account for the hypnotic spell of the technology to which a fascinated church had succumbed, surrendering its soul for a bowl of pragmatic success. In reaction to the growing suspicion, a judgmental attitude marked by technophobia emerged—an attitude of exclusivity and cultural sequestering. Cinema was a product of modernity, and conservative churches abhorred theological modernity. Fundamentalists stood firmly against the religious attitude that conflated social Darwinism, German higher criticism, a belief in the essential goodness of humans, and a denial of anything supernatural or miraculous in the Christian scriptures. And the modern technology of the screen continually reaffirmed the goodness of heroes and heroines and the possibility of man-made miracles.

Adding to the newly sacred stature of technology, modern miracles had been attributed to the medium.[30] Congregationalist writer George Anderson marveled at the miracle of Yankee ingenuity, noting that when a certain producer wished to represent the hosts of Israel crossing the Red Sea, he went with his apparatus to a "Long Island sand-bar" uncovered at low tide. He spent six hours of an ebb tide taking a few pictures every fifteen minutes. When the entire reel was displayed, it showed "a marvelous parting of the waters, true as Scripture!"[31]

Many, like poet Vachel Lindsey, attributed the miracle of temperance to the movies. According to supporters, saloons lost appeal on account of the attraction of an alternative wholesome entertainment in the moving picture. Apparently, movies made men sober, and worked even greater miracles. British psychologists in 1919 investigated the claim that "Films Make Girls Pretty," and discovered that "mental impressions unconsciously make faces more beautiful and film celebrities agree in indorsing [*sic*] the Cinematograph as a Beauty Doctor."[32] Stories of faith healing grew (corresponding to the rise of Christian Science in the Los Angeles community), with the production of films like Thanhouser's *The World and the Woman* (1916) and *The Miracle Man* (1921).[33] A spectacular event, reported by the *Los Angeles Times*, occurred when a moving picture miraculously restored speech to a little mute girl, Lillian Osterseizer—the "Miracle Maid of Temple Street." Dumb for eight years, she suddenly burst into speech while watching a dramatic movie. Her emotions had been so powerfully stirred that the film healed her of her infirmity, wrote the *Los Angeles Times*, declaring it a "miracle" that no one could deny.[34] The modern religion of the moving pictures could seemingly boast its own set of miracles, miracles that suited the modern civil religion of the cinema.

Civil Religion at the Movies

As we have seen, the drift from a verbal culture to a visual one at the turn of the century was marked by a change from Protestant cultural dominance to a new kinetic religion, namely, film. Cinematic piety differed significantly from traditional holiness. New stories, with progressive morals and visual rituals, were supplanting traditional stories. Through the emergence of a classic Hollywood narrative paradigm, which supplanted the more divinely inspired paradigms articulated by the Hudson River painters, a secular gospel of American ingenuity and self-help replaced an orthodox tradition of sin, repentance, the presence of God, and grace.

Those films in and for churches did serve as the bridge (and proverbial "wedge") to get religious middle-class audiences into the "movie habit."[35] The two most popular stars of the late teens and early twenties, Mary Pickford and Douglas Fairbanks, bowed their knees sufficiently to take on the mantle of the church in preaching new visual sermons of the moral life. One charming Mary Pickford film in particular illustrates this transfer of religious authority from the doctrines of the Protestant pulpit to American myths scripted on screen. In *Rebecca of Sunnybrook Farm*, Pickford was tempted to eat a tantalizing piece of forbidden pie left on the kitchen table. As she surveyed her temptation, she saw a sampler on the wall that commanded: "Do not steal." The biblical admonition stemmed her appetite and she walked away. However, just before she left the kitchen, she saw an American platitude woven on another sampler. This one, presumably from Benjamin Franklin, himself an early proponent of the American civil religion, encouraged her: "God helps those who help themselves." Weighing the two competing visions of religion, Mary opted for the latter and gobbled down the juicy dessert. It was a wonderfully comic moment, but also a profound sign of the direction of American film morality. In conjunction with the emerging Hollywood classical narrative paradigm, in which individuals helped themselves and dictated their own destinies, Mary's face was an icon of innocence shining in the celluloid wilderness. The new popular religion encapsulating this self-help tradition would be preached by people such as Henry Emerson Fosdick of the Riverside Church, and Norman Vincent Peale, whose *Guideposts* magazine incorporated the celebrated religious testimonies of many silent stars like Lillian Gish and Mary Pickford.[36]

Rural Church Versus Urban Cinema

While religious leaders sought to define themselves in opposition to Hollywood cinema as privileging religious and educational products over the merely commercial, they found that economic realities generally quashed their idealistic vision. The financial difficulty of producing their own film culture became even more pronounced with the advent of sound pictures. The vision for religious productions, especially that of the *Christian Herald* planners, had been for a competitive professional product, but unlike the alternative amateur movements in documentary and avant-garde film in the 1920s, religious producers' attempts to make products that were simultaneously didactic, inspirational, and commercial were generally futile.[37] The strength of biblical motion pictures lay in the familiarity of their entertainment, but their weakness of innovation led to staleness.

In contrast, Hollywood films were evolving, moving away from the sentimental piety of the late Victorian era and revealing more sophisticated, secular, and urban attitudes. Hollywood films were not the product of a heartland culture; they were no longer "homegrown." After touring America in the early 1920s, British wit and journalist G. K. Chesterton noted the contrast between heartland piety and urban sophistication in a book about his travels, entitled *What I Saw in America*. He noted that the culture and creeds reflected by American movies came from the great urban centers and "bring with them a blast of death and a reek of rotting things," and suggested that rural Americans needed to produce "their own spiritual food, in the same sense as their own material food."

> They do not, like some peasantries, create other kinds of culture beside the kind called agri-culture. Their culture comes from the great cities; and that is where all the evil comes from. . . . You would hardly find in Oklahoma what was found in Oberammergau. What goes to Oklahoma is not the peasant play but the cinema. And the objection to the cinema is not so much that it goes to Oklahoma as that *it does not come from Oklahoma*.[38]

The cultural chasm separating Oklahoma and Hollywood was fundamentally the same one that separated Hollywood and the church film movement. University of Idaho professor Carl Wells, writing in 1932, acknowledged that both film and church were community institutions that depended on voluntary support. But clear distinctions between them needed to be made; the most basic was that the church was situated in a "*rural* heritage" while the movie had evolved from an "*urban* heritage."[39] He expanded upon Frederick Collins's observation that "around the corner from what used to be the old meeting house is the motion picture theatre which is, for thousands and millions of people the new meeting house."[40] Wells saw that the church used traditional techniques to achieve its mission, appealing to memories and shibboleths like "Thus saith the Lord" to augment worship experiences, while the movie, on the other hand, employed novelty and modernistic mechanics to entertain. Helen and Robert Lynd likewise observed in their 1929 study on Muncie, Indiana, that the motion picture, like the automobile, added new dimensions to the city's leisure life. Not only had movies cut into lodge attendance, saloon going, and union activity, but they were also supplanting the church itself. According to the Lynds, movies attracted their largest audiences in this Protestant town on Sundays, with filmgoers even outnumbering churchgoers. Only a few efforts to clean up the movies by certain women's clubs and the concern of the Ministerial Association about "Sunday movies" demonstrated opposition to the trend. Middletown, and by extension Middle America seemed content to adopt the movies at "their face value—'a darned good show'—and largely disregard their educational or habit-forming aspects."[41]

Consequently, the nontheatrical Christian film movement had tried to produce its own spiritual culture. Under the auspices of the Harmon Foundation and Mary Beattie Brady, an amateur Christian film industry had come up with a grassroots product and had tried to move into the mainstream, even if its grass roots were limited to Bible and missionary films.[42] The Presbyterian Reverend John Sherman Potter extolled the virtues of movies, especially in small towns, lauding the potency of moving pictures like *The Cavell Case,* a visualization of the life story of the courageous British nurse Edith Cavell. For Potter, the film's faithful portrayal of the "triumph of faith in the Risen Savior" proved a powerful vehicle for evangelism and for wholesome entertainment for the rural community.[43] Significantly, it brought neighbors together; even Methodists and Roman Catholics joined the "Two-Seeds-in-the-flesh-Predestinarians" for a Gospel movie service. This grassroots movement had demonstrated that the marginalized voices of religious groups—who deeply feared cultural authority drifting from Protestant hegemony to Hollywood—*could* show their faith and their tradition through the visual images of the silent film. The Bible and its authentic geography *could* be shown. Sermon parables *could* be illustrated. Preaching, teaching, and community service *could* be fostered by the use of the motion picture. Most efforts at church-based exhibition and production demonstrated clearly that the motion picture and the church occupied two separate cultural realms.[44]

In the battle for cultural hegemony between the urban and the rural, the irreligious and the religious, Hollywood and Oklahoma, the movies and the church, the loud urban voice of the mass medium proved the stronger of the two by at the end of the 1920s. According to critic Harry Alan Potamkin, optimists could still try to absolve the sin of cinema by believing that: "Out of putrid matter the fairest flower may bloom." Yet the vile matter of the movies had been elevated to Art enabling it to attain the status and dignity of a religion. Hollywood became synonymous with American culture; it made American idols. As Potamkin commented caustically:

> The cry of the films as a moral agent is advanced: "The cinema is the enema of sin! The enema of the people! Sin is not the synonym of cinema. The film is Virtue!" I ply here, descriptively, the preposterous

trade of the Hollywood wisecracker, the wizard of wit [Will H. Hays].
"Religion is the worlds' greatest industry," and the *movie is the new
religion.*[45]

Film had become a religion, not simply in Marx's simplistic sense of being
"an opiate of the people" or in Freud's sense as compensation for a lost
father, but in the sense of providing worldviews that mediated meaning
through their visual myths.[46] Warner Bros.' inaugural talking film of
1927, *The Jazz Singer,* traced the religious trajectory of Jakie Rabinowitz,
a Jewish cantor's son, from the faith and orthodox tradition of his fathers
to a new existential religion, that of theatrical entertainment. Arguing
against going back to the synagogue to sing the prayers for his dying father, Jakie shouted, "We in the show business have our religion too—on
every day—the show must go on." At the end of the film, the jazz singer
had left the synagogue behind and was performing on the stage of the
new secular temple, "singing to *his* god."[47] Such films augured the changing religious values of society, and the Hollywood industry became a
repository of alternative religious expressions and visions. It became, in
Kenneth Anger's classic description, Hollywood Babylon, a factory of
idols. Unfortunately, the church's films could not compete with either the
slick professional entertainment of Hollywood or the mythic appeals of
violence, adventure, success, and romance as means to salvation. As critic
Margaret Miles suggests, the Christian churches had "relinquished the
task of providing life-orienting images" and thus the secular film culture
filled the void.[48]

The individual self functioned as its own savior, with Hollywood
films redefining human purpose and destiny and narrating how one
made one's own meaning rather than discovering it through sacred texts
or traditions. Audiences thus conformed to a material celebrity culture
rather than being transformed by a transcendent God. All aspects of the
classic Hollywood narrative paradigm seemed to provide the simulated
foundations of sand, gilded wood, and graven silver upon which
moviegoing congregations could order their lives, however tenuously.
The psalmist had once denounced those idols of silver and gold that had
eyes but could not see, had ears but could not hear, and had mouths but
could not breathe; but not only did the image makers trust in the works
of their own hands, they even *imitated* them. Mimesis was the order of
the graven image.[49] With regard to these kinetic images becoming a central contemporary site of religious activity, film scholar Christopher

Deacy explains that the secular agency of the film industry challenges and even supersedes religious institutions in their scramble for religious attention and participation. Even if the cinema has not yet moved to replace the sanctuary or the screen has not yet fully replaced the pulpit, films do enable spectators to confront their religious need for salvation and guidance.[50]

Hollywood was the new Babylon, competing with and for the chosen people of God and abducting them from their holy places; film had displaced and transposed some of the functions traditionally provided by religious communication. Generally in watching a film one enters a site of sacred time in the movie cathedral, where the cult of celebrity is as close to polytheism as a modernist can get, offering many celluloid gods and goddesses enshrined on the screens of every city and extolled in the pages of new sacred texts, the fan magazines.[51] As critic Richard Walsh wryly observes, the medium of film actually "suits polytheism, pantheism, or materialism better than monotheism."[52] By the 1930s, the cultic empire of images had overshadowed all other works of art and their memories. It was a distinct possibility that the fascination and deception of the eye could lead to a renewal of symbolic Asherim worship, sexual excess, and violence, essentially a celebration of graven and simulated flesh. Yet at the same time, the church saw in the moving pictures an opportunity to exploit the cultural apparatus for its own purposes. It is important to see that the grounding of the church's ambivalent relations to film lay in its prior struggles with both icon and theater. As the prophet Koheleth wrote, "There is nothing new under the sun."[53]

Finally, however, out of what many saw in the early thirties as the movies' slimy trail of moral sewage, a call arose for a fresh and cleansing reformation, a new vanguard of "Protest—ants," those who would stand up for what was right and true against an encroaching system of pagan immorality.[54] The vociferous remonstration against moving pictures that followed marked a noteworthy withdrawal from the early hopes and visions of the majority of church leaders at the turn of the twentieth century. Their emphasis was now on criticism, judgment, and above all, condemnation: film had become a rival religion. They feared the new cult was overthrowing the old-time religion, introducing its own pantheon of pagan celebrities. It would erase the holy words of the past and paint vivid images that hypnotized and embalmed the imagination of the people. Yet the church had to deal with its rival's formidable boast: "You ain't seen nothing yet."

Foundations for the Future of Christian Film

For the church, the first two decades of sound motion pictures were marked by hesitancy and frugality, as the Depression drew attention and resources away from the creative arts to more pressing humane concerns. It was also a season of self-assessment and consolidation in religious films, with various educators and administrators strategizing how best to deal with Hollywood, promote uplifting movies, and marshal assets for religious education. By 1931, critic Alva Johnston saw that the secular cinema still craved the church's approval, believing that the latter enjoyed a dangerous political influence. But, he suggested, the church would perform its greatest service if

> it would teach Hollywood by example rather than precept. Let the Federal Council or some other religious group produce a pious epic that grosses a million dollars. Everyone knows what imitators the magnates are: there will be an immediate stampede to dramatize purity and sanctity. It would be better still if the church would produce a series of masterpieces; three or four super pictures could be made from the money now sunk in one cathedral.[55]

Johnston lamented the fact that the Modernist brand of Christianity had "lost much of its popularity by becoming too genteel." By discarding Satan, his minions, and the menace of an everlasting bonfire, the church had lost its drama. "The enormous mileage of empty pews in the churches of America suggests that it is impossible to run a religion without a villain. Perhaps the church, after all, has more to learn from Hollywood than to teach it."[56]

But for the next twenty years, into the early 1940s, the church made no outstanding pictures because the emergence of sound technology during an era of economic depression retarded the involvement of religious bodies in film production. Sound technology had already changed the focus of church evangelism, spending its limited resources to the development and diffusion of broadcast radio as the primary, most economical, and most efficient medium for its mission. Thus, strained finances and the church's shift to radio ultimately undermined the embryonic Christian film industry of the 1920s. Christian radio offered a logocentric, far-reaching, and cheaper medium to use in propagating the faith. By the

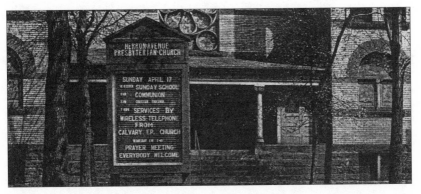

After wearying of his work regarding motion pictures in the church, Homer
Croy found another technological marvel in radio broadcasting sermons, first
experimented by Presbyterians in Pittsburgh. "Radio Announcement on the
church board," *The Christian Herald* (July 29, 1922), 531. Courtesy Library of
Congress.

mid-twenties, religious periodicals such as the previously film-addicted
Christian Herald, were heralding the advent of religious broadcasting sta-
tions and the emergence of the Radio Church.[57]

By the end of the thirties, religious radio, with its biblical dramas like
the story of Elisha and the Shunannite's son, had become a national institution, easily supplanting the visual entertainment of the churches.[58]
Aimee Semple McPherson, broadcasting out of her Angeles Temple in Los
Angeles, was a notorious and electrifying celebrity of religious broadcasting, who, journalist H. L. Mencken noted, had the "wildest nightlife"
of any movie counterpart.[59] Author Sinclair Lewis made her fictional
counterpart, Elmer Gantry, the first in his state to inaugurate a radio ministry out of his Wellspring Church (which had also once operated a motion picture booth).[60] The church's cultural fascination with radio gradually replaced much of its vision to adapt film for religious uses, for radio
was more economical and better suited to its rhetorical gifts.[61]

The advent of sound film had offered new opportunities as well as new
temptations for the church. As economics played the crucial role in de-
terring the church from engaging in further production, it wasn't until the
1940s that a cornucopia of new developments in religious filmmaking appeared with increased denominational production and with the emergence of three key Christian *auteurs:* the Episcopal Reverend James K.
Friedrich of Cathedral Films, Carlos Octavia Baptista, and Dr. Irwin

Moon of Moody Science Films offered heuristic models that served the Christian film industry well into the twenty-first century and they deserve their own memorials. Friedrich, an Episcopal minister, revived the black and white biblical stories of the early period, but creatively put the Apostle Paul in perilous cliff-hanging serials. In his vision to provide films for Sunday school education, Baptista produced an animated feature on *Pilgrim's Progress*. Dr. Moon experimented with illustrated *Sermons from Science*, incorporating electronic, photographic, stroboscopic, and sonic devices to demonstrate the kinship of the Christian faith and true science. The belief in a divine presence evident in creation was rooted in the Hudson River painters, with the subtle fingerprints of God hinting of a divine design in the mysteries and glories of nature. Moon's time-lapsed photography offered a technological version of Cropsey's oils with both pointing to the parable of the autograph of God in the beauty of nature. In the footsteps of these pioneers came Billy Graham Evangelistic Films' World Wide Pictures, Gospel Films, Family Films, Ken Anderson Films, and numerous other independent companies that exploded on the scene. In the 1960s, Roman Catholics emerged with creative parables through the artistry of the Franciscans and the Paulists. While the era saw the development of numerous instructional films such as the James Dobson series on the family, noteworthy feature films such as *The Hiding Place, The Cross and the Switchblade,* and *Romero,* all based on the witness of actual Christians, attracted a new generation to the power and excitement of filmmaking.

An influx of young Christian filmmakers opened the floodgates of experimentation in numerous genres and voices during the latter three decades of the twentieth century. Recruiting Irwin "Shorty" Yeaworth, one of the principal directors of *The Blob,* producer and Yale University graduate Russell Doughton incorporated Mark IV Pictures to specialize in horror films, scratching together one of the most haunting films of the eschatological pre-tribulation "rapture" films, *A Thief in the Night.* Such harrowing films that would try to literally "scare the hell out of people" gave birth to Regent University filmmakers like Danny Carrales and Wes Llewellyn. Supernatural horror films would reach an apex in Biola University graduate Scott Dickerson's Hollywood release of *The Exorcism of Emily Rose* (2005). Several films by young Christian filmmakers competed and won regional and national Student Academy Awards, including Bill Harris's *All Things Fanged and Carnivorous* (1985), John Newcombe's *Lovestruck* (1986), Antonio Zarro's *Bird in a Cage* (1987), and

Jim Lincoln, Jeannie Hardie, and Lisa Swain's *Turtle Races* (1990). In the field of comedy, Phil Vischer and his team, weaned on the diverse humors of Disney and Monty Python, founded Big Idea Productions in 1993 and released one of the most successful animated musical comedy series ever made, *Veggie Tales,* with Bob the Tomato and Larry the Cucumber. Other Christians would stretch the limits of comedy filmmaking with Hollywood features. Hollywood directors Tom Shadyac and Kevin Smith, both of whom happened to be Christians, broke ground with remarkably successful and hilarious productions of *Bruce Almighty* (2003) and *Dogma* (1999). A trend of assimilation into the mainstream media industries had transpired, culminating in the formation of Micheal Flaherty's Walden Media.

Significantly, churches in North America envisioned the first-ever "church theatrical premier" with the latest, low-budget movie, *Left Behind,* by Peter Lalonde's Cloud Ten Pictures.[62] The culmination of Christian involvement in the media in the early twenty-first century, marking a return to similar visionary sponsorship by the Harmon Foundation, has emerged from Philip Anschutz, the billionaire founder of Qwest Communications and a devout Christian who created the Anschutz Film Group and Walden Media. The latter is Disney's partner in producing and marketing the phenomenal best-seller by British Christian author C. S. Lewis, namely, *The Chronicles of Narnia: The Lion, the Witch, and the Wardrobe.* Numerous evangelical Christian associations, such as Focus on the Family, touted such productions, calling upon their membership to support the production. Ministers like Tom Holladay of Saddleback Church, in Lake Forest, California, coordinated advance screening for twenty-thousand members of his congregation one day before the film was to open nationwide. The old ways of evangelical marketing and exhibition have been revived. The Sanctuary Cinema movement has been resurrected.[63]

With the earlier development of religious television broadcasting, the Christian community had begun again to incorporate images, but still focused on the word, preaching, and teaching, so much so that it deserved the moniker of "talking heads" media. Remarkably, in the first decade of the twenty-first century, the church revived its vision to produce, market, and exhibit films, a vision born over a hundred years ago. Ironically, the ultimate apotheosis and apex of mediated Christian communication exploded on the scene in the early twentieth century not through a logocentric production, but with the essentially silent film work of director

In a frontispiece of the Pilgrim Tract Society of North Carolina, the alleged serpentine poisons of the moving pictures infected other visual media, including television. Courtesy of the University of Wisconsin.

Mel Gibson's *The Passion of the Christ*. As John Lyden has keenly noted, the technologically advanced film could be viewed as a predominantly visual work of art with subtitles (in Aramaic, a foreign language no one speaks) and with a great emphasis on image over story. Its phenomenal success may have had something to do with the way images, rather than words, created their own drama and resonated with Christian filmgoers. According to two separate 2005 studies by Barna and Ellison research groups, over 60 percent of American churches were using a large-screen projection system in their church communications, where hymns had once been projected on the walls of the churches one hundred years before.[64] But the story of the reembrace of the visual must await another book on the creative, economic, and technological emergence of the Christian film industry in the latter half of the twentieth century, when it would become big business.

In their work on the marginalized voices of American silent film, editors Gregg Bachman and Thomas J. Slater bemoan the fact that many contributing identities in film history have been lost.[65] It is hoped that this work has brought back into the congregations of film histories one enduring but neglected tradition, that of the early Christian Film movement. Among all the voiceless creatures and idols on the outskirts of Hollywood, the brazen serpent still slithers about silently, and its former skins are fascinating, at least to those who like to examine the transformations of these theatrical images within histories of the church and film. For the brazen serpent would shed its skin again and again, continuing to nest within the imaginations of churchmen and women, sometimes bringing poison, sometimes bringing healing, but always challenging those who would keep the company of snake handlers.

Notes

Notes to the Introduction

1. See Emanuel Levy's *Cinema of Outsiders: The Rise of American Indepen-dent Film* (New York: New York University Press, 2001). However, while Levy depicts the independent film movements of women, African Americans, Asian Americans, and regional cinemas, he is unaware of anything approaching an alternative Christian film industry.

2. John Hill and Pamela Church Gibson, eds., *The Oxford Guide to Film Studies* (Oxford: Oxford University Press, 1998), xxi.

3. George A. Kennedy, *Classical Rhetoric and Its Christian and Secular Tradition from Ancient to Modern Times* (Chapel Hill: University of North Carolina Press, 1980), 147.

4. Lee Grieveson, "Woof, Warp, History," and Donald Crafton, "Collaborative Research, Doc?" *Cinema Journal* 44: 1 (Fall 2004), 119–126 and 138–143.

5. Gustavo Gutierrez, *We Drink from Our Own Wells* (Maryknoll, New York: Orbis Books, 1984).

6. A telling contrast can be seen in Glenn Man's *Radical Vision: American Film Renaissance, 1967–1976* (Westport, CT: Greenwood, 1994), and Kristin Thompson and David Bordwell's *Film History: An Introduction* (New York: McGraw-Hill, 1994).

7. Daniel Fierman and Gillian Flynn, "The Greatest Story Ever Sold," *Entertainment Weekly* (December 3, 1999): 55, 59, 61, 64; Jeff Jensen and Gillian Flynn, "The Next Temptation," *Entertainment Weekly* (December 10, 1999): 43–44, 46, 48.

8. Lorraine Ali, "Jesus Rocks: Christian Entertainment Makes a Joyful Noise: The Glorious Rise of Christian Pop," and Marc Peyser, "God, Mammon and 'Bibleman,'" *Newsweek* (July 16, 2001), 38–48.

9. Anne Henderson-Hart, "What Makes a Film Christian?" *Eternity* (June 1982), 19–21.

10. See Richard Maltby, "The King of Kings and the Czar of All the Rushes: The Propriety of the Christ Story," *Screen* 31 (1990), 188–213; and Robert S. Birchard, *Cecil B. DeMille's Hollywood* (Lexington: University Press of Kentucky, 2004).

11. *Psalm* 101:3.

12. *MPW* (December 5, 1908), 451, in Lee Grieveson, *Policing Cinema: Movies and Censorship in Early-Twentieth-Century America* (Berkeley: University of California Press, 2004), 87.

13. As historian Lee Grieveson notes, even the rhetoric of the trade journals suggested how the cultural function of cinema could be linked to that of the church. In particular, he cites *Nickelodeon* (January 1909), 16 and *MPW* (January 8, 1910), 16; *MPW* (March 5, 1910), 339; and *MPW* (June 24, 1911), 1428.

14. Roberta Pearson and William Uricchio, "'The Formative and Impressionable Stage': Discursive Construction of the Nickelodeon's Child Audience," in Melvin Stokes and Richard Maltby, eds., *American Movie Audiences: From the Turn of the Century to the Early Sound Film* (London: BFI, 1999), 64–78.

15. "A Great Epic in Moving Pictures," *MPW* 9 (July 15, 1911), 14–16.

16. See Andrew Brodie Smith, "The Making of Broncho Billy," in *Shooting Cowboys and Indians* (Denver: University Press of Colorado, 2003), 134.

17. See Neal Gabler, *An Empire of Their Own: How the Jews Invented Hollywood* (New York: Anchor, 1989).

18. *MPW* (November 9, 1912), 538, 643, cited in Eileen Bowser, *The Transformation of Cinema, 1907–1915* (New York: Scribner's, 1990), 133.

19. Charles Musser, *Before the Nickelodeon* (Berkeley: University of California Press, 1991), 23.

20. Kay Sloan, *The Loud Silents: Origins of the Social Problem Film* (Urbana: University of Illinois Press, 1988), and Steven Ross, *Working-Class Hollywood: Silent Film and the Shaping of Class in America* (Princeton: Princeton University Press, 1998).

21. George J. Anderson, "The Case for Motion Pictures," *Congregationalist and Christian World* 95: 29 (July 8, 1910), 46. See also Terry Lindvall, "Telling Stories through Celluloid: The Congregational Church and Cinema," *Congregationalist* 155: 2 (April-May-June 1995), 8–12.

22. *MPW* (December 28, 1912), 1284, cited in Bowser, 187.

23. William D. Romanowski, "John Calvin Meets the Creature from the Black Lagoon: The Dutch Reformed Church and the Movies 1928–1966," *Christian Scholars' Review* XXV: 1 (September 1995), 47–62.

24. Willis Elliot Reynolds, "The Clergy and the Picture," *MPW* 6: 11 (March 19, 1910), 430.

25. Robert Molhant, *Catholics in the Cinema: A Strange History of Belief and Passion, 1895–1935* (Brussels: OCIC, 2000).

26. Ted Ownby, *Subduing Satan: Religion, Recreation, and Manhood in the Rural South, 1865–1920* (Chapel Hill: University of North Carolina Press, 1990), 196–97.

27. In his study of silent film star Douglas Fairbanks, Sr., author John Tibbetts compared the gymnastic evangelist of Hollywood to his dynamic counterpart, baseball revivalist Billy Sunday. John C. Tibbetts and James M. Weise, *His Majesty, the American* (New York: Barnes and Noble, 1977).

28. "Missionaries and Moving Pictures," *Nickelodeon* 1: 1 (January 1909), 16.

29. See Jon Butler, Grant Wacker, and Randall Balmer, *Religion in American Life* (New York: Oxford University Press, 2000), 331.

30. William Uricchio and Roberta Pearson, *Reframing Culture: The Case of Vitagraph Quality Films* (Princeton: Princeton University Press, 1993), 161.

NOTES TO CHAPTER 1

1. Garnet Warren, *New York Herald* (1909), as cited by Jan Olsson, "Pressing Inroads: Mapping the Los Angeles Nickelodeon Culture," in *Ephemeral Discourses* at the SCS Conference (Washington D.C., May 24, 2001).

2. Donald P. Costello, *The Serpent's Eye: Shaw and the Cinema* (Notre Dam, Ind., University of Notre Dame Press, 1965), 1–2. See George Bernard Shaw, "The Cinema as a Moral Leveller," *New Statesman: Special Supplement on the Modern Theatre* III (June 27, 1914), 1, 2, and "Education and the Cinematograph," *Bioscope: Educational Supplement* XXIII (June 18, 1914), i, ii.

3. In her rediscovery of his work, editor Florice Whyte Kovan celebrated how Hecht "veils and unveils, with a peremptory snicker and grin, the marketplace of the celluloid serpent." Florice W. Kovan, ed., *Rediscovering Ben Hecht: Selling the Celluloid Serpent* (Washington D.C.: Snickersnee Press, 1999), 6.

4. Ben Hecht, *A Child of the Century* (New York: Simon & Schuster, 1954), 469.

5. See "The Widening Trail of the Celluloid Serpent," *Current Opinion* (January 1920), 794ff.

6. Sir James George Frazer, *The Golden Bough* (1922) (New York: Macmillan, 1978).

7. A Smithsonian Institute Exhibit of Hollywood Legend and Reality showcased director Cecil B. DeMille's tinny and tacky oak wood and gold leaf construction of the Golden Calf. His facsimile was embarrassingly shoddy, but vividly reminded one how superficial idols were. Eerily enough, the Academy Award of the Netherlands, the Dutch Oscar as it were, is known as the Golden Calf Award.

8. *Exodus* 20:4–5; *Deuteronomy* 4:15

9. Worship in the Greek is προκυνεο, which literally means "pro" toward, and "kuneo" kissing. Thus to prostrate oneself and kiss the hand or feet was to surrender your allegiance and affection to the object of worship. Canaanite and Phoenician religions afforded extremely debasing forms of idol worship, with

Baal towering over the other demons. See John Bright, *History of Israel* (London: Westminster Press, 1959), 108.

10. Desiderius Erasmus, *The Praise of Folly* (trans. Hoyt Hopewell Hudson) (Princeton: Princeton University Press, 1941), 89.

11. *Isaiah* 30: 19–22. Isaiah castigated those "idols overlaid with silver," admonishing the Hebrews to defile them, throw them away like a menstrual cloth, and say, "Away with you." Israel was prone to surrender to superstition, and to worship these molten images. St. John of Damascus. *On the Divine Images* (trans. by David Anderson) (Crestwood, N.Y.: Sr. Vladimir's Seminary Press, 1994), 18.

12. The visual objectifying and commodifying of the female image, for example, would lead to its desire and consumption as an object. Feminist film theorist Laura Mulvey sees women being the exploited "object of the male gaze," while positing that the root of desire is in the encounter with the image. For all practical purposes, the gaze in the movie theater is gendered male, directed toward the eroticized female body. Yet might we mischievously suggest that one other paradigm analogy for the serpentine image might be the brazen woman called Medusa, with her unruly head of hair-snakes? She holds the power not only to make those men who gaze upon her impotent, but to transform them into deaf and dumb idols of stone themselves. The mythically divine woman condensed into a material object has her own revenge. Laura Mulvey, *Visual and Other Pleasures* (Bloomington: Indiana University Press, 1989).

13. "The gaze in the movie theater is, for all practical purposes, gendered male: the pay off for the viewer, as often as not, is the eroticized female body, and the very fact of looking at conventional films becomes a form of repressed adultery. Just as so many men *in* films have sex with more than one woman, the male or 'male' spectator comes to 'know' the women in films in addition to whatever women they know in real life." Scott MacDonald, "From Zygote to Global via Su Friedrich's Films," *Journal of Film and Video* 44:1–2 (Spring–Summer 1992), 31. See *Colossians* 3:5; *Ephesians* 5:5; and *Philippians* 3:19.

14. David Freedberg, *The Power of Images* (Chicago: University of Chicago Press, 1989), xxiii.

15. *Ibid.*, 76. See especially Freedberg's chapter on the "Arousal by Image," pp.317–44.

16. *Ibid.*, 378–79, 423. See also James L. Crenshaw, *The Psalms: An Introduction* (Grand Rapids, Eerdmans, 2001). In the book of *Proverbs*, young Hebrew men slipping away at dusk to a cultic courtesan were forewarned against becoming oxen going to the slaughter, of being enticed, excited, and executed. The apostle Paul later admonished the Corinthians with a vivid illustration of the consequences of Israel's idolatry: "The people sat down to eat and drink and got up to indulge in pagan revelry. We should not commit sexual immorality as

some of them did—and in one day 23,000 of them died. We should not test the Lord as some of them did—and were killed by snakes." *I Corinthians* 10: 7–9. The disciple John confronted a similar crisis finding in the city of Pergamos the devotees of the Nicolaitans and Balaam (those who compromised the Christian faith rather than combating it), worshiping the snake, often in orgiastic feasts that led people into idolatry and sexual immorality. *Mark* 16:18; *Revelation* 2:14–15.

17. *St. John*, 32.

18. "'To See Is to Believe,' Says Minister, Pleading for Picture Shows in Churches," *MPW* (May 15, 1920), 932. "The devil uses everything he can, but that is no reason why we should let him monopolize things with vast possibilities for good."

19. "Letter to Editor," *MPW* (February 22, 1908), 133. Putman's letter to the *Home Journal* was dated February 15, 1898.

20. Janet Staiger, "The Future of the Past," and Steven J. Ross, "Jargon and the Crisis of Readability: Methodology, Language, and the Future of Film History," *Cinema Journal* 44: 1 (Fall 2004), 127–28, 131.

21. See Ingrid Shafer, "The Catholic Imagination in Popular Film and Television," *Journal of Popular Film and Television* (Summer 1991), 50–58 and David Morgan, "The Protestant Struggle with the Image," *Christian Century* (March 22–29, 1989), 308–11.

22. Robert Hellbeck, "The Film and Protestantism," *International Review of Educational Cinematography* 3 (October 1931), 923.

23. T. J. Jackson Lears, *No Place of Grace: Antimodernism and the Transformation of American Culture 1880–1920* (New York: Pantheon Books, 1981), 192.

24. "In good Christian screenwriting, truth and beauty speak for themselves." *Our Sunday Visitor* (February 25, 2001), 14.

25. An article from the inaugural issue of the *Crayon* argued that Christianity provides a stronger basis for the arts than Greek paganism, as "Christianity does not see human beings as the center of the universe." Gene Edward Veith, *Painters of Faith: The Spiritual Landscape in Nineteenth-Century America* (Washington, D.C.: Regnery, 2001), 56.

26. Horace's conception of poetic narrative required that it be both *dulce* and *utile*, or sweet and useful, entertaining and didactic. Horace, *Satires, Epistles and Ars poetica* (trans. H. Rushton Fairclough) (Cambridge: Harvard University Press, 1978, c. 1929), (lines 180–82).

27. Richard C. Trench, *Notes on the Parables of Our Lord* (1862). (London: Sovereign Grace: 2002)

28. John Durham Peters, "Beauty's Veils: The Ambivalent Iconoclasm of Kierkegaard and Benjamin," in *The Image in Dispute* (ed. Dudley Andrew) (Austin: University of Texas Press, 1997), 9–32.

29. Walter Benjamin, "The Work of Art in the Age of Mechanical Reproduction" (trans. by Harry Zohn) in *Illuminations* (ed. Hannah Arendt) (New York: Schocken Books, 1969), 224.

30. Curiously enough, a "domestic epigram" from Goethe's *Zahme Xenien* expressed similar skepticism regarding claims by the visual graphic arts of bringing about goodness or enlightenment: "Many stupid things are often said/ As well as written,/ They do not kill the flesh or soul,/ Nor any change effect./ But something stupid offered to the eye/ exerts a magic force:/ Because it chains the senses/ The mind remains a slave." Cited in Lewis Jacobs, ed., *The Compound Cinema: The Film Writings of Harry Alan Potamkin* (New York: Teachers' College Press, 1977), xv–xvi.

31. Lionel Kochan, *Beyond the Graven Image: A Jewish View* (New York: New York University Press, 1997).

32. See André Bazin, "The Ontology of the Photographic Image," *Que-est-ce que le Cinéma?* (ed. and trans. by Hugh Gray) (Berkeley: University of California Press, 1967), 9–16.

33. M. Darrol Bryant, "Cinema, Religion, and Popular Culture," in John R. May and Michael Bird, eds., *Religion in Film* (Knoxville: University of Tennessee Press, 1982), 113.

34. Edwyn Bevan, *Holy Images: An Inquiry into Idolatry and Image-Worship in Ancient Paganism and in Christianity* (London: George Allen and Unwin, 1940). Arguing against projecting such sins upon the "suggestiveness of virile motion pictures" in modern times, the advertising manager of the French Gaumont Company, John B. Clymer, thought such blame tossing to be futile. For him, the neutral image had been abused and had become the new scapegoat of culpability. Mockingly, he suggested that the juveniles of Sodom and Gomorrah most likely "pointed the finger of accusation to art in the nude as a cause for their remiss conduct." John Clymer, "The Futility of Foisting the Sins of Our Nether Selves upon the Suggestiveness of Virile Motion Pictures," *Moving Picture News* VI: 21 (November 23, 1912), 15. He wrote with jaded candor against religious meddlers: "Instead of giving to patrons heralds of coming features, tracts will be handed around and evangelists will hold short snappy meetings, saving souls between reels."

35. Jacques Ellul, *The Technological Society* (New York: Vintage, 1964); Jacques Ellul, *The New Demons* (New York: Seabury Press, 1975); Jacques Ellul, *The Humiliation of the Word* (Grand Rapids, Mich., Eerdmans, 1985).

36. Marshall McLuhan, *Understanding Media* (New York: McGraw Hill, 1964); Mitchell Stephens, *The Rise of the Image, the Fall of the Word* (New York: Oxford University Press, 1998).

37. Richard Stivers, *Technology as Magic: The Triumph of the Irrational* (London: Continuum, 1999).

38. Chesterton mocked H. G. Wells's idea that men are like gods. If so, he wrote, "we would like to know which gods; and whether man is to be Moloch

the murderer or Mercury the thief." George Marlin, ed., *Collected Works of G.K. Chesterton Vol. 21: What I Saw in America, the Resurrection of Rome, Sidelights,* (San Francisco: Ignatius Press, 1990) 307.

39. Bright, 149. In a clever bit of mockery, St. John wrote, "The Manichaeans wrote the Gospel according to Thomas; will you now write the Gospel according to Leo?" (Bright, 63).

40. In his intellectual history of iconoclasm, Alain Besancon connected this perennial smashing of images with the destruction of the sacred groves of Phoenicia. Even after Orthodox Christianity's vindication of the acceptable nature of icons, the hydra heads of opposition to the forbidden essence of images continued to be raised by radical reformers and other philosophers. See Alain Besancon (trans. Jane Marie Todd), *The Forbidden Image: An Intellectual History of Iconoclasm* (Chicago: University of Chicago Press, 2001).

41. As the Scriptures (*II Corinthians* 4:4) indicated, Jesus Christ was the image (εικων) of the Father. Thus, the Council declared that one could "render icons the veneration of honor (*proskune-sis*), not true worship (*latreia*) of our faith which is due to the divine nature." Such an honor shown to the icon is conveyed to its prototype, passing to the One depicted. So Christ could be worshipped as God, just as Mary (τηæτοκοσ) and the saints could receive their own due veneration.

42. E. H. Gombrich, *The Story of Art* (London: Phaidon Press, 1972), 130.

43. Saint Bonaventura. Liber III, Sententiarum: Dist. IX, Art. I, Quaestio II, *Opera Theologica Selecta* (Florence: ex typo-graphia Collegii S. Bonaventura 1941), 194. While uneducated people could not read books, they could read images on a wall. Poet François Villon rhapsodized on this experience in verses written for his mother in the mid-fifteenth century: "I am a woman, poor and old,/Quite ignorant, I cannot read./They showed me in my village church/A painted Paradise with harps,/And Hell where the damned souls are boiled./One gives me joy, the other frightens me." Gombrich, 130.

44. St. Thomas Aquinas echoed Bonaventura: "The instruction of the unlettered, who might learn from them as if from books; second, so that the mystery of the Incarnation and the examples of the saints might remain more firmly in our memory by being daily represented to our eyes; and third, to excite the emotions which are more effectively aroused by things seen than by things heard." *Commentarium super libros sententiarum: Commentum in librum* III dist. 9, art. 2. qu. 2. See also Bonaventure *Itinerarium mentis ad Deum* 2: 11.

45. Gregrory the Great, *Lib. IX, Epistola LII Ad Secundinum* in PL 77, cols. 990–91. Cited in Freedberg, 470 fn9. Dionysius Areopagaticus also emphasized how meditation is enabled by the cult of images: "We are led up, as far as possible, through visible images to a contemplation of the divine." *De ecclesia hierachia,* 1.2 (trans. Kitzinger) PG 3, col. 373: 1952, 137–38.

46. In Zwingli's view, even his own visually decorated parish church, the Great Minster, abetted the veneration of relics. A Catholic legend promised that one could find protection from the plague by viewing the Great Minster's St. Sebastian, protection from epilepsy by gazing upon St. Valentin, protection of all types by viewing St. Christopher, and immunity from temptation by viewing St. Jerome. Charles Garside, Jr., *Zwingli and the Arts* (Cambridge: Da Capo Press, 1981), 88–89. Garside astutely points out in his *Zwingli and the Arts* that both educationally and physically (he was near-sighted), Zwingli was unable to appreciate art. See also Hans J. Hillerbrand, *The Protestant Reformation* (New York: HarperCollins, 1990), 160.

47. See Carlos Eire, *War against the Idols: The Reformation of Worship from Erasmus to Calvin* (New York: Cambridge University Press, 1986).

48. Even John Calvin's austere theological aesthetics utilizes metaphors that view the scriptures as "spectacles" and the world as "the theater of God's glory." See his *Institutes of the Christian Religion,* book 1, chapters 11–12, 108.

49. Calvin did argue that painting and sculpture, as gifts of God, must adhere to their "pure and legitimate use." John Calvin, *Institutes of the Christian Religion* (trans. Lewis Battles Ford) (London: Westminster Press, 1960), Book I, Chapter 11, Section 12. See also Paul Corby Finney and Jane Dempsey Douglass, *Seeing Beyond the Word: Visual Arts and the Calvinist Tradition* (Grand Rapids, Mich.: Eerdmans, 1999). See also Veith, 21–22. Calvinist churches were mostly bare and had unadorned buildings for any form of "religious art was suspect as potentially idolatrous."

50. David C. Steinmetz's *Calvin in Context* (Oxford: Oxford University Press, 1995), 59.

51. Martin Luther, "Against the Heavenly Prophets in the Matter of Images and Scaraments" (1525), in *Luther's Works* (ed. Helmut T. Lehmann) (Philadelphia: Muhlenberg Press, 1958), 85–86, 99.

52. According to Christopher Dawson, "the popular religious drama, which had such an important influence on the rise of European drama as a whole, was either a liturgical drama in the strict sense, like the Passion plays and Nativity plays, or was directly related to the cult of the saints and the celebration of their feasts." Christopher Dawson, *The Historic Reality of Christian Culture: A Way to the Renewal of Human Life* (New York: Elliots Book, 1960), 72.

53. Henry Ward Beecher, "Popular Amusements," *Lectures to Young Men on Various Important Subjects* (New York: J. B. Ford and Company, 1873), 174.

54. Henry Ward Beecher, "*Seven Lectures to Young Men*" (Indianapolis: Thomas B. Culter, 1844). See also John F. Kasson, "Idle Pleasures: Recreation or Ruin?" (Winston-Salem, N.C.: Reynolda House Museum of American Art, n.d.).

55. Tertullian, *De Spectaculis* (trans. T. R. Glover); *Tertullian* (Cambridge: Harvard University Press, 1977), 230–301.

56. *Ibid.*, 279.

57. Cyprian, *On the Public Shows* (trans. Ernest Wallis, ed. Alexander Roberts and James Donaldson), *The Ante-Nicene Father* (Grand Rapids, Mich.: Eerdmans, 1986), V, 577.

58. Cyprian, 577. Like Augustine, he acknowledged his own shame while naming the vices to be denounced as "the tricks of arguments, the cheatings of adulteries, the immodesties of women, the scurrile jokes, the sordid parasites, even the toga'd fathers of families themselves, sometimes stupid, sometimes obscene, but in all cases dull, in all cases immodest."

59. Menucius Felix, *The Octavius of Ninucius Felix* (trans. Gerald H. Rendall), *Minucius Felix* (Cambridge: Harvard University Press, 1977), 314–437.

60. Soren Kierkegaard ironically bemoaned the fact that preachers were not as effective as poets and actors in their respective rhetoric. "Whereas, alas, the Christian proclamation at times is scarcely heard, all listen to the poet, admire him, learn from him, are enchanted by him. Whereas, alas, people quickly forget what the pastor has said, how accurately and how long they do remember what the poet has said, especially what he has said with the help of the actor!" *Works of Love* (ed. and trans. Howard and Edna Hong) (Princeton: Princeton University Press, 1996), 47.

61. Jonas Barish, *The Antitheatrical Prejudice* (Berkley: University of California Press, 1981), 51.

62. See Chrysostom (trans. Elizabeth Clark), *Jerome, Chrysostom and Friends: Essays and Translations* (New York: E. Mellen Press, 1982); and Blake Leyerle, *Theatrical Shows and Ascetic Lives: John Chrysostom's Attack on Spiritual Marriage* (Berkeley: University of California Press, 2001).

63. See Robert A. Krupp, "Golden Tongue and Iron Will," and Margaret Schatkin, "Culture Wars: How Chrysostom Battled Heresy, Superstition and Paganism," *Christian History* 44 (XIII: 4, 1994), 6–11, 33–35.

64. Lactantius, *The Divine Institutes* (trans. William Fletcher), in Alexander Roberts and James Donaldson, eds., *The AnteNicene Fathers* (Grand Rapids, Mich., Eerdmans, 1986), VII, 187.

65. Clement of Alexandria, *Stromata* 1:5. Cited in Williston Walker, *A History of the Christian Church* (New York: Scribner's, 1970), 73.

66. Clement of Alexandria, *Protrepticus* 4 (trans. G. Butterworth) (Cambridge: Harvard University Press, 1953), 133.

67. They were warned against the staging of "*iocos vel ludos.*" See William Tydeman, *The Theatre in the Middle Ages* (Cambridge: Cambridge University Press, 1978).

68. Swedish director Ingmar Bergman's classic medieval film, *The Seventh Seal,* depicts such a bawdy, rollicking troupe.

69. One well-known *trope* was the Gospel pericopae called "Whom do you seek?" (*quem quaeritis*) in which monks played out parts of the Easter story.

70. Peter A. Bucknell, *Entertainment and Ritual: 600–1600* (London: Stainer and Bell, 1979), 28f.

71. See Glynne Wickham, *The Medieval Theatre* (3rd ed.) (London: Cambridge University Press, 1987).

72. John C. Tibbetts, (ed.), *Introduction to the Photoplay* (Shawnee Mission, Kans.: National Film Society, 1977), 67.

73. Elbert N. S. Thompson, *The Controversy between the Puritans and the Stage* (1903), (New York: Russell & Russell, 1966), 43. Numerous other clergy of this early Elizabethan period saw "in the stage no serious menace to Christianity."

74. In his thorough history of the Puritan attacks on the theater in the seventeenth century, Barish points out how Martinists mocked zealous preachers who were often more dramatic than stage players. One fanatical clergyman wore out three hundred pulpits "with the unreasonable bouncing of his fists." Yet curiously enough, Puritans were viewed by Papists such as Thomas More as too giddy and glad in their constitution, as "young, fierce, progressive intellectuals—very fashionable and up to date." Barish, 81. See C. S. Lewis, *English Literature in the Sixteenth Century, Excluding Drama* (New York: Oxford University Press, 1973), 18.

75. Mortimer J. Adler, *Art and Prudence: A Study in Practical Philosophy* (1937) (New York: Arno, 1978), 67.

76. The most extreme rebuke of the evil stage at this time came from Arthur Bedford; even the title of his diatribe indicates the intensity of his vehemence, *The Evil and Danger of Stage-Plays: Showing Their Natural Tendency to Destroy Religion and Introduce a General Corruption of Manners.*

77. Blaise Pascal, *Pensées* I:11 (trans. W. F. Trotter) in *Great Books of the Western World* 33 (Chicago: Encyclopaedia Britannica, 1952), 173–4. The English Puritans did not abandon the aforementioned tradition of Cyprian and Lactantius, for whom the theater, "the mother of all public amusement, was idolatry." Cyprian, *On the Public Shows,* 224.

78. W. E. Biernatzki, S.J., "Entertainment and Religion," in *Communication Research Trends* 18: 3 (1998), 14–18. See also William H. McCabe, S.J., *An Introduction to the Jesuit Theater* (St. Louis: Institute of Jesuit Sources, 1983).

79. See John Dennis, *The Usefulness of the Stage to the Happiness of Mankind, to Government, and to Religion* (London, 1698), as cited in Adler, 71–72.

80. Jacques Maritain, *Art and Scholasticism* (trans. J. F. Scanlan) (New York: Scribner's, 1924), 80.

81. Augustine H. Smith, "The Fine Arts in Religion," *International Journal of Religious Education* (November 1926), 13–16. Smith also championed the fact that the modern church had revived the use of pictures "brightening up dark corridors, illuminating the lesson material by art masterpiece, traveling to

Palestine and other lands by means of graph and stereograph. Appetites, voracious for Andy Gump and Mutt and Jeff, will continue so until Sunday supplements succumb to the immortal art of Titian, Rembrandt, etc."

82. Adler, 88. Adler concluded his section on Christian responses to art by saying: "It is not in the spirit of Savonarola that the arts must be scourged and expunged, but in the spirit of St. Thomas, who, at the end of his life and in religious ecstasy, could say of his own *Summa Theologica*—incomparably magnificent as a production of human art—'it seems to me rubbish.' It is through such manifestations of Christian vision that one can appreciate, though in a feeble way, the Franciscan impulse to make a huge conflagration of all the classics of the western world, with Hollywood film as tinder" (92).

83. Charles Johnson Post, "Motion Picture Madness," *CH* (July 1, 1922), 466.

84. Ronald Holloway, *Beyond the Image: Approaches to the Religious Dimension in the Cinema* (Geneva: World Council of Churches, 1977), 46.

85. *Ibid.*, 45. Humorously enough, vamp actress Theda Bara claimed in an August 1917 issue of *Motion Picture*, "Every mother and every minister owes me gratitude because every picture in which I appear has a clear moral. I am saving hundreds of girls from social degradation and wrongdoing." To which her biographer, Ronald Genini, responded tongue-in-cheek, "Well, perhaps." Ronald Genini, *Theda Bara* (Jefferson, N. C., McFarland, 1996), 78.

86. See James Cooper, *Knights of the Brush* (New York: Cropsey-Newington Foundation, 1999).

87. Veith persuasively argues that when Hollywood gave a "Cole-fired vision of heaven," in *What Dreams May Come,* they naturally turned to the imagery of the Hudson River School. *Painters of Faith,* 16.

88. Cooper, 6. Author Scott MacDonald also identifies the landscape paintings of Thomas Cole as a key antecedent to nonmainstream films. Scott MacDonald. *The Garden in the Machine: A Field Guide to Independent Films about Place* (Berkeley: University of California Press, 2001). See also the Western rejection of a feminized Christianity in Jane Tompkins, *West of Everything: The Inner Life of Westerns* (New York: Oxford University Press, 1992), 31–38.

89. J. Stuart Blackton, an early animator and founder of the Vitagraph Studios, drew his own "lightning sketches" of the ages of man as a comic homage to Cole's voyages. Donald Crafton, *Before Mickey: The Animated Film 1898–1928* (Cambridge: MIT Press, 1982).

90. Cooper, 15.

91. Jasper F. Cropsey, "Letter to Maria Cooley" (Hastings-on-the-Hudson, N.Y.: Newington-Cropsey Foundation, 1846). See also his "Up among the Clouds," *Crayon* 2 (August 8, 1855), 79.

92. Cooper, 79. On its cover page, The *Crayon* quoted Paul's epistle to the *Philippians* (4: 8) as a prologue to its Protestant homilies on art.

93. "Fine Arts," *Literary World* VII (November 16, 1850), 392. See also Anthony Speiser, "Fine Arts: Panorama of Pilgrim's Progress, A More Particular Notice," *Literary World* VII (December 7, 1850), 460.

94. Kevin Avery, "The Panorama and its Manifestation in American Landscape Painting, 1795–1870," Ph.D. dissertation, Columbia University, 1995, 241.

95. Avery, 243. See Alison Griffiths, "'Shivers Down Your Spine': Panoramas and the Origins of the Cinematic Reenactment," *Screen* 44: 1 (Spring 2003), 1–37.

96. Horace Bushnell, *Nature and Supernature: As Together Constituting the One System of God* (New York: Scribner's, 1858). Bushnell was the pastor of artist Frederic Church.

97. Jonathan Edwards, "Images of Divine Things," *Typological Writings* (ed. Wallace Anderson), *Works of Jonathan Edwards* II (New Haven: Yale University Press, 1993), xii, 56.

98. The Reverend Herbert Atchinson Jump found similar inspiration in the glories of these peaks to pen his own work, *The Yosemite: A Spiritual Interpretation*. Reverend Herbert A Jump, *The Yosemite: A Spiritual Interpretation* (Boston: Pilgrim Press, n.d.).

99. Cropsey, "Up among the Clouds," 80.

100. Dennis Williams, *God's Wilds: John Muir's Vision of Nature* (College Station: Texas A & M University Press, 2002).

101. An early *Ford Educational Weekly* film promoted the wonders of the Canadian Rockies, "where the hand of man has not disfigured the sheer mountain crags that stretch their straggling peaks heavenward," in a reel aptly entitled *God's Handiwork*. See "*God's Handiwork,*" *Ford Educational Weekly* (Washington, D.C.: Library of Congress Foster Files), Reel 9. Similarly, the Canadian films of Nell Shipman, shot on location in the frozen wilderness of Canada, also celebrated the wild landscapes of creation, as in the aptly titled *Back to God's Country* (1919).

102. See David Morgan, *Protestants and Pictures: Religion, Visual Culture, and the Age of American Mass Production* (New York: Oxford University Press, 1999).

103. Ruth M. Whitfield, "Old School Books and Their Illustrations," *Visual Education* (December 1922), 387–89. The Lord's Prayer illustrated from a seventeenth-century Horn Book and a 1785 English Primer set the standards for visual education in religious settings. See also H. Paul Janes, *Screen and Projector in Christian Education* (Philadelphia: Westminster Press, 1933), 45.

104. Carl Clayton Savage, *Study of Broadman Films: Department of Baptist Sunday School Board* (New Orleans: New Orleans Baptist Theological Seminary, 1966), 2–3. The father of Southern Baptist Vacation Bible School programs, Homer Grice was also one of the first to utilize audiovisuals for religious

education in his denomination. "In 1923 he bought a DeVry portable motion picture projector to show films during the Sunday night services," mostly of travelogues provided by railroads and other businesses (10). Grice became chair of the Visual Education Committee of the Baptist Sunday School Board in 1942.

105. "Visualized Religious Education," *IJRE* (October 1924), 62. See also notes on George Bond's Slide Company in "The Bible Land and Its People: The Life and Travels of Jesus: Illuminating and Clarifying the Bible Message," *IJRE* (February 1925), 1. "The Fine Arts in Religion," *IJRE* (November 1926), 13–16.

106. John Davis, *The Landscape of Belief: Encountering the Holy Land in Nineteenth-Century American Art and Culture* (Princeton: Princeton University Press, 1996).

107. Frederica Beard, *Pictures in Religious Education* (New York: George H. Doran, 1920), 83–84.

108. H. L. Mencken, *The American Scene* (New York: Knopf, 1941).

109. See Anne Hollander, *Moving Pictures* (Cambridge: Harvard University Press, 1991).

110. André Bazin, *What Is Cinema?* Vol. II (Berkeley: University of California Press, 1971).

111. Paula Marantz Cohen, *Silent Film and the Triumph of the American Myth* (New York: Oxford University Press, 2001), 73–78.

112. See the essays in both *Back in the Saddle: Essays on Western Film and Television*, ed. Gary A. Yoggy (Jefferson, N.C.: McFarland, 1998), and *Back in the Saddle Again: New Essays on the Western*, ed. Edward Buscombe and Roberta E. Pearson (London: BFI, 1998).

113. See Tom Gunning, "Passion Play as Palimpsest," and Charles Keil's "From the Manger to the Cross: The New Testament Narrative and the Question of Stylistic Retardation," in *Une Invention du Diable?* 102–20.

114. In their study of Muncie, Indiana, in the mid-twenties, Robert S. Lynd and Helen Merrell Lynd found that a majority of the population held very traditional evangelical beliefs in the Bible and Christianity. Robert Lynd and Helen Merrell Lynd, *Middletown: A Study in Modern American Culture* (New York: Harcourt Brace, 1929), 328.

115. Gerald Forshey, *American Religious and Biblical Spectaculars* (New York: Praeger, 1992), 4.

116. Joscelyn Godwin, *Athanasius Kircher: A Renaissance Man and the Quest for Knowledge* (London: Thames and Hudson, 1979).

117. For an explication of the medieval controversies regarding ghosts, daemonic apparitions, and other "straunge sightes," particularly as they related to the science of optics (and subsequently to the tricks of the magic lantern), see Stuart Clark, "The Reformation of the Eyes: Apparitions and Optics in Sixteenth- and Seventeenth-Century Europe," *Journal of Religious History* 27: 2 (June 2003), 143–60.

118. Olive Cook, *Movement in Two Dimensions* (London: Hutchinson, 1963), 82.

119. "Comenius Would Have Welcomed Movies," *EFM* VI: 2 (August 1921), 9. See also "Comenius and Pestalozzi, Fathers of Visual Education," *EFM* III: 1 (January 1920), 6.

120. John A. Comenius, *The Great Didactic* (trans. M. W. Keatings) (London: Black, 1896), 291–92. In 1958, Gene Getz cited Comenius as the evangelical father of all audiovisual instruction. Gene Getz, *Audio-Visual Media in Christian Education* (Chicago: Moody Press, 1972).

121. In the Age of Reason, his projected images of phantoms and specters among the tombs provoked the perverse delights of terror in his viewers. In 1831, Robertson wrote his *Memoires*, Vol. 1 (Paris: chez l'auteur et Librarie de Wurtz, 1831), 278–79.

122. Musser, Charles. *The Emergence of Cinema* (Berkeley: University of California Press, 1994), 24.

123. Etienne Gaspar Robertson, "Ghosts or Disembodied Spirits," *New York Evening Post* (November 4, 1803), 3.

124. See Charles Hughes, "Spirits Shown in Public," *VP* (October 9, 1921), 2; and Ernest A. Dench, "Spiritualism by the Film," in *Motion Picture Education* (Cincinnati: Standard Publishing Company, 1917), 122–57.

125. C. Lance Brockman, "Setting the Stage for Motion Pictures," in Patricia McDonnell, *On the Edge of Your Seat: Popular Theatre and Film in Early Twentieth-Century American Art* (New Haven: Yale University Press, 2002), 96. See also Richard Allen, *Projecting Illusion: Film Spectatorship and the Impression of Reality* (Cambridge: Cambridge University Press, 1995).

126. Musser, 30–31. See Edward Earle, ed., *Points of View: The Stereograph in America—A Cultural History* (Rochester, N.Y.: Visual Studies Workshop, 1979).

127. See Bey A. W. Lamar, *The Stereoptican in Sunday Night Preaching Solved or The Sunday Evening Problem* (New York: Riley Brothers, 1895), and Elizabeth Shepherd, "The Magic Lantern Slide in Entertainment and Education 1860–1920," *History of Photography: An International Quarterly* 11: 2 (April–June 1987), 91–108; and Cheryl C. Boots, "The Intersection of Technology and Religion: Magic Lantern Hymn Slides," *Magic Lantern Gazette* 5: 2 (Summer 1993), 12–14.

128. Charles Musser and Carol S. Nelson, *High-Class Moving Pictures* (Princeton: Princeton University Press, 1991), 10

129. See X. Theodore Barber, "The Roots of Travel Cinema: John L. Stoddard, E. Burton Holmes, and the Nineteenth-Century Illustrated Travel Lecture," *Film History* 5: 1 (1993).

130. Musser (1994), 37–38

131. Kathryn Oberdeck, *The Evangelist and the Impresario* (Baltimore: John

Hopkins Press, 1999), 130. See W. T. Stead, "The Magic Lantern Mission," *Review of Reviews* 1: 12 (1890), 562.

132. *Ibid.,* 42.

133. Musser and Nelson, 10.

134. Terry Borton, "Cinema before Film: Victorian Magic-Lantern Shows and America's First Great Screen Artist, Joseph Boggs Beale" (preliminary draft of work generously supplied to the author).

135. *Ibid.,* 22.

136. See Edwin Rice, *The Sunday-School Movement, 1780–1917,* and *The American Sunday-School Union, 1817–1917* (Philadelphia: American Sunday School Union, 1917).

137. Borton, xx.

138. Boots, 12–14 See also "Singing by Magic Lantern Displays," Frank Leslie's *Illustrated Newspaper* (March 8, 1879), 5, 7; Sidney Ahlstrom, *A Religious History of the American People* (New Haven: Yale University Press, 1972); Susan Tamke, *Make a Joyful Noise Unto the Lord: Hymns as a Reflection of Victorian Social Attitudes* (Athens: Ohio University Press, 1978); and David Robinson, "Introduction: Shows and Slides," in *Magic Images: The Art of Hand-Painted and Photographic Lantern Slides,* ed. Dennis Crompton, David Henry, and Stephen Herbert (London: Magic Lanterns Society of Great Britain, 1990).

139. See Kemp R. Nivers, *Motion Pictures from the Library of Congress Paper Print Collection, 1894–1912* (Berkeley: University of California Press, 1967), 330.

140. Louis Reeves Harrison, "Pilgrim's Progress," *MPW* (November 9, 1912), 538; See also *MPW* (October 26, 1912), 324; and *MPW* (December 7, 1912), 957.

141. "Church to Give Illustrated Songs and Sermons," *Motography* V: 4 (April 1911), 13.

142. Walter Hervey, Ph.d. *Picture = Work* (New York: Fleming H. Revell, 1908).

143. *Ibid.,* 20. Hervey's theology was more heavily influenced by the immanence of Frederic Schlieremacher than by historic orthodoxy, but he here focused on the pragmatic efficacy of visual images for religious work. The iconoclastic controversy tumbled out of competing interpretations of the Second Commandment, dealing with the Hebraic prohibition against graven images.

144. Arthur Edwin Krows, "So the Pictures Went to Church," *TES* (October 1938), 252–53.

145. Krows, "Motion Pictures—Not for Theatres," *TES* (September 1938), 212.

146. Krows, "So the Pictures," 252–3.

147. Albert Edward Bailey, *The Use of Art in Religious Education* (Nashville, Tenn., Abingdon Press, 1922), 110.

240 I *Notes to Chapter 1*

148. *Ibid.* 78–80. By the late twenties, two groups had defined themselves according to the Modernist/Fundamentalist split in theology. See James Carter, *The Gospel Message in Great Pictures* (New York: Funk and Wagnalls, 1929).

149. *Ibid.*, 31.

150. Rev. Chester S. Bucher, "Preaching by Pictures: Screen Sermons," *The Advance* (November 2, 1916).

NOTES TO CHAPTER 2

1. "Church Comments," *Screen*, II: 2 (August 1921), 40.

2. Douglas Gomery, *Shared Pleasures: A History of Movie Presentation in the United States* (Madison: University of Wisconsin Press, 1992) *American Silent Film: Discovering Marginalized Voices* (Carbondale: Southern Illinois University, 2002).

3. Rev. W. H. Jackson, "An Indictment: The Moving Picture, A Clergyman's Child, Has Been Neglected by the Church," *MPW* (April 13, 1918), 233.

4. See T. M. Dombey, *Reverend Hannibal Goodwin, Inventor of the Motion Picture Film* (New York: Dombey, 1921), 3, 5, 11.

5. Emmanuel Billman Joseph, "The Religious Use of Motion Pictures," unpublished B.D. dissertation (University of Chicago: August 1917); Perry Anderson Roberts, "The Social Aspect of the Motion Picture," unpublished M.A. thesis (Southern Baptist Theological Seminary, 1920); "A Study of Motion Pictures in Chicago as a Medium of Communication," unpublished M.A. dissertation (University of Chicago, April 13, 1924), 86–96; Edward Sayler, "The Use of the Motion Picture in the Church as a Means for Religious Education," unpublished B.D. dissertation (Chicago Theological Seminary, June 1925); Leah Irene Fanning, "A Study of the Use of Motion Pictures in the Program of Certain Protestant Churches," unpublished M.A. thesis (Graduate School, University of Southern California, June 1938); Ralph Marion Nichols, "A Survey of the Production of Religious Motion Pictures," unpublished M.A. thesis (University of Southern California, June 1950); Stewart Elson, "A Model for Film Education in the Local Church," unpublished D.Min. dissertation (Claremont School of Theology, June 1971); Joseph Lewis Bridges, "A Historical Study of Cooperative Protestant Religious Film in America from 1914 to 1972," doctoral dissertation (University of Southern California, Los Angeles, 1975); Vinnie Rosini, "Sanctuary Cinema: The Rise and Fall of Protestant Churches as Film Exhibition Sites, 1910–1930" doctoral dissertation (Regent University, 1998).

6. Colin Harding and Simon Popple, *In the Kingdom of the Shadows: A Companion to Early Cinema* (London: Cygnus Arts, 1996), 63.

7. "Moving Picture Evangelist," *Bioscope* (October 9, 1908), 15.

8. Joan Long and Martin Long, *The Pictures That Moved: A Picture History of the Australian Cinema, 1896–1929* (Richmond, Victoria: Hutchinson of Aus-

tralia, 1982), 20–21. See also "Army Cinematographs," *The Field Officer* (October 1906); "Animated Pictures: A Nineteenth-Century Wonder: To Go Round the Provinces," *The Officer* (March 1897); "The Cinematopraph: Its Spiritual and Financial Value," *The Field Officer* (January 1906); and Sylvie Pliskin, "L'influence du département audiovisuel de l'Armée du salut sur le développement du cinéma de fiction en Australie (1896–1910)," in *Une Invention du Diable?* 256–62.

9. John R. Hamilton, "An Historical Study of Bob Pierce and World Vision's Development of the Social Action Film," Ph.d. Dissertation (Los Angeles: University of Southern California, 1980): 56.

10. "Advertisement for *Soldiers of the Cross*," cited in Hamilton, 59. See also *The History of the Salvation Army*, V, *op. cit.* 293–94.

11. See Dean Rapp, "The British Salvation Army, the Early Film Industry and Urban Working-Class Adolescents, 1897–1918," *Twentieth Century British History* 7: 2 (1996), 157–88.

12. Hamilton, 57. Famous Players-Lasky produced propaganda for the Salvation Army in a special melodramatic feature. "*Fires of Faith*," *Variety* (May 9, 1919), 52.

13. W. Stephen Bush, "Maligners of the Moving Picture," *MPW* 3: 23 (December 5, 1908), 444–5. The church in Tuscola, Illinois, planned to draw greater crowds with its next film, *The Sailor's Last Drink*. "Church Finds Moving Pictures Successful Means of Awakening Interest," *MPW* 3 (October 24, 1908), 320; "Moving Pictures and the Sunday School," *Expositor* 11: 10 (July 1910), 539; Stephen W. Bush, "Pictures for Churches," *MPW* 10 (December 2, 1911), 701–2; Rev. Jackson, "The Moving Picture and Its Enemies," *MPW* 7 (September 24, 1910), 681–82; "Moral Lessons on the Screen," *MPW* 8 (January 14, 1911), 87; "Biblical and Religious Pictures," *MPW* 15 (1913), 54; "Moving Picture Educator: Among the Churches," *MPW* 24: 5 (May 1, 1915), 7; "The Clergyman as an Exhibitor," *MPW* (January 2, 1915); "In the Religious World," *MPW* (January 25, 1915); and "The Experience Column: Views of Our Readers Who Are Using Motion Pictures in School and Church Work," *MPW* (May 25, 1918), 1130; and *MPW* (June 1, 1918), 1277.

14. *New York Dramatic Mirror* (April 30, 1913), 28.

15. Terry Ramsaye, *A Million and One Nights: A History of the Motion Picture Through 1925* (New York: Simon and Schuster, 1926), 375. Frederick A. Talbot, *Moving Pictures: How They Are Made and Worked* (Philadelphia: J. B. Lippincott, 1912), 318.

16. Lewis Jacobs, ed., *The Compound Cinema: The Film Writings of Harry Alan Potamkin* (New York: Teachers College Press, 1977), xiii.

17. Rapp, 188.

18. Krows, "So the Pictures Went to Church," 252–53.

19. Claudine Burnett, "Long Beach Motion Picture Industry: 1911–1923," as cited in Jean-Jacques Jura and Rodney Norman Bardin II, *Balboa Films* (Jefferson, N.C., McFarland, 1999), 17.

20. Kevin Starr, *Inventing the Dream: California through the Progressive Era* (New York: Oxford University Press, 1985).

21. See Paul Tillich, "Art and Ultimate Reality," in *Art, Creativity, and the Sacred: An Anthology in Religion and Art,* ed. Diane Apostolos-Cappadona (Crossroad, 1984), 219–36; and *On Art and Architecture* ed. John Dillenberger and Jane Dillenberger (New York: Crossroad, 1987).

22. Wilbur F. Crafts, *National Perils and Hopes: A Study Based on Current Statistics and the Observations of a Cheerful Reformer* (Cleveland: O. F. M. Barton, 1910), 39.

23. Herbert A. Jump, "The Child's Leisure Hour: How It Is Affected by the Motion Picture," *Religious Education* 6 (October 1911), 349–54.

24. Musser, *Before the Nickelodeon*, xiii, xiv.

25. See Devin Lewis, "Rev. Herbert Jump and the Motion Picture," *Film History* 14 (2002), 210–15; and Richard Stromgren, "The Moving Picture World of Stephen Bush," *Film History* (Winter 1988), 19.

26. This treatise predated both the influential psychological study of the photoplay by Hugo Munsterberg and poet Vachel Lindsey's rapturous praise of the new art form. In his 1922 reprint, Lindsay attacked the "brazen pretender" Will Hays who had been promoted as a "boot-licker" for the troubled film industry. Had Hays ever devoted "one hour of his life [to] thinking and working and praying" for the health and morality of the photoplay? Lindsay thought not. In his vision to purify film and restore it to the dignity of Egyptian hieroglyphics and the Gospel of Beauty, he insisted: "Let the evangelists go to Los Angeles, and drive these movie men to their knees with whips of scorpions." *The Film: A Psychological Study, The Silent Photoplay in 1916* (New York: Dover, 1970); *The Art of the Moving Picture* (New York: Liveright, 1970). See Vachel Lindsay, *The Progress and Poetry of the Movies* (ed. Myron Lounsbury) (Lanham, Md.: Scarecrow, 1995), 88–89.

27. *Ibid.,* 22–24.

28. In 1910, Jump even published a statistical analysis on the impact of moving pictures on his town of New Britain, Connecticut. Herbert Jump, "Moving Picture Statistics in New Britain, Conn.," *Moving Picture World* 7: 27 (1910), 1541; "The Social Influence of the Moving Picture," *Playground* 5: 3 (1911), 74–84.

29. When asked to vacate his pulpit in New Britain, Jump was invited to take a new Congregational flock in Oakland, California. From Oakland, Jump led the life of a peripatetic parson, lecturing at various universities like the University of Southern California; and he finally traveled to Ann Arbor, Michigan, where as late as 1925 he was extolling the virtues of film. "The First Christian

Martyr for Moving Pictures," *MPW* 10 (December 16, 1911), 898. See also
"Another Kind of Minister," *Nickelodeon* V: 5 (February 4, 1911), 125–26.

30. George Anderson, "The Case for Motion Pictures, Part I," *Congregationalist and Christian World* 95: 29 (July 9, 1910), 46; George Anderson, "The
Case for Motion Pictures, Part II," *CCW* 95: 29 (July 16, 1910), 78. See also
Jump, *op. cit.*, 13; see also "Religious Use of Moving Pictures," *Literary Digest*
41 (July 30, 1910), 170–72; "Sermon Pellets for Motion Picture Services," *Expositor* 26: 5 (February 1925), 715. Jump also wrote *The Yosemite: A Spiritual
Interpretation* (Boston: Pilgrim Press, circa 1924).

31. Jump, 3.

32. See Edward H. Chandler, "The Moving Picture Show," *Religious Education* VI: 4 (October 1911), 344–49, as well as Jump's companion article, "The
Child's Leisure Hour—How It is Affected by the Motion Picture," *Religious Education* VI: 4 (October 1911), 349–54. See also Jump, "The Ideal City," *Independent* 69 (July 21, 1910), 126–27.

33. "The Motion Picture Sermon," *Nickelodeon* V: 7 (February 18, 1911),
190. See also "How to Make Sermons Interesting," *Nickelodeon* V: 8 (February
25, 1911), 216.

34. "Advocates Films for Churches," *Motography* V: 6 (June 1911), 136.

35. Robert F. Y. Pierce, "Eye Preaching," *Pictured Truth* (New York: Fleming
H. Revell, 1895), cited in Morgan, 248–49. The Reverend J. Webster Bailey of
the Congregational Church in Ottawa, Illinois, echoed the thought that the
Gospel could be preached through the eye as well as the ear, in his presentation
of Selig's *Holy City.* "Moving Pictures at Church Services," *MPW* 3 (December
26, 1908), 522.

36. "Motion Pictures to Replace Sermon, Skowhegan Pastor Will Show *Life
of Moses,* says Boston Globe," *MPW* 7 (December 10, 1910), 1342. Down in
Macon, Georgia, a Baptist pastor substituted his lectures with songs and motion
pictures of Jerusalem and other biblical places as well. "Moving Pictures in the
Church," *MPW* 5 (August 21, 1909), 250. See also "Moving Pictures to Invade
the Church? Rev. W. G. Archer Who Has Already Introduced Stereopticon
Views and Illustrated Hymns, Thinks So," *MPW* 2: 26 (June 27, 1908), 542.

37. "Moving Pictures in Church," *Literary Digest* 40: 23 (June 4, 1910),
1123.

38. "Religious Use of Moving Pictures," *Literary Digest* 41 (July 30, 1910),
170–72.

39. "A New Use of Moving Pictures," *Moving Picture World and View Photographer* I: 1 (March 9, 1907), 6.

40. "Notes of the Week," *Motion Picture News* V: 4 (July 27, 1912), 14.

41. "Vaudeville on a Roof Garden," *MPW* I: 15 (June 15, 1911), 233. "St.
Louis Church Opens Picture Show," *MPN* VI: 7 (August 17, 1912), 20.

42. *MPW* II (January 1908), 6.

43. "Moving Pictures at Revivals," *Motography* VI: 3 (September 1911), 110.

44. "Church to Use Films," *Motography* VI: 4 (October 1911), 190; "Wants Pictures in Churches," *Motography* (July 20, 1912), 65.

45. Musser, 83.

46. "The Editor's Chair," *Photographic News* (January 14, 1898), cited in Harding and Popper, *op. cit.,* 79.

47. Carl Holliday, "The Motion Picture and the Church," *Independent* 74 (February 13, 1913), 353; "The Power of Pictures," *Motography* IX: 7 (April 5, 1913), 220. See also Holliday citing Jump at a University of California lecture, in which he described film as the "hand-maiden of education." Carl Holliday, "The Motion Picture Teacher," *The World's Work* 26 (May 1913), 39–49.

48. Dench, 122–57.

49. See "The Churchmen Say," *Film Progress* 6:8 (September 1922), 4. Emphasis in original. See also C. N. Lathrope, "Motion Picture and the Church," *Playground* 16 (October 1922), 307–8; "Motion Pictures and the Churches: Part Three," *Playground* 16 (December 1922), 416–17 and "Motion Pictures and the Churches: Part Four," *Playground* 16 (January 1923), 451–52.

50. "DeVry Portable Motion Pictures for Church Schools," *IJRE* (May 1926), 71; "DeVry," *IJRE* (June 1926), 77; "Victor Animatograph Corporation," *IJRE* (November 1944), 39. The 16mm industry for church and educational markets was born on August 12, 1923 through the inventions of Alexander F. Victor.

51. Charles Banning, "Church Problems in the Use of Motion Pictures," *IJRE* (July–August 1925), 14–15.

52. "More Necessary than the Church Bell," *CH* (April 17, 1920), 493. On another note, Marcel Proust compared the magic lantern to moving stained glass windows in *Remembrance of Things Past,* suggesting another instance of the continuity of religious communication.

53. Orrin Cocks, "The Successor of the Saloon," in Herbert Sherwood ed., *The Bulletin of the Affiliated Committees for Better Films* 3:2 (New York: National Committee for Better Films, February 1918), 1. See also Charles Stelzle, "Movies Instead of Saloons," *Independent* (February 25, 1916), 311.

54. Alfred Hill, "What Are the Substitutes for the Saloon?" *CH* (May 10, 1919), 530.

55. John Flinn, "The Movies and Morals," *CH* (September 6, 1919), 937; Orrin Cocks, "The Movies as Substitute," *CH* (May 10, 1919), 530; S. I. Rothapfel, "Always the Saloon's Rival," *CH* (May 10, 1919) 530; Charles Stelzle, "Substitutes for the Saloon," *CH* (April 26, 1919), 492; Charles Sheldon, "After the Saloon—What?" *CH* (June 7, 1919), 637.

56. "Manager in Church: Arthur Merriman to Study for Episcopalian Orders," *Variety* (August 26, 1921), 39; and "Gives Up Films for the Pulpit," *Variety* (April 1, 1925), 27.

57. "Cleric Abuses Courtesy: Clergyman in Donated Theatre Heaps Tirade on Other Houses," *Variety* (February 18, 1921), 1.

58. Frederick James Smith, "Making the Movie Do Its Bit: Organizing the Church, School and YMCA for the Presentation of Motion Pictures," *Photoplay* 12 (November 1917), 85–86, 112.

59. "Protestant Sects Now Unite to Show Films in Churches," *Variety* (September 9, 1919), 57.

60. "Personally Conducted Church Film Review," *TES* (October 1925), 484.

61. "The Hymnbook of the Screen," *IJRE* (April 1945), 38.

62. The Reverend John Koontz even coordinated a conference on Kodachrome slide usage. Otto Nall, "A Quarterly Conference in KODACHROME," *CA* (September 26, 1946), 1228.

63. However, a hymnologue like *Onward Christian Soldiers* could be harshly criticized as merely depicting poorly illustrated soldiers marching about. "Hymnologues," *IJRE* (July–August 1945), 28.

64. H. Paul Janes, "How to Illustrate Hymns with Pictures," *TES* (June 1933), 170–71.

65. "Personally Conducted Church Film Review," *TES* (September 1925), 414. See also "Moving Pictures in the Church," *Church Management* 3: 8 (May 1927), 457, for a "synchronized evening service" order from organ prelude through the motion picture, *Main Street the World Over,* and the sermon on "Why Some Marriages End in Divorce." Marceille Conkling, "Movies Fill This Church," *Church Management* 4: 9 (June 1928), 597–98.

66. "Moving Pictures in Danville Church," *VP* (July 3, 1917), 9.

67. Dr. Carl Patton, "Why We Use the Movies," *VE* IV (June 1923), 189. "Motion Pictures in the Sunday Evening Services," *Congregationalist* CIX: 13 (March 27, 1924), 402, 415; Arthur Marble, "Sunday Evening Movies," *Photo-Era Magazine* 63 (July 1929), 46–47. See also "Sunday Evening Movies," *Photo Era* 63 (July 1929), 46–47; and Will Hays, *The Memoirs of Will H. Hays* (Garden City, N.Y.: Doubleday, 1955), 375.

68. "Idle Wives' Film Sermon at Fotosho," *VP* (July 8, 1917), 18.

69. Rom Pettey, "Movies—Friend or Foe? *CH* (October 20, 1928), 1101, 1102.

70. One successful young man confessed: "I was one of the dirty-faced urchins who in childhood came to your free motion pictures. The addresses and the atmosphere of those church movies gave me the deep inspiration which has finally brought me to this responsible position." *Ibid.,* 1101.

71. See also Chester Marshall, "Motion Pictures in the Church," *CH* (April 24, 1920), 523 "As One Minister Sees Us," *MPW* (May 1, 1920), 653.

72. *Ibid.,* 1101, 1102.

73. Butler, 352.

74. Churches in small towns in particular were urged to cooperate with the "little photoplay theatre" in their vicinity. "Says Movies Offer Lesson to Church," *New York Times* 75 (January 30, 1926), 18

75. Elisha King, "How Ministers Use Motion Pictures," *Congregationalist* CIX: 13 (March 27, 1924), 394–95. See also "Motion Pictures in the Church to Stay," *Church Management* 4: 2 (December 1927), 112–13.

76. William Jennings Bryan, quoted in Rae Henkle, "The Puzzle of the Pictures," *CH* (September 16, 1922), 647. See also "Biblical Picture Road Show," *Variety* (July 14, 1922), 47; and "Bible Film Showing," *Variety* (March 3, 1922), 44. The Artclass Picture was touted as an "Italian picturization."

77. "Billy Sunday on the Educational Power of the Movie," *EFM* VII: 1 (January 1922), 11; "Evangelist Filmed Unaware," *MPW* (April 10, 1915), 258. See also "Some Things to Be Thankful For: That Evangelist Billy Sunday Says Picture Shows Are All Right!" "William Lord Wright's Page," *MPN* VI: 21 (November 23, 1912), 14. However, earlier *Variety* had sighed in relief: "Philadelphia theatrical managers are thankful this is the last week of Billy Sunday's revivals in this city. He has lasted 11 weeks." "Billy Sunday's Last," *Variety* (March 19, 1915), 3.

78. William Mitchell, "How to Use Motion Pictures in the Pulpit," *VE* (October 1921), 4–8, reprinted from *The Expositor* (August 1921); Frederic Fay, "Motion Pictures and Worship," *VE* (1921), 172–173. See also Mitchell's article, "The Film as Introduction to the Sermon," in *EFM* VI: 65 (November 1921), 13, 19–20 A young Italian parishioner told the preacher: "Gooda picture. God lika dat!" Reverend John McAfee, "Purpose of Pictures Is to Preach," *EFM* VI: 6 (December 1921), 12; "Neighborhood Night," *Simpson Historical Volume* (Minneapolis, MN: Simpson United Methodist Church, 1919), 59–63. A detailed blueprint of "Simpson's New Church Building" shows a giant auditorium with a "movie booth above" (May 1924).

79. The Reverend Dr. Leslie Willis Sprague identified four distinct ways in which churches had used films: "for recreation, for popular attraction, for religious and moral instruction, and as aids to worship and the strengthening of spiritual emotion." Leslie Willis Sprague, "Four Ways in Which Churches Use Movies," *EFM* III: 2 (February 1920), 18. Through his Community Motion Picture Bureau, Sprague also taught young preachers at Boston Theological Seminary how to preach with the aid of motion pictures. See "Teaching Preachers Via the Screen," *EFM* III: 4 (April 1920), 15–16.

80. A. B. Hollis, "Movies in the Church School," *IJRE* (May 1926), 33–34. Emphasis added. See also Grace Harris, "The Use of Pictures in the Vacation Church School," *IJRE* (April 1925), 36–37; "Use of Motion Pictures in Teaching Religion," *IJRE* III (November 1926), 26–27; and Hazel Lewis, "Effective Use of Pictures in Church School Work with Children," *IJRE* (April 1927), 19–20. "The Movies and the Children," *IJRE* (September 1932), 3.

81. Uthai Vincent Wilcox, "Motion Pictures at the Sunday Services," *Homiletic Review* 95 (June 1928), 448–50.

82. Josephine Baldwin, "Motion Pictures," *IJRE* (July–August 1926), 11–12.

83. *Ibid.*, 12.

84. Walsh, 18–19.

85. Charles Banning, "The Purpose of Motion Pictures in Religious Education," *IJRE* (June 1925), 17–18.

86. "Moving Pictures in the Church: How a Minister Aims to Teach Christ in Pictures," *Photoplay* 8 (November 1915), 150. See also "Minister Uses Screen in His Social Service Work," *MPW* (January 10, 1920), 254.

87. *MPW* I:16 (June 22, 1907), 249. The Catholics at St. Jude's Church in Beloit, Wisconsin, conducted a five-cent theater during the week before Lent even as Chicago Presbyterian women were arranging picture shows for children. "Pastor Conducts Picture Theater," and "Picture Show in a Church," *Nickelodeon* I: 5 (May 1909), 124, 140; "Moving Pictures in Church," *Nickelodeon* II: 5 (November 1909), 146. Of special interest was the Reverend William Smothers, "pastor of the Ebenezar Baptist Church, Negro" who added a moving picture machine to his equipment in Atchison, Kansas. "Moving Pictures in Church," *Nickelodeon* III: 2 (January 15, 1910), 32.

88. "Church Service in Moving Picture Theater," *MPW* 8 (January 21, 1911), 136; "Clergymen Patronize Moving Picture Exhibitions," *MPW* 6 (March 5, 1910), 329. The Reverend Edward Dempster of Olivet Presbyterian Church in Lima, Ohio, gained publicity by displaying his sermon topic on the local Lima Picture Theater marquis all week. "Strange Use for Picture Theater," *Nickelodeon* III: 9 (May 1, 1910), 240. See also how the Rochester Theatre proprietors chose "not to compete with the Lord on Sundays," but wanted to advertise the minister's sermons. "Movies Propose Help for Churches," *MPW* (May 3, 1919), 651.

89. "Turning Moving Picture Theaters into Churches," *MPN* 5: 2 (January 13, 1912), 17–18.

90. "The Church, the School and the Moving Picture," *MPW* XIX: 13 (March 21, 1914), 1513; "Church for Pictures," *Variety* (December 18, 1905), 14. *Variety* announced on Christmas Day that William Fox took another New York church for his exhibition enterprises. "Fox to Convert Church," *Variety* (December 25, 1909), 10. The New Orpheum purchased the Old St. Patrick's Church in Brockton, Massachusetts, for similar purposes. "Theater on Church Site," *MPW* (January 2, 1915), 79. *Variety* reported that the problem of what to do with the "large barren structures that were left in the wake of a Billy Sunday sojourn" was solved when the tabernacle was reconstructed into a theater for returning servicemen. "Tabernacle a Theatre," *Variety* (March 7, 1919), 1.

91. "Church Movie Theaters," *EFM* IV: 2 (August 1920), 12. See also Rev. James D. D. Empringham, "The Photoplay Theatre as a Church Enterprise,"

The Churchman CXXI: 19 (May 8, 1920), 15. Earlier, however, churches had been "corrupted" into becoming theaters. See "Trade Notes," *MPW* (March 16, 1907), 23.

92. "Sunday Movies in Theater," *EFM* V: 3 (March 1921), 17; "Non-Theatrical Exhibitors—Take Heed," *EFM* V: 4 (April 1921), 5.

93. Even conservative Baptists held a major unification meeting in the Academy. "Extension Rally Early in New Year" (December 2, 1908), 3. See also "Large Attendance at Noon-Day Service," *VP* (March 11, 1909), 6; "Noonday Services at the Wonderland," *VP* (March 16, 1909), 3; "Dr. Bell Speaks during Holy Week at the American Theatre," *VP* (April 16, 1919), 10; "Episcopal Church Congress Will Convene in Norfolk," *VP* (April 30, 1916), 3.

94. "Bishop Strange to Large Audience," *VP* (March 17, 1911), 10; "Large Attendance at Noon-Day Services," *VP* (March 7, 1911), 4; "Good Attendance at Monday Services," *VP* (March 9, 1911), 5; "Professing Christians Are of Little Good at Granby," *VP* (March 24, 1911), 3; "Preached on Love of God and Love of Man," *VP* (April 4, 1911), 13; "Last Monday Service at Granby: Dr. F. C. Steinmitz," *VP* (April 14, 1911), 3; "Through Ideals Is Created Character," *VP* (March 28, 1911), 7; "Larger Crowds at Noon Services," *VP* (February 23, 1912), 7; "Another Big Crowd Hears Bishop Strange," *VP* (February 29, 1912), 3.

95. "The Fall of Babylon: How? When? Why?" *VP* (January 12, 1918), 2.

96. "To Lecture on World, War, and Bible," *VP* (January 20, 1918), 4.

97. "Evangelist Richardson Tells of Rules of Righteous and New Jerusalem at the Colonial," *VP* (February 4, 1918), 3; "Second Coming of Christ in This Generation," *VP* (February 17, 1918), 10.

98. "Millions Now Living Will Never Die," advertisement *Ledger-Dispatch* (December 20, 1919), 11; "End of the World Seems to Have Been Postponed," *VP* (December 17, 1919), 1; "Sun Shines for First Time since World's End," *VP* (December 24, 1919), 1.

99. "Evangelist Claims Empires Will End," *VP* (January 27, 1918), 17.

100. "YMCA Meeting Today," *VP* (January 19, 1908), 5; "'Self Control' Theme of Rev. Booker," *VP* (March 31, 1908), 5.

101. "At Barton's Theatre Tuesday," *VP* (April 25, 1908), 2. See "Barton on Bended Knee, Seeks Blessings of God," *VP* (April 29, 1908), 7.

102. "Noonday Services in the Granby Today," *VP* (March 1, 1911), 2. With major social and religious events occurring in theaters, the paper suggested: "What Norfolk Must Have: A Modern Auditorium," *VP* (May 21, 1916), 21. "Lenten Services Begin Next Week: Will Be Held at Granby Theatre under Auspices of Brotherhood of St. Andrew," *VP* (January 29, 1913), 3; "The Wonder of the Gospel," *VP* (February 21, 1913), 3; "Rev. George Stuart to Speak Here Today," *VP* (January 2, 1916), 3; and "What Was the Religion of Jesus?" *VP* (January 13, 1916), 2.

103. Thomas Doherty, "This Is Where We Came In: The Audible Screen and the Voluble Audience of Early Sound Cinema," in *American Movie Audiences* (ed. Melvyn Stokes and Richard Maltby) (London: BFI, 1999), 148. "What exhibitors dubbed the 'Lenten slump' was a yearly reminder of the impact of Catholics on the box office."

104. "Church Observances Confuse Theatres," *Variety* (April 7, 1922), 1. Soon it was not unusual for revivalists and preachers to proclaim their message at the best auditoriums in the city. While many such sermons were merely moralistic, some were very evangelistic, decrying sin (which did not seem to be defined as one's presence in theaters) and calling for conversions. (Following one sermon, however, there was to be a wrestling carnival. Also, not all presentations at these theaters were so orthodox, as the Royal Theatre addressed the topic of reincarnation.) See "Revivalist at Colonial Today," *VP* (March 20, 1921), 22; "Engineer Urges Christ Be Given Right of Way: Gaining Pleasure in Sin Will Bring Sorrow in End, Preacher Asserts at Colonial," *VP* (March 21, 1921), 12; "Reincarnation the Topic of Sunday Night Lecture at the Royal Theatre," *VP* (March 15, 1910), 12.

105. "Is There a Devil?" *VP* (April 11, 1915), 2; "To Excommunicate Satan," *VP* (May 16, 1916), 6.

106. "Methods to Attract Worshippers," *VP* (July 12, 1908), 16; "Pictures Lure for Non-Churchgoers," *VP* (December 3, 1911), 44.

107. "The Way Our Bible Came to Us," *VP* (October 31, 1915), 2.

108. H. L. Lambdia, "A la Hollywood," *CH* (September 14, 1933), 871; "Sermon Titles," *CH* (October 5, 1933), 959.

109. "Col. Dean to Speak at Arcade Today," *VP* (September 19, 1915), 7; "Baptist Dr. Swope Will Speak at the Majestic Theatre on 'The Way of Transgression Is Hard,'" *VP* (October 9, 1915), 4.

110. "Rain Interferes with Revivals," *VP* (October 8, 1915), 4.

111. "Increased Interest in Baptist Revival," *VP* (October 7, 1915), 3; "Religious Matters: Noonday Worship at the Academy," *VP* (March 29, 1916), 8; and "The Gospel at the Academy," *VP* (April 19, 1916), 5.

112. "Dr. Hillis's Sermon on Censorship," *Film Progress* 7: 5 (May 1923), 6. And "Better Films in Negro Theatres" and "Motion Pictures in Sunday Evening Services," *Film Progress* 7: 7 (September 1923), 3–4; "Pastor Has Novel Plan for Sermons," *NJG* (September 16, 1922), 1; "Church Vote Acquits Theatre Goers of Sin," *NJG* (September 23, 1922), 1.

113. "Bishop Ward to Open Crusade at Attucks Sunday," *NJG* (February 5, 1927), 8. There was also an advertisement for the Grace Episcopal Choir to "Render the Crucifixion" and "Handel's Messiah" at the Attucks for Easter celebration.

114. "A Special Sermon to Men Only" (March 12, 1921), 4 ("No boys nor women will be admitted," the Attucks warned). See also "Bishop Ward to Open

Crusade at Attucks Sunday," *NJG* (February 5, 1927), 8; and "To Render the 'Crucifixion' at Attucks Sunday," *NJG* (April 9, 1927), 8.

115. "Church or Devil to Entertain Young of This Century," *VP* (August 21, 1909), 5.

116. "Mass Meeting for Women at Colonial Next Sunday," *VP* (March 23, 1919), 7. See also "Salvation Army to Distribute Gifts at the Majestic," *VP* (December 21, 1915), 4.

117. "Will Operate Movie Theatre for Charity," *VP* (January 4, 1920), 2: 1, 6.

118. "Entertainment at Kempsville," *VP* (January 23, 1921), 1: 9.

119. For some, however, "the five-cent theater is the devil's apothecary shop, an awful curse to the boy. . . . The five-cent theater undoubtedly is a sin producer." "The First Church in the World to Show Motion Pictures," *EFM* 2: 1 (July 1919), 15–16; "Seek Sin at a Bargain," *MPW* I: 37 (November 16, 1907), 594. "Wicked Five-Cent Theatres," *MPW* I: 38 (November 23, 1907), 615. J.M. B. of *MPW* reported that in 1906 a man was making a comfortable living as the booking agent for motion pictures for churches. "Pictures for Church Work," *MPW* 6: 4 (January 29, 1910), 121. Even a Baptist in southern Macon, Georgia, adopted illustrated songs and motion pictures in lieu of a sermon, which prompted one wag to retort: "Who wouldn't?" "Moving Pictures in the Church," *MPW* 5: 8 (August 21, 1909), 250.

120. "Motion Pictures at the New York Labor Temple," *Film Educational Magazine* 2: 2 (August 1919), 18, 20. In contrast to Chambers's success, the Episcopalians lost 54,000 children within a two-year period, as they hadn't realized the magnetic power of movies. See "Sunday School Movies," *EFM* 2: 6 (December 1919), 6.

121. *Ibid.*, 20.

122. *MPW* (December 28, 1912), 1285. See Sloan, 111, 113.

123. "Free Movies for Children," *New York Times* 64 (December 12, 1914), 11.

124. "Orphans Invited to Free Entertainment: 'Pilgrim's Progress' will be shown at Cumberland St. Church Tonight," *VP* (October 18, 1917), 4; "Pilgrim's Progress and Parsifal in Pictures," *VP* (November 17, 1917), 7; "The Frederick Ray Cinemalogues: Pilgrim's Progress and Parsifal," *VP* (November 18, 1917), 27.

125. "Moving Picture Shows," *Expositor* 14: 7 (May 1913), 503–4.

126. "The Church's Duty to the Movies," *LD* 64 (February 21, 1920), 38.

127. "'Movies' in Church and Out," *LD* 49 (July 4, 1914), 24.

128. See also "Church Picture Plan Tried Out," *MPW* XXI: 1 (July 4, 1914), 41.

129. "Methodist Centenary Committee Favors Use of Moving Pictures in Religious Services," *MPA* (August 1920), 20.

130. Hilda Jackson, "Church Motion Pictures—Its Development and Growth," *Screen* 1: 8 (April 13, 1921), 6–7.

131. William Gardner, "Moving Pictures and the Church," *MPM* 18 (November 1919), 38–40, 112–22.

132. Ronald Walter Greene, "Y Movies: Film and the Modernization of Pastoral Power," *Communication and Critical/Cultural Studies* 2: 1 (March 2005), 20–36.

133. Ronald Greene, "(Wh)Y Movies: Early Cinema and the Art of Liberal Governance" (Miami: NCA Convention, November 22, 2003).

134. John Collier, *Motion Pictures in Public Education* (New York: Industrial Department International, YMCA, 1913), 3–4.

135. Alexander's early study on Sunday schools, adolescents, and moving pictures inquired whether anyone had facts regarding the effects of Sunday moving pictures upon boys. (Regarding whether sexual wrongs were prompted by "suggestive pictures," the author found that "in one college library, scientific books on sex hygiene were so worn with much use by students" that a professor was put in charge of them; but nothing in the motion pictures had, in 1912, titillated young boys. Of course, everyone knew that French films were wicked. J. L. Alexander, "Theaters, Nickelodeons, and Amusements," *The Sunday School and the Teens* (New York: Association Press, 1913), 282–87, 311–13; O. C. Helming, "Moving Pictures in the Sunday School," *Independent* 75 (July 31, 1913), 277–78.

136. Otis Caldwell, *VE* I: 1 (January 1920), 2.

137. C. L. Hultgren, "Teaching English to Foreigners through Motion Pictures," *VE* 1: 5 (September–October 1920), 25–28; "One Thousand Film Subjects at Your Service," *VE* (May 1920), 59. With many parishes buying projectors, companies like Atlas offered a *"gradual payment plan for your church."* Emphasis added. See *Churchman* (May 8, 1920), 19.

138. Henry Atkinson, *The Church and the People's Play* (New York: Pilgrim Press, 1913), 137–38; Herbert Wright Gates, *Recreation and the Church* (Chicago: University of Chicago Press, 1917).

139. Frederick Talbot, *Moving Pictures* (Philadelphia: J. B. Lippincott, 1912), 317.

140. Christian Reisner, *Church Publicity* (New York: Methodist Book Concern, 1913); Carolyn Sherwin Bailey, "Church 'Movies' This Summer," *Ladies Home Journal* 34 (June 1917), 35; Frederick James Smith, "Making *the* Movie Do Its Bit," *Photoplay* XII: 6 (November 1917), 85–86, 112; "Dr. Reisner Adopts Screen for All Religious Instruction," *Reel and Slide* I: 1 (March 1918), 3–4; Rev. Charles McCarthy, "Motion Pictures in the Church," *CH* (September 6, 1919), 937; Rev. Ernest Miller, "The Movies in the Church," *CH* (May 10, 1919), 530; Chester Marshall, "The Motion Picture in Church Work: How the Motion Picture Has Helped Me in My Church," *CH* (December 13, 1919),

1273; Rev. Wm. Whear (Lanesboro, Iowa), "Motion Pictures and the Church," *CH* (December 13, 1919), 1273. Marshall wrote a five-part installment series on movies and their relationship to the church in *CH* (March 13, 1920), 318; *CH* (April 3, 1920), 422–23; *CH* (April 17, 1920), 488; *CH* (April 24, 1920), 523; and *CH* (May 15, 1920), 596–97.

141. Greene, "Y. Movies: Film and the Modernization of Pastoral Power," 24.

142. "Pictures at Church Entertain Sailors: Big Audience Attends Screen Show at Cumberland Street Methodist Church," *VP* (September 14, 1917), 7; "Entertainment at Spurgeon Memorial," *VP* (September 25, 1917), 10; "Enlisted Men Entertained at Cumberland St. Church," *VP* (September 28, 1917), 4; "Park View Church to Entertain Men," *VP* (October 2, 1917), 7; "To Entertain for the Enlisted Men: Catholic Women of Norfolk to Be Hostesses at YMCA," *VP* (October 19, 1917), 7; "Moving Picture Exhibition at Sunday School," *VP* (November 2, 1917), 11.

143. Carlyle Ellis, "The Parson Who Believed in Pictures," *Everybody's Magazine* 36 (February 1917), 140–43.

144. "Moving Pictures in the Church: How a Minister Aims to Teach Christ in Pictures," *Photoplay* 8 (November 1915), 150.

145. P. Marion Simms, "Modern Methods in Church Work," *Biblical World* 46 (December 1915), 359. See ground and balcony floor plans for motion pictures. "Moving Pictures in the Church," *Expositor* 17: 4 (January 1916), 375–76.

146. R. H. Rolofson, "Great Sunday Evenings with Pictures," *TES* (September 1924), 266–68.

147. *Ibid.*, 16.

148. "The element of controversy increases when dogma, theology or biblical interpretation, or the person of the Deity is presented," it announced. *Motion Picture Principles for the Church* (National Board of Review Collection, Box 30, National Religious Advisory Committee, Rare Manuscripts Division, Astor, Lennox, and Tilden Foundation, New York Public Library, 1913).

149. In 1907, Dr. N. W. Tracy used the moving picture, *The Footsteps of the Prodigal Son,* as an illustrated parable in pantomime during his evangelistic tent revival in Lexington, Kentucky. At the same time, William Buckman of the Trenton, New Jersey, Presbyterian Church was illustrating his lecture for missionary funding with striking actualities. "Leaving the Harbor, Storm at Sea," *MPW* I: 7 (April 20, 1907), 103.

150. Rev. Stanley Hunter, "Use of Stereopticon and Motion Pictures in Our Christian Work," *The Presbyterian Banner* 103: 17 (October 5, 1916), 12–14; Rev. W. H. Jackson, "The Clergyman as an Exhibitor," *MPE* (January 2, 1915), 64.

151. George White, "Missionary Messages," *MPA* V: 3 (March 1922), 11.

152. Ernest Dench, "The Effect Motion Pictures Have on Heathens," *Motion Picture Classic* 2 (June 1916), 17–18.

153. Eva Chappell, "Interchurch Movement Turns to Film Producing," *EFM* III: 1 (January 1920), 18–19.

154. "Slides and Pictures Used in Interchurch World Work," *MPA* 3:5 (May 1920), 13–14.

155. "Interchurch Officers," *Variety* (February 17, 1922), 41.

156. E. N. Walnes of the Southern Baptist film exchange directed exhibitions in Tokyo. "Visual Activities the World Over," *VE* (April 1922), 215. The underlying end and aim of all visual education, according to Homer Rodcheaver of Shentung Christian University was, "making known the Gospel of Christ to all who visit the English Baptist Mission." "The Religious Note: Pictures Models, Charts Bring World Ideas to Chinese Masses," *VE* (September 1924), 290–91.

157. Harry Myers, "Missionary Education through Pictures," *IJRE* 3 (February 1927), 21–22; Sydney Cox, "How an Australian Pastor Regards Movies," *VE* (October 1924), 352.

158. Hanford Judson, "*As Ye Sow,*" *MPW* 23: 1(January 2, 1915), 58.

159. John Stapleton, "The Film Parable: A New Move in Movies," *Congregationalist* 109: 29 (May 22, 1924), 655–56.

160. Thomas Opie, "How We Use Motion Pictures," *Churchman* 139: 3 (January 19, 1929), 15–16. Opie estimated that by 1929 film exhibition extended among 7,000 Methodist churches, 3,000 Presbyterians, 1,000 Congregationalists, and hundreds of Episcopal churches.

161. "Thomas Fletcher Opie," *Churchman* (February 15, 1957); Margaret Elizabeth Gant, *The Episcopal Church of the Holy Comforter, 1879–1979, 100 Years* (1980), 14.

162. Beulah Amidon, "New Guises for Old Truths," *Survey* 58 (April 15, 1927), 105.

163. "Missions and the Movies," *CC* (May 8, 1924), 598–99.

164. H. F. Huse, "The Picture an Agency in Aggressive Church Work," *TES* (September 1925), 409–14. Huse recommended *Silas Marner* for its immense "homiletical usefulness."

165. "Methodists Using Motion Pictures," *Motography* IX: 12 (June 14, 1913), 420.

166. "Missionary Takes Bible Films to Savages," *Screen* I: 8 (April 13, 1921), 20.

167. "Why the Church Must Show Movies," *EFM* 2: 1 (July 1919), 6–7. Emphasis added.

168. Gross W. Alexander, "Motion Pictures and the Motion Picture Theater," *Methodist Review* LXVII: 3 (July 1918), 520–21.

169. Charles M. Sheldon, "Choked with Pleasures," *CH* (May 24, 1919), 592.

170. "*Martyrdom of Philip Strong,*" *Variety* (December 1, 1916), 27.

171. "A Community Show Conducted by a Church," *FP* 1: 3 (March 1924), 10; "Special Lenten Shows: Religious Meetings in Theatres," *MPW* (February 27, 1915), 330; "Lenten Drop Begins," *Variety* (March 3, 1922), 1, 11; "Church Observances Confuse Theatres," *Variety* (April 7, 1922), 1; "Church and Theatre Cooperate in Lenten Exhibitions," *FP* 1:4 (April 1924), 7.

172. Henry F. Cope, *Organizing the Church School* (New York: George Doran, 1923), 250.

173. "A Question for Every Minister and Church Member," *CH* (April 3, 1920), 410.

174. H. V. Mather, "Community Movies in San Diego Church," *EFM* III: 3 (March 1920), 14; Rev. Dr. E. C. Horn, "Educational Movies in Minnesota Church," *EFM* III: 3 (March 1920), 15; "Church Screens Children's Programs on Saturday Afternoons," *EFM* III 4 (April 1920), 14; "The Church Is Being Born Anew," in "Motion Picture Activities in the Country's Churches," *EFM* III: 4 (April 1920), 15.

175. Chester Marshall, "Pictures and the 'Church Night,'" *TES* (April 1924), 156–57.

176. Rev. C. C. Fisher, "Are Motion Pictures in the Church a Success?" *TES* (January 1924), 30.

177. Homer Croy, "Making a Friend of the Movies," *CH* (January 24, 1920), 93.

178. *Ibid.,* 93. In spite of his enthusiasm, however, it wasn't long before Croy championed another religious medium, the radio. Homer Croy, "What the Radio Means to the Church," *CH* (July 29, 1922), 531.

179. "Entertainment and the Church," *MPA* V: 4 (April 1922), 7–8, 37–38.

180. "This Preacher's Gumption Filled His Empty Pews," *American Mercury* 94 (June 1922), 64–65.

181. Rev. D. T. Robertson, "The Moving Picture in the Program of the Church," *TES* (December 1925), 612. Florence Baer, "The Open Letter Column," *TES* (November 1925), 554–55.

182. Atkinson, 136.

183. Christian Reisner, *The Church as a Social Center* (Philadelphia: American Baptist Publication Society, 1915), 20.

184. George Esdras Bevan, *Motion Pictures: The Experience of One Church* (New York: Educational Department Board of Home Missions of the Presbyterian Church in the U. S. A., n.d.), 4. "The Church must go out into the highways and constrain them to come in" with moving pictures. City authorities provided a free license and a fire insurance agent secured waivers regarding permits. *Ibid.,* 6.

185. Roy Smith, "How Our Church Uses Moving Pictures: III. Organizing to Handle 'Neighborhood Night,'" *MPA* IV: 1 (January 1921), 7–8, 15–16; Rev.

C. J. Sharp (pastor of Christian Church in Hammond, Indiana), "Films' Place on a Church Program," *Reel and Slide* I: 10 (October 1918), 7; Charles Banning, "Pictures in the Educational Program," *IJRE* (September 1925), 17–18.

186. Roy Smith, *Moving Pictures in the Church* (New York: Abingdon Press, 1921), 22–23.

187. Roy Smith, "How Movies Made the Church a House of Happiness," *EFM* 2: 6 (December 1919), 17–18. See also the Pastor of First Baptist Church, Grafton, West Virginia. Rev. Em M. Rhoades, "'Children's Hour' Movies Attract 13,000 Sunday School Pupils." *Ibid.*, 18.

188. "Unfair Competition by Churches," *MPW* (November 25, 1916), 1213.

189. It is worth noting that a decade before in Minneapolis, a theater called the Milo, catering mostly to Russian immigrant Jews, chose to show only biblical films. "A Theater Showing Only Biblical Films," *Motography* VI: 6 (December 1911), 258. The article lists only Hebrew Bible narratives like *Mordecai and Esther* and *The Life of Moses*.

190. *Ibid.*, 17.

191. "Third Bible Picture Study Awards," *CH* (May 24, 1919); Frank Brown, "Sunday School Methods: Missionary Entertainments and Pageants," *CH* (March 1, 1919), 252. Rev. Adam Chambers, "Winning the Children with Motion Pictures," *CH* (November 8, 1919), 1178.

192. J. A. Steward, "A 'Movie' Theater Sunday School," *CH* (December 20, 1919), 1327.

193. Charles Banning, "Pictures in the Educational Program," *IJRE* (September 1925), 17–18.

194. Clinton Wunder, *The Conversion of the Motion Picture* (New York: August Gauthier, 1927), 11, 18. Since the "movie" is being converted, Wunder wrote, the scriptures thus demand that "the industry is working out its own salvation." *Ibid.*, 22.

195. William Stidger, *That God's House May Be Filled: A Book of Modern Church Methods and Workable Plans* (New York: George Doran, 1924). Stidger also advocated radio ministry, suggesting that "with a mere nominal expenditure the church could install receiving sets in the homes of the old and the sick and they could hear the services just as if they were well," broadcasting into "hotel lobbies where the indifferent gather." *Ibid.*, 152.

196. Thomas Tiplady, *The Cinema Church: What It Is and What It Is Doing* (London: University Library, 1935).

197. Mitchell recognized that the advent of the talkies produced another problem for the church producer, because silent films quickly became as superannuated as the old nickelodeon material. William S. Mitchell, *A Seven-Day Church at Work* (New York: Funk and Wagnalls, 1929), 65–66, 68, 71. As far as preferred films went, Al Christie's comedies were a big hit with Father Neal Dodd, rector of "the Little Church around the Corner," Saint Mary's of the An-

gels of East Hollywood. "Christie Pictures Boost Motion Picture Church," *MPW* (January 24, 1920), 607. See also Rob Wagner and Rupert Hughes, *Two Decades: The Story of a Man of God—Hollywood's Own Padre* (Los Angeles: Young and McCallister, 1936). Dodd labored diligently with the Motion Picture Relief Fund and was known as "the Father Damien" of the Hollywood lepers.

198. "Sunday Hurts in K. C.," *Variety* (May 5, 1916), 1, 3.

199. "Afraid of Bill Sunday," *Variety* (November 17, 1916), 3.

200. "Holy Rollers Like Ice Water," *Variety* (January 14, 1925), 1, 47.

201. "Conn. Evangelist Killing Theatre Biz: Draws 3,000 Nightly at So. Norwalk—Record Low Grosses for Theatres," *Variety* (October 21, 1925), 1.

202. "Church Observances Confuse Theatres," *Variety* (April 7, 1922), 1; "Easter Week Brings Boost Followed by Another Slump," *Variety* (April 28, 1922), 44; "Frisco Houses Improve despite Holy Week," *Variety* (April 21, 1922), 45; "Business Minimum Holy Week at Loop's Picture Houses," and "Week and Weather Hit Buffalo Hard: Saturday Was Worst Day," *Variety* (April 5, 1922), 30; "Holy Week Hits Frisco Houses Hard," and "Lent's Bad Business Held Up Until Last: Holy Week Gave Light Business to Picture House," *Variety* (April 23, 1922), 18.

203. "Passes for Ministers," *Variety* (March 25, 1925), 26.

204. Selig Advertisement, *Saturday Evening Post* (April 3, 1915), 23.

205. William Johnston, "Selig Advertisement," *Motion Picture News* 11: 18 (May 8, 1915), 32.

206. Allan Dwan's "Billy Sunday" movie, *Jordan Is a Hard Road,* had been shown at the Wells Theatre in Norfolk, Virginia. *Jordan Is a Hard Road, VP* (December 26, 1915), 7.

207. "The Reverend Billy Sunday Says," *VP* (September 30, 1917), 10, "A hundred million people ought to see the play—for the play is the thing."

208. "God Help Poor Girls—Says Billy Sunday," *VP* (March 19, 1922), 2: 8.

209. "Church to Compete with Picture Shows," *Motography* (April 1911), 35; "Minister Will Give Film Shows to Children," *Motography* V: 5 (May 1911), 78.

210. "Church Competes with Picture Shows," *Nickelodeon* V: 7 (February 18, 1911), 184.

211. "Lindsay Advocates Films for Churches," *Motography* IX: 5 (March 1, 1913), 178.

212. "The Church to Establish Theatres?" *TES* (March 1925), 185.

213. "Community Shows as Competitors," *EFM* IV: 3 (September 1920), 5.

214. "Community Exhibitors Have Church Opposition, in Films," *Variety* LIV: 17 (April 11, 1919), 59.

215. "License Necessary for Church Show," *Variety* (April 7, 1922), 1.

216. "Churches and Schools in Omaha Heavy Film Buyers," *MPW* (January 31, 1920), 730.

217. "Church and Theatre Opposition in L.A.: Show Films across Street from One Another—Church Makes 'Lobby' of Vestibule," *Variety* (January 12, 1923), 38.

218. "Church-Theatre Compete," *Variety* (May 3, 1923), 23.

219. "Kansas Exhibitors Fight Non-Theatrical Pictures," *Variety* (April 7, 1922), 44.

220. *Catechism on Motion Pictures in Interstate Commerce* (Albany, N.Y.: New York Civic League, 1922), 87. Chase had vociferously opposed nickelodeons in 1907 for breaking the Lord's Day.

221. "MD. Church Is Exhibitors' Competitor: Hagerstown Sees Regular Picture Business in House of Worship," *Variety* (October 15, 1924), 23.

222. "Church Pictures," *Variety* (January 24, 1924), 1; "'Love Harbor' in Church: Pastor Resumes Sunday Film Showings," *Variety* (January 24, 1924), 20.

223. "Church Film Shows Stopped by Pa. Dept. of Labor; Inspectors Allege Violation of Panic Law—Must Have Permit to Exhibit Pictures—Structural Changes Required," *Variety* (March 12, 1924), 21.

224. "Memphis Churches Do Capacity on Sundays: Theatres Obliged to Close on Sabbath—'Moral Pictures'—'Free Will' Admissions," *Variety* (February 14, 1924), 1.

225. "Movies for Sunday School Lesson—Free in Church," *Variety* (July 15, 1925), 24.

226. "Bible Film Showing," *Variety* (March 3, 1922), 44.

227. "Inside Stuff on Pictures," *Variety* (March 12, 1924), 32.

228. "Minister's Promotion through Pictures: Crowded Small Town Church," *Variety* (January 31, 1924), 1.

229. "Inside Stuff," *Variety* (March 5, 1924), 19.

230. "Church-Exhibitors' Fight," *Variety* (December 27, 1923), 1–2.

231. "Report Atheists Attacking Sunday Church Movies," *Variety* (October 28, 1925), 27.

232. Hays (1995), 375. Hays described the film mechanism in momentous biblical terms as a "new language that leaps the barriers of Babel."

233. "Visual Activities as Noted in the Daily Press," *Visual Education* (November 1921), 15–16.

234. "Preaching by Pictures: How the Film Is Becoming the Strongest Ally of the Teachers of the Gospel," *Photoplay* 11 (February 1917), 60; it was won by the Reverend Dr. C. S. Bucher of Lima, Ohio.

235. "Visual Activities as Noted in the Daily Press," *VE* (January 1922), 103–4.

236. Stephen Leacock, "What Shall We Do with Our Churches?" *Vanity Fair* 12: 5 (July 1919), 25; Alva Johnston, "Pictures Which Have Discarded Satan for Mother Church," *Vanity Fair* 27 (October 1931), 55, 84.

237. J. T. Brabner Smith, "The Centenary Celebration Teaching the Church to Smile Again," *CA* (July 10, 1919), 879. Emphasis added. Dr. S. Earl Taylor is the one credited with bringing the smile to the church. "There is a Cana as well as a Calvary in Christianity—a place for laughter as well as a place for tears."

238. Elmer T. Clark, "Conception and Development of the Centenary," *Story of the Centenary Celebration: Missionary Centenary of the Methodist Episcopal Church Pamphlet* Vol. 2, New York Public Library (New York: Methodist Centenary Celebration Souvenir, 1919), 9.

239. "Big Boss of Centenary Never Talks Weather—He Doesn't Have Time," *Columbus Citizen* 21:95 (June 19, 1919), 1. Tyler Bennett, "Who's Who at the Centenary Celebration," *Ohio State Journal* (June 20, 1919), 3.

240. "Methodist Hosts Invade Columbus for Greatest Missionary Event in the History of the Christian Church," *Centenary Bulletin* (June 26, 1919), 1; "Methodism Leads the Way to Columbus to Celebrate the Centenary of Its Missions," *Ohio State Journal* (June 17, 1919), 1. "Movie Men Said Large Projector Was Impossible," *Columbus Evening Dispatch* (June 25, 1919), 3. "Gigantic Screen for Stereopticon Views," *Centenary Bulletin* (June 5, 1919), 3; "When Johnny attends the Centenary exposition with dad and takes his seat in the oval at night, he will witness the largest pictures on the largest screen, projected by the largest and most powerful lantern ever made." "Lantern Piles Up Heat at Centenary," *Ohio State Journal* (June 25, 1919), 3. A Simplex projector was used, equipped with extra light shutters, special lenses, and 150-ampere light, "three times the strength of ordinary movie light." "Screen Record Smashed," *Columbus Citizen* 21: 108 (July 4, 1919), 2.

241. The technical challenges of its construction were a drama in their own right. Lawrence Rich, Taylor's staff photographer, accomplished the daunting feat, even as he directed "many of the thousands of foreign pictures now in the possession of the Board of Foreign Missions." See "An Eight-Story Picture," *Christian Advocate* (June 19, 1919), 782–83.

242. "An Eight-Story Picture," *Zion's Herald* (June 18, 1919), 786.

243. Griffith and his cameraman Billy Bitzer arrived to record the Centenary as a "mammoth dramatic picture story of Christianity" for posterity and as a "Memorial to Film King's Mother." "Griffith to Stage Big Celebration," *Ohio State Journal* (July 4, 1919), 3."Whatever I may do," said Griffith, "will be in memory of my mother who was a devoted Methodist. I have no commercial connection with the celebration. I have been astounded beyond measure at the breadth, extent and scope of the entire scheme. My last experience with a Methodist celebration was in the days of my youth in a little church 20 by 30 where a little organ and a lame soloist furnished the entire entertainment." "Griffith Honors Memory of Mother by Filming Church Pageant Free," *Columbus Citizen* (June 6, 1919), 2. "Man with Big Camera Directs Centenary Opening Ceremony," *Ohio State Journal* (June 21, 1919), 12. "Here to Film Events,"

Ohio State Journal (June 19, 1919), 3. "To Take Films Today," *The Ohio State Journal* (June 20, 1919), 3. The Reverend S. R. Vinton, the head of the stereopticon slide department of the Board of Foreign Missions, saw that "the Church needs the moving pictures to add realism to the beauty of the slides." "Moving Picture Men Meet," *Christian Advocate* (July 17, 1919), 915.

244. "World to See Centenary Celebration," *CA* (June 26, 1919), 814.

245. "Movie Stars Scorn Rain," *Columbus Citizen* (June 27, 1919), 11. See also "How They Brought the World to Columbus," *CA* XCIV: 31 (July 31, 1919), 974–78.

246. "Methodists Spend $500,000 for Huge Centenary Celebration," *Variety* LV: 4 (June 20, 1919), 12. Film critic Noel Burch caustically noted that Methodists were likely to support moving pictures, as its "popular roots [were] especially suited to a task in which its terroristic, guilt-instilling methods found fertile ground." *Ibid.*, 83.

247. Lamont Warner, "'Movies' at the Methodist Centenary Celebration," *EFM* 1: 5 (May 1919), 14.

248. "Movies at the Methodist Centenary," *EFM* 1: 6(June 1919), 15; "Methodist Church Movies," *EFM* 1: 6 (June 1919), 6.

249. "Motion Pictures a Great Success," *Columbus Journal* (July 9, 1919), 3.

250. "Millions for 'Movies' in Methodist Churches," *EFM* 1: 5 (May 1919), 16.

251. "The Methodist Centenary Convention Adopts Motion Pictures," *Bulletin of the Affiliated Committees for Better Films* 3:8 (September 1919), 4. Within a year articles were celebrating the growing use of films by Methodist congregations: "All Michigan Methodist Churches to Show Movies," *EFM* III: 4 (April 1920), 16. "To Hold Church Conference on Movies," *EFM* 2: 1 (July 1919), 16. See also Mary B. MacKellar, "*Missionarylogs* at Baptist Convention," *EFM* IV: 1 (July 1920), 17. "Methodist Centenary Committee Favors Use of Moving Pictures in Religious Services," *Moving Picture Age* III: 8 (August 1920), 20.

252. "The Solution of Your Motion Picture Problems: Graphoscope Ad," *Christian Advocate* (September 4, 1919), 1145; "The First Essential: DeVry Portable Projector Ad," *Christian Advocate* (September 11, 1919), 1179; and "An Approval That Means Something: Victor Safety Cinema," *CA* (September 25, 1919), 1241.

253. J. E. Crowther, "The Wayfarer: A Pageant of the Kingdom," *Story of the Centenary Celebration: Missionary Centenary of the Methodist Episcopal Church Pamphlet*, Vol. 2, New York Public Library (New York: Methodist Centenary Celebration Souvenir, 1919), 14. "The Wayfarer: A Pageant," *CA* (July 10, 1919), 880–82; J. E. Crowther, "Methodism and the Theatre," *CA* (September 18, 1919), 1191–92.

254. "Griffith to Stage Big Celebration," *Ohio State Journal* (July 4, 1919), 3. Griffith also used the event as an opportunity to prerelease his picture *Boots*.

255. "John Wesley," *EFM* VI: 6 (December 1921), 14; and "Reviews: God and the Man—Central Film," *Screen* 2: 4 (October 1921), 36.

256. "Pathe Pictures Will Show Columbus Rallies," *Centenary Bulletin* (June 5, 1919), 3.

257. "Ticket Holders in Protest," *Columbus Citizen* (July 8, 1919), 11; "Scalpers Busy at Expo," *Columbus Citizen* (July 11, 1919), 6.

258. "Value of Moving Pictures Shown to Church Workers," *Centenary Bulletin* (July 17, 1919), 2.

259. "Biggest Movie Crowd Sees Largest Film," *Centenary Bulletin* (July 17, 1919), 1. For impressive photographs, see "The Bigness of the Big Exposition," *CA* (July 31, 1919), 978.

260. "Motion Pictures a Great Success," *Columbus Journal* (July 9, 1919), 3. "Attendance Reaches Million Mark as Centenary Celebration Closes; Everybody Votes it a Real Triumph," *Centenary Bulletin* (July 17, 1919), 1. "Griffith at Work on Centenary Films: Over 10,000 Feet to Be Put into Picture Story of Christianity and World Programs," *Centenary Bulletin* (July 17, 1919), 1.

261. Cocks had advocated a church-film alliance for many years. See Orrin Giddings Cocks, "Urging an Alliance of Church and Motion Picture," *LD* 53 (August 5, 1916), 308–9; and "The Motion Picture in the Church," *EFM* 2: 4 (1919), 17–18; Skeffington, "A Conception of Screen as Handmaid of Church Expressed by Clergymen," *MPW* (September 6, 1919), 1450, 1493; "Giant Screen on Stereopticon View," *Centenary Bulletin* 2.73 (1919), 3; "Biggest Movie Crowd Sees Largest Film," *Centenary Bulletin* 2.79 (1919), 1; and "An Eight-Story Picture," *CA* 94. 25 (1919), 915. One such film promoted by Methodists was *The Chosen Prince—David and Jonathan* by Lyman I. Henry. "A Biblical Photodrama," *CA* (October 2, 1919), 1273.

262. "Explains Why Centenary Is Great Success," *Columbus Evening Dispatch* (July 8, 1919), Part II, 6. See also "World to See Centenary Celebration," *Zion's Herald* XVIII: 26 (June 25, 1919), 821.

263. *New York Times* (June 27, 1920), Section 2, 1. By 1924, however, *the Christian Century* was warning of Hollywood's "universal language" being spread around the world. "The influence of this industry upon the missionary cause is just beginning to be felt." America, an ostensibly "Christian" nation, was exporting impressions that were not in keeping with what a Christian faith espoused, making the missionary's work more difficult. "Missions and the Movies," *Christian Century* (May 8, 1924), 598–99.

264. "Missionaries and the Cinema," *International Review of Educational Cinematography* 4 (July 1932), 557–58. As a minority voice later reflecting on the church's infatuation with moving pictures, Canon Brohee protested

that even the documentary film tends to annul the reverent nature of sacred events. Canon Brohee, "The Cinema and Religion," *Intercine* 7 (March 1935), 146.

265. Janet Priest, "Films and Your City's Welfare: How City Officials Apply the Ideals of the Better Photoplay League—the Columbus Festival of Church and Screen," *Photoplay* (Chicago) 16 (August 1919), 53–54, 129.

266. "Films for Church and School Use Indorsed [*sic*] at Des Moines," *MPW* (June 12, 1920), 1450.

267. Julian Johnson, "Let There Be Light!" *Photoplay Magazine* 16 (1919), 46–48. For Julian, "the prevailing note, the motive, the master-key, the tone of this great whole, . . . the kaleidoscope of the world" at this great religious gathering was the huge motion picture show.

NOTES TO CHAPTER 3

1. K. S. Hover, "Motography as an Arm of the Church," *Motography* V: 5 (May 1911), 84–86.

2. "Earmarks of Makers," *New York Dramatic Mirror* 60: 1560 (November 14, 1908), 10.

3. "Three Hundred Clergymen See *Civilization*," *MPW* (October 14, 1916), 249.

4. Vachel Lindsay, *The Art of the Moving Picture* (New York: Liveright, 1970), 6, 251, 305.

5. James Ecob, "The Bible and Moving Pictures," *Homiletic Review* (March 1916), 216.

6. Jonathan Edwards, "Images of Divine Things," in Wallace Anderson, ed., *The Works of Jonathan Edwards,* Vol. II (New Haven: Yale University Press, 1993) xxviii, 38.

7. "Gospel by Film Drama: 5,000 Persons See 'The Creation,'" *New York Times* (January 12, 1914), 9.

8. *Scenario of the Photo-Drama of Creation* (Brooklyn, N.Y.: International Bible Students Association, 1914). Controversy arose not because of its subject matter or treatment, but over its use as a tool of religious propaganda by the cult of Jehovah's Witness.

9. "*The Creation,*" *MPW* 19: 3 (April 21, 1914), 1512; "In Defense of Features," *Motography* 10:3 (August 9, 1913), 108.

10. "Growth of 'Movies,'" *Billboard* 25, 26 (June 28, 1913), 20.

11. *Scenario, op. cit.,* 39.

12. Richard Alan Nelson, "Propaganda for God," in *Une Invention du Diable?* 234.

13. This culminating "year of grace" and peace came, ironically, in the year that saw the outbreak of the Great War. "Bible Pictures," *op. cit.,* 39.

14. *The Mena Film Company* (Dayton, Ohio: General Printing Company, n.d.), 2. The official periodical of the Jehovah's Witness, *The Watch Tower,* chronicled the work's progress and delays. "Photo-Drama of Creation," *TWT* 34, 19 (October 1, 1913), 5338; "The Photo-Drama of Creation," *TWT* 35, 4 (February 1, 1914), 5410.

15. See Leonid Ouspensky, *Theology of the Icon,* Vol. I, trans. Anthony Gythiel (Crestwood, N.Y.: St. Vladimir's Seminary Press, 1978), 138.

16. "Using Motion Pictures to Save Souls," *VP* (May 17, 1914), 39; "'Movie Films to Save Souls; Pictures Presenting the Story of Human Development as Told in the Bible," *VP* (May 15, 1914), 8.

17. *Ibid.,* 39.

18. "Bible Pictures," *VP* (May 26, 1914), 9.

19. "Motion Pictures Tell Story of the Creation: Bible Students' Association Begins Unique Religious Campaign at Wells Theatre," *VP* (May 18, 1914), 3.

20. "'Movie' Films to Save Souls," 39.

21. Kevin Brownlow, "Lillian Gish," *American Film* IX: 5 (March 1984), 22; Lillian Gish (with Ann Pinchot), *Lillian Gish: The Movies, Mr. Griffith and Me* (New York: Prentice Hall, 1969), 358.

22. Pastor Charles Taze Russell, founder of the *Watch Tower* and the Jehovah's Witness dispensational cult, predicted the end of the world in 1914. See Paul Boyer, *When Time Shall Be No More: Prophecy Belief in Modern American Culture* (Cambridge: Harvard University Press, 1992).

23. "The Creation," *Moving Picture Educator* 19: 13 (March 21, 1914), 1512.

24. "Creation Photo-Drama," *TWT* 35, 9 (May 1, 1914), 5456–57; "Proper and Improper Advertising," *TWT* 36, 14 (July 15, 1915), 5729.

25. *Mena Film Company,* 6.

26. "The Photo-Drama of Creation," *TWT* 38, 3 (February 1, 1917), 6041; "Photo-Drama of Creation," *TWT* 38, 5 (March 1, 1917), 6050–51.

27. "The Gospel by Film Drama," 9.

28. *The Laodicean Messenger* (Chicago: Bible Educational Institute, 1923), 125.

29. For more information on Russell, Mormonism, and the religious productions of Nell and Ernest Shipman, see Arthur Krows, "Motion Pictures—Not for Theatres," *TES* (January 1939), 13–16.

30. Cited in "Miscellany: Films in Church and Sunday Schools," *VE* (November 1921), 21.

31. *Ibid.,* 22–23.

32. "The Editorial Forum: Two Pictures," *CH* (October 14, 1922), 720; Charles Sheldon, "Wanted: A New Amusement," *CH* (June 10, 1922), 413–14.

33. "Church Picture Plan Tried Out," *Moving Picture World* 21: 1 (July 4, 1914), 41.

34. James Shields, "The Church and the Motion Picture: Films Can Be Made Which Carry the Gospel Message," *CH* (November 19, 1921), 839.

35. See Patricia King Hanson, ed. *The AFI Catalogue of Feature Films, 1911–1920.* (Berkeley: University of California Press, 1988), 893.

36. "Shields's Story Is told on Screen: *The Stream of Life* Is Visualized Version of His *Philip Maynard,*" Frances Agnew, "Review: *The Stream of Life*" (Washington, D.C.: Library of Congress, Foster Files, Community Motion Picture Bureau Scrapbooks), Reel 21.

37. Chester Marshall, "Preaching with Motion Pictures," *CH* (May 15, 1920), 596–97.

38. Gladys Bollman, *"The Stream of Life," EFM* 2: 5 (November 1919), 22–23.

39. "Ballyhooing" for the film was done by means of a young lady on a trumpet. "A Methodist Picture," *Variety* (April 9, 1920), 65.

40. Several church leaders appealed to Jesus and Moses as ideal motion picture men: J. O. Knott, "Visual Instruction for Churches" *IJRE* II (May 1926), 44. "Moses gave a very good illustration of a 'movie' in his first appearance before Pharaoh." See Henry H. Barstow, "Jesus Christ, Story Teller," Calvary Presbyterian Church, Auburn, New York, *IJRE* (June 1927), 7–8.

41. Reviewer Thomas C. Kennedy critiqued this Epic Pictures Corporation production as a trifle too long and a bit mawkish. Thomas C. Kennedy, *"The Stream of Life,* a Religious Picture" (Washington, D.C.: Library of Congress, Foster Files, Community Motion Picture Bureau Scrapbooks), Reel 21. Reviewer Tom Hamlin found the film a preachment drawn out over seven thousand feet of film, echoing Kennedy in pointing out that while *The Stream of Life* would have little appeal to regular motion picture fans, it was an ideal production to show "on Sundays where no Sunday shows are permitted. For it preaches the gospel and if properly exploited among the church people would draw many new faces into the theatre—at least once." Hamlin recommended that exhibitors who booked the film should use the church lists and "improve the presentation by securing a choir leader to lead the audience in community singing." However, he was skeptical that the film could register as a "regular picture." Hamlin confessed that it "brought back memories to the reviewer of the days when he warbled in a little Methodist church choir." Tom Hamlin, *"The Stream of Life"* (Washington, D.C.: Library of Congress, Foster Files, Community Motion Picture Bureau Scrapbooks), Reel 21. Finally, *Wid's Daily*'s critic keenly recognized *The Stream of Life*'s appeal to the rural element of American religion, as the story begins out in the natural country, "long before there was a Broadway." It dealt with a true-to-life story of the country, rather than the big cities, where spiritual health meant as much as physical vigor, and both more than worldly success. "Narrative Which Teaches Lesson Given Artistic Production," *Wid's Daily* (October 26, 1919), 16.

42. Reviews of his film are in *MPN* (November 1, 1919), 3345; *MPW* (January 17, 1920), 472; *Wid's* (October 1919), 16; *ETR* (January 17, 1920), 711; and *NYMT* (October 26, 1919).

43. Rev. Carl Nau, "Sermons on the Screen Are Bringing Unchurched People to Services," *MPA* III: 7 (July 1920), 16.

44. Shields, 839.

45. Shields did not shy away from heralding his own work by publishing a pamphlet of endorsements from numerous clergy, mostly from the New York and New Jersey areas. The pamphlet praised the film as heart-gripping, inspirational, full of poetry and pathos, uplifting, instructive, entertaining, spiritual, and a sublime masterpiece. The Reverend Dr. Ferdinand Iglehart confirmed Shields's evaluation, confessing that the film gripped him as "few things have ever done in literature, oratory, or any realm of fine art. It has a touch of pathos that melts the heart and sanctifies the soul. At the close of the play I thought I was the only weak one, but when the lights were turned on I found nearly every one in the audience was crying also." Another clergyman, the Reverend Dr. W. A. Knox, went so far as to declare that it would help to establish the Kingdom of Christ on earth. James Shields, *The Clergy Endorse the New Photo-Drama "The Stream of Life"* (Newark, N .J.: Plymouth Film Corporation, 1920).

46. *Ibid.,* 839.

47. Clifford Putney, *Muscular Christianity: Manhood and Sports in Protestant America, 1880–1920.* (Cambridge: Harvard University Press, 2001). Shields was an Anti-Saloon League leader—which seems quite surprising for an Episcopalian.

48. Frank Field, "The Town That Forgot God: Illustrating a New Kind of Moving Picture Sermon," *TES* (June 1924), 237–39.

49. Arthur Krows, "A Quarter-Century of Non-Theatrical Films," *TES* (June 1936), 169–73; "Motion Pictures—Not for Theatres," *ESM* (September 1938), 211–14; (October 1938), 249–50; "Motion Pictures—Not for Theatres," *ESM* (September 1941), 333.

50. Shields continued his work in 1921 with another six-reel film, *A Maker of Men,* released through his Plymouth Film Corporation (while also being handled by New Era Films). Shields believed that *A Maker of Men* would reach indifferent church members, being a modern drama designed to "emphasize the value and comfort of righteous conduct." One review praising it for its dignified and serious purpose saw it as communicating a "certain heaviness." "It frankly preaches, and people are used to thinking of a picture as recreation." "*A Maker of Men,*" *VE* (November 1921), 36–38.

51. James Shields, *The Life of John Wesley* (Bridgeport, Conn.: John Wesley Pictures Corporation, n.d.).

52. Charles Johnson Post, "Motion Picture Madness," *CH* (July 1, 1922), 465. Post emphasized that the motion picture was essentially the "evolution of the printing-press and *not of the theater.*"

53. "Miscellaneous Notes: Visual Activities," *VE* (January 1921), 32.

54. Charles Sheldon, "In His Steps Today: What Would Jesus Do with the Drama?" *CH* (December 4, 1920), 1247–48.

55. Sheldon, "The Church and the Theater," *CH* (December 3, 1927), 1060; and "In His Steps Today: What Would Jesus Do with the Drama?" 1247–48. *In His Steps* had already been "picturized" as well as his earlier book, *The Crucifixion of Philip Strong.* "*In His Steps* Picturized," *MPW* (February 26, 1916), 1332. See also *In His Steps: Special Photoplay Edition* featuring Eric Linden and Cecilia Parker (New York: Burt Company). N.D. (photoplay edition had no date in book)

56. Sheldon, "How to Use Pictures in the Church," *CH* (October 14, 1922), 719. Sheldon preached that "when Jesus was on the earth, he emphasized Truth by telling stories, made vivid by picturization." No book, he argued, "contains so [many] dramatic images and illustrations as the Bible." Herein one could find an astonishing collection of biographical bits, stories of sin, virtues, struggles with God and others, earthly ambitions and joys. Sheldon, "Ethics in the 'Movies,'" *CH* (January 17, 1920), 76.

57. Dean Charles Lathrop, "The Motion Picture Problem: Survey of the Social Service Committee of the Federal Council of Churches of Christ in America," *VE* (October–November 1922), 360.

58. *Ibid.,* 466. E. H. Packard, "Forward: New England Essays" (Cambridge: 1926), 21. (Located in Box A, John Hay Library, Manuscripts Division, Brown University Library, Providence, R.I.). "New England Essays (1927), 22.

59. Post, "Motion Picture Madness," 466.

60. *Ibid.,* 466.

61. "The Little Giant," *Time Magazine* (January 11, 1937). See also Rosenbloom "From Regulation to Censorship," 55.

62. "Movies at Canon Chase's Church," *EFM* 1: 6 (June 1919), 14–15.

63. Rev. Dr. William Sheafe Chase, "$20,000,000 Fund for Religious Films," *EFM* III: 2 (February 1920), 18. "Let Us Have Free Motion Picture Libraries," *EFM* III: 5 (May 1920), 9, 26.

64. *Ibid.,* 3 William Sheafe Chase, *Catechism on Motion Pictures* (Albany: New York Civic League, 1922).

65. "Clean Picture Sentiment Crystallized," *CH* (October 28, 1922), 756.

66. "Wholesome Movies for Church and School," *Literary Digest* 75: 3 (October 21, 1922), 35–36.

67. Rae D. Henkle, "Give Us Clean Pictures!" *CH* (June 23, 1923), 497.

68. "Clean Picture Sentiment Crystallized," *CH* (October 28, 1922), 756. "Are They Better?" *CH* (November 18, 1922), 812. See a rejoinder indicating the audience's culpability. Honore Morrow, "It Isn't All Hollywood's Fault," *CH* (July 1932), 24.

69. "Call on Churches," *Variety* (January 27, 1922), 11.

70. Rae D. Henkle, "The Puzzle of the Pictures," *CH* (September 16, 1922), 647.

71. The Reverend Frank Robertson warned in 1919 that such activities to "throw open the doors" for Sunday showings "may possibly conceal an ulterior design. If we let the bars down to provide entertainment, have we any assurance that things will not gradually widen until the first thing we know we shall have a continental Sunday." "Nobody Agreed at Meeting on Sunday Movies," *VP* (March 25, 1919), 2.

72. *Ibid.*, 2.

73. *Variety* noted, too, that the main problem identified by the Methodist Episcopal conference was that they believed that motion picture interests were determined to "get a foothold" on the Sunday showing issue, with the "use of pictures in churches to help sermons acting as a wedge for Sunday pictures in the theatres." "Church Discusses Pictures," *Variety* (March 26, 1920), 58.

74. Musser, "Passions and the Passion Play: The Theater, Film and Religion in America, 1880–1900," *Film History* 5: 4 (1993), 447. Major Truxton reminded the council, "But Norfolk, it should be remembered, was a seaport town, and because of that fact was facing certain conditions that few other American cities had to contend with," namely, prostitution. In contrast, moving pictures looked downright pious.

75. "Churches Want "Positive" Ads on Theatrical Pages," *Variety* (February 14, 1924), 1. "Methodist Church Again: Dignitaries Considering Advertisements of Pictures," *Variety* (May 5, 1922), 39.

76. "Methodist Memorial," *Variety* (October 18, 1923), 1.

77. Haviland Haines Lund, "Unshackle the Motion Picture," *CH* (October 20, 1923), 820.

78. Russell Conwell, "Letter to the Editor," *CH* (June 9, 1923), 458.

79. "Putting the Bible on the Screen," *CH* (September 27, 1919), 1042. Ernest A. Phillips, "Filming the Bible," *CH* (October 25, 1919), 1138.

80. Rev. Richard Braunstein, "The Movies: Right and Wrong," *CH* (April 17, 1926), 345.

81. Anonymous, "How to Preach by Moving Pictures," *Literary Digest* 53 (November 25, 1916), 1410.

82. Paul Maynard, "What the People Want: Clean, Wholesome Pictures," *CH* (May 8, 1920), 576.

83. "How One Pastor Uses the Movies," *CH* (April 3, 1920), 423.

84. "Announcing the CHRISTIAN HERALD MOTION PICTURE BUREAU," *CH* (September 2, 1922), 623; (September 30, 1922), 677.

85. "Ministers, Let Burton Holmes into Your Church," *CH* (October 21, 1922), 736.

86. "The Christian Herald Presents the Holy Bible in Moving Pictures," *CH* (September 16, 1922), 676.

87. Edgar Swan Wiers, "Experiences of One Church," *TES* (March 1924), 111–13.

88. Henkle had argued that the devil had captured the motion picture, "the most tremendous force yet found, for the transmission of thought," but only temporarily. Its very neutrality as technology enabled its users to shape its influence for either good or bad. In his view, "We have let it be bad. Let us use it to tell of the glories of God. Christian people, wake up!" Henkle, "Give Us Clean Pictures!" 497; "Making the Devil Useful," *English Journal* 2 (December 1913), 658.

89. Rae Henkle, "The Church or the Theatre," *CH* (August 19, 1922), 579–80; and Henkle, "The Puzzle," 655.

90. Rae Henkle, "Churches Sure of Films," *CH* (September 2, 1922), 613.

91. Henkle acknowledged that the plan "first disconcerted and then angered the picture industry," so that *CH* "has been denounced and threatened. We have traced the inception of a venomous campaign against us, but we are not especially disturbed." "Announcing the CHMPB," 623.

92. Henkle, "'Give Us Clean Pictures!'" 495–96. Henkle would soon turn to the new medium of radio. Rae D. Henkle, "The Radio and the Gospel," *CH* (January 13, 1923), 26.

93. Joseph Emmanuel Bilman, *The Religious Uses of the Motion Picture*, BD dissertation (Chicago: University of Chicago, August 1999), 49.

94. "Constructive—or Destructive—Pictures?" *CH* 47: 30 (August 2, 1924), 631.

95. Henry Clay Foster, "What Radio Means to Religion," *CH* 49: 1 (January 2, 1926), 3–4; Homer Croy, "What Radio Means to the Church," *CH* 45: 36 (July 29, 1922), 531–32.

96. "Do You Know There Is Now an Eighth Fine Art?" *CH* (December 11, 1920), 1284; Channing Pollock, "*The Fool:* Illustrated with Pictures from the Wm. Fox Motion Picture," *CH* (December 27, 1924), 1074–75, 1082. The *Christian Herald* had published the serialized novel from January 3, 1925 through February 28, 1925.

97. "The Creation, Cain and Abel, the Deluge," *VE* III (January 1922), 35–36.

98. "Filming King David's Story," *New York Times* 71 (March 23, 1922), 13.

99. "Geographic Film Company of Cincinnati, Enters State Rights Field with Biblical Films," *MPW* 56: 2 (May 13, 1922), 176.

100. "Films Viewed and Reviewed," *VE* II: 2 (February 1921), 36.

101. "Putting the Old Testament on the Screen," *Current Opinion* 74 (February 1923), 209–11.

102. Edgar J. Banks, "New Movies: "Reconstructing Abraham's Life at Ur," *CH* (April 7, 1923), 277, 281.

103. Edgar Banks, "Motion Pictures in the Church," *RE* (August 1923), 234–36. Banks lauded "one company which has survived, and is far on the way towards success. I refer to Sacred Films, Incorporated, of Burbank, California."

104. "The Whole Bible in Pictures," advertisement *IJRE* (December 1926), 41.

105. Catherine B. Ely, "The Screen as Humanizer," *Visual Education II: 2* (February 1921), 17–20. The Reverend Lewis Stark of Gallup, New Mexico, counted over five thousand churches with full equipment for film projection, along with hundreds of Roman Catholic churches. "Inevitable," *MPA V: 11* (November 1922), 10–11. Stark's fight against the "modern 'holier than thou' Pharisees" of the church and his boostering of church films stemmed from his view that "motion pictures are but parables on the screen."

106. Harwood Huntington, "The Bible in Motion Pictures," in "Challenge of the Films," *VE* (December 1921), 17–19, 56. See also A. P. Hollis, "The Screen and the Book," *VE* (May 1921), 22–23. Hollis was the Visual Instruction Service Director of North Dakota Agricultural College, and the author of *The Celluloid Prayer*. A. P. Hollis, "The Film Prayer," *VE* (January 1922), 41.

107. *TES* (October 1926), 503–4.

108. Charles M. Sheldon, "How to Use Pictures in the Church," *CH* (October 14, 1922), 719.

109. "The Bible Land and Its People," *VE* V (April 1924), 112–13; J. E. Holley, "What Ministers Think of the Pictural Set: The Bible Land and Its People," *VE* V (April 1924), 116.

110. "Tours around the World," with advertisement for "5 Special Reels on the Holy Land" through the *Christian Herald* Motion Picture Bureau. *CH* (October 21, 1923), 737.

111. "City Churches to Use Movies," *VP* (June 21, 1914), 16.

112. Edward Packard, "Letter: Christian Pictures Inc," (Watertown, Mass.: N. p., 1925), Archives of the New York Public Library for the Performing Arts (MFL n.c.4). See also his *Christian Pictures, Inc. Supplying the Kind of Pictures Churches Want* (Watertown, Mass.: N. p., 1925), 3pp.

113. Kathryn Oberdeck, *The Evangelist and the Impresario: Religion, Entertainment, and Cultural Politics in America, 1884–1914* (Baltimore: John Hopkins University Press, 1999), 105.

114. Delphia Phillips, "How One Clever Pastor Filled the Church Sunday Evenings," *Homiletic Review* 95 (May 1928), 385–86; Helen Lockwood Coffin, "A Minister as a Movie Maker," *Homiletic Review* (June 1931), 8–9, 15.

115. Stockton, "The Picture in the Pulpit: *But the Greatest of These Is Charity*," *MPW* xiv (1912), 543.

116. S. R. Bratcher, "Pictures in the Church," *TES* (October 1927), 393–95, 397. See also the article by Dwight Furness, Director of Publicity for the Methodist Episcopal Board of Education, "Amateur Films for Churches," *TES* (January 1929), 30.

117. See "Pastor Defends His Film," *New York Times* (July 1, 1918), 9; Commissioner Gilchrist opined that the film about vice and "white slavery" in San Francisco (and an indictment against the city government) taught no moral, but was "immoral and indecent," while Mrs. O'Grady suggested it would be better propaganda for every motion picture house to print The Ten Commandments (one at a time) on its screen every night to give people time for reflection. "Sees City Officials Belittled in Film," (July 3, 1918), 11; "Court Upholds Ban against Photo Play" (July 4, 1918), 13; "Attacks City Censorship" (July 6, 1918), 11; "A Censor in Action" (July 7, 1918), III: 5; "Replies to Mrs. O'-Grady" (July 8, 1918), 8.

118. Paul Smith, "A Pioneer Preaching Method: The Movies for a Pulpit," *CA* 93.7 (1918): 194; "Work of International Church in Producing and Distributing Shows New Ministerial Attitude," *Screen* 1.2 (1921): 9.

119. "The Motion Picture Goes to Church," *Epworth Herald* 31: 40 (October 2, 1920), 942. See "Churches to Film Own Movies with Players Unnamed," *Sun and New York Herald* LXXXVII: 315 (July 11, 1920), Section 4: 4.

120. Paul Smith, "A Pioneer Preaching Method: The Movies for a Pulpit," *CA* 93: 7 (February 14, 1918), 194. His film was called spiritual dynamite, the incendiary Uncle Tom's Cabin of the cinema era, a most trenchant sermon by Baptists, Presbyterians, and Methodists, and Dan Brummitt, editor of the *Epworth Herald*. "Prizes Offered to Ministers for Best Sermons Based on the Modern Magdalene," *MPW* (April 17, 1920), 404.

121. Elisha King, "How Ministers Use Motion Pictures," *Congregationalist* CIX: 13 (March 27, 1924), 394–95.

122. "Famine in Religious Films Nearing Its End," *EFM* 2: 3 (September 1919), 18.

123. "Bible Stories on the Screen," *Literary Digest* 67 (November 13, 1920), 36–37.

124. "Production of Church Film Programs," *EFM* IV: 3 (September 1920), 15.

125. "The Greatest Force for Good Outside the Church," *EFM* V: 1 (January 1921), 14.

126. "New Biblical Films Released," *EFM* V: 3 (March 1921), 16.

127. Trade publications were awash in mention of churches using moving pictures. For example, one claimed the first church in Los Angeles to "adopt the motion picture as a means of arousing interest in religious work was Salem Congregational Church." "Church to Give Illustrated Songs and Sermons," *Motography* V: 4 (April 1911), 13; "Minister Will Give Film Shows," *Motography* V: 5 (May 1911), 78; "Church to Use Films," *Motography* VI: 4 (October 1911), 190; and "Pictures Swell Church Attendance," *Motography* VI: 5 (November 1911), 234.

128. "International Church to Release Interchurch Missionary Subjects," *Screen* 1: 2 (March 2, 1921), 13.

129. Smith and Edgerton continued to promote religious films, establishing the American Motion Picture Corporation (AMPC) in 1925, headquartered in the New York Masonic Temple building (which housed numerous budding film-makers, including Shields's Plymouth Pictures and John Holley's Holy Land Pictures). However, very few films, if any, were produced, although it did attract a flock of small investors, including "many church widows and orphans who were attracted by a crusading minister." *Ibid.*, 28.

130. *"The Expanding Years," EFM* IV: 1 (July 1920), 16. A second film, *Methodism in Action,* gave an "Interboard statistical review of Methodist activities." "Home Mission Report Made in Film," *op. cit.,* 16. See also "The Expanding Years: Home Missions in Motion Pictures at the General Conference," *CA* (June 16, 1920), 778.

131. John Wesley Jackson, "Along the Years from Yesterday: Early Methodism Made Real in Motion Pictures," *CA* XCV: 41 (October 7, 1920), 1343. The Committee on the State of the Church pronounced its report on "Recreation and Amusements" in 1920, affirming that while "improper amusements are a fruitful source of spiritual decline," "social and recreational instinct is God-given, and if properly guided will strengthen rather than injure the spiritual life." Rev. Edmund M. Mills (ed.), *Journal of the Twenty-Eighth Delegated General Conference of the Methodist Episcopal Church* (Cincinnati: Methodist Book Concern, 1920), 587. The conference delegates voted to establish exchange agencies to secure high-grade motion picture film: "Whereas, the use of moving pictures has become a means of education in the church; and Whereas, there is great difficulty in securing suitable films for such use; therefore be it RE-SOLVED, that we commend the work already accomplished by the Centenary Conservation Committee (and request it) to establish depositories and exchange agencies of Moving Picture Films and Lantern Slides in order that churches, Sunday Schools, and kindred societies may be assured of the highest grade service at a minimum expense." *Ibid.,* (644).

132. Arthur Krows, "Motion Pictures—Not for Theatres," *TES* (September 1941), 292.

133. Paul Smith, "Work of International Church in Producing and Distributing Shows New Ministerial Attitude," *Screen* 1: 2 (March 2, 1921), 9, 30, 32. South American churches were targeted as well, with the American Church of Buenos Aires, Argentina, popularizing the *biografo* for its Latin American audiences. Willis Jones, "The Instructional Reel and Slide in South American Churches," *MPA* III: 1 (January 1920), 13.

134. Krows, "Motion Pictures—Not For Theatres," *TES* (May 1942), 180–82.

135. *Ibid.*

136. Bridges, 24.

137. Edgar Banks, "Educational Bible Films," *TES* (October 1922), 249.

138. Edgar Banks, "Archaeology and Motion Pictures," *Art and Archaeology* XV: 1 (January 1923), 3–13.

139. Edgar Banks, "New Movies: "Reconstructing Abraham's Life at Ur," *CH* (April 7, 1923), 277, 281.

140. Edgar Banks, "Letter to John Chambers" (Burbank, Calif.,: Sacred Films Incorporated, April 6, 1922).

141. "Will Use Bible Stories in Films: Popularity of 'Good Book' Is Expected to Be Greatly Increased," *VP* 53 (December 2, 1921), 17.

142. *Ibid.*, 17. According to Vroom, "It will be a strict rule of the company that everyone connected with it in any way must be a Christian in good character."

143. "Film Bible Stories," *Variety* (September 9, 1919), 57. Actor Vroom had just finished acting in a Lew Cody production.

144. "Western Promoter Plans Complete Picturization of the Bible," *Variety* (December 5, 1919), 66. Part of his vision was to promote a Holy City, built in San Fernando Valley, a replica of scriptural Jerusalem.

145. William L. Stidger, "Taming the Movies: Story of Cecil B. DeMille" *CH* (October 1932), 14, 15, 32.

146. Rogers, 8. Holley sought to stimulate interest in his film work in the Holy Land by publishing a complementary picture book entitled *Touring the Holy Land* (Cincinnati: Sacred Pageant Society, 1927).

147. *Ibid.*, 35.

148. "Filming the Bible," *EFM* 2: 5 (November 1919), 20.

149. "Story of the Bible in Moving Pictures," *MPA* III: 7 (July 1920), 10.

150. *Variety* (January 9, 1920), 55.

151. "Sea of Galilee," *Screen Education* (April 1926), 232–34. See also "Religious and Biblical Scenes," *Descriptive List of Pathescope Films Classified* (New York: Pathescope Co. of America, Inc. Aeolian Hall), 114–16.

152. "Inspiration and Entertainment," *The Shepherd Boy of Galilee, IJRE* II (December 1925), 42.

153. Frank H. Madison, "Form Church Film Circuit," *MPW* (September 4, 1915), 1696.

154. Orrin G. Cocks, "Studies in Social Christianity: Motion Pictures" *Homiletic Review* (March 1916), 217–23. "Films for Churches," *The Survey* 33 (March 27, 1915), 698. See also "Why I Opened a Moving Picture House," *MPW* (January 2, 1915), 8; Frederick James Smith, "Bringing the Motion Picture to Church," *Photoplay* 125 (October 1917), 47–48; Frederick James Smith, "Making *the* Movie Do Its Bit," *Photoplay* XII: 6 (November 1917), 85–86, 112; and Carlyle Ellis, "The Parson Who Believed in Pictures," *Everybody's Magazine* 36 (February 1917), 140–43. Later in the decade, the Community

Motion Picture Bureau in New York appealed to mercenary motives (find funds for new seats, furniture, fresh paint, hymn books, or "an increase in the minister's pay "without begging by letting "Charlie Chaplin Do It"), using movies to make money. See "Let Charlie Chaplin Do It," *Survey* 42 (July 19, 1919), 607.

155. Dr. F. F. Nadler, "Motion Pictures and Education in the Great Northwest," *Screen* 2: 4 (October 1921), 4–5, 37.

156. The Corporation, or Bureau, boasted a board of prominent religious leaders and distinguished educators such as the Reverend Charles Parkhurst, the Reverend Josiah Strong, Hamilton Holt, editor of the *Independent,* and the Reverend John Grier Hibben, president of Princeton University. "Church People in Picture Fields," *MPW* 20: 13 (June 27, 1914), 1808–9; and "The Church and Social Service Bureau," *MPW* 22: 10 (December 5, 1914), 1358. See also "Church People in Picture Field," *MPW* XX: 12 (June 20, 1914), 1808–9.

157. "Church and School Film Bureau," *MPW* (July 3, 1915), N. P.

158. William L. Rogers and Paul H. Vieth, *Visual Aids in the Church* (Philadelphia: Christian Education Press, 1946), 3.

159. "Bible Film Begins Work in New Mexico," *Motion Picture News* 15:1 (1917), 102.

160. "Bible Film Co.," *MPW* (January 6, 1917), 80.

161. Actually it was Bradt himself who puffed his production. See Rev. Charles Bradt, "First Missionary Photoplay Produced by Religious Body," *Reel and Slide Magazine* II: 6 (June 1919), 9–10. *Reel and Slide* published a book called *Showing Movies for Profit in School and Church* in 1919. "The Increasing Ministry of Moving Pictures," *Expositor* 21: 242 (November 1919), 146. See also Alexander Gibson, "Motion Pictures in the Church," *Expositor* 21: 241 (October 1919), 26–28.

162. Bradt, 'P. Cit., 9–10. "A Missionary Drama Produced by a Religious Body," *Bulletin of the Affiliated Committees for Better Films* 3:7 (July 1919), 2.

163. "The Motion Picture Goes to Church," *Epworth Herald* 31: 40 (October 2, 1920), 941–42. Its many productions varied from *Satan's Schemes* and *The Great Miracle* to *The Trip through China* and *The Story of Plymouth Rock.*

164. "Rumors Materialize—Bible Films Now Available," *MPA* 3:9 (September 1920), 20.

165. Betram Willoughby, "What One Church Did with Movies," *MPA* IV: 5 (May 1921), 9. See also Rev. Frederic H. von der Sump, "Vitalizing the Gospel through Films," *MPA* V: 10 (October 1922), 12–13.

166. Rev. George Esdras Bevans, "Church-Film Data," *MPA* V: 9 (September 1922), 9; and *Motion Pictures: The Experience of One Church* (New York: Board of Home Missions of the Presbyterian Church in the U.S.A., 1922), 14 pp.

167. Rev. M. C. Mackinnon, "The Church Cinema in Operation," *EFM* V: 6 (June 1921), 12–13; "Film Thoughts from a City Pastor," *EFM* V: 6 (June

1921), 13. On how film is a "God-Given Medium for World Evangelism," see Rev. George Esdras Bevans, "How One Presbyterian Church Capitalizes the Movies," *EFM* VI: 1 (July 1921), 10; Rev. John Sherman Potter, "Movies in Small-Town Church Potent in Evangelism," *EFM* VI: 1 (July 1921), 9, 16; and on how Presbyterians and Methodists shared uplift missions, William Vaughan, "Combined Churches Give Community Movies Shows," *EFM* VI: 2 (August 1921), 9.

168. Ray Johnson, "Church Film Service Now a Reality," *EFM* IV: 5 (November 1920), 13–14.

169. "Moving Pictures and the Church," *CM* 3: 9 (June 1927), 526.

170. "Moving Pictures in the Church," *CM* 3: 8 (May 1927), 457.

171. "Moving Pictures for the Church," *CM* 3: 7 (April 1927), 389.

172. Besides the Ideal Company there was also the very ephemeral, but aptly and strategically named Uplift Motion Picture Company of Los Angeles. Another company with a seemingly fitting name, Inspiration Pictures, was actually a corporation to release Richard Barthelmess pictures. "Current Releases Announced," *The Church, the Child and the Movies* 1: 4 (October 1925), 8; "How Our Church Uses Moving Pictures: IV: Using Films in Church Educational Work," *MPA* IV: 2 (February 1921), 9–10, 24.

173. Dolph Eastman, "The Church as a Film Producer," *EFM* V: 2 (February 1921), 5; "Methodist and Episcopalian Churches Enter the Film Business," *EFM* V: 2 (February 1921), 13.

174. From a readers' poll in 1921, *Photoplay* magazine listed it as the best film made to date.

175. "Protestant Churches Giving Own Motion Picture Shows," *Variety* (November 14, 1919), 63.

176. "God and the Man—Central Film," *Screen* 2:4 (October 1921), 36. A later scenario on "The Life of John Wesley" was written by James Shields and copyrighted by The John Wesley Pictures Corporation (Bridgeport, Conn., n.d.).

177. "*Out of the Christian College*," *EFM* V: 4 (April 1921), 19.

178. "Moving Pictures on Christian Education," *Christian Education Monthly* XI: 1 (January 1921), 5.

179. Rev. O. Hagedorn, "The Film as a Messenger of the Gospel," *EFM* IV: 2 (August 1920), 13, 22.

180. Frank Jensen, "The Church and Pictures—Church Film Review, *Martin Luther: His Life and Times*," *TES* (June 1925) 368; James MacRae, "An Exceptional Opportunity for Co-Operation by the Church," *TES* (October 1925), 486.

181. O. H. Pannkoke, "Living Pictures to Bring the Church at Large to its Members," *American Lutheran* (February 1924): 15–16.

182. J. F. E. Nickelsburg, "A Successful Publicity Tour," *American Lutheran* (February 1926): 8–9.

183. "The Life of Christ as Shown in the Movies," *Current Opinion* 57 (September 1914), 192; Richard Muckermann, "Religion and the Film," *International Review of Educational Cinematography* 2 (January 1930), 476; Robert Hellbeck, "The Film and Protestantism," *International Review of Educational Cinematography* 3 (October 1931), 924.

184. "M. E. Church in Pictures," *Variety* LXI: 9 (January 21, 1921), 1.

185. Chester Marshall, "Pictures and the Church," *TES* (January 1925), 26; R. F. H. Johnson, "The Church Field," *TES* (December 1930), 313; Dwight Furness, "Amateur Film Making," *TES* (December 1930), 316.

186. Rogers and Vieth, 11.

187. "Special Denominational Films of Religious and Educational Value," *TES* (January 1926), 43; Frank Jensen, "The Church and Pictures," *TES* (January 1926), 39.

188. "Editorial," *CA* (February 20, 1936), 172.

189. Otto Nall, "Our Advancing World: Movie Tip," *CA* (August 18, 1938), 846.

190. Don Carlos Ellis and Laura Thornborough, *Motion Pictures in Education* (New York: Thomas Y. Crowell, 1923), 114, 143.

191. Elisha King, "Motion Pictures in the Church to Stay," *TES* (September 1927), 335–36.

192. *Ibid.*, 366. William Stidger, "Great Motion Pictures as Sermons," *CM* (May 1928); Bernard Clausen, "When *The King of Kings* Came to Our Town," *CM* (September 1928).

193. In contrast, some clergy continued to condemn the ways in which church movies were being used, as exhibition became a commercial activity within the sacred spaces of God. The Presbyterian Reverend William Duff decried the use of moving pictures in the church, claiming that while people were crying for their souls to be fed, the churches were simply serving entertainment and failing to give them what they truly needed. Duff declared that through these sins of omission, the church was neglecting to address the spiritual burdens and sufferings of those who came not to see moving pictures or any other attraction, but to hear the word. He lamented this failure, and fiercely indicted the Interchurch movement, describing movie-crazy churches as "broken cisterns which could hold no water." "Church Condemns Movies," *New York Times* (April 18, 1921), 10.

194. "Methodist-Made Pictures" and "Church Wants to Hold Attendance of Younger Generation—Making Only Shorts at Present—May Turn to Biblical and Fictional Subjects—But Must Make All Pictures Interesting to Draw to Church Halls, Where They Will Be Exhibited," *Variety* (March 5, 1924), 1, 33; "Inside Stuff on Pictures," *Variety* (February 7, 1924), 21; and "Church Film Circuit Is a Possibility: Pastor Plans Lineup to Cover All New York State," *Variety* (September 17, 1924), 22.

195. "Church 'Dark': Churchly Films Don't Draw," *Variety* (July 22, 1925), 22.

196. "Church Films Very Active," *Variety* (November 4, 1925), 30.

197. Chester Marshall, "What Shall We Do with the Movies: A Questionnaire Sermon," *TES* (October 1924), 315–16.

198. Marshall, "What Shall We Do with the Movies: A Questionnaire Sermon," *TES* (November 1924), 359.

199. *Ibid.*, 26.

200. Marshall, "What Shall We Do with the Movies: A Questionnaire Sermon," *TES* (January 1925), 24–25.

201. H. F. Huse, "The Picture an Agency in Aggressive Church Work," *TES* (September 1925), 409–14. Huse offered four subheadings to his arguments: "1. The Church Needs the Picture. 2. The Picture in a Religious Service. 3. The Picture in the Social Work of the Church. 4. The Sermonic Usefulness of the Picture."

202. "Why Not a Christian Film Foundation?" *EFM* 2: 6 (December 1919), 5.

203. *TES* (December 1926), 620.

204. William E. Harmon, *The Religious Motion Picture Foundation* (New York: Harmon Foundation, 1927), 1.

205. The Federal Council of Churches, founded in 1908, focused more on radio and broadcasting. See Ralph Jennings's doctoral dissertation, "Policies and Practices of Selected National Religious Bodies as Related to Broadcasting in the Public Interest, 1920–1950" (New York University, 1968). Charles Lathrop did investigate the medium of film for the FCC during the silent era. See *The Motion Picture Problem* (New York: Department of Research and Education, Federal Council of Churches of Christ in America, 1924).

206. "The Church and Motion Pictures as a Tool," (New York: unpublished pamphlet of the Religious Motion Picture Foundation, 1925), 2. See also "Finds Movies Aid Churches," *New York Times* 3 (October 23, 1925), 23.

207. Gilbert Simons, "Christ in the Movies," *World's Work* 56 (May 1928), 68–74; and Gilbert Simons, "Christ in the Movies: New and Bold Efforts to Interpret His Life," *World Today* 52 (June 1928), 26–33. See also Gilbert Simons, "Filming Christ for the Church," *Literary Digest* 97 (May 12, 1928), 26–27.

208. Simons, "Filming Christ," 30.

209. "Religious Motion Picture Foundation," *TES* (December 1926), 619. See also Rev. George Reid Andrews, "The Church and the Drama: The Motion Picture Influence," *TES* (March 1927), 152–53; and "The Church and the Motion Picture," *National Board of Review Magazine,* (NY Public Library, n. d.), 9, 10, 17.

210. George Reid Andrews, "Use of Motion Pictures in Teaching Religion," *IJRE* III (November 1926), 26–27. He addressed the National Better Films Conference held in New York to answer three pivotal questions: "What is the Religious

Motion Picture Foundation?" "What does it propose to do to supply the churches with pictures?" and "How is the RMPF related to the Federal Council?"

211. *Ibid.,* 7. Harmon emphasized that they did not wish to create a *"twilight zone* verging on the field of amusement." Emphasis added.

212. Part of Andrews's strategy was to convince clergy that films should serve as sermon illustrations, and this idea became his slogan. "Work of the Religious Motion Picture Foundation Analyzed," *TES* (June 1926), 366. In his personal correspondence with D. W. Griffith and Adolph Zukor, Andrews, representing himself and the Congregational Education Society, sought in 1924 to produce a motion picture on "the Life of Christ" entitled "Story of Jesus." Zukor indicated interest in cooperating with him and Griffith if conditions could be agreed upon. (Adolph Zukor to Mr. L. Roy Curtis. Personal correspondence, April 14, 1924.) However, in a letter to Will H. Hays, Andrews protested that the movie czar seemed to be helping Earl Hudson with his plans to produce Papini's "Life of Jesus" (October 6, 1924). As a property, the sacred story was seemingly hot. Hays responded that such a story "should be placed under the auspices of a religious organization than by a commercial company" (October 14, 1924). Andrews responded that he should control production (December 11, 1924). Politically, Hays tried to encourage Andrews that the motion picture industry and the churches "can and should work together," but also sought to maintain his distance and noninvolvement (December 17, 1924; December 19, 1924; and January 22, 1925). By 1928, Andrews's dissatisfaction with Hays (Andrew was now with the Church and Drama Association) was clearly evident (October 1, 1928). Correspondence was discontinued over squabbling about funding policy. ("Personal Correspondence from Secretary of the MPPDA, Carl E. Milliken, to Rev. George Reid Andrews," October 11, 1928.) In another letter from E. A. Talbot (March 29, 1923), Andrews was told that their friend DeMille had a studio that "is about the worst, out there, morally." Ironically it was DeMille who would realize Andrews's dream of such a film. (Letters from the Southern Historical Collection, the Library of the University of North Carolina at Chapel Hill.)

213. Arthur Edwin Krows, "Motion Pictures—Not for Theatres," *TES* (May 1942), 180–82.

214. Rev. Frank Jensen, "The Church and Pictures," *TES* (September 1926), 425.

215. "Church Films Very Active," *Variety* (November 4, 1925), 30.

216. George Reid Andrews (FCC), "Use of Motion Pictures in Teaching Religion," *IJRE* III (November 1926), 26–27. Citing Professor George Albert Coe, Andrews argued that film would get to "the heart of the message" of Bible stories, giving them graphic treatment. Picture of "David Livingston, amidst beautiful African scenes, would be made complete with preparatory study; for impressions plus knowledge leads to full education." For him the problems were

simply that "the supply is very inadequate. The pictures produced up to the present time for religious purposes are lacking in artistic, dramatic and religious merit." *Ibid.*, 27. See also Dean Rapp and Charles Weber, "British Film, Empire, and Society in the Twenties: The 'Livingstone' Film, 1923–1925," *Historical Journal of Film, Radio and Television* 9: 1 (1989).

217. Will H. Hays, "Church Pictures Are Assured," *The Church, the Child and the Motion Picture* 1: 4 (October 1925), 2, 7, 8.

218. The exhaustive canvassing and study was done with ten suburban churches within fifty miles of New York City to judge how "such an adjunct to the services would affect attendance and also to obtain information regarding the type of picture that would best convey a spiritual message." *Ibid.*, 7. See also how the Harmon Foundation initiated this "quiet investigation" to see if the truly religious picture could "sustain interest without reverting to mere entertainment," and provide an "important supplemental contribution to spiritual life and worship." "The Religious Motion Picture Foundation," *Harmon Foundation Yearbook, 1924–1926* (New York: Harmon Foundation, 1926), 72–75.

219. "The Religious Motion Picture Foundation, Inc.," *TES* (November 1925), 552–53.

220. Suggested forms of service and suggested hymns and sermon topics for these films were included in the Foundation's pamphlet: Harmon, *The Religious Motion Picture Foundation* (New York: Harmon Foundation, 1927), 3–10.

221. Evelyn Brown, "Religious Motion Pictures Produced for Use in Church Service," *TES* (December 1926), 620. Directed by Herbert Dawley, who worked at the Metropolitan Museum of Art and was "also the inventor of the jointed figures used in the production of *The Lost World*," the films were shot in Chatham, New Jersey.

222. Janes, *Screen and Projector*, 66–71.

223. "Productions of the Religious Motion Picture Foundation," *TES* (May 1927), 246.

224. Simons, "Filming Christ for the Church," 27.

225. "To Enrich the Spoken Word," *CH* (December 1932), 35.

226. "The Religious Motion Picture Foundation," 75. Founders of the movement stressed both the homiletic and aesthetic traditions of religious films, believing them to be descended from the stained glass found in cathedrals. Historian Melvyn Bragg described the medieval cathedral as a sort of early precelluloid cinema, "where congregations gather to see the great illuminated stories in glass, to watch the ritual performances on the stage of the altar, to follow, through the calendar, the great epic of Christianity with its heroes, its villains, its disputes and digressions, its strange character parts, its compelling storyline." Melvyn Bragg, *The Seventh Seal* (London: BFI, 1993), 10–11. Bragg's observation was not lost on early advocates of church films such as Gilbert Simons's writing in *The World's Work*. "Add the appeal of motion to the beauty

of a twelfth-century window and you have the ideal toward which the studio of Religious Motion Picture Foundation at Chatham, New Jersey is working." Simons, "Filming Christ for the Church," 26–27; and Simons, "Christ in the Movies," 28. Lecturing at the University of Southern California on March 6, 1929, producer Paul Bern acknowledged the creative foundation of the church in the building of cathedrals and communicating through the eye to the common people. In morality plays, for example, the "various characters, so that they might be easily understood by the simple audiences which saw them, were named Envy, Sin, Lust, Weakness, Love—something like some of the pictures of today." Tibbetts, *Introduction to the Photoplay*, 67.

227. "Motion Pictures on a Non-Commercial Basis," *TES* (September 1926), 426

228. By promoting "Old Truths in New Garments," the Harmon Foundation sought to empower young people in local congregations to help make motion pictures. With professional 16mm amateur equipment becoming more accessible, almost any church group could produce "simple Biblical and other inspirational pictures and keep historical records of the Church." "Directory of Rental Films," *The Religious Motion Picture Foundation* (New York: Harmon Foundation, 1936).

229. Simons, "Christ in the Movies," 68–74.

230. Brady hired an experienced movie man, Major Herbert Dawley, who recruited theological students from Drew Seminary to play in the film. Rogers, 9.

231. "Says Fewer Oppose Christ in Film Role," *New York Times* 77 (September 28, 1927), 52.

232. Rogers and Vieth, 14.

233. H. Paul Janes, *Screen and Projector in Christian Education: How to Use Motion Pictures in Worship, Study and Recreation* (Philadelphia: Westminster Press, 1932).

234. "Pictures in Church: Supernatural Powers Claimed for New Camera," *Variety* (February 14, 1924), 20.

235. Rogers and Vieth, 13.

236. Mary Beattie Brady, "The Motion Picture in Religious Publicity," *TES* (April 1935), 106.

237. Beulah Amidon, "New Guises for Old Truths," *Survey* 58 (April 15, 1927), 105.

238. Rev. A. M. Hanson, "The Use of Movies in Worship: Successful Minnesota Experiment," *Congregationalist* CIX: 13 (March 27, 1924), 397–98; Edward Tallmadge Root, "Meeting the 'Menace' of the Movies," *Congregationalist* CIX: 13 (March 27, 1924), 398–99.

239. Associate Professor of Religious Education in the Divinity School of Yale University, Dr. Paul Vieth conducted a course and helped to direct various

film projects. See Rogers and Vieth, 15. The authors suggest that the short "life situation" films done at Yale coincided with the "first course in visual education to be offered in a theological school." *Ibid., 16.* "News Notes," *Educational Screen Magazine* (June 1940), 261.

240. *Visual Materials for Your Program* (New York: Division of Visual Experiment/Harmon Foundation Inc., n.d.).

241. *Visual Materials for Your Program* (New York: Harmon Foundation, 1949), 4.

242. "Against the Odds," *Video Librarian* (July–August 1994), 7.

NOTES TO CHAPTER 4

1. "Pictures Are God-Given," *MPW* (July 17, 1915), 520.

2. "In Search of Better Films: What Are the Facts?" *IJRE* (April 1936), 20, 40.

3. "YMCA: Motion Picture Handbook," *EFM* IV: 2 (August 1920), 12.

4. Billman listed several pages of films and suppliers in an Appendix. *Op. cit.,* 62–75. See the four New Era sermonettes written by Rev. Betram Wiloughby, "Screen Sermonettes," *EFM* V: 3 (March 1921), 16; "Motion Picture Sermons," *Screen* I: 10 (April 27, 1921), 12–13; and Thomas Bruce Butler, "How One Church Conducts a Moving Picture Service," *Screen* I: 12 (June 1921), 18. The editor of *Moving Picture Age* distinguished between the sermon as discourse and the sermonette as a moving picture telling "the old, old story in a new way." The first title to be produced by Commonwealth Pictures was "The Christmas Message" and suggested more concern with the "divine nature of humanity" and the higher life than with orthodoxy. "Screen Sermonette on the Nativity, First of a New Series," *MPA* III: 1 (January 1920), 11–12.

5. "Illustrated Sacred Songs on Film," *EFM* V: 4 (April 1921), 19.

6. Elisha King, "How Ministers Use Motion Pictures, *Congregationalist* CIX: 13 (March 27, 1924), 394–395; "Church Use of Motion Pictures," *Ibid.,*388.

7. Shields prepared the film for the League of Nations. "*Hell and the Way Out,*" *TES* (September 1926), 428.

8. "Personally Conducted Church Film Review," *TES* (September 1925), 413.

9. "Film Reviews," *TES* (November 1926), 566–67; "*The Protestant Prince,*" *TES* (September 1926), 428.

10. Numerous tidbits clutter the trajectory of companies involved in religious production and distribution. For example, King points to how Huntington's Sacred Films and Christian Herald Motion Pictures were taken over by the United Cinema Company and the International YMCA, which distributed free films to over one hundred churches.

11. "Personally Conducted Church Film Review," *TES* (February 1926), 101.

12. "Special Note," *TES* (November 1926), 566; and *TES* (February 1926), 102.

13. Elisha King, "Motion Pictures for Churches," *CA* 100: 16 (April 16, 1923), 495; "Sunday Evening Pictures in the Church," *Screen* 1: 6 (March 30, 1921), 13–14.

14. Donald Crafton, *Before Mickey: The Animated Film, 1898–1928* (Cambridge: MIT Press, 1982), 137–39.

15. Elisha King, "Motion Pictures for Churches: Commended Sources of Supply," *Congregationalist* (February 19, 1925), 236–37.

16. Pictorial Clubs, formerly known as the Historical Film Corporation and the Kelly Clubs, produced and distributed Sterling Films and took over the distribution of the Urban-Kineto Library.

17. Arthur Edwin Krows, "Motion Pictures—Not for Theatres," *TES* (April 1942), 138–40.

18. "*As We Forgive*," *EFM* IV: 3 (September 1920), 14. The Historical Film Corporation had planned a series of one hundred two-reel films promoting "Americanization."

19. "Personally Conducted Church Film Review," *TES* (October 1925), 483–84; "Personally Conducted Church Film Reviews: *Blood Will Tell*," *TES* (December 1925), 613. See also *TES* (March 1926), 169; "*The Man Nobody Knows*," *TES* (December 1925), 614. See also *TES* (January 1926), 41. The review acknowledges that the film is an "interpretation of the purely human side of the life of Jesus, the Christ." It claims to be "a picture of the places where Jesus lived and worked—of the sort of people He knew—of the sort of things He did—of the very hills and streams and rocks that touched His feet." For Barton, a redesigned or reconstructed Jesus as a Savoir from Wall Street rather than a manger fit the times and appealed to a modern masculine, business model. See *The Man Nobody Knows* (New York: Grosset & Dunlap, 1925).

20. *Ibid.*, 613. Alexander Savine composed the musical score from familiar hymns.

21. See *TES* (February 1926), 102; and *TES* (March 1926), 169.

22. "Special Note," *TES* (June 1926), 366. The story is about how a missionary engages a prosperous man and challenges him to realize it is only the fool who says in his heart, "There is no God." Also SEE *TES* (April 1926), 235.

23. "Bland Talks to Churchgoers," *MPW* (January 30, 1915), 658.

24. Orrin G. Cocks, "Motion Pictures: Facts Concerning Instructional and Selected Motion Pictures for Use in Churches and Church Schools," *Religious Education* (February 1920), 41–43.

25. "*A Pilgrimage to Palestine*," *TES* (April 1926), 232.

26. "*A Pilgrimage to Palestine*," *TES* (November 1925), 553; Charles Jones, "The Church and Pictures," *TES* (April 1926), 234.

27. W. Stephen Bush, "'The Glad Tiding' in Motion Pictures," *MPW* 13 (August 31, 1912), 846. For Bush, the images secured by the cinematograph were monuments "more enduring than brass or stone." Bush also praised the initiative of a First Baptist Church in showing *Eugene Wrayburn, Our Mutual Friend,* and *The Work of the Red Cross* as well as Vitagraph's superb *The Life of Moses.* Stephen Bush, "Pictures for Churches," *MPW* 10 (December 2, 1911), 701–2.

28. W. Stephen Bush, "Are Sacred Pictures Irreverent?" *MPW* 14 (December 7, 1912), 957.

29. "Preaching by Pictures: How the Film Is Becoming the Strongest Ally of the Teachers of the Gospel," *Photoplay* 11 (February 1917), 60.

30. Orrin Cocks, "The Meaning of the Better Films Movement," *EFM* 1: 3 (March 1919), 13. In a letter to President Henry Churchill King of Oberlin College, Cocks delivered his *Motion Picture Principles for the Church* (New York: National Committee for Better Films, October 1919). See also Orrin Cocks, "Motion Pictures: Facts concerning Instructional and Selected Motion Pictures for Use in Churches and Church Schools," *Religious Education* (February 1920), 41–43.

31. Alongside the popular magazines of the day, films like *The White Terror* (about tuberculosis) helped to mobilize the middle class into an institutionally constituted audience for progressive uplift films. See Shawn Shimpach, "A-Massing the Early Film Audience: Popular and Progressive Representations of the 1910s Filmgoers" (Miami: NCA Convention, November 22, 2003).

32. "Better Pictures Assured," *IJRE* (March 1926), 68; Frederick James Smith, "Bringing the Motion Picture to Church," *Photoplay Magazine* (October 12, 1917), 47–48. The Better Films Committee was an outgrowth of the Parent Teacher Association and kept abreast of national trends as reported in a section entitled "School and Screen" in the *Child Welfare Magazine.* "Women Take Stand for Better Films: Ideas Set Forth in Resolutions Submitted to Owners of Theaters," *VP* (March 4, 1924), 5.

33. Orrin G. Cocks, "The Motion Picture in the Church, Address at the Methodist Centenary Celebration, Columbus, July 8, 1919," *Bulletin of the Affiliated Committees for Better Films* 3:8 (September 1919), 1–3. Cocks listed five steps which the church should adopt in order to utilize motion pictures satisfactorily: 1. Recognize that suitable films exist. 2. Standards of acceptability for church use need to be defined (higher than standards of the National Board of Review). 3. Kinds of pictures should include those stories and parables used by the Savior rather than mere educational or nondramatic films which should be secondary. ("The motion picture today possesses many of the characteristics of the parable.") 4. Churches should be willing to pay manufacturers and distributors their just due, or be content with older films. 5. The church should be served only the finest films.

34. Orrin Cocks, "Questions," *Bulletin of the Affiliated Committees for Better Films* 3:8 (September 1919), 5. A history of Cocks's forward movement in the National Committee for Better Films was recorded in the *Bulletin*'s successor, *Film Progress* 6: 8 (ed. by Alice Belton Evans) (New York: National Committee for Better Films, September 1922), 1–2.

35. "Fairbanks Heads *Non-Sense* Film Ridiculing Censorship," *Variety* (April 15, 1921), 44

36. University of Iowa professor of philosophy, Herbert Martin addressed the crucial difference between morality and religion in film later in the decade. See "Moral and Religious Values of the Motion Picture," *Religious Education* XXII: 10 (December 1927), 1008–14.

37. "Against Bare Knees' Pictures in Church," *Variety* (March 10, 1922), 44.

38. G. J. Fritz, "The 'Movie' in the Church," *CH* (December 27, 1919), 1368.

39. W. O. Benthin, "The Community Picture Shows," *CH* (December 4, 1920), 1255; E. V. Lee, "Church Movies on Business Basis: Good Church Business," *VE* (November 1923), 273–74; "Cultural Film Programs in Church," *EFM* V: 1 (January 1921), 11. See also "The Greatest Force for Good Outside the Church," *EFM* V: 1 (January 1921), 14.

40. Charles F. Banning, "Church Problems in the Use of Motion Pictures," *IJRE* (July–August 1925), 14–15. See also "Bible Stories on the Screen," *Literary Digest* (November 13, 1920), 36–37.

41. Advertisement, *Congregationalist* CIX: 13 (March 27, 1924), 408.

42. "Best Motion Pictures for Church Entertainments," *EFM* III: 6 (June 1920), 12. See Margaret Farrand Thorp's discussion of Better Film Councils in her *America at the Movies* (New Haven: Yale University Press, 1939), 117–ff.

43. "*The Chosen Prince*," *EFM* III: 6 (June 1920), 16–17, 20.

44. "In Connection with the Sermon," *VE* (May 1922), 311. See also the recommendation of Burton Holmes's *Solomon's Temple* and the Sacred Films in "The Film Field: Religious and Inspirational," *VE* (October–November 1922), 383.

45. The *International Journal of Religious Education* was published by the Department of Education Development, National Council of Churches. The name of the column was changed to "Current Film Estimates" by 1931, with many of its research findings summarized in the 1940 Educational Bulletin, *Visual Method in the Church*. Committee on Visual Education, *Visual Method in the Church* (Chicago: International Council of Religious Education, 1940).

46. See "Current Film Estimates," *IJRE* (November 1931), 33, 48.

47. "Film Council Recommendations for May," *TES* (May 1925), 296.

48. Rev. Frank Jensen, "The Church and Pictures: Editorial," *TES* (May 1927), 244; Nelson Greene, *1000 and One: The Blue Book of Non-Theatrical Films*, 4th edition (Chicago: Educational Screen, Inc, 1926). Rev. Frank E.

Jensen, "The Motion Picture Sermon," *TES* (January 1927), 45. Jensen also advertised Rev. Roy L. Smith's book, *Motion Pictures in the Church.*

49. The Church also prepared a large poster announcing the subject for the week's sermon and film. "Motion Picture Activities in the Country's Churches," *EFM* 2: 5 (November 1919), 19–20. "Motion Pictures in the Country's Churches," *EFM* VI: 3 (September 1921), 13, 18.

50. J. Caleb Justice, "Motion Pictures in the Church," *Congregationalist* CIX: 13 (March 27, 1924), 392–94.

51. "Methodists' White List of Players," *Variety* (April 22, 1921), 42. Topping the list was the prototypical Western hero, a Protestant William S. Hart, whose films were packed with Calvinist theology and morality. Conspicuously absent from the list were the notable figures of Charlie Chaplin, Douglas Fairbanks, and Mary Pickford, because of the vulgarity of the first and the divorces and remarriage of the latter two. "Methodist Church Regular Film House," *Variety* (June 24, 1921), 1; "Churches in Theatres," *Variety* (December 13, 1923), 1; and "Churches Agitating Against Pictures," *Variety* (September 23, 1921), 46.

52. "Miscellaneous Notes: Does the Motion Picture Kill the Imagination?" *VE* (March 1921), 33.

53. L. C. Everard, "Visual Material: Spur or Sedative?" *VE* (September 1920), 29–33

54. Catherine B. Ely, "The Screen as Humanizer," *VE* II: 2 (February 1921), 17–20; Henkle, "Give Us Clean Pictures!" 495.

55. For a fuller understanding of the history British relations between of silent films and the church, see the thorough research by Dean R. Rapp, "A Baptist Pioneer: The Exhibition of Film to London's East End Working Classes, 1900–1918," *Baptist Quarterly* 40 (January 2003), 6–21; Rapp, "Sex in the Cinema: War, Moral Panic, and the British Film Industry, 1906–1918," *Albion* 34: 3 (Winter 2002), 422–51; and Rapp, "The Reception of the Silent Film Industry by British Anglicans and Their Response to Jesus Films, 1912–1939" (paper presented at the American Culture Association in San Antonio, Texas: April 9, 2004). Such entertainment followed the cultural tradition of the church arranging amusement in former centuries for people in cities and secluded villages. The chief agency promoting the religious use of film in Great Britain was the Church Pictorial Movement. From Vicar J. J. Langham, writing in the *Challenge,* an official organ of the Established Anglican Church, emerged a vision for utilizing the church's own buildings and the "brightening of our village life by the provision of pure and healthy amusement." But as one vicar pleaded to those who attended the films in his sanctuary, "Please remember we are a church, not a picture palace. Be reverent—and no smoking, please." "Church Pictorial Movement," *EFM* IV: 4 (October 1920), 21. See "The Motion Picture as a 'Handmaid of Religion,'" *Literary Digest* 65 (May 15, 1920), 46–47.

56. Reisner, "Dr. Reisner Adopts Screen," 3–4.

57. Henkle, "Give Us Clean Pictures!" *op. cit.,* 496.

58. J. M. Bradlet, "The Lord's Prayer—Illustrated," *MPW* 7 (July 9, 1910), 82–83.

59. Harwood Huntington, "The Challenge of the Films," *VE* (December 1921), 17–19, 56.

60. "European Bible Films," *EFM* V: 4 (April 1921), 18.

61. "William Lord Wright's Page," *MPN* VI: 21 (November 23, 1912), 14. See also "Biblical History Pictured: Interview with the Kalem Company's President," *Bioscope* (1912), 403; and "Review of *From the Manger to the Cross*," *New York Dramatic Mirror* (October 23, 1912), 28.

62. Cited in Campbell and Pitts, *op. cit.,* 81.

63. W. Stephen Bush, *MPW* (December 7, 1912), 957. See also *MPW* (October 26, 1912), 324. Inexplicably, director Olcott had hired British actor Robert Henderson Bland to play Jesus in the *silent film* because "his voice sounded right!" Bland ended up publishing two books, *From the Manger to the Cross* (1922) and *Actor-Soldier-Poet* (1939), dealing with his role in the film. Costing about $100,000 to make, it reaped a handsome gross of over a million. Its success met a little resistance among clergy who felt uneasy about a dramatic presentation of the Savior and from at least one film critic who complained that it would be "both bad taste and artistically ineffective to sandwich the picture between a juggler's act and a Broadway song and dance." *New York Dramatic Mirror, op. cit.,* 28. Moreover, some Protestants expressed reservations about using the film due to the narrative's end at the cross, without a Resurrection scene. After some maneuvering, it was later reedited to six reels to include a Resurrection episode, quashing the concerns of Protestant churches. In fact, in renting the adapted film, such churches were now advised to have "the music synchronized with the picture as far as possible," using hymns like *Hark, the Herald Angels Sing, Fairest Lord Jesus, When I Survey the Wondrous Cross,* and the like. Elisabeth Edland, "The World's Supreme Tragedy Reverently Told," *EFM* III: 3 (March 1920), 16–17.

64. Gauntier claimed to have received the inspiration in a hallucinatory vision. See André Gaudreault, "La Passion du Christ," and Tom Gunning, "Passion Play as Palimpset," in *Une Invention du Diable?* 91–120; and Charles Musser, "Passions and the Passion play," *op. cit.* (1993), 419–56.

65. Rev. Boudinot Stockton, "The Picture in the Pulpit: *The Holy City*," *MPW* xii (1912), 1138.

66. "All Roads Leading Again to Oberammergau," *VP* (May 3, 1910), 12; "Two Divergent Views as to Famous Passion Play," *VP* (August 14, 1910), 21. Others argued that there was "No Commercialism in Great Passion Play," *VP* (December 7, 1911), 13. The *Literary Digest* reported on stringent comments on a debate in the *London Church Times* regarding an old feud between

Church and Stage, now exacerbated by cinematographers shooting the Passion Play, or faking it. "Sacred Subjects in the 'Movies,'" *Literary Digest* 45 (November 30, 1912), 1016.

67. Rev. Boudinot Stockton, "The Religious Value of Pathe's *Life of Our Savior,*" *MPW* xx (1914), 188.

68. W. Stephen Bush, "Review of *Life of Our Savior,*" *MPW* 20: 2 (1914), 188. This praise echoed Bush's review of *From the Manger to the Cross,* in which he found embodied "thousand paintings and statues" of the Christian tradition. *MPW* 14: 4 (1912), 324.

69. Lawrence Marston, "How I Made *The Star of Bethlehem,*" *MPW* xiv (1912), 1305.

70. "Want Their Film in Church Use," *MPW* xv (1912), 979.

71. "Advertising for Exhibitors," *MPW* xv (1912), 987.

72. "Pulpits Advertise Films," *MPW* xv (1912), 788.

73. "Biblical Pictures," *Nickelodeon* II: 6 (December 1909), 167.

74. "Review of *The Life of Moses—Part I,*" *MPW* 5: 27 (1909), 878.

75. Louis Reeves Harrison, "The Christian," *MPW* 19: 13 (March 28, 1914), 1656.

76. Hanford C. Judson, "Review: *As Ye Sow,*" *MPE* (January 1915), 58.

77. "Holy Land Films," *TES* (October 1925), 487–90. Also recommended were *Behold the Man* and *Other Man's Shoes.* See advertisement, *TES* (October 1925), 493, which promised "not a dull, lifeless, badly-titled 'scenic,' but an intelligent and human portrayal of Palestine in its geographical, historical and biblical significance."

78. "Life of Christ as Shown in the Movies," *Current Opinion* 57 (September 1914), 192.

79. Ernest Dench, "Spiritualism in the Film," *Motion Picture Education* (Cincinnati: Standard Publishing Company, 1917), 124.

80. *MPW* I: 43 (December 28, 1907), 706. However, Pathe's *Life of Christ* scored a great hit when it was shown to the Doughboys during World War I. "The religious spirit of a half-million American soldiers was awakened by this remarkable picture and the beneficial results can hardly be measured," claimed Walter A. Morton, sponsor of the Knights of Columbus. "Soldiers Partial to Religious Film," *MPW* (June 21, 1919), 1768.

81. Gilbert Seldes, "Christ in the Movies," *New Republic* (1927), 298–99.

82. Bush was lashing out against a certain "revolting " religious film entitled *The Broken Vows.* W. Stephen Bush, "No Sectarian Films," *MPW* 9 (August 19, 1911), 438–39.

83. Stockton, "The Picture in the Pulpit," *MPW* IX (1911), 439.

84. The Episcopal Reverend Harry Belamy speaking for the National Commission on Pageantry and Drama raised another unrelated conflict among artists within the church. He saw "an imminent fight to the finish between mov-

ing pictures and [his] own realm of church drama, competing for the allegiance of youth." "Dr. Silverman Advises 'Keep Religion Out,'" *Variety* (September 29, 1922), 47.

85. Carl Milliken, "Motion Pictures: Two Views," *CM* (January 1929). In the same issue, see Arnold Keller, "The Gospel on the Screen," *CM* (January 1929).

86. Rev. Frederic Fay, "The Use of Feature Films in the Sunday Evening Service," *TES* (December 1926), 617–19. Evelyn Brown, "Religious Motion Pictures Produced for Use in Church Service," *TES* (December 1926), 619–20.

87. On the continuing success of *King of Kings,* see P. R. Hayward, "The King of Kings," *IJRE* (April 1928), 7.

88. See Richard Maltby, "The *King of Kings* and the Czar of All the Rushes: The Propriety of the Christ Story," *Screen* 31: 2 (Summer 1990), 188–ff.

89. Gretta Palmer, "Greatest Movie Success," *CH* (April 1944), 23.

90. Cecil B. De Mille, "The Screen as a Religious Teacher," *Theatre Magazine* 45: 6 (June 1927), 45–76.

91. "Conference on Movies," *Banner* 61 (March 19, 1926), 168.

92. Paul Frederick Cressey, "Influence of Moving Pictures on Students in India," *American Journal of Sociology* 41 (November 1935), 341–50.

93. "The Screen Will Be What YOU Make It," Paramount ad, *CH* (April 30, 1921), 327.

94. William L. Stidger, "Taming the Movies: The Story of Cecil Blount De-Mille, the Man Who Made "The King of Kings" and "The Ten Commandments," *CH* (October 1932), 14–15, 32.

95. "Yale Becomes a Film Producer," *VE* IV (January 1922), 160–61. No film was released without the recommendation of Dr. Max Farrand, Professor of American History, and Dr. Frank Ellsworth Spaulding, head of the Department of Education, editors-in-chief. See Nathaniel W. Stephenson, "Filming the Story of America," Yale History Films, *VE* (February 1923), 40–42.

96. Robert S. Lynd and Helen Merrell Lynd, *Middletown: A Study in Modern American Culture* (New York: Harcout Brace, 1929), 199.

97. See Daniel Knowlton and J. Warren Tilton, *Motion Pictures in History Teaching* (New Haven: Yale University Press, 1929).

98. Lynd and Lynd, 199.

99. *Ibid.,* 266.

100. Dolph Eastman, "*Evangeline,* a Work of Art in Film," *EFM* 2: 4 (October 1919), 20. Eastman also praised *Deliverance,* Helen Keller's biographical "Message to the World."

101. Gladys Bollman, "*The Stream of Life,*" *EFM* 2: 5 (November 1919), 22–23.

102. "Popularity of Semi-Religious Picture Fast Increasing, Says Benjamin Prager," *MPW* (October 9, 1920), 828.

103. "Powerful Religious Picture: *The Ninety and Nine*," VE V (June 1924), 169.

104. "The Christian," *VE* (April 1923), 129.

105. "Catholic Art Association Produces *The Blasphemer*," VE V (June 1924), 167.

106. In the film, an arrogant businessman, Johnny Harden abandoned his wife in order to dally with his mistress, neglected his children, and defied God. His Mother had told him as a boy about St. Peter of Verona, directing his gaze upon Victorian pictures in an illustrated Bible. He pointed to a biblical picture hanging on the wall and asked caustically, "Why do you persist in such old-fashioned beliefs and superstitions?" At the peak of his success, he threw a party during a gathering storm, boasting that he was master of his fate and captain of his soul. "I answer to none but myself! To the Strongman belongs the spoils and I drink to him (myself)!" Harden lost his fortune and became a bum. Living on the streets, he saw a legion of men marching in a "Holy Name Parade." In a visionary moment, Harden then saw a stained glass window of St. Peter coming to life. St. Peter immediately rebuked him: "*Thou* shalt not take the name of the Lord in vain." As Harden gazed upon the portrait icon, a narrative drama ensued in which St. Peter was martyred. The saint was stabbed in the back, wrote CREDO in the sand, and was then beheaded. Overcome with anguish over the blood of the martyr, Harden repented: "If this man could die bravely for the name of God, why can't I live bravely?" Harden returned home penitent, begging forgiveness from his wife, from his Mother who sobbed, "My prayers have been answered," and from his children. At the end, he confessed his sinful ways, blessed the holy name of God, and received a Divine benediction.

In the tradition of St. John of Damascus against the iconoclasts, *The Blasphemer* justified the visual image as a means to religious redemption. The moving visual icon of St. Peter's martyrdom triggered the conversion of its prodigal protagonist, a sermon communicated through Harden's viewing of an image. Thus, if stained glass images could preach and elicit religious guilt, provoke reflection, and spark personal transformation, how much more effective could a movie like *The Blasphemer* be to unconverted spectators? According to film scholar Tom Gunning, a similar effect occurred in a D. W. Griffith short film, *The Drunkard's Reformation* (1909). In the film, an alcoholic and abusive father saw the errors of his waywardness when a performance of a moral stage play by Emile Zola dramatically reflected his own life. Both secular moving pictures enhanced their own efficacy as sermons by demonstrating how motion pictures produced by nonsectarian producers could function effectively as religious or moral discourse. Robert Sherwood, *The Best Moving Pictures of 1922–1923* (Boston: Small, Maynard, & Company, 1923): 27; Tom Gunning, "From the Opium Den to the Theatre of Morality: Moral Discourse and the Film Process in Early American Cinema," *Art and Text* 30 (September–November 1988): 30–41.

107. "Bible Stories," *MPW* (March 17, 1917).

108. "Famine in Religious Films Nearing Its End," *EFM* 2: 3 (September 1919), 18–19.

109. Charles Stanley Jones, "Church Service with Motion Pictures," *TES* (March 1925), 151–53, 158. Jones recommended various features from Hollywood like *The Miracle Man, Shadows, The Man Who Played God, Nanook of the North, The Little Church around the Corner,* and *Orphans of the Storm.*

110. B. F. Wahlstad, "The Distribution Problem Reviewed for Church Pictures," *Screen*.1: 5 (March 23, 1921), 9, 27. See also "Motion Pictures Suitable for Churches, Schools and Colleges," *Screen* (March 23, 1921), 23–27; and James Kelly, "Film Man Outlines Methods for Church and School Distribution," *Screen* 1: 3 (March 9, 1921), 6–7.

111. "Moreover," wrote Harwood Huntington, "there are doctrinal questions and theological controversies to act as traps for those who are not omniscient." Harwood Huntington, "The Challenge of the Films," *VE* (1921), 17–19, 56.

112. "Dr. Aked on Church Movies," *New York Times* 72 (September 9, 1923), 9.

113. "Interchurch Officers," *Variety* (February 17, 1922), 41. The ICFC was established in 1920 in Troy, New York, to furnish specialized films; all its officers and directors were clergymen or social workers.

114. Roy Smith, *Sentence Sermons* (New York: Fleming H. Revel Company, 1925), 19.

115. Justice, "Motion Pictures in the Church," 392–94.

116. King, "How Ministers Use Motion Pictures," 394–95.

117. William Horton Foster, "Eyes That Are Opened," *Congregationalist* CIX: 13 (March 27, 1924), 395–96.

118. Oscar Mehus, "Wholesome Motion Pictures: An Approved List of Entertainment Films," *Congregationalist* CIX: 13 (March 27, 1924), 399.

119. "The Motion Picture by Ministers Who Have Used Them," *Congregationalist* CIX: 13 (March 27, 1924), 407–9, 410.

120. "Clergy Split on Film: Violent Division on *Inside of the Cup*," *Variety* (March 4, 1921), 42.

121. Herbert Jump, "College Students Run Movie Service," *Congregationalist* CIX: 13 (March 27, 1924), 409–10. Edward Tallmadge Root, "Meeting the 'Menace' of the Movies," *Congregationalist* CIX: 13 (March 27, 1924), 398–99.

NOTES TO THE CONCLUSION

1. Rev. Dr. Percy Stickney Grant, "If Christ Went to the Movies," *Photoplay* 17 (March 1920), 29–30, 121. According to this self-confessed liberal, "broad-minded" churchman, Christ would approve of "anything that makes for the happiness of mankind." See also "Entertainment and the Church" on Grant's

use of film for the poor and homeless in his parish. *Motography* XI: 12 (June 13, 1914), 414.

2. Bob Thomas, *King Cohn: The Life and Times of Harry Cohn* (New York: G. P. Putnam, 1967), 243.

3. James MacRae, "A Symposium on the Motion Picture Situation," *TES* (January 1926), 41.

4. Alva Johnston, "Hollywood Gets Religion," *Vanity Fair* 27 (October 1931), 55–84.

5. Ben Singer, *Melodrama and Modernity: Early Sensational Cinema and Its Contexts* (New York: Columbia University Press, 2001).

6. Leo Charney and Vanessa R. Schwartz (eds.), *Cinema and the Invention of Modern Life* (Berkeley: University of California Press, 1996).

7. See Lynne Kirby, *Parallel Tracks: The Railroad and the Silent Cinema* (Chapel Hill: Duke University Press, 1997).

8. Vachel Lindsay, *The Progress and Poetry of the Movies,* (ed. Myron Lounsbury) (Lanham, MD: Scarecrow, 1995), 94.

9. Herbert Martin, "Moral and Religious Values of the Motion Picture," *Religious Education* XXII: 10 (December 1927), 1009–10.

10. Miriam Hansen, *Babel & Babylon,* (Cambridge: Harvard University Press, 1991), 19.

11. What the film communicated effectively was the truth that to break God's laws is fatal, that "the wages of sin is death." Chester Marshall, "The Ten Commandments," *TES* (February 1924), 68–69.

12. George Bernard Shaw, "Among the Magazines," *TES* (November 1924), 360. See also Marion Lanphier, "Among the Magazines and Books," *TES* (March 1930), 78.

13. See John Dillenberger, *The Visual Arts and Christianity: From the Colonial Period to the Present* (New York: Crossroad, 1989).

14. "Camera Convictions," *Christian Herald* (February 12, 1931). Based on I Kings 21:17–22.

15. R. Laurence Moore, *Selling God: American Religion in the Marketplace of Culture* (New York: Oxford University Press, 1994).

16. Robert Bellah, "Civil Religion in America," in *Beyond Belief: Essays on Religion in a Post-Traditional World* (New York: Harper and Row, 1970).

17. Dr. Remsen Dubois Bird, "Education and Pictures," *American Cinematographer* 3: 9 (December 1922), 4, 21.

18. John Henry Newman, *The Idea of a University* (1852) (ed. Martin Svaglic), (Notre Dame, Ind.: University of Notre Dame Press, 1982), 59.

19. Emile Durkheim, *The Elementary Forms of the Religious Life* (trans. by Karen D. Fields) (New York: Free Press, 1995), 9, 429.

20. W. W. Charters, *Motion Pictures and Youth: A Summary* (New York: Macmillan, 1935), 4.

21. *Ibid.*, 38–39.

22. Henry James Forman, *Our Movies Made Children* (New York: Macmillan, 1933), 170–71.

23. Grant, *op. cit.*, 29–30, 121.

24. David Bordwell, Janet Staiger, and Kristin Thompson, *The Classical Hollywood Cinema: Film Style and Mode of Production to 1960* (New York: Columbia University Press, 1985).

25. For a very insightful cultural and economic analysis of DeMille's epic, see Richard Maltby, "The King of Kings and the Czar of All the Rushes: The Propriety of the Christ Story," *Screen* 31:2 (Summer 1990): 188–213.

26. "Religious Education in Motion Pictures," *Church Management* 3: 10 (July–August 1927), 580.

27. Quentin J. Schultze, *Christianity and the Mass Media in America* (East Lansing: Michigan State Press, 2003).

28. See Jose Casanova, *Public Religions in the Modern World* (University of Chicago Press, 1994); and Charles H. Lippy (ed.), *Twentieth-Century Shapers of American Popular Religion* (New York: Greenwood Press, 1989).

29. "Pictures Are God-Given," *MPW* (July 17, 1915), 520.

30. For example, French director George Melies showed Jesus walking on water.

31. George Anderson, "The Case for Motion Pictures, Part 1," *Congregationalist and Christian World* 95: 29 (July 9, 1910), 46.

32. "Films Make Girls Pretty," *VP* (October 5, 1919), 7: 5; "Are Movies Making Girls Lovelier the World Over?" *VP* (October 12, 1919), 5: 6.

33. Louis Reeves Harrison, "*The Faith Healer!*," *MPW* xiv (1912), 533.

34. W. Boyd Gatewood, "Girl, Dumb Eight Years, Speaks after Seeing Thrilling Moving Picture," *Los Angeles Times* (December 14, 1919), 4: 13.

35. Andrews, "The Church and the Motion Picture," *op. cit.*, 17.

36. See Roy Anker, "Self-Help Tradition and Popular Religion," in *Handbook of American Popular Culture*, (ed. M. Thomas Inge) (New York: Greenwood Press, 1989).

37. See Jan-Christopher Horak, "Avant-Garde Film," in Balio's *Grand Design*, 388–ff.

38. G. K. Chesterton, *As I Was Saying . . .* (Grand Rapids, Mich.: Eerdmans, 1985), 37–38. Emphasis added. Over sixty years later, Chesterton's cultural observation was echoed by independent filmmaker John Sayles, who envisioned a "democratizing of the filmmaking process." Through a decentralization of financing, distribution, and delivery systems, he hoped for more demographically narrow casting of film audience. John Sayles, "The Big Picture" *American Film* (June 1985), 10.

39. Carl D. Wells, "The Motion Picture versus the Church," *Journal of Applied Sociology* 16 (July–August 1932), 540.

40. Frederick L. Collins, "Shall We Bury Our Dead Churches?" *Woman's Home Companion* (November 1929), 21.

41. Robert Lynd and Helen Merrell Lynd, *Middletown: A Study in Modern American Culture* (New York: Harcourt Brace, 1929), 263, 269.

42. See "Church Organizes to Make Scriptural Dramas," *MPW* (February 7, 1920), 909. "We are going to edit and film the great thrilling dramatic stories of the Bible," declared Captain G. Charles Gray, a chaplain attached to Fort Riley, Kansas.

43. Rev. John Sherman Potter, "Movies in Small-Town Church Potent in Evangelism," *New Era Magazine* 27 (January 1921), 3. The church of for another Presbyterian minister put Sunday movies out of business and drew in many men "who never darkened a church door" and now seldom missed a service. Rev. William Jobush, "Church Puts Sunday Movies Out of Business," *NEM* 27 (September 1921), 529.

44. The Reverend John Peters in Manhattan, New York, however, studied the effects that moving pictures had on his own parish of three thousand people, and found the uplifting and educational power of the picture houses falling short. "Motion Picture Educator: The Church and the Photoplay," *MPW* (October 28, 1916), 550.

45. Lewis Jacobs, ed., *The Compound Cinema: The Film Writings of Harry Alan Potamkin* (New York: Teachers College Press, 1977), 238. Emphasis added.

46. Author Norman Mailer echoed this notion that the cinema offers a religious experience. "When the religious enter a church, they feel a sense of relaxation and of death which is equivalent to the way movie-lovers feel when they enter a movie house." "Psychology of Cinema" in Geoffrey Atheling Wagner (ed.), *The Novel and the Cinema* (New York: Associated University Press, 1975), 151.

47. Read Mercer Schuchardt astutely reviews *The Jazz Singer* as a three-step progression of the death of God. See "Cherchez la Femme Fatale: The Mother of Film Noir," in *The Philosophy of Film Noir* (ed. Mark Conard) (Lexington: University Press of Kentucky, 2006), 49–68.

48. Margaret Miles, *Image as Insight: Visual Understanding in Western Christianity and Secular Culture* (Boston: Beacon Press, 1985), 152.

49. *Psalm* 135: 15–18.

50. Christopher Deacy, *Screen Christologies: Redemption and the Medium of Film* (Cardiff: University of Wales, 2001), 4.

51. Peter Williams, *Popular Religion in America: Symbolic Change and the Modernization Process in Historical Perspective* (Englewood Cliffs: Prentice Hall, 1980), 202.

52. Richard Walsh, *Reading the Gospels in the Dark: Portrayals of Jesus in Film* (New York: Trinity Press, 2003), 188.

53. *Ecclesiastes* 1:9.

54. Frederick Brown Harris, "Wanted—Protest-ants," *CH* (December 28, 1933), 1244.

55. Alva Johnston, "Pictures Which Have Discarded Satan for Mother Church," *Vanity Fair* 27 (October 1931), 55, 84.

56. In contrast to the effete liberals, Johnston pointed to another entertaining fundamentalist: Accordingly, Satan was last seen when he traded "bites, scratches and gouges with Billy Sunday under the auspices of John D. Rockefeller Jr." *Ibid.*, 84.

57. "Religious Broadcasting Station," *CH* (February 23, 1924), 183; "The Radio Church," *CH* (February 7, 1925), 23; "Teaching by Religious Drama (at Auburn Theological Seminary)," *CH* (March 7, 1925), 9; Rev. J. K. Pfohl, "What Radio Means to the Pastor," *CH* (January 9, 1926), 24, 36; Henry Clay Foster, "What Radio Means to Religion," *CH* (January 2, 1926), 3. See especially Robert Fortner, "The Church and the Debate over Radio, 1919–1949," in *Media and Religion in American History* (ed. William David Sloan) (Northport, A.L.: Vision Press, 1999).

58. Margaret Widdemer, "The Bible on the Radio," *CH* (August 1937), 28–31, 44; Daniel Poling, "National Religious Radio," *CH* (August 1938), 34–35.

59. H. L. Mencken, "Interlude in the Socratic Manner," in *The Movies in Our Midst: Documents in the Cultural History of Film in America* (ed. Gerald Mast) (Chicago: University of Chicago Press: 19).

60. Sinclair Lewis, *Elmer Gantry* (1927) (New York: Dell, 1954), 410, 413.

61. See Donald Crafton, *The Talkies: American Cinema's Transition to Sound, 1926–1931* (Berkeley: University of California Press, 1997).

62. See *Publishers Weekly Religion Bookline* (October 26, 2005); Hanna Rosin, "Can Jesus Save Hollywood? From the Passion of the Christ to The Chronicles of Narnia, the Christian Audience Is Making Spirits Rise," *Atlantic Monthly* (December 2005).

63. Elise Soukup, "Hollywood: Praise the Movie," *Newsweek* (November 21, 2005).

64. http://www.barna.org/ and http://www.ellisonresearch.com/PastorStudy .htm

65. Gregg Bachman and Thomas J. Slater (eds.), *American Silent Film: Discovering Marginalized Voices* (Carbondale, Ill.: Southern Illinois University Press, 2002).

Bibliography

Addams, Jane. *The Spirit of Youth and the City Streets*. New York: Macmillan, 1909.

Adler, Mortimer. *Art and Prudence* (1937). New York: Arno, 1978

Alexander, J. *The Sunday School and the Teens*. London: Association Press, 1913.

Allen, Robert, and Douglas Gomery. *Film History: Theory and Practice*. New York: Knopf, 1985.

Anderson, Milton. *The Modern Goliath*. Los Angeles: David Press, 1935.

Atkinson, Henry. *The Church and the People's Play*. Boston: Pilgrim Press, 1915.

Barrett, Wilson. *The Sign of the Cross*. New York: Grossett and Dunlap, 1924.

Bevan, Edwyn. *Holy Images*. London: George Allen and Unwin, 1940.

Blumer, Herbert. *Movies and Conduct*. New York: Macmillan, 1933.

Bordwell, David, Janet Staiger, and Kristin Thompson. *The Classical Hollywood Cinema: Film Style and Mode of Production to 1960*. London: Routledge, 1985.

Bowser, Eileen. *The Transformation of Cinema, 1907–1915*. New York: Scribner's, 1990.

Bright, John. *A History of Israel*. Louisville, KY: Westminster John Knox Press, 1990.

Brownlow, Kevin. *Behind the Mask of Innocence*. New York: Knopf, 1990.

Campbell, Richard, and Michael Pitts. *The Bible on Film*. Metuchen, N.J.: Scarecrow Press, 1981.

Cope, Henry. *Organizing the Church School*. New York: George H. Doran, 1923.

Cosandey, Raland, Andre Gavdreault, Tom Gunning (eds). *Une Invention du Diable?* Lausanne: Editions Payot Lausanne, 1992.

Crafton, Donald. *Before Mickey: The Animated Film, 1898–1928*. Cambridge: MIT Press, 1982.

Ellul, Jacques. *Humiliation of the Word* (trans. Joyce Main Hanks). Grand Rapids, MI: Eerdmans, 1985.

Encyclical Letter of His Holiness Pope Pius XI on Motion Pictures. Boston: St. Paul Editions, 1936.

Encyclical Letter of His Holiness Pope Pius XII on Motion Pictures, Radio and Television. Boston: St. Paul Editions, 1957.

Federal Council of the Churches of Christ in America (Department of Research and Education). Moving Pictures: Their Impact on Society: The Public Relations of the Motion Picture Industry. 1931. Jerome Ozer, Publisher, 1971.

Feldman, Charles. The National Board of Censorship of Motion Pictures, 1909–1962. New York: Arno Press, 1977.

Forman, Henry James. Our Movie Made Children. Norwood, Mass.: Norwood Press Linatype, 1933.

Freedberg, David. The Power of Images. Chicago: University of Chicago Press, 1989.

Fuller, Kathryn H. At the Picture Show: Small-Town Audiences and the Creation of Movie Fan Culture. Washington, D.C.: Smithsonian Institution Press, 1996.

Gardner, Gerald. The Censorship Papers: Movie Censorship Letters from the Hays Office. New York: Dodd, Mead, 1987.

Gates, Herbert Wright. Recreation and the Church. Chicago: University of Chicago Press, 1917.

Godwin, Joscelyn. Athanasius Kircher. London: Thames and Hudson, 1979.

Gombrich, E. H. The Story of Art. London, Phaidon Press, 1972.

Handy, Robert T. A Christian America: Protestant Hopes and Historical Realities. New York: Oxford University Press, 1971.

Hays, Will H. Memoirs of Will H. Hays. Garden City, N.Y.: Doubleday, 1955/

Hays, Will H. See and Hear. New York: Doubleday-Doran, 1929.

Holloway, Ronald. Beyond the Image. Geneva, Switzerland: World Council of Churches, 1977.

Jacobs, Lewis (ed). The Compound Cinema: The Film Writings of Harry Alan Potamkin (New York: Teachers College Press, 1977.

Janes, Paul. Screen and Projector in Christian Education: How to Use Motion Pictures in Worship, Study, and Recreation. Philadelphia: Westminster Press, 1932.

Jura, Jean-Jacques, and Rodney Norman Bardin II. Balboa Films (Jefferson, N.C.: McFarland, 1999.

Johnston, Robert K. Reel Spirituality: Theology and Film in Dialogue. Grand Rapids, MI: Baker, 2000.

Kochan, Lionel. Beyond the Graven Image: A Jewish View. (New York: New York University Press, 1997.

Koszarski, Richard. An Evening's Entertainment: The Age of the Silent Feature Picture, 1915–1928. New York: Scribner's, 1990.

Lane, Tamar. What's Wrong with the Movies? Los Angeles: Waverly Co., 1923.

Lindvall, Terry. The Silents of God. Lanham: Scarecrow Press, 2001.

Lindsay, Vachel. The Art of the Moving Picture. New York: Liveright, 1970.

Lindsay, Vachel. *The Progress and the Poetry of the Movies*. Lanham, MD: Scarecrow, 1995.

Lyden, John C. *Film as Religion: Myths, Morals and Rituals*. New York: New York University Press, 2003.

Lynd, Robert, and Helen Merrell Lynd. *Middletown: A Study in Modern American Culture*. New York: Harcourt Brace, 1929.

Lynes, Russell. *The Lively Audience: A Social History of the Visual and Performing Arts in America, 1890–1950*. New York: Harper and Row, 1985.

Marsden, George. *Fundamentalism and American Culture: The Shaping of Twentieth-Century Evangelicalism 1870–1925*. New York: Oxford University Press, 1980.

Marty, Martin (ed.). *Modern American Religion, Vol. 1. The Irony of It All*. Chicago: University of Chicago Press, 1986.

May, Lary. *Screening Out the Past: The Birth of Mass Culture and the Motion Picture Industry*. Chicago: University of Chicago Press, 1980.

McDannell, Colleen. *Material Christianity: Religion and Popular Culture in America*. New Haven: Yale University Press, 1995.

Molhant, Robert. *Catholics in the Cinema: A Strange History of Belief and Passion, 1895–1935*. Brussels: OCIC, 2000.

Morgan, David. *Protestants and Pictures*. New York: Oxford University Press, 1999.

Musser, Charles. *The Emergence of Cinema: The American Screen to 1907*. New York: Scribner's, 1990.

Musser, Charles, and Carol Nelson. *High-Class Moving Pictures: Lyman H. Howe and the Forgotten Era of the Traveling Exhibition, 1880–1920*. Princeton: Princeton University Press, 1991.

Oberdeck, Kathryn. *The Evangelist and the Impresario: Religion, Entertainment, and Cultural Politics in America, 1884–1914*. Baltimore: John Hopkins Press, 1999.

Ouspensky, Leonid. *Theology of the Icon, Vol. 1*, (trans. Anthony Gythiel). Crestwood, N.Y.: St. Vladimir's Seminary Press, 1978.

Perlman, William (ed.). *The Movies on Trial*. Norwood, Mass.: Norwood Press, 1936.

Peters, Charles. *Motion Pictures and Standards of Morality*. New York: Arno Press, 1970.

Ramsaye, Terry. *A Million and One Nights: A History of the Motion Pictures through 1925*. New York: Simon and Schuster, 1926.

Reisner, Christian. *Church Publicity*. New York: Methodist Book Concern, 1913.

Rogers, Williams L. and Paul H. Vieth, *Visual Aids in the Church*. Philadelphia: Christian Education Press, 1946.

Rolfo, Luigi. *James Alberione: Apostle for Our Times*. New York: Alba House, 1987.

Ross, Steven. *Working-Class Hollywood: Silent Film and the Shaping of Class in America*. Princeton: Princeton University Press, 1998.

Sheldon, Charles M. *In His Steps: Special Photoplay Edition*. New York: A.L. Burt Co.

Shenton, Herbert. *The Public Relations of the Motion Picture Industry*. New York: Department of Research and Education, Federal Council of the Churches in Christ in America, 1931.

Sloan, Kay. *The Loud Silents: Origins of the Social Problem Film*. Urbana: University of Illinois Press, 1988.

St. John of Damascus. *On the Divine Images* (trans. David Anderson). Crestwood, N.Y.: Sr. Vladimir's Seminary Press, 1994.

Sumner, Robert. *Hollywood Cesspool*. Murfreesboro, Tenn.: Sword of the Lord Publishers, 1955.

Tibbetts, John C. and James M. Weise. *His Majesty, the American*. New York: Barnes and Noble, 1977.

Tozer, A. H. *Menace of the Religious Movie*. Grand Rapids: Christian, 1974.

Urrichio, William, and Roberta E. Pearson. *Reframing Culture*. Princeton: Princeton University Press, 1993.

Veith, Gene Edward. *Painters of Faith: The Spiritual Landscape in Nineteenth-Century America*. Washington, D.C.: Regnery, 2001.

Walsh, Frank. *Sin and Censorship: Catholic Church and the Motion Picture Industry*. Yale University Press, 1996.

Walsh, Richard. *Reading the Gospels in the Dark: Portrayals of Jesus in Film*. New York: Trinity Press, 2003.

Waller, Gregory. *Main Street Amusement*. Washington, D.C.: Smithsonian Institute Press, 1995.

Wilson, John F. *Public Religion in American Culture*. Philadelphia: Temple University Press, 1979.

Wilson, Wayne A. *Worldly Amusements*. Enumclaw: Wine Press, 1999.

Index

About the Author

TERRY LINDVALL occupies the endowed C. S. Lewis Chair of Communication and Christian Thought at Virginia Wesleyan College. He previously taught at Duke University School of Divinity, Regent University, and was the Walter Mason Fellow of Religious Studies at the College of William and Mary. He is the author of *Surprised by Laughter: The Comic World of C. S. Lewis* (Thomas Nelson, 1997); *The Silents of God: Selected Issues and Documents in Silent American Film and Religion, 1908–1925* (Scarecrow, 2001); and *The Mother of All Laughter: Sarah and the Genesis of Comedy* (Broadman Holman, 2003). He is also the executive producer of over fifty films. An ordained Congregational minister, he received his B.A. from Vanguard University, M.Div. from Fuller Theological Seminary, and Ph.D. from the University of Southern California. He and his wife, Karen, have two merry children, Chris (15) and Caroline (12), and live in Virginia Beach, Virginia.